MW00560026

FILIPINO STUDIES

Filipino Studies

Palimpsests of Nation and Diaspora

Edited by Martin F. Manalansan IV
and Augusto F. Espiritu

NEW YORK UNIVERSITY PRESS
New York

NEW YORK UNIVERSITY PRESS
New York
www.nyupress.org

References to Internet websites (URLs) were accurate at the time of writing. Neither the author nor New York University Press is responsible for URLs that may have expired or changed since the manuscript was prepared.

ISBN: 978-1-4798-2905-7 (hardback)
ISBN: 978-1-4798-8435-3 (paperback)

For Library of Congress Cataloging-in-Publication data, please contact the Library of Congress.

New York University Press books are printed on acid-free paper, and their binding materials are chosen for strength and durability. We strive to use environmentally responsible suppliers and materials to the greatest extent possible in publishing our books.

Manufactured in the United States of America

10 9 8 7 6 5 4 3 2 1

Also available as an ebook

CONTENTS

ACKNOWLEDGMENTS

This anthology began as a conference, "Philippine Palimpsests: Filipino Studies in the 21st Century," held on March 7–8, 2008, at the University of Illinois at Urbana-Champaign. The conference and this anthology were fueled by the enthusiasm and support of many individuals and institutions. To be clear, this collection is not a record of the conference proceedings; instead it is composed of mostly original essays that were written after the event. Initial seed money was provided by the Department of Asian American Studies. The conference's main funding came from the Office of the Provost, Center for Advanced Study, the CIC Big Ten Consortium in Asian American Studies, and the State of the Art Conference grant from the College of Liberal Arts and Sciences. Additional funding came from the Asian American Cultural Center, the Center for East Asian and Pacific Studies, the Center on Democracy in a Multiracial Society, the Department of Gender and Women's Studies, the Department of Human and Community Development, International Students and Scholars Services, the Illinois Program for Research in the Humanities, and the Unit for Criticism and Interpretive Theory. This anthology was made possible by research assistantship funding and a publication subvention grant from the Research Board.

The Department of Asian American Studies at the UIUC was the home for this project, and the faculty and staff have been pivotal in helping shepherding it along. The editors acknowledge the generosity of Kent Ono and Lisa Nakamura for their unequivocal support. We especially thank Nancy Abelmann, Lisa Cacho, Jose B. Capino, and David Coyoca for being part of the steering committee. Former graduate students who are now colleagues, Aide Acosta, Genevieve Clutario, and Stanley Thangaraj, offered their valuable ideas, voices, and energies to the conference. We would like to thank the departmental staff (both former and current), Mary Ellerbe, Viveka Kudaligama, Christine Lykes, and Pia Sengsavanh for their hard work. Special thanks go to Constancio Arnaldo, who was the research assistant and the virtual backbone of this project. He kept the project moving and prevented major pitfalls. Anna

Gonzales was the instigator of this project—she strongly suggested that the energies and ideas around the conference be harnessed into a book.

The editors acknowledge the contributions of the fine scholars and intellectual leaders from all over the United States (including colleagues from our own campus) who graced our home in the Midwest with their presence during the conference weekend, including Deidre Agbayani, Kimberly Alidio, Nerissa Balce, Rick Baldoz, Francisco Benitez, John D. Blanco, Rick Bonus, Lucy Burns, Richard Chu, Denise Cruz, Robert Diaz, Kale Fajardo, Anna Guevarra, Emily Ignacio, Julian Go, Theodore Gonzalves, Allan Isaac, Moon-kie Jung, Soo Ah Kwon, Linda Maram, Dina Maramba, Cynthia Marasigan, Joyce Mariano, Victor Mendoza, Mimi Nguyen, Jan Padios, Joanna Poblete, Martin Joseph Ponce, Dylan Rodriguez, Robyn Rodriguez, Jeffrey Santa Ana, Sarita See, Neferti Tadiar, Antonio Tiongson, and Benito Vergara. The conference was buoyed by the wonderful words and generous intellectual presence of our keynote speaker, Professor Reynaldo Ileto. Professor Ileto is the exemplary model of a Filipino scholar who the younger generation of scholars at the conference aspire to become.

At NYU Press, gratitude is extended to Eric Zinner for believing in the project and Alicia Nadkarni for guiding it. Vincenz Serrano graciously gave permission to reprint Neferti Tadiar's essay in *Kritika Kultura*. Finally, here and elsewhere, we acknowledge the inspiration from the works of several Filipino and Filipino American scholars such as Eufracio Abaya, Patricio Abinales, Ponciano Bennagen, Oscar Campomanes, Randolph David, Gary Devilles, Carol Hau, John Labella, Ferdinand Lopez, Francisco Nemenzo, Vicente Rafael, Laura Samson, Michael Tan, and many others in the transnational network of Filipino scholars.

Augusto F. Espiritu: I thank Anna K. Gonzalez and Rafa, for helping sustain and encourage me always. Last, but not least, I thank my colleague, friend, and partner in this enterprise, Martin Manalansan, whose vision, leadership, tremendous hard work, and devotion to the scholarship of the Filipino diaspora and Filipino American studies, American Studies, and Asian American Studies has been unstinting, generous, and deeply moving. It has been a tremendous pleasure to work with Martin through all the vicissitudes of this project, from its inception in 2005 to the arrival of this book a decade later.

Martin F Manalansan IV: I extend my heartfelt gratitude to Augusto Espiritu, my partner in crime, for helping me weather the ebbs and flows of this project. Special thanks also go to the contributors for their patience with a rather protracted process. I also want to express my warm regards to all members of the "Filipino mafia" (including but not limited to the Filipino caucus at the Association for Asian American Studies), a wide-ranging web of friendships and intellectual partnerships. Finally, I want to express my love to my family, dispersed across thousands of miles like the typical family of modern-day Philippines. My late father has been unable to see any of my published work. As I get older, I realize that I bear the imprint of his generous personality and gentle nature. I am forever grateful and truly blessed.

The Field

Dialogues, Visions, Tensions, and Aspirations

MARTIN F. MANALANSAN IV AND AUGUSTO F. ESPIRITU

Filipino Studies: Palimpsests of Nation and Diaspora is a collection of chapters that offers both critical commentaries on the state of Philippine Studies as well as innovative works that offer novel frameworks and alternative vantages for the study of the Philippines and its diaspora. Written by a group of Philippine-, US-, and Canada-based Filipino and Filipino American scholars, the chapters are also critically aware of the positionalities, constraints, and opportunities that make this work possible. After years of occupying a vexed and ambivalent position in area studies and Asian American Studies, Philippine, Filipino, and Filipino American Studies have emerged in the past fifteen years as a trenchant and vibrant academic presence. Proof of this ascendancy is a long list of notable works that have become widely read not only in North America and Europe but also in the Philippines where many of these works have been republished by local university and private presses. The circulation of ideas in the field has been transnational, though sometimes fraught and problematic, as is reflective of the kinds of work presented in this volume.

This anthology is the outcome of a series of conversations, shared wishes, and fervent longings for an intellectual forum for the ideas of several US-based Filipino, Filipino American and Filipino Canadian scholars.

Many contributors to this collection incidentally come from the Big Ten or the group of land-grant universities mostly in the American Midwest that hosted a wave of Filipino scholars in the early twentieth century called *pensionados*. These pensionados were sent by the American colonial government to study in US universities and eventually assisted in the integration of the Philippines into American imperial rule as part of its tutelary project. Ironically, they would also become crucial to the rise of Filipino cultural nationalism and the prelude to Philippine independence. The papers in this volume struggle to engage and assess the legacies of imperial power and its ideas, and redirect the trajectories of American empire by creating a set of critical optics to frame ongoing intellectual engagements with the exigencies of colonialism and postcolonialism, as well as the contemporary challenges of transnationalism, globalization, and diaspora.

Propelled by a pivotal semantic inspiration from the word "palimpsest," the chapters in this collection attempt to uncover the mercurial "layerings" or shifting stratigraphy of power that obscure or erase and at the same resurrect specific historical, cultural, and political experiences. Like the palimpsest, these chapters are not isolated reflections but rather emerge alongside, parallel to, against, and despite other writings, thoughts, and ideas in other sites and spaces. In her magisterial ethnography of Bicolano rural poor, Fenella Cannell (1999) deployed the idea of the palimpsest to think about subaltern practices that are part of structured and structuring relationships between rural Bicolanos and more powerful "others," such as rich urban Filipinos, the Christian God, or America. Therefore, under the sign of the palimpsest, this collection is a moment in a continuing power struggle that forms a series of stratigraphic shifts, movements of layers, of inscriptions, erasures, and reinscriptions or overwritings. Whether addressing Filipino coloniality, the contested memories of World War II, the "voyage" of Filipino men and women into the US metropole, or the state of migrant labor, the chapters assembled in *Filipino Studies* build over old ones, never fully obliterating previous ideas, scratching away obfuscating strata, and deciphering the links between the past and present with a hopeful longing for various kinds of futures.

Time, History, Layers

To understand the rich variety of essays produced under in this collection requires a historical contextualization albeit in very broad and abbreviated strokes. Laying down such a context is admittedly a difficult task given that each of the chapters seeks the revision of that very history. It is easy enough to recount *modern* Philippine history, if one means its history *after* the arrival of colonialism. For four centuries, the archipelago was a Spanish colony, a Catholic country, and a military outpost of Spain in the Far East. The Philippine colonial economy was bound to the trans-Pacific Manila-Acapulco galleon trade, administered by the Viceroyalty of New Spain (Mexico) for two centuries, until the Latin American independence movements ended the connection. In the mid to late nineteenth century, as part of a reorganized and liberalized Spanish empire, the Philippine economy developed and an economically prosperous middle class made up of Spanish, Chinese mestizo, and *indio* background emerged to challenge Spanish hegemony. The children of this class studied in Spain, and their wider horizons provided the basis for the emergence of Filipino nationalism and the decolonization movement that culminated in the country's first declaration of independence on June 12, 1898, and the founding of the Philippine Republic.

Philippine independence was short-lived, however, as the United States invaded the country and made it a US colony through the Spanish-American and Philippine-American Wars. The United States, in the throes of its own Age of Progressivism, that is, of full-scale movements of social and political reform, established a public education system in which English became the official language, a civil service system, a US-style system of political representation, in addition to improvements in public health, transportation, and communication. During the Commonwealth phase (1935–46), a women's suffrage law was passed and a ten-year timetable for independence was established. At the same time, it cannot be doubted that US colonial rule left a problematic legacy, creating economic dependency, instilling colonial patronage politics, and establishing racial hierarchies, as for instance, expanding the Chinese Exclusion Laws to the Philippines. As before, Filipino elite political leaders as much as the Filipino masses were extremely engaged in independence agitation from the United States. Then followed four years of Japanese occupation under the "East Asia Co-Prosperity Sphere." A Second Philippine Republic under Japan's protection was proclaimed. Despite the American departure, Filipinos launched a guerrilla war against the Japanese, especially in response to various atrocities committed by the Japanese military. One of these was the forced enslavement of Filipino "comfort" women for sex and recreation, which only came to be known several decades later. After World War II, and American reoccu-pation, the Philippines was granted independence, though with so many strings attached to the United States as to make it a virtual neocolony.

The Philippine Republic has properly been a postcolonial nation for close to seventy years, its existence punctuated by economic prosperity al-ternating with economic crises, widespread poverty, political corruption, and indebtedness. It has experienced a serious peasant rebellion, nearly two decades of authoritarian rule, a long-standing communist insurgency, and an even longer protracted struggle with its Muslim minority. In the process, the Philippines has developed strong traditions of dissent, mass mobilization, and a national media unifying an extremely diverse popula-tion. Globalization has, on the surface, helped lead to economic growth in the twenty-first century, although the most powerful super storm in all history, Typhoon Haiyan, has slowed down that progress.

Migration has always been a crucial element in the making of the Philippines and of the Filipino overseas communities. In the Spanish colonial period, this involved internal migrations that led to the popu-lation of "frontier" areas in the Philippines, transoceanic crossings to Mexico through the galleon trade, which led to unexpected twists as in the founding of a pre-US Civil War Filipino settlement in Louisiana, and to the European sojourns of the *ilustrados* (elites). In the twentieth cen-tury, waves of migrants, regular and irregular, have come back and forth from the United States, as labor migrants, members of the US military, professionals, and political exiles.

While men had dominated the migrant pool to the United States for most of the century and women had been a distinct minority, the pas-sage of the 1965 Immigration Act led to a gender transformation among Filipino Americans, with women now the clear majority in the com-munity. As is the case with other immigrants, Filipinos have undergone the same difficult struggles of adjustment, discriminatory barriers to employment, and hostility to their presence. The vast majority of immi-grants decided to remain in the United States although economic global-ization and transportation have facilitated their visits to the Philippines as tourists ("*balikbayans*") with their visible "balikbayan box" (package of goods for the homeland visit) or as return migrants, alongside their second-generation children who may be visiting the country for the first time. The challenges of being in between two countries, two continents divided by great oceanic distance, and two different cultural formations have led to hyphenated identities and biculturalism or multiculturalism, indeed a common questioning of self and identity.

During the 1960s, Filipinos in the United States were swept up in several overlapping strands of political activism, from the antidictatorship struggle against Ferdinand Marcos to the Asian American movement to the Filipino American movement to sporadic participation in American Indian, Puerto Rican, African American, and anti-Vietnam War activism. Filipino American women and men were also actively involved in gay liberation, feminist, and Third World feminist movements. As with many other American ethnic groups, Filipino American identity, culture, and institutions emerged during the 1970s and 1980s in response to this surge in mass democratic politics, its critique of American racism, and its positive embrace of racial identity. While the surge in civil rights and black power had a positive impact upon the rise of various ethnic empowerment movements, these also made possible the critique of the very black/white binary that afflicts American racism, viz. the way race, racism, racists, and racial victims are interpreted in the larger society as matters pertaining only to white oppressors and black victims, excluding all other ethnic groups that do not fit the paradigm.

In recent years, there has been an ongoing attempt to resurrect buried artistic and political models, including Carlos Bulosan's writings and the poetry and autobiographical memoirs of early Filipino and Filipina migrants and activists, as well as those of diasporic, literary intellectuals like Ben Santos, Jose Garcia Villa, and N. V. M. Gonzalez. There was a surge in literary and artistic activity among Filipino Americans, including poetry (Jeff Tagami, Virgie Cerenio, Jessica Hagedorn), plays (Melvin Escueta, Jeanie Baroga), novels (Peter Bacho, Linda Ty-Casper, Ninotchka Rosca, Jessica Hagedorn, Tess Uriza Holthe, Brian Ascalon Roley, R. Zamora Linmark), and artwork (Carlos Villa, Manuel Ocampo) displaying artistic innovation circuitous routes and the multivalent, complex sensibilities of Filipino-ness.

Organization of the Anthology

This collection of chapters is organized into four intersecting parts. While all the chapters are advancing specific frameworks and research itineraries, the first section puts together the more explicit agenda-setting and field-wide critical inquiries. Looking at both the genealogy as well as the politically necessary future trajectory of the field, chapters by Tadiar, Rodriguez, and Blanco explore what it means to have a relevant and vibrant project of analyzing the Philippines and its diaspora in the present time as well as attempting to envision possibilities for the future.

The next section, "Colonial Layerings, Imperial Crossings" is a combination of period-specific studies by Alidio, Rodriguez, Go and Bascara that strongly maintain a recalcitrant approach to traditional historiographic renditions of Filipino and Filipino American histories and more specifically interrogating the conceptual viability and the historical contingencies of colonialism and empire. From histories of Philippine elites, racial ontologies, and colonial education to the Japanese occupation of the islands and the subsequent intrusion of the Cold War and decolonization/"independence" from the United States, these chapters are compelling pronouncements about how and what should be studied under the sign of "Philippine colonial history."

The Filipino Body section focuses on the notions of embodiments, aesthetics, and desire where processes of Filipino racialization, gendering, and sexualization as constitutive of colonial, postcolonial, and national projects. The chapters by Cruz, Diaz, Ponce, and See are cartographic exercises on the ways in which womanhood, queerness, and desire are culturally produced and historically situated within and fleshed out through the exigencies of Filipino national and transnational institutions, personhoods, and affective ecologies.

"Philippine Cultures at Large: Homing in on Global Filipinos and Their Discontents" is the final section. It brings together the chapters by Benitez, Bonus, Guevarra, and Ignacio all of which investigate the transnational and diasporic mediated predicaments of Filipinos and Filipino Americans. From undocumented migrant status to return migration to the workings of arts, these chapters partake of the ethos behind the critical historical reframing and unraveling that works contained in the second section have offered. These chapters also direct theoretical and conceptual attention to what "should" be important to understand about the Filipino diasporic/transnational (im)mobilities and settlement in the twenty-first century. Home and return are no longer mere spatial endpoints or temporal nodes of ontological completion in the diasporic cycle; rather, they are scattered in ambivalent moments and spatial elsewheres.

Overall, the chapters in this anthology are far from just being explorations of various sorts of genres, sites, and texts. These chapters put forward bold and formidable declarations about the productive and innovative frameworks that open up new archives and landscapes of knowledge for Filipino/Philippine/Filipino American Studies in contemporary times.

Philippine Studies, Filipino Studies, Filipino American Studies: Tensions and Challenges

To put it simply, this anthology is neither the first nor the final statement on the Philippines and its diaspora. Numerous interdisciplinary anthologies about the Philippines and its diaspora have been published before. We acknowledge our indebtedness to that work for helping spur and stimulate the project for this collection. Tiongson et al. (2006) and Coloma et al. (2012) are collections that deal with Filipinos in the United States and Canada, respectively. They are focused on issues of invisibility and representation and are projects that seek to put forward archives of experiences of Filipinos in both countries. Tolentino's (2011) edited volume of *positions: east asian cultures critique* provide critical perspectives on late twentieth- century- and early twenty-first-century cultural productions marked by the end of martial law and shaped by the oeuvre of one of the foremost film director, the late Lino Brocka. Rafael (1999) is a collection of mostly previously published works of United States, Philippine-, and Australian-based scholars and aims to "call attention to the frayed and porous passages between what is inside and outside not only of the Philippines but also that which is commonly thought of as the 'West'" (xv). Patajo-Legasto (2011) is a voluminous collection with a sizeable section on Filipino American experiences but depends on an eclectic telos and genealogy of Philippine Studies.

The chapters in this volume speak from a particular transnational location, the American academic landscape, and other social locations. They do not speak "for" all Filipinos and Filipino scholars everywhere and at all times; instead, the contributors speak "from" structurally, historically, and politically positioned viewpoints and perspectives. The collection does not purport to speak as the sole and primary source about

Philippine subject matters, but clearly emerges from several strong intellectual traditions and angles, one of which is Filipino American Studies.

Filipino Studies goes beyond identity and invisibility questions, to think more capaciously about cultural production, social justice and transformation, structural politics, historical passages, and collective actions. We recognize the undercurrents and histories around the building of Filipino American Studies that opened up new and strong spaces for the study of the Philippines in the American academy where it previously occupied a marginal and lowly status in area studies, more specifically, Southeast Asian Studies. While Filipino American presence was limited in the US academia throughout most of the twentieth century, scholarly productions on Philippine and Filipino American subjects has skyrocketed in the late twentieth and twenty-first centuries. As one indicator, while in the early years, Filipino American academics were but a small presence in the annual meetings of the Association of Asian American Studies, the Filipino caucus now includes more than eighty members, most of them tenured or tenure-track faculty, postdoctoral scholars, and advanced doctoral students, each actively engaged in every facet of associational life. As humanities and/or social science scholars, they are especially passionate about migration studies, queer studies, race, gender, class, colonialism, postcolonialism, and labor studies.

While recognizing the importance of this visible presence and emergent status in the American academy and in bringing area studies and ethnic studies in conversation with each other, the contributors in this collection do not consider themselves and their works as uncritically applying ethnic studies ideas on race and other so-called American theories to the Philippine context. Rather, they are involved in an exploration of the tenability and plasticity of ideas and concepts. Instead of focusing on the exceptional character of the Philippines, the chapters seek capacious ways to calibrate the dangers, pleasures, and possibilities of cutting across knowledge formations and traditions to then set them against the geographic reach of Filipinos scattered all over the world.

In addition to recognizing the strong ethnic studies undercurrent of the various chapters in this collection, it is equally important to note that this collection is not solely a product of ethnic studies scholars as can be gleaned from the biographies of the contributors. Contributors include scholars trained in area studies and other disciplines. As such, *Filipino Studies* brings together conversations between fields such as critical ethnic studies, cultural studies, area studies, and the traditional disciplines (for example, literature, anthropology, and so on).

In bringing this collection together, the editors acknowledge the tangled web of "roots and routes" of intellectual production around these objects of study. In this anthology, Philippine Studies, Filipino Studies, and Filipino American Studies are used in various contexts. While it is instructive to attend to the various ways in which these categories are used—while Philippine Studies is popularly seen as the area studies based concentration on the nation and the state, Filipino Studies involves the global diaspora and Filipino American Studies focuses on the Filipino experiences in the United States—the chapters in this anthology defy these seemingly static notions and fields. This collection, because of its central organizing or core metaphor of the "palimpsest," suggests that knowledge production is about the layering, erasures, and reinscriptions of histories, spaces, and cultures or a deep engagement with the "porousness" and permeability of intellectual, cultural, and political borders as Rafael (1999) astutely suggests.

However, the problems of borders are not just semantic; they are also issues of unequal power distribution. Reynaldo Ileto (2014), Caroline Hau (2014), and Francisco Benitez and Laurie Sears (2014) have trenchantly presented and skillfully mapped the tensions and issues that are at the heart of numerous debates and polemics around the study of the Philippines and its diaspora. The issues of collaboration and the politics of citationality are just two of the numerous pressing issues that pervade projects such as this collection. The problem of authority and authenticity—who speaks for whom—calls to mind what Hau (2014) has termed as "epistemic privilege," which points to the unequal and situated distribution of intellectual range and prominence, or to put it another way, the politics of intellectual location. The evaluation of one's scholarship and its mode of circulation depend on one's distance from the center of power. In this case, research works on the Philippines are subjected to divergent standards, nativist impulses, eruptions of "Western" guilt, elitist language, and various modes of academic chauvinisms and exclusions. The circulation and reception of *Philippine Palimpsests* will not be an exception.

We look toward possible links and strategies to overcome the difficulties. Many of the contributors are typically the only "Philippine experts" on their campuses. While this virtual isolation places an extraordinary burden on pedagogy, research and institutional visibility, and survival, the meeting of various scholars through conferences may be one way to assuage this onus. The Palimpsests conference together with those at the University of Hawai'i Center for Philippines Studies and the biannual ICOPHIL (International Conference on Philippine Studies) are just among a few attempts to link and connect scholars into a communal hub and network of collaboration, conversation, and debate.

Clearly, these are not enough. More creative and effective strategies and activities need to be forged to address the various issues discussed briefly mentioned above. However, because of the Global North site of this anthology's publication, distribution/dissemination and the institutional affiliations of most of its contributors, we are aware of the limits and possibilities of reaching various reading communities across regions and borders. Nevertheless, we offer these chapters as a contribution toward expansive dialogue between and among scholars and other audiences in various sites. We recognize the difficulties and hurdles, but as a collective effort, *Filipino Studies,* true to the organizing semantics of the word palimpsest, are open to the revisionary and trace-like qualities of knowledge formations. We reject the static hierarchical formations of native versus stranger, nation versus diaspora, and of the here and there. However, we also appreciate and concede the multidirectional, striated, and inter/intra scalar power arrangements in the production of academic knowledges about the Philippines. We are open to more hopeful and sometimes ambivalent thoughts and longings for a viable future or set of futures. We remain committed to exploring other processes of building alternative strategies for collaborative knowledge formations. In the final analysis, we go by what Caroline Hau (2014:56) has wisely admonished scholars on the Philippines which is to interrogate our own positionings, to think of our works not as final statements that excludes other scholarship but are open, generous gestures, and attempts toward new conversations and collaborations, in order to think more broadly and aspirationally about emancipatory politics and futures, and to open up capacious vistas of "what it means to live as, and call oneself, Filipino."

Works Cited

Benitez, J. Francisco, and Laurie J. Sears. "Passionate Attachments: Subjectivity and Diaspora in the Transpacific." In Janet Hoskins and Viet Nguyen (eds.), *Transpacific Studies: Interventions and Intersections*. Honolulu: University of Hawai'i Press, 2014. Print.

Cannell, Fenella. *Power and Intimacy in the Christian Philippines*. Cambridge: Cambridge University Press, 1999. Print.

Coloma, Roland Sintos, Bonnie McElhinny, Ethel Tunghanm, John Paul Catungal, and Lisa M. Davidson, eds. *Filipinos in Canada: Disturbing Invisibility*. Toronto: University of Toronto Press, 2012. Print.

Hau, Caroline. "Privileging Roots and Routes: Filipino Intellectual and the Contest Over Epistemic Power and Authority." *Philippine Studies: Historical and Ethnographic Viewpoints* 62, no. 1 (spring 2014): 29–65. Print.

Ileto, Reynaldo C. "Nation and Empire in the Intellectual Biographies of Southeast Asian Scholars." *Asian Studies* 23, no. 4 (2014): 59, 9–17.

Patajo-Legasto, Priscelina, ed. *Philippine Studies: Have We Gone Beyond St. Louis?* Diliman: University of the Philippines Press, 2008. Print.

Rafael, Vicente, ed. *Discrepant Histories: Translocal Essays on Filipino Cultures*. Manila: Anvil Publications, 1995. Print.

Tiongson, Antonio T., Jr., Edgardo Gutierrez, and Ricardo V, Gutierrez, eds. *Positively no Filipinos Allowed: Building Communities and Discourse*. Philadelphia, PA: Temple University Press, 2006. Print.

Tolentino, Rolando, ed. *Positions: East Asia Cultures Critique*. "Special Issue: Vaginal Economy: Cinema and Sexuality in the Post Marcos Post-Brocka Philippines" 19, no. 2 (fall 2011): 229–56. Print.

PART I

Where from? Where to? Filipino Studies

Fields and Agendas

Challenges for Cultural Studies under the Rule of Global War

NEFERTI TADIAR

Although it would appear that the times we live in, following the launching of the "war on terror" by the United States in October 2001, with the bombing of Afghanistan—that these current times are no different from the previous twelve to fifteen years under the undisputed global reign of the United States (whether you date it from the fall of the Berlin wall or the first Gulf War), we are, I believe, living in a changed and changing historical situation whose import for our shared futures we have yet to fully grasp.[1] I do not intend today to speculate on the future implications of the current global situation. After all, we have yet to adequately account for the specific features comprising this current situation, in which, I would argue, the economic globalization of capital is being reharnessed to the ends of political-military domination by means of war. My purpose rather is to think about the present implications of this situation for cultural studies.

Many parallelisms with past, well-known historical situations have been and continue to be made by both those who are critical of the global-US "war on terror" and those who openly advocate the rule of empire: early twentieth-century US colonization of the Philippines, Puerto Rico, Cuba, Hawaii, Samoa, and Guam; British conquest of Mesopotamia (present-day Iraq) and the division of the former Ottoman Empire between Britain and France; the First World War among the imperialist nations; the Second World War and the ascendance of US world hegemony and the onset of the Cold War; as well as the long, ignominious, and bloody track record of US foreign interventions in the last hundred years. These past wars are often invoked as the historical precedents of, if not the legitimate models for, the blatant political-military actions currently undertaken by the United States and its network of complicit states, including the Philippines, and thus also as guides for possible scenarios in the near future.

In the 1967 preface to *Imperialism*, Part Two of her three-volume work, *The Origins of Totalitarianism*, Hannah Arendt comments on the resemblance between contemporary events then—particularly the US war against Vietnam—and the events of imperialism during the period preceding the outbreak of World War I, about which she writes. As she concludes, however:

> To stress the unhappy relevance of this half-forgotten period for contemporary events does not mean, of course, either that the die is cast and we are entering a new period of imperialist policies or that imperialism under all circumstances must end in the disasters of totalitarianism. No matter how much we may be capable of learning from the past, it will not enable us to know the future.[2]

The past will not enable us to know the future inasmuch as the future is the result not of an abstract logic, whose tendencies might be discerned across historical times, but rather of peoples' liberatory social struggles and the efforts on the part of ruling elites to contain and defeat them.

Indeed, what ensued after 1967, when Arendt wrote this preface, was not totalitarianism, but instead tremendous social unrest and revolution, much of which was cut short and undermined by the installation of reactionary regimes the world over. We have only to look at our own historical experience here in the Philippines, with the social upheaval and nascent revolutionary movement during the late 1960s followed by the declaration of Martial Law by the authoritarian Marcos regime, to ascertain this fact. The liberatory struggle of the Vietnamese people was itself a material testimony to the powerful force of the Third World that challenged US world domination, and the anti-Vietnam War movement in the United States, with which the broad Civil Rights movement of the 1960s and 1970s was importantly aligned, only served to strengthen this challenge and the sense of international solidarity that grew around it. Decolonizing nationalist movements worldwide, marked by the triumph of Vietnam against the United States and the victory of the Nicaraguan revolution against the US-backed Somoza regime, were met with fierce and relentless counterinsurgency campaigns, funded and equipped by the US military-industrial complex. These counterinsurgency campaigns were coupled with an equally fierce and relentless program of financial capitalist expansion to stave off the world economic crisis of the early 1970s, produced precisely as a consequence of the struggles of labor worldwide and the challenge of Third World nation-states to First World hegemony.[3] And neoliberalist restructuring processes during the last two decades, which have often been referred to as globalization, comprised an effort to capitalize upon this long cultural revolution of minoritized populations in the Third and First Worlds alike.

In some ways, then, the global-US "war on terror" now being waged on diverse fronts can be understood as a retaliatory measure on the part of a right-wing faction of the global elite bent on rebuilding its hegemony in the face both of rival powers (notably the European Union and the tiger economies of the Asia-Pacific, including China) and of the gains of people's struggles against global corporate and state powers (institutionally expressed for example in the Kyoto Protocols, the World Conference on Racism, the International Criminal Court, and so on). The formation of the new "security" state in the United States, with repressive policies such as the Patriot Act and the Domestic Security Enhancement Act (or Patriot Act II), points to the visible tendencies of fascism that are in evidence there, domestically, as well as in "coalitional" states, such as the Philippine state, which currently embrace the "war on terror" as an alibi for continued and new forms of political repression and cronyist war profiteering. The execution of human rights activists in Mindoro several months ago, the mounting cases of harassment and "disappearances" of individuals linked to radical political organizations, and the egregious military abuses and atrocities in Southern Mindanao since the Philippine government joined forces with the United States only show the ambition and retaliatory political and military opportunism driving the Philippines' part in this global crusade. In the meantime, while offspring and beneficiaries of the previous fascist regime propose refurbished antisubversion decrees (in the guise of antiterrorism measures), economic opportunism goes hand in hand with rising authoritarianism. Besides the US$356 million security-related assistance granted by the United States to the Philippine government, plenty of opportunities for economic gain are to be had with the proliferation of sites of state "war." The recent quarrel on the front pages of Philippine news over departmental jurisdiction in the antidrug campaign, expressed by some journalists as a "turf war" taking over the "drug war," reveals the underlying motivation of the ostensibly moral campaign, which is precisely cronyist war profiteering. Today the close links between the military police and the underworld of drug trafficking, illegal gambling, and the kidnapping business have all but been formalized into state rule, creating an ascendant cronyist class power ready to take charge of the national war economy.

Like the fascism of Germany and Italy in the earlier period, these trends toward fascism arise precisely out of a context of intensified imperialist competition and crisis, particularly for the United States, which has found itself increasingly marginalized by other national and regional economies and yet continues to be the greatest military superpower on earth. If the new period of imperialism that Arendt saw looming in 1967 did not immediately end in the disasters of totalitarianism, at least on the scale that they did in the middle of the century, perhaps now we are witnessing the beginnings of that conclusive end to US empire, that is, global fascism.

Some progressive scholars in the United States are in fact calling for a new analysis and at least recognition of the emergent conditions of fascism that confront not only the people in the United States, but also all the peoples in the paths of the global-US "war on terror." The question of "culture" in this context is, as it was under European fascism in the midtwentieth century, once again paramount for politics. It is, I believe, an important challenge for cultural studies to provide an account of the role that culture plays in this present situation, which can be characterized by the ascendancy of the rule of war. The war on terror, the war on drugs, the war against crime, the war against poverty—these are all instantiations of the rule of war. War has become a bureaucratic matter, with the military turned into police (which we have seen before, under Martial Law) and constitutionality and law overturned for a government run by decree. Witness the Macapagal-Arroyo government's willingness to sign on to decrees issued by the United States, such as the latter's decree of refusal to participate in the International Criminal Court, which could very well try the United States as a war criminal for its preemptive war against Iraq. Despite the fact that the Philippines was among the signatories to the 1998 Rome Statue creating the ICC, the Macapagal-Arroyo government has signed on to what amounts to a unilateral decree of immunity from international criminal prosecution for the US and Philippine states.[4] The rule of war is not only the rule of might, but also the rule of absolute and arbitrary power as the normal and legitimate state of affairs.

While now, perhaps more than ever, the exercise of naked power seems to reign over and above all ideological window-dressing (in contrast to the Marcos era, when the state invested heavily in cultural propaganda), "culture" as a realm of social action is no less crucial to power. But I think it is a challenge for cultural studies to figure out the *ways* that "culture" is crucial, that is, *how* cultural practices serve to maintain this power based on the rule of war and, furthermore, how cultural practices are reproducing and changing contemporary social relations of production or, more specifically, the social conditions of the exploited and the marginalized. In other words, it is a challenge for cultural studies today to interpret, articulate, and participate in the social struggles taking place in and through cultural practice.

This injunction is, of course, not new. In the Philippines we have heard it before in the words of Recto, Constantino, and Sison. And we have seen this injunction heeded in the vast amount of partisan cultural work carried out by writers, artists, and filmmakers since the political ferment of the 1960s. Feminists have been particularly attentive to the crucial importance of culture to social struggle. For feminists, such as Sr. Mary John Mananzan and Lilia Quindoza Santiago, culture refers to concrete, everyday habits historically embedded in women's relations to others as well as to themselves, relations that are fundamental to present and past orders of social oppression. This Philippine tradition of anti-imperialist, nationalist, and feminist cultural critique has long emphasized the role of culture in securing and enabling prevailing forms of domination. What is new or changed today are the specific conditions under which cultural practice is converted into socioeconomic infrastructure supporting the rule of war. For example, the ways in which narco-culture supports the mutually dependent "war on drugs" and narco-trafficking; the ways in which global media culture supports the forced export of Western-style bourgeois democracy via preemptive war, with the war on Iraq setting the precedent; and the ways in which the entrepreneurial ethic governs virtually all major efforts to revitalize or strengthen Philippine "culture" at the expense of sustaineable relations of community and solidarity. Beyond merely securing the consent for the rule of war, these cultural practices comprise the "software" for social relations on which the rule of war, in both its political and economic aspects, depends.

Those of us engaged in cultural studies are thus confronted with a pressing question. What cultural practices enable the transformation in global social relations wrought, on the one hand, by the emergence of a global network of quasi-militarist states in tributary relations to the US super security state and, on the other hand, by the emergence of a global counterpublic or constituency, which found representation in the unprecedented worldwide protests against the US-UK-led war on Iraq? I am suggesting that these recent political developments—the rise of both global, imperial fascism and popular transnational opposition to it—depend on cultural shifts that have occurred as the combined result of the long, world cultural revolution since the late 1960s and of the political and economic counterrevolution staged by state, corporate, and financial powers, which sought to co-opt and capitalize upon the gains of the former (culminating in "globalization"). On this view, cultural histories of the last three and a half decades or more would be a vital component of any politicized account of the conditions that have led to, as well as that might lead beyond, the current world crisis.

While the global network of complicit states attempts to refurbish an older territorial world-system and its geopolitical categories by reconfiguring old territorial boundaries and drawing new ones (for example, the new boundaries along the so-called axis of evil, from North Korea to Iraq, or from East to West Asia, and along the line from Central Asia to Eastern Europe), the global counterconstituency or, if you will, "transnational-popular" depends on transformed and largely deterritorialized conditions of social and political identification.[5] Witness one message on activist t-shirts: We are all Palestinians now. It is, of course, true that these deterritorialized conditions of social and political identification run both ways, politically speaking, so that a transnational imagined community like a global civil society can very well also support the neoliberalist wing of the new security state. By this I mean to imply that, as simultaneously the conditions of free trade promoted by neoliberalism and the conditions underlying emergent transnational imaginaries such as that of a global civil society, "globalization" is not necessarily incompatible with imperial fascism.[6] Or, we might say, imperial fascism is an attempt to overcome the real crisis of world social struggles that "globalization" was itself a complex attempt to resolve. Insofar as it addresses and depends upon the prevailing interstate system and, in relation to the latter, it plays the role of social conscience in what is at base a free world market economy, such a global civil society only succeeds in bolstering the logic of turning to authoritarianism and repressive militarist state power to control any threat to this world capitalist hegemony. Immanuel Wallerstein notes how, in the process of exerting pressure on states, human rights organizations that have mobilized around the notion of civil society "have come to be more like the adjuncts of states than their opponents and, on the whole, scarcely seem very antisystemic."[7] The important point here, however, is that the political direction and meaning of emergent social conditions and the activisms that depend on and foster them are not determined from the outset. Social relations on a global scale are in the thick of transformation, and only struggle will determine the political outcome. Moreover, the cultural dimensions of what might appear to be principally the political and economic restructuring of the contemporary world order are of no secondary importance to this struggle. Indeed, if we do not have an understanding of the complex, creative role that cultural practice plays in this struggle, we will be reduced to, at worst, making the most fundamentalist assumptions about the politics of culture (as in the current violent realization of "the clash of civilizations") and, at best, surrendering its transformative political potential to both the neoliberals and the neoconservatives.

When we take on the category of culture, as we do in cultural studies, we need to interrogate its easily assumed equivalence with territory (for example, of the nation-state, such that Philippine or Filipino culture would refer only to the peoples originally defined by the boundaries of the Philippine nation-state). This questioning of the territoriality of the nation does not mean an eschewing of nationalism or a dismissal of the continuing importance of the nation-state as a unit of political regulation and surplus-value extraction on a global scale (we know very well that the denial of this fact has often been crucial to the neoliberalist promottion of a free global market). To interrogate culture's assumed equivalence with territory means rather to take into account the plasticity of cultures.[8] It means to a certain extent taking care not to understand culture predominantly as a noun, as in "a culture," however historically specific we might want to be when we do so. As social ways of *doing*, cultural practices do not have hard and fast lines of demarcation, even if principles of social organization such as gender, class, and nation may appear to confine particular ways of doing to given social groups (for example, women, workers, Filipinos). It is important, especially at this conjuncture, to be attendant to the minute shifts in social formations that have been enabled through sea changes in cultural practice. I am thinking, for example, of how the nationalism and mass-orientation of cultural practice that was cultivated in the radical movements of the late 1960s and early 1970s also came to be articulated in a hegemonic key. Today, state and corporate culture industries as well as local community development programs tout reified versions of "Filipino culture" or the values and ways of "the Filipino people" that are greatly appealing to the middle classes as well as to the vast Filipino diaspora. I am also thinking of how youth cultures across diverse contexts have come to be increasingly closer to one another (in codes of behavior, communication, and affect) than to their own immediate and "traditional-cultural" communities. Sea changes in cultural practice are supporting and shaping changes in conventional rural-urban social relations, both nationally and transnationally, such that a rural milieu from Malaybalay, Bukidnon can be found alive and well in New York.

It is equally important to be cognizant of the diversity or differences of cultural practice within given social groups as well as of the sharing, migration, and influence of cultural practices between and among constituted social groups. OFW communities shape and change—and in turn are shaped and changed by—their "host" cultures. At the same time, those OFW communities are far from homogeneous in their cultural ways. This is where strict class or regional categorizations need to be inflected and intersected with other operative principles of social organization such as gender and race. On the West Coast of the United States, many second- and third-generation Filipino American youth share and participate in cultures of hip-hop and the inner city, often identified as Black and/or Latino, while in other parts of the world, immigrant Filipina workers find themselves in fragmented cultural enclaves isolated from both dominant and other marginalized communities.

We cannot presume to know in advance the social groups for whom particular practices comprise certain "cultures," which subsequently serve to define such groups (in the current fashion of cultural racism). I would go so far as to suggest that there are levels of social constitution that operate below the threshold of current codings of social identity—which I would call forms of *infra-sociality*. This is the level of emergent social constitution, whereby imagined communities both beneath and beyond hegemonic categories of nationhood, regionality, ethnicity, gender, and so on, are in the process of being created. Or, put differently, the micropolitical, subjective level at which dominant social relations of production are undergoing transformation. Indeed, it is an important part of cultural struggles to set the defining limits and identifying marks of emergent social formations produced out of new configurations of cultural practice (for example, for example, whether one identifies forms of sociality as Ilocanos, Filipino Americans, OFWs, or peasants and their respective practices as Ilocano, Filipino American OFW or peasant "culture"). That is to say, cultural struggles are also importantly struggles over the construction of effective political subjects. We can see such efforts in the conservative instantiations of "the Filipino character" that abound, even or especially today, in the midst of global phenomena such as the neoliberal global market, terrorism, and epidemics like HIV/AIDS. These conservative instantiations seek not only to territorialize the realm of culture, so that it becomes simply another area of state management, but also to separate it from the realm of political economy, in the idealist, transcendent form of "values," that are to fall under the jurisdiction of dominant social institutions such as the educational system.

Take, for example, the recent Asian Social Institute commencement speech given by Presidential Adviser on Culture, Leticia Ramos-Shahani, which provides an example of the refurbishment of values-oriented inquiries of the 1960s and 1970s in the context of revanchist fascism.[9] In this speech on "Politics and Spiritual Values," Shahani emphasizes the particular urgency of the issues of values today in the face of "threats like terrorism, regional armed conflicts, SARS, HIV/AIDS" and in the context of a world of growing inequality and injustice. She asks, "Is not the widening gap between the rich and the poor also an indication of the felt absence of a moral order which should guide the lives of individuals and nations in the modern world?" Diagnosing the "diseases of poverty, passivity, graft and corruption, exploitative patronage, factionalism" and other pathologies afflicting our "sick nation," Shahani proposes to revitalize the Moral Recovery Program that she had advocated in the Senate in 1987. Besides interpreting the 1986 EDSA uprising as essentially a moral event, the Moral Recovery Program commissioned leading Filipino social scientists to conduct an analysis of "the strengths and weakness of the Filipino character," which would serve as the basis of rebuilding the nation. To continue this program, Shahani recently prepared a handbook to disseminate the methodology of moral and spiritual education, through "self-analysis, self-purification and self-awareness" as well as "regular spiritual discipline," that, it is hoped, would result in people demanding high standards of moral values from electoral candidates. This program of cultural transformation does not only seek to institute yet another "revolution from the center," in which the dictates of discipline and moral development are decreed by a small authoritative group. As its vision of change in our political culture makes clear, it also seeks to recalibrate, but essentially preserve, the prevailing state in a manner that better coordinates it with a semiliberal capitalist socioeconomic order: "We should elect men and women who understand that public office exists to serve the people, to enable the private sector to function dynamically and to cooperate with civil society in common concerns." How different, in the end, is the Christian vision of "a new world order of spiritual values, and economic prosperity" based on the quest for divine redemption and righteousness and worldly compensation, which Shahani puts forth, from the civilizationist discourse that undergirds Bush's mandate to wage the "war on terror"?

I hope it is by now evident that when I speak of cultural practices I do not mean peculiar habits of thought or action detached from economic conditions and political events. After all, social thought, action, and experience do not occur in a vacuum, detached from the historical situations that the dominant organization of production and power plays a fundamental part in generating and shaping. To take account of the material force or world-making effects of cultural practice, one must first recognize the continual subsumption of people's labor—physical, mental, experiential, and psychical—into systems of domination and exploitation. Subsumption here can be likened to taxation, in the sense of exacting payment or tribute from those who perform the whole range of labor that maintains the overall economic order. I would suggest in fact that this tributary or enforced taxation system is one that has not been outmoded in peripheral nations such as the Philippines but in fact today generalized, even if largely informalized. We can, on this view, understand the rule of war to be also the rule of taxation, best represented by the "tong" capitalism of the military-police-criminal syndicate. The exaction of monetary "cuts" and/or fees at all levels of the current drug war, from the drug test fee to get one's driver's license to protection fees for the drug lords (or their "profit-sharing" schemes with government), is supplemented and matched by the expropriation of people's cultural practices of accommodation and resistance. I mean, for one, the way the consumption of drugs itself often serves as a cultural form of accommodation to prevailing social conditions of profound alienation, debasement, and/or exploitation. I also mean, for another, the way the antidrug campaign of the state and its facilitation of "tong" capitalism enjoins the civic participation of precisely those who would oppose this criminal-state alliance. This expropriation of sociocultural technologies of resistance against the ruling system can be seen in Alex Magno's call for a "people's war" against "the drug menace."[10] Invoking the Maoist phrase of radical democratic struggle, Magno argues for the necessity of "an information infrastructure that allows for broad involvement" of "the people." This information structure, which would not entail any additional budgetary allocation and, moreover, would provide the means for "a fully developed social movement," will "network the power of the mass media and private communications (such as web groups and mobile phones) to provide enforcements information dominance against the enemy." Clearly, what is proposed here is no less than an appropriation of the notion and motivation of progressive social movements, as well as socially developed means of communication and community (web groups and mobile phones), for the purposes of a state intelligence that is completely embroiled in the cronyist war economy.[11] Given the close links between the antidrug and antiterrorist campaigns under the current rule of global war, it may come as no surprise to find the Pentagon thinking along similar, though much more ambitious, lines. The latest US Defense Department's antiterrorist plan is to create an online futures trading market in which speculators could bet on forecasts of terrorist attacks, assassinations, and coups, thereby providing a way of predicting and preventing future attacks.[12] Although heavy criticism has apparently laid this latest plan to rest, there is no better example of the way the US security state is seeking to reharness the "new economy" (of speculative finance capital) to the military-political apparatus and its resource- and rent-based economy; of the way it seeks to create the conditions for its own reproduction and growth (by inducing, through the profit incentives of speculation, the very future events it purportedly is trying to prevent); and of the way social desires, as expressed by and played out on the Internet, are to be appropriated for the purposes of this security state and its new economy.

Beyond the continual subsumption of cultural practice, one must however also recognize the equally continual inventiveness on the part of people in their efforts to survive and thrive, and even to partake of the spoils of exploitation (that is, to participate in the system of expropriation). Here we have to distinguish between life-making, liberating, and democratizing practices of resistance and forms of "resistance" that displace the deleterious effects of systems of domination, which they help to preserve.[13] In the present situation, the realms of freedom being carved out of the ever-expanding realms of necessity, dictated by the rule of war (and the capitalist system which underwrites it), are getting smaller and smaller, and more difficult to recognize in particular spatial or social zones, even as realms of more formal progressive political action are getting broader (for example, the World Social Forum). At the same time, small spaces of creativity and freedom are won in what appear to be thoroughly commodified sites (for example, popular music), even as progressive initiatives are at an ever-quickening pace subjected to both commodification and co-optation by dominant political agendas.

In this light, the challenge for cultural studies is to locate and extend these spaces of creativity and freedom, and to extricate the cultural practices that have made such spaces as well as their political potential from those cultural practices that contribute to the containment, expropriation, and alienation of people's labor, processes which operate everywhere, even in the most politically radical sectors.

To begin, we might examine the notions of culture that are used and invoked in the contemporary context as well as the political significance these notions bear. We might take a critical look at proposals for the incorporation of indigenist or traditional cultural practices in dominant institutions, such as in F. Landa Jocano's *Towards Developing a Filipino Corporate Culture (Uses of Filipino Traditional Structures and Values in Modern Management)*, or the growing body of analyses of "Filipino political culture" and its implications for "democracy," which would include work sponsored by both state and nongovernment agencies (for example, Shahani's Moral Recovery Program and the Philippine Democracy Agenda series put out by the Third World Studies Center). It would be important to place these works in the context of the shifts in political, economic and social orders, such as I have described, to see the role "culture" plays or is expected to play in such projects of nation-building.

In view of the instrumentality with which culture is both understood and deployed in many of these largely hegemonic projects, it would also be useful to examine its invocation and use in more critical or counter-hegemonic projects, such as recent efforts to assess the historical legacy of US colonialism (for example Sangandaan conference) and, in general, the varied streams of contemporary Philippine cultural criticism (for example, the works of Alice and Gelacio Guillermo, Edel Garcellano, E. San Juan Jr., Bienvenido Lumbera, Nick Tiongson, as well as those of younger critics, Caroline Hau, Roland Tolentino, Flaudette May Datuin, and others). A closer examination and reassessment of these critical projects and their political implications for cultural intervention in the current situation will, I believe, help us come up with conceptual frameworks for viewing culture and history that can, at the same time, serve as crucial components of struggle against the looming threat and actual reality of global fascism and its pernicious rule of war.

I have tried to briefly describe and demonstrate above some aspects of such a framework. My own engagement with feminist and women's work has led me to view cultural practice through the notion of invisible labor and its vital role in producing and shaping the broader social order and its system of economic wealth. Hidden in the banality of naturalized subjective capacities, such invisible yet vital labor can help us understand the historical materiality and political potential of cultural practice. Moreover, insofar as it deals with precisely banal and mundane experiences of daily living, which are given form in cultural objects, cultural studies can find the words, images, and affects to recognize and articulate invisible practices of cultural labor, the political potential of which we might better deploy. Specific questions for a cultural studies that takes up the challenges posed by the current crisis might include:

What are the cultural resources and practical philosophies of everyday struggle, which the current global war on terror is an extensive effort to recontain and defeat? As I have already suggested, we need to view both neoliberalist "globalization" and the emergent security state system as complex efforts to coopt, capitalize upon, and undo the gains of the long, cultural revolution of the last three and a half decades. Moreover, we need to locate those practices of cultural transformation that have not been subsumed by these counterrevolutionary efforts.

How can we provide a specific vocabulary and syntax for those cultural resources and practical philosophies that at once differentiate Filipino social formations from and put them in relation with other peoples in struggle (for example, Afghanis, Iraqis, Palestinians—a geopolitical context that the Philippines has been ideologically and politically separated from, even if economically connected to for the last few decades)? This is not only a matter of highlighting common structural features (for example, the similarity between US suppression of Iraqi "insurgents" today and US suppression of Philippine "insurgents" a century ago) but, more importantly, of foregrounding and bolstering real living relations and their historical precedents. Françoise Verges has written about the historical world of Afro-Asian exchanges and political solidarity that took place via routes across the Indian Ocean, in particular the South-South connections of Third World decolonization.[14] While noting current tendencies to reconstruct African-Asian connections either under the sign of the market or in the hierarchical mode of civilizationist pursuit, creating new layers of inequalities, Verges remains attentive to the ways that both formal policies and informal practices of Afro-Asian exchange create unforeseen consequences. As she writes:

> The decentering of Europe and the reconstruction of African-Asian links open new possibilities for the revision of former politics of solidarity, the circulation of narratives of resistance, alternative forms of hybridization, and creation of new politics of solidarity among the urban poor, peasants, artists, and scholars. The connections between the urban poor, peasants, artists, and scholars. The connections between the urban poor in Bombay

and Cape Town, between trade unions in Madagascar and Malaysia, between musicians in Mauritius and South Africa bespeak these emergent formations.[15]

We would, I believe, do well to similarly explore the real, living connections and cultural exchanges between Filipino communities and other communities across the vast Asian continent, including Islamic and non-Islamic communities of Southeast, Central, and West Asia. This would mean an attention not only to relations of cooperation among communities but to relations of contradiction as well.

This last point leads us to consider what kind of social and cultural geography of resistance and struggle we want to help make through scholarly as well as activist writing. In exploring connections that defy the geopolitical map drawn by the current global imperialist project, we contribute to the creation of alternative political imaginations.

It goes without saying that the creation of alternative political imaginations can only be a collective accomplishment. It remains to be said, however, that the transformative potential of cultural work lies not simply in organizing people according to preconceived notions of political action and strategy, where "culture" serves as the mere means of this mobilization and organization. It lies rather in bringing cultural practice to bear on our actionable understanding of the logics underwriting and undermining the prevailing social order, that is, of bringing culture to bear on politics (instead of only analyzing the politics of culture, as in more conventional forms of ideological critique). Although the instrumental use of culture remains important, just as the practice of "demystification" in unveiling the lies of the Bush, Blair, and Macapagal-Arroyo regimes remains politically useful, we have to view culture as also the very realm of transformation that we might otherwise see as the priority of economic and political action. We must view cultural practice not only as the means of a transformation we would finally seek elsewhere but as part and parcel of that very transformation we hope and strive for, that transformation which would indeed comprise "another world" here and now.

Notes

1. This is a revised talk given on 1 July 2003, at Ateneo de Manila University, not long after the United States launched its so-called war on terror in Iraq in the aftermath of the September 11 attacks.

2. Hannah Arendt, *Imperialism, Part Two of the Origins of Totalitarianism* (San Diego, New York, and London: Harcourt Brace Jovanovich, Publishers, 1968), ix–x.

3. See Giovanni Arrighi, "Tracking Global Turbulence," *New Left Review* 20 (Mar./Apr. 2003): 5–72; and Jose Enrique Africa, "Paper Tiger: U.S. Imperialism's Struggle Against Economic Crisis," in *Unmasking the War on Terror: U.S. Imperialist Hegemony and Crisis* (Philippines: Center for Anti-Imperialist Studies, 2002), 101–80.

4. "Guingona wants gov't to bare immunity pact with U.S." [http://www.inq7.net/brk/2003/jun/17/text/brkpol_15-1-p.htm] As Guingona is correct to point out, this "executive agreement" demonstrates the Philippines' subjection to US domestic law, specifically, the US Homeland Security Act, which greatly expands, by limiting prior legal restrictions on, the powers of the federal government and its agencies. The rule of war means the ruling out of the political participation, or at least its semblance, of the nation-state's public constituency.

5. By "transnational-popular," I allude to Gramsci's notion of "national-popular," which is a construction of the people or the general constituency of the nation against the ruling state(s) (in this case, the ruling transnational inter-state system).

6. As Nick Beams shows, the aggressive, militarist behavior of the new security state under Bush Jr. was already clearly a part of the Clinton administration's foreign policy. In 1993, as "globalization" was underway, Clinton's national security adviser Anthony Lake announced, "We have arrived at neither the end of history nor a clash of civilizations, but a moment of immense democratic and entrepreneurial opportunity. We must not waste it. . . . The successor to a doctrine of containment must be a strategy of enlargement—enlargement of the world's free community of market democracies. . . . [O]nly one overriding factor can determine whether the U.S. should act multilaterally or unilaterally, and that is America's interests. We should act multilaterally where doing so advances our interests—and we should act unilaterally when that will serve our purpose." Quoted in Nick Beams, "The Political Economy of American Militarism: Part 1" [http://www.wsws.org/articles/2003/jul2003/nb1-j10_prn.shtml]

7. Immanuel Wallerstein, "New Revolts Against the System," *New Left Review* 18 (Nov./Dec. 2002): 29–40. For critiques of the normative predications of current invocations of "civil society," see John Beverley, "Civil Society, Hybridity, and the '"Political" Aspect of Cultural Studies' (on Canclini)" in his *Subalternity and Representation: Arguments in Cultural Theory* (Durham, NC, and London: Duke University Press, 1999), 115–32; and Mahmood Mamdani, *Citizen and Subject: Contemporary Africa and the Legacy of Late Colonialism* (Princeton, NJ: Princeton University Press, 1996), which describes the racial exclusion fundamental to the operation

of civil society in postcolonial African nations. In light of the current authority of the concept of civil society deriving in part from its use to account for anti-Soviet movements in Eastern Europe and the Soviet Union in the 1980s, Beverley points out that Gramsci's own criticism of the state and civil society distinction takes up the parent form of neoliberalism, that is, "*laissez-faire* liberalism." "The core idea of laissez-faire liberalism is, Gramsci writes, that 'economic activity belongs to civil society and that the State must not intervene to regulate it.' But the distinction of state and market here is 'merely methodological' rather than 'organic'; 'in actual reality civil society and the State are one and the same,' since '*laissez-faire* too is a form of State "regulation," introduced and maintained by legislation and coercive means.'" Beverley, *Subalternity and Representation*, 118.

8. Here I invoke Samir Amin's notion of the plasticity of religions with regard to particular modes of production and implied notions of progress. Writing against the absolute judgments made about Christianity, Islam, Hinduism, Buddhism, Confucianism, Taoism, and animism, Amin asserts, "In fact, the plasticity of religions and the possibility of adapting them in ways that allow them to justify differing relationships among people invite us to ponder the fact that ideologies formed at one moment in history can subsequently acquire vocations very different from those of their origins." Samir Amin, *Eurocentrism*, trans. Russell Moore (New York: Monthly Review Press, 1989), 84.

9. Leticia Ramos-Shahani, "Politics and Spiritual Values," *The Philippine Star* (June 25, 2003).

10. Alex Magno, "People's War," *The Philippine Star* (June 24, 2003).

11. For a discussion of the historical genealogy and complex political valence of the use of cell phones, particularly in People Power 2, see Vicente L. Rafael, "The Cell Phone and the Crowd: Messianic Politics in Recent Philippine History" [http://communication.ucsd.edu/people/f_rafael.cellphone.html].

12. "New Pentagon Plan Bets on Future Terror," *San Jose Mercury News* (July 29, 2003). I thank Jonathan Beller for calling my attention to this news report and its implications.

13. I have argued elsewhere about informal practices of economic survival, including low-level practices of "graft and corruption," in these terms. See "Petty Adventures in (the) Capital" in my book, *Things Fall Away: Philippine Historical Experience and Subaltern Makings of Globalization* (Durham: Duke University Press, 2009).

14. Françoise Verges, "Writing on Water: Peripheries, Flows, Capital, and Struggles in the Indian Ocean," *positions: east asia cultures critique* 11.1 (2003): 241–57.

15. Verges, "Writing on Water," 253.

Works Cited

Africa, Jose Enrique. "Paper Tiger: U.S. Imperialism's Struggle Against Economic Crisis." In *Unmasking the War on Terror: U.S. Imperialist Hegemony and Crisis,* 101–80. Philippines: Center for Anti-Imperialist Studies, 2002. Print.

Amin, Samir. *Eurocentrism.* Trans. Russell Moore. New York: Monthly Review Press, 1989. Print.

Arendt, Hannah. *Imperialism, Part Two of the Origins of Totalitarianism.* San Diego, New York, and London: Harcourt Brace Jovanovich, Publishers, 1968. Print.

Arrighi, Giovanni. "Tracking Global Turbulence." *New Left Review* 20 (2003): 5–72. Print.

Beams, Nick. "The Political Economy of American Militarism: Part 1." http://www.wsws.org/articles/2003/jul2003/nb1-j10_prn.shtml

Beverley, John. "Civil Society, Hybridity." In *Subalternity and Representation: Arguments in Cultural Theory,* 115–32. Durham, NC, and London: Duke University Press, 1999. Print.

———. "'Political' Aspect of Cultural Studies' (on Canclini)." In *Subalternity and Representation: Arguments in Cultural Theory,* 115–32. Durham, NC, and London: Duke University Press, 1999. Print.

Gramsci, Antonio. *Further Selections from the Prison Notebooks,* Minneapolis: University of Minnesota Press, 1995. Print.

"Guingona wants gov't to bare immunity pact with U.S." http://www.inq7.net/brk/2003/jun/17/text/brkpol_15-1-p.htm.

Magno, Alex. "People's War." *The Philippine Star,* June 25, 2003. Online. June 28, 2003.

Mamdani, Mahmood. *Citizen and Subject: Contemporary Africa and the Legacy of Late Colonialism.* Princeton, NJ: Princeton University Press, 1996. Print.

"New Pentagon Plan Bets on Future Terror." *San Jose Mercury News,* July 29, 2003. Online. Accessed on December 30, 2003.

Rafael, Vicente L. "The Cell Phone and the Crowd: Messianic Politics in Recent Philippine History." *Public Culture* 15:3 (2003): 399–425. Print.

Ramos-Shahani, Leticia. "Politics and Spiritual Values." *The Philippine Star,* June 25, 2003. Online. June 28, 2003.

Tadiar, Neferti. "Petty Adventures in (the) Capital." In *Things Fall Away: Philippine Historical Experience and Subaltern Makings of Globalization.* Durham, NC: Duke University Press, 2009. Print.

Verges, Françoise. "Writing on Water: Peripheries, Flows, Capital, and Struggles in the Indian Ocean." *positions: east asia cultures critique* 11.1 (2003): 241–57. Print.

Wallerstein, Immanuel. "New Revolts Against the System." *New Left Review* 18 (2002): 29–40. Print.

2

Toward a Critical Filipino Studies Approach to Philippine Migration

ROBYN MAGALIT RODRIGUEZ

After more than a century of emigration from the Philippines and settlement in the United States, the US Filipino population continues to be largely foreign born. Indeed, during different periods of time over the last decade, Filipinos were the largest im/migrant group in the United States, second only to Mexicans. According to the 2010 Census, Filipinos are the second-largest Asian group after the Chinese.[1] At the same time, the Philippines is one of the top migrant-sending countries in the world. As of 2012, nearly 4,500 Filipinos boarded airplanes to work far from home on a daily basis.[2]

This chapter outlines a Critical Filipino Studies approach to understanding processes of contemporary Philippine e/migration. My use of the term(s) e/migration, as opposed to immigration, is purposeful. A focus on e/migration processes shifts analysis away from the United States's Immigration Act of 1965. This Act dominates both scholarly and popular accounts in explaining contemporary migration from the Philippines to this country. However, to attribute the ever-growing presence of Filipinos in the United States through the Immigration Act of 1965, I would argue, has the effect of reifying US nationalist ideologies of liberal multiculturalism and the idea of the United States as a "country of immigrants," not one of empire. A Critical Filipino Studies approach to Philippine migration to the United States, however, is one that is attentive to the legacies of US imperialism, especially neocolonial state formation on processes of e/migration.

I argue that the neocolonial Philippine state, what I call elsewhere, a "labor brokerage" state, plays a crucial role in producing Filipino labor for the United States today.[3] Analyzing contemporary Philippine e/migration through the lens of the Philippine labor brokerage state, more-over, exposes how the globalization of Filipino workers as short-term, contract workers is directly tied to the neocolonial relationship between the Philippine state and the United States. Filipinos not only labor in the territorial United States, but also for both transnational US firms and the US military around the world. US capital even manipulates (former) US colonial borders to better exploit workers from the Philippines. By outlining an analysis that centers the Philippine state in understanding contemporary Filipino community formation in the United States and beyond, I build on radical traditions in Filipino Studies.

Furthermore, by attending to the ways that the Philippine labor bro-kerage state plays a role in the formation of the US Filipino community, the new sets of struggles Filipino im/migrant workers face in the con-temporary period become more visible. Recently arrived im/migrants from the Philippines in the United States, many of whom are profession-ally trained, might appear to be more privileged than their early twenti-eth-century counterparts. Yet as a labor brokerage state, the Philippines engages in what amounts to nothing less than legal human trafficking. The im/migrants who come to come to the United States, though in many cases highly educated, face new and more complex forms of ex-ploitation. As US immigration policy has become increasingly more restrictive, on the one hand, and the family reunification backlog per-sists, on the other, Filipinos desperate to find employment in the United States and/or anxious to rejoin their relatives are preyed on by private labor recruiters, in collusion with US employers and ultimately sanc-tioned by the Philippine labor brokerage state, who are trafficked into low-wage work and often rendered undocumented.

The Historiography of Filipino (Im)migration

Much of the scholarship on the history of Filipino-US immigration has characterized it, either explicitly or implicitly, as being defined by "waves."[4] Though sometimes the demarcations for the beginnings and ends of particular waves differ, generally speaking there have been three waves identified in the literature: the colonial period from the turn of the twentieth century to just before World War II; post World War II; and 1965 to the present. The flows and ebbs of these "waves" as understood in the scholarship as linked primarily to shifts in US immigration law tied to racialized labor demand.

Beginning during the American colonial period, the "first wave" of Filipino immigration to the United States is explained by most scholars as linked to the United States's occupation of the Philippines and violent subjugation of the Filipino people after it wrested the Philippines away from Spain in 1898. Many scholars agree that the economic, political, and social conditions in the colonial Philippines and the active recruitment of Filipinos to fill new forms of racialized labor demand in the United States and its territories provide the historical and structural context for early Filipino "immigration."[5] Indeed, the recruitment of Filipinos was a response to immigration restrictions on previous sources of labor, namely, the Chinese and the Japanese. As "wards" of the United States, Filipinos could more facilely be brought into the country as compared to other foreign workers.

Beyond the demand for cheap labor in agriculture, the political and military exigencies of the colonial state structured the outflow of Filipino "immigrants." The colonial project of "Benevolent Assimilation" with its expansion of general public education and the US training of would-be colonial bureaucrats (for example the *pensionados*), as well as the expansion of public health and the necessary training, also in the United States, of health personnel would form pools of prospective and unintentional "immigrants." Moreover, education produced a kind of "culture of migration" among many Filipinos.[6] Finally, Filipinos' colonial subject-status as "nationals" enabled their relatively smooth entry into the United States in any capacity, whether as a worker or student.

The end of World War II marks the "second wave" of Filipino immigration to the United States in the literature. To characterize this period as a "wave" belies the new forms of restriction imposed by the United States limiting the immigration of Filipinos. Nevertheless, what marks this period are the restrictions placed on immigration from the Philippines. Restrictions on Filipino immigration to the United States occurred alongside the Philippines' "independence." Indeed, these were seen as complementary measures when the 1934 Tydings-McDuffie Act was introduced. Significantly, the moment Filipinos were constituted as Filipino citizens in the Philippines and no longer American colonial subjects, they were simultaneously constituted as aliens in the United

States. In other words, Philippine nation-state formation and citizenship was predicated on Filipinos' exclusion from and inassimilability in the United States. Filipino immigration during this period, limited to a mere fifty per year, was comprised of primarily Filipino World War II veterans and their families as well as the war-brides of American soldiers who served in the Pacific theater. The Philippines' "special" military relationship to the US military allowed Filipinos to evade immigration restrictions.[7]

The third "wave" of Filipino immigration to the United States is marked by the introduction of new immigration legislation in 1965, which dropped national origins quotas, offered family reunification as a mode of entry into the United States, and favored the immigration of skilled professionals. This third wave of Filipinos is cited as being especially important in the formation of contemporary US Filipino communities. Scholars have found, for instance, that in the immediate period after the enactment of the 1965 Immigration Act, a majority of Filipinos entered the United States as professionals and other highly trained individuals and that they eventually settled in areas outside of the California and Hawaii, regions typically the home for Filipino immigrants in earlier decades. Over time, however, these same immigrants have come to use family unification preferences to help facilitate the immigration of relatives from the Philippines.[8] Indeed, this latter form of immigration can even be considered the fourth "wave."

The temporalization of pre-1965 Filipino immigration in "waves" is important because, at least from a Critical Filipino or what Campomanes might call a "radical epistemological" perspective, it highlights the way US imperialism and the colonization of the Philippines distinguishes the movement of Filipinos to United States and their racialization from other Asian groups. In an essay in *positions* entitled, "New Formations of Asian American Studies and the Question of U.S. Imperialism,"[9] Oscar Campomanes calls on Asian Americanists to resist both "contributionism" and "domestication" in their scholarship of Asian immigration, a rejection of both forms the basis of a radical epistemology. Contributionism, according to Campomanes, "effectively valorizes the United States as the supreme nation of immigrants." To domesticate Asian American studies meanwhile is to fail to adequately square with US imperialism in contemporary diasporic formations. Philippine migration to the United States, according to scholars like Campomanes, is an especially important site for disturbing dominant narratives of immigration as the migrations of Filipino and Filipina laborers at the turn of the twentieth century was a direct consequence of the United States's colonization of the Philippines in 1898.

Yet, examinations of Philippine im/migrant community formation after 1965, often suspend an analysis of the legacies of empire such as underdevelopment or neocolonial state formation in the Philippines. The scholarship often takes for granted that 1965 was a watershed year in Philippine (and other Asian) immigration. Responding to domestic demands for civil rights by racialized minorities as well as to international pressures within the context of the Cold War to exhibit truly democratic ideals, it was in the field of immigration policy that the United States sought to remake itself and live up to its self-proclaimed status of being a "nation of immigrants" by eliminating all forms of racist immigration legislation. This sort of understanding of Philippine im/migration after 1965, however, tends toward the "domestication" that Campomanes warns us against.

Moreover, because post-1965 im/migration from the Philippines has a fundamentally different character from earlier waves (characterized by highly educated, professional rather than low-skilled, low-status workers), more recent im/migrants from the Philippines may be analyzed as (and may think themselves as) having had more agency and choice in e/migrating than their predecessors. In this way, conventional understandings of Filipino im/migration can fall into the trap of "contributionism" that Campomanes fears.

What is less analyzed in post-1965 Filipino im/migration scholarship is the lasting legacy of colonization for Philippine nation-state formation after "independence," the underdevelopment that has resulted as a consequence of neocolonialism and the active role the neocolonial state would eventually play in both promoting and facilitating out-migration. The demarcation of latter twentieth-century im/migration from the Philippines as "post-1965" is therefore problematic because it fails to recognize that not long after the United States introduced the 1965 Immigration Act, the Philippine government institutionalized the export of labor in 1974 as a developmental intervention.[10] The institutionalization of labor export, which marks the Philippines' emergence as a "labor brokerage" state is linked to neocolonial state formation and the underdevelopment the elites at the helm of the Philippine state have actively facilitated.

The neocolonial state allied itself with US imperialist interests in ways that would ultimately give rise to labor brokerage. First, the newly "independent" Philippine state closely complied with the dictates of multilateral institutions like the World Bank and the International Monetary Fund (IMF) adopting developmental initiatives that favored export-oriented industrialization through major influxes of foreign (often US) capital both in the form of investments and loans. Borrowing heavily from the World Bank and the IMF, the Philippines was subject to conditionalities, so-called structural adjustment, which often required the diversion of national funds away from public services (including education and health) to loan repayment. Additionally, structural adjustment required the liberalization of trade, labor contractualization, and other policies that were aimed at making the Philippines more attractive to foreign investors. Structural adjustment, perhaps not surprisingly, elicited much resistance from the Filipino people. In the early 1970s, the Philippine state's resolution to controlling this resistance was through the imposition of Martial Law in 1972. Another resolution instituted shortly after the declaration of Martial Law was the introduction of the labor export policy or Presidential Decree P.D. 442 in 1974.

Building on earlier structures established during the colonial period (the Philippines' culture of migration, American colonial education as well as the Philippines' close economic, political, and military ties to the United States), the labor export program was expected to generate much-needed foreign exchange to service the government's growing debts. At the same time, it was hoped that the active promotion of overseas employment would alleviate the social pressures that were feeding oppositional movements. US imperial legacies, specifically the institutionalization and normalization of labor migration under the US colonial state, on the one hand, and neocolonial socioeconomic conditions after colonialism, on the other, made labor export both necessary and practicable as a developmental intervention in the Philippines by 1974. US colonialism's impacts on Filipino (im)migrations are not limited to formal colonialism but extend to neocolonial Philippine state formation.

The labor export policy gave rise to a vast transnational labor brokerage apparatus through which the state mobilizes Filipino migrant labor for export. The state's consular offices abroad facilitate the distribution of Filipino migrants as Philippine labor attaches actively market Filipino migrants abroad through conventional advertising techniques and through diplomacy. Then, through what is literally a kind of bureaucratic assembly line based in the Philippines, the state trains and "officializes" migrants, that is, it provides migrants with the necessary skills and documentation for immediate employment overseas.

Through the labor brokerage apparatus, the Philippine state produces e/migration from the Philippines to the territorial to the United States and to key sites (countries) vital to US global capital and empire. While US immigration law might have changed in 1965, what has not changed is US capital's demand for racialized, Philippine labor. Now footloose, US capital need no longer be encumbered by the thorny issues of restriction and exclusion that characterizes US nativist immigration politics past and present; it can instead depend on a long-reliable source of labor, the Philippines, which can (unlike before) be easily secured and at the same time easily rendered back to its home country. US capital has globalized; so too have Filipino workers. The globalization of Filipinos is, furthermore, specifically tied to the US military as it operates around the world. Moreover, as the American empire, the military-industrial complex, along with globalizing US capital spread across the world, Filipino labor, as a preferred and accessible pool of labor, has followed suit by finding its way to the territorial United States as well as to the US empire's reach globally.

In this moment of neoliberal globalization, the Philippines is all the more dependent on labor export to reproduce the social order. The state can promise jobs overseas as it imposes "flexible" work regimes at home. As remittance money flows into the Philippines to support and sustain Filipino families and communities, the state can reduce its expenditures for social goods. In effect, through labor brokerage, the state can mask the displacements and inequalities that are endemic to neoliberalism. The Philippines has developed a transnational migration apparatus, which serves as a veritable export-processing zone to facilitate the outmigration of workers. What I call labor brokerage is an economic strategy by the neoliberal Philippine state through which it draws from its overseas' citizens earnings abroad to pay for its exorbitant debts. It is, moreover, a political strategy through which it aims to absorb growing discontent among its citizens at home. Filipino families can draw from a source of income, albeit abroad, from which they can pay for education and health care, public services that the state is increasingly privatizing. There is a way that the historiography characterizes Filipino immigration pre-1965 as more conscripted and coerced because of the US colonial labor system than post-1965 e/migration, yet given the conditions wrought by neoliberal globalization that make it nearly impossible for many Filipinos to have secure livelihoods at home belies the notion that post-1965 is more voluntaristic than early e/migrations.

The contemporary im/migration of Filipinos to the United States as well as the migration of Filipinos as contractual workers beyond the United States must be linked to legacies of US imperialism. It is the neocolonial labor brokerage state that facilitates both processes. My work complicates mainstream understandings of im/migration and how migrants labor for the United States, as I suggest that Filipinos labor for empire both within its territorial boundaries and the globalized spaces it occupies through the intervention of the neocolonial state. What I contribute is an attention to specific sets of neocolonial state practices that allow us to better understand these linkages. I examine the collusions between the Philippine and US state officials as their particular interests in foreign aid, military expansion, cheap labor, or access to labor markets coincide.

Methods

The research I discuss here is based on nearly fifteen years of transnational research. My work included participant-observation or ethnography along the Philippines' transnational migration apparatus, which includes a number of offices in the Philippines as well as the Philippines' consular or embassy offices overseas. In addition to ethnographic work, I conducted in-depth interviews of migration officials. These officials ranged from lower-ranked program administrators to top-ranked bureau heads. During the course of my research, I was also able to secure internal as well as publicly available government documents. In addition to examining the state, I conducted in-depth interviews with prospective migrants in different stages of the migration process including those considering migration for the first time, migrants being redeployed for overseas work, as well as return migrants.

Alongside nearly fifteen years of research, the issues discussed here draw from my even longer history as a Filipino im/migrant rights advocate. I turn now to a discussion of the mechanisms by which workers from the Philippines are actively mobilized by the Philippine state to labor in the United States and globally and how Filipino migrants' globality is connected with US imperialism.

The Labor of Empire

When the United States declared its global "war on terror" during the administration of George W. Bush, Philippine president Gloria Macapagal Arroyo was among the first heads of state in Asia to pledge membership to the "coalition of the willing." In addition to expressing a willingness to host US troops in the Philippines for joint military exercises, the Philippine government exhibited a willingness to deploy Filipino migrant workers to assist in US militarization and occupation efforts. Shortly after President Arroyo's visit to the United States, the Philippines' main migration agency, the Philippines Overseas Employment Administration began posting public announcements about the availability of ten to fifteen thousand jobs in the Middle East "due to the presence of U.S. forces" (Rodriguez 2010).

The globalization of Filipino labor is crucially linked to the globalization of US empire as well as US capital. The Philippine state plays an active role in facilitating the placement of Filipino workers in the various sites where the US military and firms are located around the world.

Philippine state officials use both formal and informal diplomatic relations as part of its labor brokerage work. In President Arroyo's case, a formal diplomatic mission to the United States aimed at publicly affirming the Philippines' commitment to the global war on terror and therefore securing military aid also became a marketing mission to prospective employers of Filipino workers. Though the Philippines has now banned Filipino migration to Iraq, the fact that Filipino workers were successfully deployed to that country and its neighbors for US military forces in the region after a successful marketing campaign by the Arroyo administration illustrates how the Philippines' neocolonial status vis-à-vis the United States continues to shape processes of Filipino e/migration.

The scholarship on Philippine im/migration to the United States documents how joining the US military has been an important strategy by which Filipinos enter the United States. Their ability to do so was directly connected to highly unequal bilateral agreements penned between the United States and the putatively "independent" Philippines in 1946. The legacies of colonialism, however, run deeper than these agreements as they also shape the orientation of the Philippines' migration program. Filipino laborers today can be flexibly and comprehensively employed to provide for the US military's various needs without actually immigrating and settling in the United States. This indicates a major shift in the ways Filipinos labor for the US military, a shift that is facilitated by the Philippine government.

My research, furthermore, suggests, Filipinos' global dispersal is significantly linked to negotiations between the Philippines and US firms. One high-ranking migration official in the International Labor Affairs Service recounted that he was part of a "marketing mission" to the United States with major construction contractors who had operations in the Middle East in the early 1970s when the labor export policy was first institutionalized. He describes how "instead of dealing with these companies' Middle Eastern middlemen, we went straight to the head offices to get a head start over other bidders of foreign labor." Clearly, this marketing work has had an impact on out-migration to Saudi Arabia as it continues to be among the top-ten destination countries for Filipino workers. Moreover, this interview reveals how Filipinos' employment in Saudi Arabia is ultimately linked to the expansion of US firms. This highlights the deep linkages between the neocolonial labor brokerage state, the globalization of US capital, and the formation of the contemporary Philippine labor diaspora.

If US capital globalizes production to maximize profits, Filipino workers, in some cases, are the preferred laborers from whom to extract profits. In the garments industry, for instance, many Filipinos work in foreign countries producing clothing for US markets. Through field research in Brunei, I learned that a significant number of Filipinos labor in the country's garment factories. In the factories I examined, Filipino migrants produced garments mainly for US-based retailers like the Gap and Old Navy. According to a Brunei-based labor recruiter who had worked throughout Southeast Asia supplying garments factories with low-wage workers, "When [a clothing tag] says 'Made in Brunei,' or 'Made in Indonesia,' it should really say, 'Made by Filipinos.'"

US capital, however, need not go too far to set up shop. Garments manufacturers have located to sites within the territorial jurisdiction of the United States, yet they are virtually exempt from US labor and immigration laws. These sites include places like Saipan in the Commonwealth of the Northern Marianas Islands (CNMI). The CNMI has long instituted a guest worker program; indeed, the foreign worker population there outnumbers the native (local) population. A majority of these workers are Filipinos. Many have lived in the CNMI for many years but are ineligible for the rights of US citizenship, a right that is reserved for CNMI natives. Indeed, even the goods produced in the CNMI can claim "Americanness" as all goods produced there can legitimately carry the label, "Made in the U.S.A." Perhaps not surprisingly, many migrant workers are employed in the garments industry.[11]

As short-term, foreign contractual workers in places like Brunei, Filipinos are a cheap labor force subject to exploitation. Indeed, I decided to do research in Brunei when Filipino garments and textiles workers went on a wildcat strike to demand higher wages, back wages for unpaid overtime, and safer working conditions. Meanwhile, Filipinos can be lured to work in places like Saipan with promises of jobs in "America" where they labor under similar conditions. In 1999, a mainstream media exposé revealed that Filipina migrants labor in garments factories there suffered extreme forms of abuse. American borders, here, are manipulated for US profits. The logics that have always informed the United States's unincorporated (colonial) territories are still operable here as they are characterized by "suspended undecidability: U.S. and not-U.S.; foreign and domestic."[12]

Labor brokerage is not merely about the export of workers, but indeed on the state-to-state relations on which they depend. Seemingly paradoxically, labor brokerage also means the facilitation of the repatriation or deportation of Filipino workers when they are economically redundant to foreign employers or politically contentious for host states.

In the wake of the wildcat strike of Filipino and Filipina garments workers employed in Brunei-based factories producing clothing for US markets, for instance, Philippine embassy officials, including the vice president of the Philippines, instructed workers to go back to work.

Many refused and continued to press the Philippine government to help them secure better terms of employment for workers. Government officials, however, ultimately encouraged migrants to accept the employer's counteroffer. When workers declined it, embassy officials mobilized government funds to "repatriate" workers back to the Philippines because the Philippine state is invested in sustaining diplomatic relations with the Brunei government in order to continue exporting workers to this lucrative labor market. Workers' demands are secondary to the requirements of a labor brokerage state.

The Philippine State and E/migration to the United States

The US Filipino population can be understood as linked to the Philippines' labor brokerage program. This is perhaps most clear in the H1B visa program. The H1B program is a work authorization visa for non-immigrant professionals in the United States. As of 2010, the Philippines was among the top-five countries supplying workers to the United States through the H1-B visa program. The Philippines brokers labor by directly marketing Filipino workers to firms hiring temporary labor in the United States. It also brokers labor by providing the employment-related training that would qualify e/migration from the Philippines for H1B visas.

I learned from interviews of Philippine migration officials in the early 2000s that former president Joseph Estrada along with other government representatives had made efforts to promote Filipino workers in Silicon Valley during a state visit to the United States. An official of the Philippine Overseas Employment Administration's Marketing Branch, she stated, "There we met directly with employers. Because this industry hires temporary workers, it is a market for Filipino workers. Unlike the Canadian IT industry which favors immigrants, there is no prospective market there." This quote demonstrates that Philippine state officials do not merely supply temporary, contractual workers to the United States's globalized military complex or US global capital operating outside of the country, but they supply temporary, contractual workers directly to firms within the United States.

Alongside a transnational labor marketing apparatus, which actually includes the Philippines' head of state, is the Philippines' migration assembly line. In the Philippines, prospective migrants are swiftly processed through several migration bureaucracies where they receive whatever training they may be required to complete by their employers or host countries prior to leaving for overseas jobs. Moreover, it is on the assembly line where their passports and employment visas are secured. From migrants' perspectives, training becomes an opportunity to secure a much-valorized US visa.

Chiari, a practicing dentist, and her husband Lorenzo, who ran a small carwash from their home, decided to get training and certification as caregivers in order to secure an employment visa from a relative who owned a home-care business in California. The US embassy denied Chiari and Lorenzo's tourist visa applications two times. Though I did not discuss it with Chiari and Lorenzo, it seemed that they ultimately planned to overstay their temporary visas and live and work illegally in the United States once they arrived. Chiari described how difficult the interview process was: "They ask you a lot of questions but you can't explain your answers in Tagalog, only English. I don't think we gave good answers when we were interviewed [for the tourist visa]. We hope this will be a good avenue for migration because my uncle handled our H1B visa papers since we're going to work for him." Chiari believed that after completing the caregiver-training course and receiving official certification, she and her husband might be more successful in getting their US visas: "At least when we are finished with this course we will get a certificate. When they interrogate us at [US] immigration, we can prove to them that we're really interested in working there. We can't fake it because we'll have the certificate." She noted, "We could never go to the US embassy without the certificate proving that we have graduated. They get so suspicious." Lorenzo joked, "You can actually buy a [fake] certificate. But if they ask you at the embassy if you understand this course that you finished, then it's good to complete it anyway."

Chiari and Lorenzo's experience not only points to the importance of officialized training in securing US visas, it also points to the complex ways Filipinos use family networks to manipulate immigration legislation. Chiari's uncle serves not as a "family sponsor" under 1965 immigration law, which most scholarship attributes to the growth of the Filipino population in the United States, but as an "employer sponsor."

A US visa (regardless of the visa type) can almost guarantee a prospective migrant a job in any other part of the world. A. J., a private English tutor in South Korea, believes that her previous travel experience to the United States, facilitated by her father, formerly employed as a construction worker in Saudi Arabia, helped her when she first decided to work abroad. In fact, an examination of visa application requirements to South Korea in the Philippines reveals that A.J. may have been right. The South Korean embassy in the Philippines exempts "holders of valid visas to the U.S.A., Canada, Japan, Australia, and New Zealand" from applying in person perhaps making it easier for prospective migrants to secure work in that country.

Peter's case also illustrates how a US visa can help prospective migrant to secure employment in third countries. Hired to work as a manager for a US-based restaurant chain, Peter was sent to training at the chain's Los Angeles headquarters. He was laid-off, but eventually he got employment at another US-based chain. Though he was laid-off again, Peter believed that his experiences in the United States would help him migrate to a different country for employment.

> Since I went to the United States for training and I came back to the Philippines when it ended, I think I can prove to other countries that I can be a responsible worker; that I'm not going to overstay my visa. When I was in the States, [my relative] joked that I should just [overstay my visa] because there are a lot of Filipinos who do that, but I couldn't. If I [overstayed my visa] I would be separated from my family for too long. Anyway, at least I can apply for a visa somewhere else. Also, since I worked for US companies, I can prove that I have good skills.

For Peter, both travel to the United States and work experience at major US multinational restaurant and café chains provides him with the potential to successfully apply for work visas in other countries.

Beyond directly (and indirectly) facilitating e/migration through bilateral or diplomatic relations, and the bureaucratic assembly line, the Philippine state facilitates e/migration by promoting the private labor recruitment industry. Indeed, the private labor recruitment industry cannot thrive without some kind of assistance from governments. If labor-importing states do not offer visas for foreign workers, labor recruiters have no market. Yet, at the same time, if labor-sending states do not also forge relationships with labor-importing states, visas are less likely to be offered to their citizens. Again, labor recruiters lose out. However, Philippine-based labor recruitment agencies (or those recruitment agencies who specialize in the overseas placements of Filipino workers) profit from the Philippine states' labor brokerage strategy. That Filipinos constitute one of the top-groups with H1B visas, I would argue, is directly linked to the Philippine government's labor export program.

There is more and more evidence that private labor-recruitment agencies, both Philippine and US-based, are playing a crucial role in mobilizing Filipino migrant workers through the H1B visa program. The Baltimore public schools system, for instance, imported Filipino teachers with the assistance of private labor recruiters after learning of successful cases of Philippine labor recruitment by the states of California and Louisiana among others.[13]

Finally, one way the Philippine state facilitates e/migration to the United States is by representing it as "natural" result of US-Philippine relations. In an account of the history of Philippine migration by the Philippine Overseas Employment Administration, it reads "in the 1900s when Hawaii experienced severe manpower shortage. Two hundred Filipinos initially went there and followed by more until they formed about 70% of Hawaii's plantation labor." It further describes how "then Filipinos became in demand in California as apple and orange pickers and gained a reputation as fruit pickers, prompting plantation owners to increase incentive for manpower recruitment."[14] Early Philippine labor migration to the United States is characterized as voluntary; Filipinos, "went there" the POEA explains, not that they were practically conscripted as colonial-subjects to work in the United States (and its territories). The by-now well-documented experiences of abuse and exploitation suffered by Filipino *manongs* as stoop laborers in California is elided and the state represents it as a sort of asset; Filipinos "gained a reputation." Furthermore, the term "manpower," a term the labor brokerage state uses to describe Philippine migrant labor today is used in the POEA's characterization of early Philippine migration historically as if the contemporary labor export system is continuous with the colonial one (indeed, in many ways it is).

Similarly, in 2006, a Filipino American Contribution Resolution passed by the Philippine Congress stating:

> Whereas the United States and the Philippines have enjoyed a long and productive relationship, including the period of United States governance between 1898 and 1946, and the period post-independence starting in 1946, during which the Philippines has taken its place among the community of nations and has been one of our country's most loyal and reliable allies internationally [. . .]
>
> Whereas the story of America's Filipino-American community is little known and rarely told, yet is the quintessential immigrant story of early struggle, pain, sacrifice, and broken dreams, leading eventually to success in overcoming ethnic, social, economic, political, and legal barriers to win a well-deserved place in American society.[15]

This resolution captures in stark ways how the labor brokerage state participates in rendering legacies of imperialism, colonialism, and neo-colonialism in the formation of the Filipino diaspora invisible in favor of celebrating, commemorating, and normalizing Filipinos' "well-deserved place in American society." Yet what exactly is Filipino e/migrants' place in American society?

New Forms of Exploitation

The system of labor brokerage has led to new forms of exploitation suffered by US Filipinos. This has become more apparent very recently as Filipinos seeking to come to the United States have become more reliant on this system to get here. Though after the 1960s and 1970s, many Filipinos came to the United States on family-reunification visas, these visas have taken much longer to secure. Filipinos are experiencing a tremendously long waiting period as certain family members are prioritized over others. As a consequence of this visa backlog, Filipinos are pursuing other visa categories, including the H1B to come to the United States. I would suggest that it is because the H1B holds out the promise, though not the guarantee, of legal permanent residence (that is, the acquisition of a green card), prospective e/migrants are lured into seeking the assistance of private labor recruitment agencies to e/migrate.[16] The involvement of private labor recruitment agencies in the deployment of Filipino migrants to the United States, however, has led to widespread exploitation, abuse, and "virtual servitude".[17]

Filipino im/migrant rights advocate, the National Alliance for Filipino Concerns (NAFCON), documents numerous cases of illegal labor trafficking of health-care workers and teachers through the H1B program. It finds that labor recruiters charge migrants exorbitant fees for their services, which are supposed to include the securing of visas, jobs, and residences. Meanwhile, recruiters dupe migrants about the sorts of jobs they will be employed in and/or the wages they will be earning and then house migrants in substandard residences. What is striking is that many of the workers suffering abuse are professional workers quite unlike their low-skilled counterparts who came to work in the United States in earlier "waves."

In 2007, ten Filipino nurses sat in a New York State courtroom, indicted on criminal charges for patient endangerment because they had walked off their jobs, along with seventeen other nurses, to protest low wages and bad working conditions. "We were brought to the staff house where we were stay for two months for free and save money we need when we move to an apartment. . . . I shared the room with other Filipino nurses. We took turns sleeping on the bed and on the floor. It wasn't comfortable, but I didn't complain," said James Millena, a nurse-turned-doctor. He also revealed that he was assigned to handle one hundred patients by himself throughout his shift. It was for ultimately "complaining" by walking off the job and filing suit against the private recruitment agency that facilitated his employment in the United States that James and others found themselves countersued by the facility where they worked.[18] In another case, forty physical and occupational therapists hired through the H1B visa program by a health-care staff agency in Florida to work in fifteen different states were found by the US Department of Labor to be owed back wages.[19]

Teachers recruited to work in Louisiana were forced to pay $16,000 for placement fees before leaving the Philippines and were required to sign over 10 percent of their monthly salaries for two years to pay for the housing provided by their agency. If they were unable to pay the placement fees, they were directed to loan companies that charged them exorbitant interest rates. Those who complained about these debt obligations were threatened with deportation.[20]

In the case of the teachers brought to work for the Baltimore schools, their wages were garnished to pay for the processing of their H1B visas.

Though the Department of Labor demanded that the school district pay the teachers back wages for their illegal deduction of migrants' salaries and barred the district from further hiring under the H1B program, it ultimately rendered the migrants undocumented by terminating the teachers' employment with the district. Since H1B visas are employer-based, teachers without jobs were therefore no longer eligible for visas.

Besides the H1B visa, another visa category through which migrants from the Philippines secure employment in the United States is the H2B. Unlike the H1B, which brings in professional workers on a temporary visa and offers the possibility of legal permanent residence if migrants' employers petition them, the H2B program is one that brings in seasonal, nonagricultural workers. Under this visa category more and more cases of abuse have surfaced as reported by immigrant and workers' rights advocates.

For example, NAFCON reports of a case of fifteen workers who were recruited, to work as housekeepers for Florida-based hotels under the H2B program. The workers paid exorbitant fees to get employment in the United States. In addition to being paid much lower wages than their counterparts (they were often paid late), they had to pay the loans they had secured from lenders to pay the fees demanded by their recruitment agency. Later, they would find themselves undocumented because the recruitment agency failed to renew the H2B visa, which is only a one-year visa (though it is renewable for up to three years).[21]

In Hawaii, according to labor activists with the International Longshore and Warehouse Union (ILWU), some hotels began to turn to importing workers from the Philippines on H2B visas in the mid-2000s.[22] While employers attribute this to labor shortages locally, activists counter that it was actually a tactic to undermine long-running labor struggles in the hotel industry there. From the mid-1990s to the late 2000s, the Pacific Beach Hotel, located on Honolulu's highly touristic Waikiki Beach, was the site for regular protests, including an international boycott, in support of the hotel workers' right to unionize. An independent commission found that workers at the Pacific Beach Hotel that management created a climate of fear to prevent workers from joining the union.[23]

Finally, when Gloria Macapagal Arroyo pledged to help "rebuild the land for the people of Iraq," by supplying the United States with migrant labor as part of its commitment to President Bush's "coalition of the willing," she simultaneously pledged to keep "terror" at bay. As immigrants have come to be increasingly characterized after 9/11 as potential terrorists based on their country of origin or potential criminal menaces since President Clinton's signing of the Illegal Immigration and Immigrant Responsibility Act of 1996 criminalized undocumented immigrants, the Philippine state has cooperated with the United States to help facilitate mass deportations of undocumented Filipino immigrants. A report from the Critical Filipino Studies Collective on Filipino removals from the United States since 2001 reveals that Filipinos are a disproportionate share of the deportee population.[24] The CFFSC attributes this phenomenon to the Philippine state's commitment to allying itself with the United States. I would further suggest that Filipino immigrant removals from the United States are enabled by the labor brokerage state, which has the bureaucratic mechanisms to facilitate that process. The process that facilitated the "repatriation" of the migrant workers who went on strike in Brunei is the same process that facilitates deportation from the United States.

Conclusion

This chapter's main contribution is in cultivating a Critical Filipino Studies approach to understanding contemporary US Filipino community formation. I argue, through the notion of the labor brokerage state, that Filipinos' ever-increasing presence in this country is a consequence of specific neocolonial state practices in collusion with US empire.

Notably, the phenomenon of contractual labor migration around the world, which has been a key feature of Philippine e/migration over the last nearly forty years, is too often considered only remotely (if at all) related to Filipino immigration to the United States and its erstwhile territories (namely, Hawaii) in the scholarship. I suggest alternatively that Filipinos' global and US migrations must be understood as inextricably linked because both migrations are attributable to US imperial legacies in the Philippines, specifically the formation of the neocolonial Philippine state as a labor brokerage state. The globalization of Filipinos is linked to the globalization of US capital and the expansion of its military-industrial complex. If Filipinos labored for the American empire from the turn of the century to the present in the United States and its territories, as the American empire globalizes, Filipinos are laboring for empire globally, and the neocolonial labor brokerage state has facilitated that process.

Accounting for the legacies of empire in the formation of the neocolonial labor brokerage state in our understandings of the contemporary Filipino labor diaspora in the United States and beyond, I would offer, opens up the development of what Campomanes calls a radical epistemology, a Critical Filipino Studies, an intellectual project that is especially vital today if we hope to fully grasp the new complexities of the Filipino migrant experience.

Notes

1. "Asian/Pacific American Heritage Month: May 2011." Facts for Features & Special Editions. U.S. Census, 29 Apr. 2011. Web. 29 June 2012. http://www.census.gov/newsroom/releases/archives/facts_for_features_special_editions/cb11-ff06.html.
2. "Philippine Overseas Employment Administration (POEA)." Philippine Overseas Employment Administration (POEA). Philippine Overseas Employment Administration, 29 June 2012. Web. 29 June 2012. http://www.poea.gov.ph/.
3. Rodriguez, R. M. 2010. *Migrants for Export: How the Philippine State Brokers Labor to the World*. Minneapolis: University of Minnesota Press.
4. The notion of "waves" has been in wide currency in studies of Filipino immigration to the United States for several decades. Even scholarship that does not explicitly discuss Filipino immigration in terms of "waves," I would argue, rests on historical demarcations on which wave scholarship depends.
5. Many scholars have been hesitant to actually identify early Filipino migration to the United States as immigrants given the nature of their colonial subject-status. See Campomanes, O. 1997. "New Formations of Asian American Studies and the Question of U.S. Imperialism," *positions* 5(2): 523–50.
6. Choy, C. C. 2003. *Empire of Care*. Durham, NC: Duke University Press; Fujita-Rony, D. B. 2003. *American Workers, Colonial Power: Philippine Seattle and the Transpacific West, 1919–1941*. Berkeley: University of California Press.
7. Espiritu, Y. L. 1995. *Filipino American Lives*. Philadelphia, PA: Temple University Press.
8. Pido, A. J. A. 1986. *The Pilipinos in America: Macro/Micro Dimensions of Immigration and Integration*. New York: Center for Migration Studies.
9. Campomanes 1997.
10. Espiritu, for instance, discusses how the "ferocity of U.S. (neo)colonial exploitation, the mismanagement of the Philippines by the country's comprador elite, and

the violence of globalized capitalism have flung Filipinos 'to the ends of the earth,' as contract workers, sojourners, expatriates, refugees, exiles and immigrants" (p. 23). Significantly, she does not discuss some of the consequences of neocolonialism, namely, the specific intervention on the part of the Marcos administration in the 1970s to institutionalize labor export. Espiritu, Y. L. 2003) *Homebound: Filipino American Lives Across Cultures, Communities, and Countries.* Berkeley: University of California Press.

11. Krikorian, Mark. 2005. "Back in the CNMI: The Commonwealth of the Northern Mariana Islands Is No Model When It Comes to Immigration." *National Review*: 22–23.

12. Isaac, Allan Punzalan. 2006. *American Tropics: Articulating Filipino America.* Minneapolis: University of Minnesota Press, 24.

13. Coates, Te-Nehisi Paul. "Looking Abroad For A Few Good Teachers," *Time Magazine.* 21 Nov. 2005. Web. 24 Sept. 2015.

14. "Brief History of Philippine Migration." *Philippine Overseas Employment Administration (POEA).* N.p., n.d. Web. 21 Mar. 1999.

15. From Office of the Press Secretary Republic of the Philippines. 2006. "House Passes Filipino American Contribution Resolution." Retrieved March 2006, from http://www.ops.gov.ph/records/proc_n0954.htm.

16. *Employment-Based Immigration to the United States: A Fact Sheet.* 2011. Rep. Washington, DC: Immigration Policy Center.

17. Toppo, Greg and Icess Fernandez. "Federal Complaint: Filipino teachers held in 'servitude'," *USA Today.* 27 Oct. 2009. Web. 24 Sept. 2015.

18. Foz, Rico. N.d. *Conflicting Findings of Facts: The Sentosa Nurses' Cases.* Rep. New York: National Alliance for Filipino Concerns.

19. Department of Labor. Wage and Hour Division. *US Labor Department Obtains More than $134,000 in Back Wages for 40 Therapists Employed by Orlando, Fla., Company under H-1B Visa Program Health Care Workers in 15 States Affected Wage and Hour Division.* Department of Labor, 24 Oct. 2011. Web. 1 July 2012. http://www.dol.gov/whd.

20. De Castro, Cynthia. "Victimized Pinoy Teachers Demand Justice at the White House," *Asian Journal.* 10-12 Aug. 2011. Web. 1 Jun. 2014.

21. National Alliance for Filipino Concerns. *Florida 15, Sentosa 27Human Trafficking of Filipinos in the US Continues Under PNoy Administration—NAFCON.Http://nafconusa.org/.* National Alliance for Filipino Concerns, 16 July 2011. Web. 16 July 2011.

22. Arakawa, Linda. 2006. "Start of Trend? Hotel Hires Foreign Workers." *The Honolulu Advertiser* [Honolulu] 1 Dec.: n.p.

23. *Hard Labor: Scared Workers, Exhausted Employees, and Declining Standards at a Hawai'i Hotel.* 2009. Rep. Honolulu: Commission to Investigate Labor and Management Practices at the Pacific Beach Hotel.

24. See Critical Filipino and Filipina Studies Collective. 2004. Resisting Homeland Security: Organizing Against Unjust Removals of U.S. Filipinos. San Jose, CA: Critical Filipino and Filipina Studies Collective, 29.

Works Cited

Arakawa, Linda. 2006. "Start of Trend? Hotel Hires Foreign Workers." *The Honolulu Advertiser* [Honolulu] 1 Dec., n.p.

"Asian/Pacific American Heritage Month: May 2011." *Facts for Features & Special Editions*. U.S. Census, 29 Apr. 2011. Web. 29 June 2012.

Bonus, Rick. 2000. *Locating Filipino Americans: Ethnicity and the Cultural Politics of Space*. Philadelphia, PA: Temple University Press.

"Brief History of Philippine Migration." *Philippine Overseas Employment Administration (POEA)*. N.p., n.d. Web. 21 Mar. 1999.

Campomanes, Oscar V. 1997. "New Formations of Asian American Studies and the Question of U.S. Imperialism." *positions: east asia cultures critique* 5.2: 523–50.

Choy, Catherine Ceniza. 2003. *Empire of Care: Nursing and Migration in Filipino American History*. Durham, NC: Duke University Press.

Coates, Te-Nehisi Paul. "Looking Abroad for a Few Good Teachers." *Time Magazine*, 21 Nov. 2005. Web. 24 Sept. 2015.

Dept. of Labor. Wage and Hour Division. *US Labor Department Obtains More than $134,000 in Back Wages for 40 Therapists Employed by Orlando, Fla., Company under H-1B Visa Program Health Care Workers in 15 States Affected. Wage and Hour Division*. Dept. of Labor, 24 Oct. 2011. Web. 1 July 2012.

Employment-Based Immigration to the United States: A Fact Sheet. 2011. Rep. Washington, DC: Immigration Policy Center.

Espiritu, Yen Le. 2003. *Home Bound: Filipino American Lives across Cultures, Communities, and Countries*. Berkeley: University of California Press.

Foz, Rico. N.d. *Conflicting Findings of Facts: The Sentosa Nurses' Cases*. Rep. New York: National Alliance for Filipino Concerns.

Hard Labor: Scared Workers, Exhausted Employees, and Declining Standards at a Hawai'i Hotel. 2009. Rep. Honolulu: Commission to Investigate Labor and Management Practices at the Pacific Beach Hotel.

Isaac, Allan Punzalan. 2006. *American Tropics: Articulating Filipino America*. Minneapolis: University of Minnesota Press.

Krikorian, Mark. 2005. "Back in the CNMI: The Commonwealth of the Northern Mariana Islands Is No Model When It Comes to Immigration." *National Review*: 22–23.

Lan, Pei-Chia. 2006. *Global Cinderellas: Migrant Domestics and Newly Rich Employers in Taiwan*. Durham, NC: Duke University Press.

National Alliance for Filipino Concerns. *Florida 15, Sentosa 27Human Trafficking of Filipinos in the US Continues Under PNoy Administration—NAFCON*. National Alliance for Filipino Concerns, 16 July 2011. Web. 16 July 2011.

"Philippine Overseas Employment Administration (POEA)." *Philippine Overseas Employment Administration (POEA)*. Philippine Overseas Employment Administration, 29 June 2012. Web. 29 June 2012.

Reader on United States History: From Pre-colonial America to the War in Vietnam (with Discussion Questions). 197[?]. Oakland, CA: Union of Democratic Filipinos (KDP).

Rodriguez, Robyn Magalit. 2010. *Migrants for Export: How the Philippine State Brokers Labor to the World*. Minneapolis: University of Minnesota Press.

Toppo, Greg and Icess Fernandez. "Federal Complaint: Filipino Teachers Held in 'Servitude.'" *USA Today*. 27 Oct. 2009. Web. 24 Sept. 2015.

Tyner, J. A. 1999. "The Global Context of Gendered Labor Migration From the Philippines to the United States." *American Behavioral Scientist* 42.4: 671–89.

3

Oriental Enlightenment and the Colonial World

A Derivative Discourse?

JOHN D. BLANCO

Orientations and Orientalizations

In Reynaldo Ileto's controversial 2001 essay, "Orientalism and the Study of Philippine Politics," he begins with the question of "whether elements of colonial discourse continue to inhabit . . . recent writing on Philippine politics. Mesmerized by the trappings of modern scholarship, have we failed to interrogate the conditions for positing what is 'true' and 'essential' about Filipino political behavior?" (41).[1] His critique invokes Edward Said's equally controversial book *Orientalism* (first published in 1978), in which Said attempts to historicize the politics of *reading and interpreting politics* (and culture) in the Middle East and even more broadly, Asia, in ways that at once presume and reify the irreducible and irreconcilable difference between West and East. Let us recall Said's argument briefly:

> Orientalism is a *style* of thought based upon an ontological and epistemological distinction made between 'the Orient' and (most of the time) 'the Occident.' Thus a very large mass of writers . . . have accepted the basic distinction between East and West as the starting point for elaborate theories, epics, novels, social descriptions, and political accounts concerning the Orient, its people, customs, "mind," destiny, and so on. (2–3)

Said's argument has been dissected, contested, and revised extensively since the work's publication in 1978.[2] Ileto's invocation of Said's work merely intends to critique a set of unexamined assumptions about Philippine politics and political authority in (largely US-based) academic scholarship. Yet it touches on a deeper question that constitutes one of the fundamental cultural and political debates of the twentieth century—from the work of late nineteenth-century Filipino writers, intellectuals, and revolutionaries to the postwar generation of cultural nationalists. What does it mean for Filipinos to "think for ourselves" if and when that very project entailed the reiteration and elaboration of Oriental(ist) reason—to repeat Said, "an ontological and epistemological distinction made between 'the Orient' and (most of the time) 'the Occident'?"[3] What would be the limits of imagining Philippine independence along the lines of European Enlightenment, if that very claim to independence was based on what Said has called "the Orientalization of the Orient" (Said, *Orientalism*, 65)?

Recent scholarship has approached this question primarily in and through the elusive, shifting category of an educated Philippine elite—the so-called *ilustrado* and the historical circumstances of his emergence (Hau, "'Patria é intereses,'" 10). Some scholars are content to consider the term as synonymous with "educated" and with educational opportunity in the colonial period being restricted mostly to elite families (the *principalía*), ilustrado almost always implies "elite" or class of elites. Resil Mojares and Megan Thomas, however, have shown how nineteenth- and turn-of-the-century Filipino expatriate students and writers received their education in the Oriental sciences and the politics of Spanish republicanism in Europe. Ileto, in contrast to both, underlines the projection or perhaps *interpellation* of this "class" of leaders during the US invasion and takeover of the Philippines, at the very moment Filipino revolutionaries (under the leadership and president of the First Republic General Aguinaldo) were attempting to consolidate the basis of declaring the Philippines to be a sovereign and independent nation. As Ileto says elsewhere, "*it was enough that a leading class could be identified*, through whose collaboration the colonial system could be established" (*Knowing America's Colony*, 24; italics in original). Indeed, it would not be a far stretch to claim that a great deal of Philippine historiography of the twentieth century tends to conflate ilustrado with "collaborator," whether this refers to collaboration with the United States or with imperial Japan.

None of these approaches to the ambiguity of the term are necessarily incompatible with one another. Yet as Caroline Hau points out in a recent essay, *Ilustración*, enlightenment carried a philosophical as well as political and sociological meaning, which Filipino writers and their intellectual peers began to use the word ilustrado to refer to themselves and each other. She writes:

The etymology of the word plays on the metaphor of "light" in the "enlightenment," holding up knowledge (via education) against the "darkness" of ignorance, error, and obscurantism. Here, the ilustrado is not defined sociologically by mere acquisition of wealth, education, or power, but politically by a *critical* stance that linked the term with words like *progresista*, *reformista* or *reformador*, *librepensador* (often appearing in the English form, "freethinker"), *liberal*, *volteriano* (Voltairian), and, most famously, *filósofo* and *filibustero*. ("'Patria é intereses,'" 11–12; see also Majul, 49–56)

It is precisely and paradoxically this critical stance that makes the various approaches to the term ilustrado contradictory. I trace the manifestations of this contradiction—premise and promise of Oriental Enlightenment—throughout the first half of the twentieth century, in order to evaluate its contribution to both the promotion and sabotage of national independence and decolonization.

Slouching toward Asia to Be Born

The inescapable reality that faced national martyr José Rizal and his compatriots advocating colonial reforms at the end of the nineteenth century was that colonial culture and politics had converged to the degree that it was impossible make statements about one without simultaneously invoking the other.[4] The simultaneous incorporation of Filipinos into the project of Spanish colonial reforms and the denigration of colonial subjects as "ill bred children, but big children, with their passions fully developed" resulted in the kinds of cultural racism publicized and promoted by Spanish writers in the Philippines during the second half of the nineteenth century: sometimes involving the vulgar adaptation of social Darwinism; other times invoking the Spanish "prestige of the race" (*prestigio de la raza*) against native inferiority.[5]

In responding to the racialization of natives (*indios*) by the colonial press, particularly with the growth and spread of newspapers during the latter 1800s, Filipino writers and later, statesmen under US colonial rule began to explore the political implications of an authentic Philippine culture: whether culture referred to the pre-Hispanic "origins" of native societies; or it referred to the absorption and accommodation of those societies to almost three and a half centuries of Spanish Christianity and colonial institutions. As Resil Mojares and Megan Thomas make clear, it is here that the immersion of writers such as Pedro Paterno and Isabelo de los Reyes, as well as the aforementioned Pardo de Tavera and Rizal, in the Oriental(ist) sciences of philology, ethnology, and linguistics generated narratives of the past, which disrupted rather than confirmed Spanish hegemony, and, more broadly, the Eurocentric bias of Darwinism, positivism, and the philosophy of history. By inhabiting the fields of "Orientalist" discourse and thereby accepting in part the premises and prejudices on which such knowledge was developed (for example, "civilization" as a Eurocentric historical process), these writers and propagandists attempted to reverse or redirect the assumptions and implications of race-thinking, Eurocentrism, and Spain's providential and presumably civilizational mission in the archipelago.

Paradoxically, then, for the educated Filipino expatriate writers in Europe arguing for the abolition of colonial rule and the dismantling of Spain's attempt to create and maintain the legislation of "Special [that is, colonial] Laws" in the archipelago, the Oriental sciences provided a language and archive for asserting Philippine belonging to a comparable, if hierarchically "inferior" or less developed, genealogy of world civilization.[6] In these texts, the location of the Philippines in Ultramar and its interlocking histories of migrations, economies, wars, and diasporas, betokened an allegiance to a culture or cultures that was irreducibly heterogeneous to Spanish rule. This is, of course, one of the central tenets of Orientalism as a discourse, but one turned back upon its original manipulation as a justification for Western colonial enterprises.

While engagements with the Philippines's Asian heritage ranged from Trinidad H. Pardo de Tavera's work on the Sanskrit roots of Filipino languages and grammars, as well as Pedro Paterno's somewhat fanciful theses on precolonial Tagalog civilization, it is in Rizal's work where the revaluation, perhaps transvaluation, of the "Oriental" sign first emerges as a political weapon, without which our Asian heritage would have remained a purely academic question. Let us recall briefly a key passage from his well-known essay, "The Philippines a Century Hence": "Oriental peoples in general and Malays in particular," he writes, "are cultures of sensitivity [*sensibilidad*]: the delicacy of sentiments prevails in them" (cited in *La Solidaridad*, I: 430). This sensitivity, a trait that seems innocent enough, becomes under Rizal's interpretation the historical catalyst that yokes together Filipinos across the archipelago as inheritors of an emerging racial consciousness. Between the growth of infrastructure and (with it) travel and public media like the newspaper, colonial subjects became gradually aware of Spanish *casticismo* (racial prestige) and the denigration of the natives. In an oft-quoted passage, Rizal observes:

> Today there exists a factor that did not exist before: the spirit of the nation has been awakened, and the same misfortune, the same abasement has united all the inhabitants. Now factor in a numerous enlightened *class* [*clase ilustrada*] within and outside the Archipelago, a *class* created and propelled to grow in ever greater in numbers by the bungling efforts of certain governors, who force [the country's] inhabitants to expatriate, to educate / enlighten themselves [*ilustrarse*] in foreign lands, and maintain themselves and fight thanks to the disturbances and to the system of herding them off. This *class*, whose number grows continually, is in constant communication with the rest of the Islands, and if today it forms no more than the country's cerebrum, in a few years it will form [the country's] entire nervous system and will manifest the country's existence in all its actions. ("Filipinas dentro de cien años," *La Solidaridad*, I: 434. Translation modified; italics added)

> [Hoy existe un factor que no había antes; se ha despertado el espíritu de la nación, y una misma desgracia y un mismo rebajamiento han unido á todos los habitantes de las Islas. Se cuenta con una numerosa *clase ilustrada* dentro y fuera del Archipiélago, *clase* creada y aumentada cada vez más y más por la torpezas de ciertos gobernantes, obligando á los habitantes á expatriarse, á ilustrarse en el extranjero, y se mantiene y lucha gracias á las excitaciones y al sistema de ojeo emprendido. Esta *clase*, cuyo número aumenta progresivamente, está en comunicación constante con el resto de las Islas, y si hoy no forma más que el cerebro del país, dentro de algunos años formará todo su sistema nervioso y manifestará su existencia en todos sus actos.]

The coincidence in this essay between Rizal's act of self-Orientalization ("Oriental peoples, and Malays in particular . . . "), the awakening of "the spirit of the nation," and the emergence of an "enlightened" or ilustrado class, and the awakening of the nation more broadly, is striking. To what degree did this nation's "awakening" correspond with its insertion into an Orientalist discourse predicated on the unbridgeable difference between East and West? Did Filipino "enlightenment" entail a rejection of the Orientalist principle—to recall Said's words, "an ontological and epistemological distinction made between 'the Orient' and (most of the time) the 'Occident'"—in order to embrace a universal, Kantian promise of living in an "age of enlightenment," or did colonial enlightenment mean the internalization and politicization of such a division?

From Rizal's schematic essay, as well as his other works, Filipino ilustrados and revolutionary leaders alike derived a number of implications. One was that the inhabitants of the archipelago shared a consciousness that was rooted in a precolonial sense of national or perhaps even pan-(Southeast) Asian belonging, as well as a future project of emancipation from colonial rule. Another was that the history of these forms of international commerce, diplomacy, and war with the Muslim, Buddhist, and Hindu worlds of the Indian Ocean and the China Seas, not to mention the Pacific Ocean, had been violently suppressed or written out of history by Spanish officials and missionary friars throughout the three centuries of colonial rule.[7] But the most dangerous implication, which radicalized the "Orientalist" insistence on the irreconcilable cultural difference, was that Filipinos belonged to an irreducibly different *nature* than that of Spaniards, perhaps even Europeans. It is this contention that brings out the full ambiguity of Rizal's veiled threats against colonial rule:

> History does not register in its annals one example of lasting domination exercised by one people belonging to one race, with foreign customs and habits, and with opposed or divergent ideals, over another . . . . It is against every natural and moral law for a foreign body to exist within another endowed with force and activity. Science teaches us that [the foreign body] is assimilated, eliminated, encysted; or it destroys the organism. (*La Solidaridad*, II: 33; italics added)

> [La historia no registra en sus anales ninguna dominación duradera ejercida por un pueblo sobre otro, de razas diferentes, de usos y costumbres extrañas, y de ideales opuestos ó divergentes . . . . Es contra todas las leyes naturales y morales la existencia de un cuerpo extraño dentro de otro

dotado de fuerza y actividad. La ciencia nos enseña, ó que se asimila, destruye el organismo, se elimina ó se enquista.]

On the one hand, then, Oriental Enlightenment might lead one to imagine—as Rizal did—future Philippine independence, by revolution or divine providence, under the leadership of an "educated / enlightened class." On the other hand, and as we know, the Orientalist premise of the superiority of Western civilization and progress could also be employed to argue against revolution or independence, in favor of the inevitable and universal spread of technological, industrial, and secular "progress" . . . as Rizal *also* argued.

The heirs of Rizal's thought followed the parallel lines of reasoning Rizal set out in essays like "Filipinas dentro de cien años" and his novels. For some, race thinking and the irreducible foreignness of Spanish colonialism infused the revolution with a radical and messianic edge, which helped to catalyze revolutionary sentiment around the Katipunan and later, the revolutionary government (see Ileto, *Pasyon and Revolution*, 115–208). In contrast, for ilustrados like Pedro Paterno and Trinidad H. Pardo de Tavera, Oriental(ist) "difference," which had served as a frame for their earlier studies of Tagalog and Philippine history and culture, had to be revaluated, perhaps "reoriented" toward the military, industrial, and economic supremacy of Europe and the United States over its transpacific colonial frontiers. It is in this context that Trinidad H. Pardo de Tavera, the Filipino appointee to the Philippine Taft Commission (the primary vehicle of colonial government in the Philippines between 1901 and 1906), develops the ideology of cultural assimilation to US colonial policies and institutions, or "Americanization" through the curious and paradoxical invocation of the "Filipino soul."

Americanize to Asianize

Scholarship on Trindidad H. Pardo de Tavera has always been (and will probably continue to be) divided.[8] Trinidad's uncle, Joaquin, was a Creole lieutenant belonging to a group of prominent advocates of colonial reform informally known as the "Committee of Reformers." After the outbreak and suppression of the Cavite mutiny in 1872, Joaquin and his associates were accused of fomenting sedition and exiled to the

Marianas Islands. The family's implication in Joaquin's reform advocacy, which brought about Joaquin's subsequent marginalization in the Philippine colony, later led to their emigration to Paris. There, the Pardo de Tavera home became host to a younger generation of Filipino students belonging to the educated elite, who received their education and voiced their protest against colonial rule in Europe.[9] Trinidad earned a medical degree at the Sorbonne and one in Malay language from the Ecole Nationale des Langues Orientales Vivantes. He published a number of short works that demonstrate his philological training in Oriental studies, which included *Contribución para el estudio de los antiguos alfabetos Filipinos* (1884) [Contribution to the study of the ancient Philippine alphabets], *El sanscrito en la lengua Tagalog* (1887) [Sanskrit in the Tagalog language], and *Consideraciones sobre el origen de los Números en Tagalog* (1889) [Considerations of the origin of numbers in Tagalog].

At the outbreak of the 1896 revolution, Pardo de Tavera was appointed director of diplomacy under the revolutionary government of Emilio Aguinaldo, but resigned soon afterward. As we know, he quickly came to promote the political annexation of the Philippines to America and cultural Americanization. Even before the official defeat of revolutionary forces by the United States in 1902, Tavera had organized a Federal platform "directed to Americanizing ourselves . . . in order that through its agency the American spirit may take possession of us, and that we may so adopt its principles, its political customs, and its peculiar civilization that our redemption may be complete and radical" (Pardo de Tavera, cited in M. Kalaw, 276).

Excoriated by revolutionaries and early members of the Nacionalista Party, alternately embraced and repudiated by the US colonial government under the Philippine Taft Commission (headed by future US president William Howard Taft), Tavera witnessed and participated in both the failure of the revolutionary government under Aguinaldo and the compromised beginnings of an "official" nationalist movement under US rule. While Rizal came to be regarded as a national hero invoked by virtually every political persuasion and civic interest group at the turn of the century, Pardo de Tavera's life and intellectual career ended with him as a marginalized and largely forgotten figure. As a final irony, perhaps the Philippines' "most respected champion of Americanism" in all its cultural, linguistic, and political dimensions ended up as the chairman of the Department of Oriental Languages at the University of the Philippines, before spending his last years as director and archivist of the Philippine National Library (Mojares, 230).

In hindsight, we tend to regard Rizal and Pardo de Tavera as sitting on opposite sides of history: while one became the national martyr and harbinger of Philippine enlightenment and independence, the other made the term ilustrado virtually synonymous with the term "collaborator," usually with the United States or Japan.[10] Yet behind this superficial contrast, Pardo de Tavera and his co-Federationists's "Americanism" was in certain respects perfectly consistent with Rizal's awareness of the geopolitics of Western imperialism at the turn of the century (see M. Kalaw, 276–77). Of immediate concern, ilustrados saw in revolutionary general and president of the First Republic Emilio Aguinaldo's failure to secure international recognition a sign of foreign interests in Asia: a sign that did not bode well for a fledgling nation's prospects for maintaining its independence (Paredes, 22).[11]

What makes Pardo de Tavera's advocacy of US colonial rule more complex, however, is that it stems less explicitly from either purely strategic considerations of Western powers in Asia or individual opportunism, but rather from what he and his commentators have called his "social philosophy." His major speeches reveal this philosophy to consist mainly of five arguments, which Pardo de Tavera would reiterate (with slight variations) throughout the first two decades of US rule. All of them appear, to varying degrees, in a lecture delivered before American and Filipino teachers in 1906, "El Alma Filipina" (The Filipino Soul).[12]

The first argument is that Spanish colonialism bequeathed to the archipelago a military and religious civilization, which, while bringing certain benefits (particularly Christianity), also inculcated Filipinos into various customs, which were for the most part backward, conservative, reactionary, and ignorant.[13] Second, Philippine nationalism owed itself—indeed the very conception of the Philippines as a nation and people—to this ilustrado class mentioned by Rizal earlier, one that imbibed the ideas of the West in the travels and studies of these young men throughout Europe in the nineteenth century. In his words:

The pro-Filipino movement was not made by the uneducated classes of our country—which, at first glance, should have been presumably responsible for conserving a genuinely Filipino soul—but rather those educated in the University and in Europe, whose souls had been profoundly adulterated. But such adulteration was only for their perfection; and while their sentiments remained the same, the ideas changed and their cultivated intelligence became capable of understanding . . . new ideals and sentiments, through which they came to know how to cultivate their language, respect their race, venerate the customs of their forbears, discover all manner of beauty in the nature of their islands. . . . (cited in de los Santos, 11)

[El movimiento filipinista no se hizo por la clase ineducada de nuestro país, que debía, al parecer, conservar un alma genuinamente Filipina, sino por los educados en la Universidad y en Europa, cuyas almas se habían adulterado profundamente, pero aquella adulteración fue de perfeccionamiento, y mientras los sentimientos permanecían los mismos, las ideas fueron otras y la inteligencia cultivada fue capaz de comprender . . . ideales y sentimientos nuevos por los cuales supieron cultivar su lengua, respetar su raza, venerar las costumbres de sus antepasados, descubrir bellezas en la naturaleza de sus islas . . .].

Third, the political domination of the Philippines by the United States was an insurmountable fait accompli; moreover, the only long-term solution to/against political domination by a foreign power would be neither political resistance nor collaboration, but rather the intellectual preparedness of Filipinos for independence.[14] This intellectual preparedness could only be secured through a rigorous and enlightened system of education/public instruction and through the Philippines's integration into the world economy. Indeed, Pardo de Tavera would say that public instruction was itself "the principal factor of civilization" ("The Filipino Soul," in Quirino and Hilario, 138).[15]

Fourth, even beyond reasons of political expediency in the Pacific region, US colonial rule was desirable in the short-term because Anglo-Saxon civilization had reached its "hour of world supremacy and splendor" ("The Filipino Soul," 147) in world history and was destined to serve as the "trustee" of universal values from which the human race would collectively benefit. Chief among these (paradoxically) was "independent thinking," which served as the prerequisite for political independence.

Fifth and finally, by accepting and adopting US rule, Filipinos would undergo a tutelage in the arts of government and "civilization" that would ultimately allow us to realize our fullest potential (*perfecciona-miento*), which was nothing more or less than the maturation of our original "soul."

Taken at face value, the first two of these arguments appear at first glance to repeat the basic arguments to be found in Rizal's earlier essay, "The Philippines a Century Hence," which was published seventeen years before Pardo de Tavera's (in 1889). And yet, how remarkably different are the implications that Pardo de Tavera drew from his position as an il-ustrado under the early years of US colonial rule than those of Rizal at the end of the Spanish regime. For Rizal, oppression under the Spanish military government and the religious orders served as the catalyst for Filipinos to look inward both individually and collectively, to recognize in each other the common basis of their degradation and denigration, and to cast a glance backward in time to an all but obliterated pan-Asian civiliza-tion that lay in the distant, pre-Hispanic past. The Orientalist archive pro-vided Rizal with all the ammunition he would need to basically reaffirm and radicalize the divide between colonizer and colonial subject: *we* are absolutely different from *you* (Spaniards), Rizal would conclude from his analysis; *you* (Spaniards) remain fundamentally, even after three centuries of colonial rule, *foreign* to *this* country and *this* people.[16]

By contrast, for Pardo de Tavera the legacy of Spanish civilization and Spanish colonialism was the generative seed of Filipino identity and consciousness itself. "The synthetic result of Spain's intervention in our archipelago," he wrote in his speech "La mentalidad Filipina" (1913) (The Filipino Mentality), "was the foundation of the Filipino nationality and [its] brain, translated in the terms of desire and the necessity of national independence" (cited in de los Santos, 19).[17] Two immediate implica-tions derived from this argument. First, and in stark juxtaposition to Rizal's "Philippines a Century From Now," Pardo de Tavera contended that, whatever their ethnic or racial origins, Filipinos were/had become members of a *European* (Latin) civilization, *not* an Asian one. "And what is the Filipino mentality but the Latin type transplanted into our islands by the Spaniards?" Tavera declared in "The Filipino Soul": "After three centuries of subjugation, the Filipino people of Malayan origin, of the yellow race, have come to form a member of the group of countries under Latin civilization and is *entirely different* from its sister-races of Asia" ("Filipino Soul," 144–45; italics added). Fifteen years later, his commencement address to the students of the University of the Philippines would repeat more or less the same assertion: "We must bear in mind that what we call the Filipino soul is a completely foreign mentality from the outside [mentalidad extranjera], which has been transmitted to a small portion of the Filipino people either through the education given in our centers of learning or through contact with the Spaniards during the long period of their domination" (278).

The second implication is that those cultural elements, which many took to be native or indigenous, and which the more ardent nationalists of Pardo de Tavera's time sought to politicize in the service of the revolutionary cause, were in fact *Spanish* and, even worse, *Spanish colonial* elements that only strengthened the fetters of a colonized mind. Speaking, for example, of the saturation of Philippine culture and society by religion in "El legado del ignorantismo" (The Legacy of Studied Ignorance), Pardo de Tavera rails against the disastrous consequences of novenas as one of the primary forms of literary education for Filipinos:

With this said, we have sufficient reasons for explaining the origin of immorality, which is the true cause of [our] predisposition to vice, the absence of any sense of responsibility: it explains perfectly that incomprehensible character, formed by a mix of expressed sentiments, which the missionaries ascribed to the Filipino, Indio, Spaniard, and Chinese, who were all implicated by that poisonous spirit informing that [religious] literature, completely at odds with reason. ("Legado del ignorantismo," 32)

[Con lo dicho hay bastante para explicar el origen de la inmoralidad, la verdadera causa de la predisposición al vicio, la ausencia del sentido de responsabilidad, la explicación natural de ese carácter incomprensible formado de una mezcla de sentimientos encontrados que los misioneros han atribuido al filipino, indio, español, y chino, incluidos todos por el espíritu nocivo que informa toda esa literatura completamente perturbadora de la razón.]

While ilustrado education exposed the Filipino elite to European "centers of learning," the religious education of the Spanish friars retarded the moral development of the rest of the Philippine population: "What I seek to do is to prevent the eventuality that, under the pretext of preserving and cultivating what we call our own that which is *not* our own, we accomplish only the sad and sure result of retarding our progress . . . of vitiating Filipino intellect."[18]

Perhaps no part of Pardo de Tavera's essay better expresses his break with the anticolonial politics of inverted- or counter-Orientalism we see in nineteenth-century ilustrado writing (including Pardo de Tavera's own, earlier work), than his invocation of Japan as a nation to be emulated by the Philippines. For what elicits Pardo de Tavera's enthusiasm has nothing to do with any sense of a common Asian heritage or belonging shared by Japan and the Philippines, but rather the success with which Japan "has absorbed in the span of one generation much of the spirit of occidental civilization" ("The Filipino Soul," 149). He adds:

> [The Japanese] too had the same fears which now assail some Filipinos: the fear that the Japanese soul would disappear under the thralldom of Anglo-Saxon education and leave enslaved the Japanese nation by the power of America and England. Fortunately, in the strife between the upholders of tradition and the defenders of progress and civilization, the latter won; and now . . . Japan ranks among the Great Powers of the world. (150)

With a gentle but firm emphasis, Pardo de Tavera detaches himself from the racial antagonism brimming just beneath the surface of Rizal's sober indictment of colonial rule, and which still smoldered in the aftermath of the Philippine revolution against Spain and the Americans. "[Racial] inferiority," Pardo de Tavera reasons, "is purely a matter of historical evolution, that the inferior races are those that preserve changeless and unchangeable their national spirit through the course of ages" (142). Not coincidentally, the very conceit that animates Pardo de Tavera's argument for the necessity of US colonial rule in the Philippines—the questioned future of a quasi-religious national identity or "soul"—turns out to be an eminently dispensable one:

> [T]he term Filipino soul is a poetic expression that reveals the existence of a poetic mentality. Such a mentality is ineffectual as it is not sufficient

to direct a country's advance on the highway of modern civilization. But I do not propose to discard or destroy it, though I do desire to give it practical attributes, so that . . . there may come others more practical and more useful to life, that will qualify better our country to win a place among the civilized nations. (155)

The isomorphism of Pardo de Tavera's social philosophy and Rizal's anti-colonial critique belies the inversion of the first by the second, however noble the intentions of the author may have been and however consistent the author believed himself to remain vis-à-vis the revolutionary sentiments of many nineteenth-century ilustrados. If Rizal's enlightenment project sought to turn the cultural difference between Spaniards and "Malays" into a political one, Pardo de Tavera's insisted instead on the indefinite suspension of political reflection by any except the educated class, in order to create a system of education "free from the unnatural pressure which represses the reason of man and subjects it to the reason of another by means of religious, political, or social dogmas" (279). Where Rizal flirted with the radical implications of racial division and conflict through the exploration of distinctly Asian (or in any case Malay) cultural traits, Pardo de Tavera would pronounce, "We Filipinos should not continue our former error of speaking of our race, because there is no such Filipino race . . . . Our origin should not engage our attention, but rather our orientation, our future" ("The Conservation of the National Type," 282). And where Rizal once mused that the constitutional and democratic traditions of US republicanism would deter it from ever coveting overseas colonial possessions in Asia like the Philippines, Pardo de Tavera reasoned that those same constitutional and democratic traditions would help the Philippines *as a US territory* to prepare to meet its destiny as a postcolonial national republic.[19] The (self-) orientalization of ilustrado discourse had come around full circle: the enlightenment of Filipinos to a knowledge of our ancestral Asian heritage, through a study of and identification with the Orientalist premise of irreducible difference between a European Self and Asian Other, had given way to the self-critique of Filipinos as the unwitting and ingenuous followers of a colonial ideology under the guise of Spanish Catholicism; and the corresponding urgency of acculturating to the technological-industrial and civic-secular aspects of American "civilization" in preparation for eventually joining it. Paradoxically, in Pardo de

Tavera's vision, the Americanization of Filipinos would neither diminish nor eliminate the "Filipino" or Asian character of the archipelago's culture and institutions. On the contrary, only through such acculturation to the English language, US customs, and the values of industry and scientific investigation, could the charting of a Filipino or Asian destiny even begin.

Re-Orientations of World Civilization

Sadly, the gift of hindsight does not allow for either the easy dismissal of Pardo de Tavera as a colonial lackey or our vindication of him as a progressive pragmatist in the age of wild messianic hopes of national liberation. In an unforeseen way, his fear of social fragmentation brought about by the premature and partial introduction of electoral politics in the archipelago anticipated John S. Furnivall's much more famous and celebrated theses on the anarchic development of "plural societies" with the weakening of colonial regimes (see Furnivall). Conversely, however, Pardo de Tavera's strident refusal to engage with what he saw as the "tyranny . . . [of] politics enthroned" (274); his conviction in the nationalizing and ultimately liberating tendencies of Anglo-Saxon education; his willful naïveté regarding the ability and willingness of an educated elite to represent "the interests of the popular class (who confide in it) as well as its own" (cited in de los Santos, 14); and his unflinching faith in the identity of science, industry, and "free trade" with the United States as the guarantors of eventual individual and national independence, all conspire to portray him as the enabler of what Spanish-educated writers and statesmen of the period called Anglo-Saxonism [*sajonismo*].[20]

Yet regardless of how we evaluate Pardo de Tavera's "enlightened" opinions in hindsight, the frame of Oriental Enlightenment that he and Rizal established for speculating on the future direction and ultimate ends of Philippine politics proved to be remarkably enduring. Take the following two examples. "The difficulty of knowing the Filipino," writes Norberto Romualdez in 1928, "is due, in my judgment, to the difference in the manner of thinking and acting between Occidentals and Orientals. . . . The people of these Islands are essentially religious. . . . This inborn religiousness is imposed on the very character of the Filipino, who inherited it from his forefathers in India and Sumatra" (cited in Quirino and Hilario, 20).[21] A contrary point of view appears in a 1927 speech by José Laurel, future president of the short-lived Philippine Second Republic under imperial Japan (1943–45), who focuses not on the religiosity of Filipinos as "Orientals" but rather the Oriental origins of "Western civilization." Despite this common origin, however, Laurel contends, "What generally characterizes Western peoples is the spirit of individualism and aggressiveness—a spirit, however, that too often has been conducive to that disregard of righteousness which has reduced the Christian religion to a refined and scientific form of intolerance and oppression" (ibid., 67). While Romualdez and Laurel seem to be taking juxtaposed positions to the question of religion in Philippine culture and its political implications, the Orientalist frame is the same.

On a larger level, the transformation of Rizal and Pardo de Tavera's critical Enlightenment stance to a discourse of racial(ized) and/or spiritualized civilizational difference was fated to repeat itself in succeeding generations of Philippine nationalism, just as Kant's Enlightenment morphed into nineteenth-century romantic nationalism and the philosophy of history more broadly.[22] In fact, the tendency of nationalists to portray the Oriental-Occidental divide in terms of a division between spiritual and material values in many ways parallels the *Arielista* tradition of pan-Latin Americanism.[23] In 1924, Pardo de Tavera's younger contemporary Jorge Bocobo (soon to be president of the University of the Philippines) warned Filipinos about the dark side of Americanization, beyond the recognition of its bankruptcy as an ideology: "Why all this learning and all this training for useful citizenship," writes, "if the rising generation of Filipinos, in consequence of this Godless system, is to worship the golden calf of materialism? How indeed, shall this generation profit if it loses its own soul?"[24] Several years later, director of the National Library Teodoro M. Kalaw was even more explicit:

Americanization, as an ideology, has in effect been dead in the Philippines for some time now. [I]t had already died with the two deaths of Pardo de Tavera: his political death in 1907, when nationalism surged up, and his natural death twenty years after. . . . Thus, from that time to this day, but especially today, in these days of fervid Asianism, we cannot hear talk of Americanization without an immediate protest from some lips. . . . [Yet] we are Americanizing ourselves faster than it looks and with the worst kind of Americanization . . . because it is the Americanization of material needs, of the needs which form the individual's habits and which now cannot be shaken off. (Lumbera and Maceda, 155–56)[25]

As the "American" and "Asian" sides of Philippine culture and society became polarized, so too did they become increasingly abstract and schematic, representing a material-spiritual divide that demanded resolution. Correspondingly, the critical and utopian dimensions of Oriental Enlightenment became increasingly difficult to distinguish, with a critique of US imperialism giving way to a reflection on the ultimate destiny, even providential mission, of the Philippines and Asia in world history. As Laurel states at the end of his 1927 speech, "The Orient should unmask the true nature of Western imperialism and understand its real spirit and designs" (73). Several years later, Bocobo proclaimed in his acceptance speech as university president (in 1934), "The University of the Philippines . . . has a mission to do its share in the rise of a new civilization that shall draw the breath of life from the character of the Far East. . . . I dare harbor the hope that the generations yet unborn will witness in the Far East . . . a new order and a new culture" (Bocobo, cited in Gonzalves, 41).[26] Departing from the task of critically interrogating the Eurocentric pretensions of inalienable rights, material progress, skepticism, and scientific method, and so forth, the Orient becomes the wellspring of a "new order and a new culture" capable of fusing genealogies of ethnic and linguistic ancestry with the promise of future independence and a competing narrative for the future of globalization.

How do we assess the degree to which the emergence of this underlying theme in nationalist discourse contributed to the success with which imperial Japan's (1942–45) vision of a pan-Asian realm would answer this call for "a new order and a new culture?" On the eve of the capture of Manila by Japanese forces—which coincided, strangely, with Rizal Day, December 30 [1942]—Lieutenant General and Fourteenth Army Commander Masaharu Homma (then commanding officer of the imperial Japanese army in the Philippines), explained to Philippine Commonwealth president Manuel Quezon:

The true aim of our forces is to drive out the evil influences and power of the United States of America, which has persisted in availing itself of each and every opportunity to obstruct the natural development and healthy growth of nations in East Asia. The Imperial Forces hold themselves responsible for the realization of their sacred mission, the establishment of Asia for the Asiatics, Philippines for the Filipinos (December 30, 1942).[27]

That same day, Manila mayor and chairman of the Japanese-sponsored Philippine government, or Philippine Executive Commission, Jorge B. Vargas (a former student of Bocobo's) commemorated Rizal Day by celebrating the "liberation of the Philippines from the American regime . . . [and] that final and long delayed redemption from Occidental domination, which was the ardent aspiration of Rizal. . . . Western imperialism has been expelled from Greater East Asia and to this day has been thwarted in all its efforts to return" (Vargas, "Address").[28] In Vargas's many speeches and statements during Japanese Occupation, we see the same themes that preoccupied Bocobo, Kalaw, and Laurel in crystallized and polemical form. Here is a typical example:

> Freed from the degenerating influence of Occidental civilization imposed on us for nearly four centuries, we are privileged now to draw inspiration from the Japanese nation and benefit in its guidance as we set ourselves to perform the great task of reviving our own culture and enriching it with what we should assimilate from other Oriental peoples . . . . The early Filipinos were known to be endowed with the best of oriental virtues . . . . [But] More than three centuries of Spanish rule . . . *and forty years of American influence* have caused a metamorphosis in Filipino individual and national life. The original virtues of the East were replaced by the acquired weaknesses of the West . . . . The importance given to the things of the spirit gave way to the excessive love of pleasure and comfort. (174; italics added)

The story Vargas tells should sound familiar: since Rizal's essay "The Philippines A Century Hence," revolutionaries and nationalists in the colonial government have retold the same narrative. The main differences, of course, concern the historical representation of a colonial "interlude" ("three centuries of Spanish rule . . . and forty years of American influence") and the Philippines's emancipation from it, as well as the designation of the foreign Other (from Spain versus the Philippines to the West versus the East). Finally, instead of looking ahead toward the turbulent and uncertain possibilities of revolution, anarchy, or political controversy, as Rizal did, Vargas looks ahead to another indefinite period of "tutelage" in the arts of civilization . . . as Pardo de Tavera once did. This one-time nemesis of the Nacionalista Party, unrepentant apologist for "Americanization" in all its dimensions, had paradoxically contributed to the nationalist vision of the Philippines's assimilation into a Greater East Asia.

Historians ranging from A. V. H. Hartendorp to Teodoro Agoncillo have questioned the sincerity of Vargas's loyalty to imperial Japan. Hartendorp emphasizes the degree to which Filipinos were coerced into reproducing this rhetoric for the sake of their lives: "with the exception of perhaps a very few of these Filipinos, not an American . . . who was familiar with the country and the people believed that they spoke voluntarily" (1:216). Agoncillo goes further, claiming that men like Vargas "had to issue statements . . . that appeared treasonous. In difficult circumstances, prudence is the better part of valor, and Vargas and company chose not to play the role of heroes for the sake of the people's safety" (Agoncillo, *Fateful Years*, 2:911).

What remains certain in either case, however, is that the rhetoric of national and Asian redemption touched the substratum of Filipino ilustrado dreams that had existed since the time of Rizal and the young Pardo de Tavera, both of whom found themselves engaged in resolving the contradiction between Enlightenment and the Orient. Seen in this light, President José Laurel's October 14, 1943, inaugural address to a nation under Japanese occupation does not so much anticipate the much-maligned "propaganda" issued by Japanese Prime Minister Hideki Tojo during the Greater East Asia Conference in Tokyo several weeks later, so much as it recapitulates and condenses what nationalists had been saying for the past two decades.[29] "We can combat the evil of excessive materialism," Laurel says, "which we inherited from the West only by a return to the spiritual ways of the East where we rightfully belong" (cited in Agoncillo, *Fateful Years*, 2: 1006). Was Laurel alone in this assessment? "Laurel," Agoncillo contends, "[unlike Vargas] had been known to be a nationalist whose basic postulate rested on knowledge of Oriental culture and the re-acquisition of those Oriental virtues necessary to counteract American materialistic proclivities" (ibid., 913–14). Yet Laurel's beliefs were by no means idiosyncratic: they had formed a major current of nationalist thought for the past ten years, if not since the end of the nineteenth century.

Imperial Japan recognized this synchronicity from the very beginning. The (Second) Republic of the Philippines was inaugurated on October 14, 1943, with former (and only) president of the First Republic, 1896 revolutionary general Emilio Aguinaldo and exiled revolutionary general Artemio Ricarte on hand to hoist the flag of independence.[30] Little did either know that less than three years later, with the defeat of the Japanese imperial army, Filipinos would be celebrating July 4 *again*—not, however, as a US holiday, but as the official recognition of the Philippines as a sovereign republic *by the United States*, which formally renounced its claim to the archipelago. The resulting palimpsest of Philippine independence was best captured by Nick Joaquin in his essay, "The Filipino as Sajonista":

> No decade in our history was more eventful than [the 1940s] . . . we passed through four different governments; had six chief exclusively . . . inaugurated two republics; and underwent a total war, two invasions, and a great peasant uprising . . . . So vast now seems the difference between what we have become and what we were before disaster struck that, in the Philippine vernacular the term "peacetime" means exclusively all the years before December 8, 1941. There has been no "peacetime" since then. (Lumbera and Maceda, 234–35)

Joaquin's words leave the reader with a profound sense of disorientation, brought about by the convolutions of imagining enlightenment from the wrong side of world. The freedom and authority of Filipinos to "think for ourselves" had constituted the one discourse that had kept alive a certain innocence regarding the future prospects of the Philippines as a modern, independent, national republic, in a world of equally (and putatively) "enlightened" nations, throughout the decades of US and Japanese rule. Yet emerging from the destruction of Manila by Japanese suicide demolition and US firebombing, and into a world-historical context in which a fledgling national republic's greatest aspiration would be to maintain and strengthen ties of dependency with its former colonial master, the question was no longer when the advent of enlightenment would begin but rather when it would end, and to what degree a Third

Republic (or for that matter, a Fourth, or Fifth) would succeed in doing what the First and Second Republics did not.[31]

The dreaming sleep of Oriental reason had produced monsters: a woman with two navels, revolutionary doppelgangers, CIA-employed *aswang* or vampires, a populist Frankenstein.[32] For nations undergoing decolonization, the age of national allegories had presumably just begun. For writers like Joaquin, perhaps the only sane path lay in bringing that age to a close.

Notes

1. See Hau, "Privileging Roots and Routes," 29–65.
2. One of the early explorations of Orientalism as a heterogeneous set of imaginaries, narratives, and discourses on the philosophy of history was Lisa Lowe's *Critical Terrains: French and British Orientalisms.*
3. In the landmark collection of essays published in 1928, under the title *Thinking for Ourselves: A Collection of Representative Filipino Essays* (in Quirino and Hilario), one of the main points of debate among statesmen and scholars alike is whether the anticipated future of Philippine independence would lead to a retrenchment in the archipelago's Asian "roots" or culturally assimilate the English language and US political traditions. See Pineda Tinio, "The Triumph of Tagalog and the Dominance of the Discourse on English," 197–207.
4. One may argue that the history of this convergence takes us even further back in time, to the 1761–62 British invasion of Manila and Spain's attempt to preserve its colonial power overseas through a series of reforms propelled by the Bourbon monarchy. See Fradera; Blanco, *Frontier Constitutions,* 27–63; and Sánchez Gómez. Some of the immediate consequences of these reforms were the militarization of the Philippine colony, the opening of the Philippines to the world market and the institutionalization of colonial racism among the clergy and military offices.
5. *Official Report for the Philippine Exposition at Madrid in 1887.* Cited by Pardo de Tavera, in *Character of Rizal,* 5. See also Blanco, *Frontier Constitutions,* esp. 184–227; and "Race As Praxis," 356–94.
6. A case example occurs in the appendix to Hegel's "Introduction" to his *Lectures on the Philosophy of World History* (1837); see appendix (152–220).
7. See Rizal's annotated edition to Antonio de Morga's seventeenth-century *Sucesos de las islas Filipinas.*
8. See de los Santos; although Ruby Paredes's analysis of Pardo de Tavera during the period of US rule is exhaustive (see Paredes). The history of the Pardo de Tavera family provides a snapshot of the major events that shaped Philippine nationalism between the nineteenth and twentieth centuries (see Paredes, 347–427; and Mojares, 121–51).

9. José Rizal, as well as the Luna brothers and the Paterno brothers, publicist Graciano López Jaena, and various contributors to the Filipino-run Spanish newspaper *La Solidaridad* between 1889–95, were among those who stayed at the Pardo de Tavera home in their travels across Europe and en route to and from the Philippines.

10. Constantino: "The collaboration of the *ilustrados* provided the Americans with a ready justification for their colonization of the Philippines. With the *ilustrados* as their prime exhibits, they were able to foist on the American people the myth that the Filipinos welcomed American rule with open arms" (*The Philippines*, 1: 243).

11. See Felipe Buencamino's statements in 1902 (cited in Paredes, "*Ilustrado* and the Proconsul," 22–23).

12. See "The Filipino Soul," in Quirino and Hilario. Santos's biography reproduces selections from the original Spanish: see Santos. For an insightful discussion of the language and culture debates taking place in the Philippines throughout the first two and a half decades of US rule, and particularly the passage of the Jones Law (1915), see Pineda Tinio, 197–207.

13. For the full expression of this conviction, see "El legado del ignorantismo," which was originally given as a speech given before the Teachers Assembly in Baguio (23 Apr. 1920). For a partial English translation, see Pardo de Tavera, "Heritage of Ignorance," in Quirino and Hilario, 1–17.

14. "For the oneness of our rights, the singleness of our duties, the harmony of our aspirations, and the unanimity of our ideals—all of which constitute our soul,—we need a common language; and this common language we are beginning to acquire with the spread of Anglo-Saxon education. This education is the only factor that can enable the Filipino people to manage and maintain their own government" (Pardo de Tavera, "The Filipino Soul," in Quirino and Hilario, 154–55).

15. This explains the urgency with which Pardo de Tavera and fellow ilustrados pursued the secularization of the administration of San José College, against the unified opposition of the religious orders. See Wilfley Lebbeus Redman et al.

16. This argument constitutes the foundation of Constantino's seminal book of essays, *Dissent and Counter-Consciousness*. For an analysis and deconstruction of this contention, see Rafael.

17. "El resultado sintético de la intervención de España en nuestro archipiélago fue la fundación de la nacionalidad filipina y del encéfalo, traducido en deseo y necesidad de la independencia nacional"

18. Pardo de Tavera, "Conservation of the National Type," in Quirino and Hilario, 280.

19. "Mis deseos no tienen nada que ver con que la soberanía que tengamos sea extranjera como hoy o domestica como aspiramos: quiero preparar al pueblo para que no sea oprimido por el gobierno, para que no pueda ser explotado por las autoridades políticas, para que no vea como únicos ejemplos dignos de imitar y dignos de conquistar situaciones oficiales" ("Autoridades sociales," cited in de los Santos, 13).

20. See Joaquin, "The Filipino as *Sajonista*," *Discovery*, 219–36.

21. Among his many accomplishments as writer, statesman, Supreme Court Justice, and educator, Romualdez was one of the seven members of the 1934–35 Constitu-

tional Convention, which drafted the 1935 Constitution of the Philippine Commonwealth. The Philippine Commonwealth effectively replaced the US insular government that had ruled the Philippines since the US invasion of the Philippines at the turn of the century. The Constitution provided for a ten-year interim administration in preparation for the US "granting" of Philippine sovereignty as promised in the 1935 Tydings-McDuffie Act. The Constitution chose Tagalog to be the national language, although Romualdez himself was from Leyte and had published works on the Waray-Waray language. He also founded the Academy of the Visayan Language of Samar and Leyte.

22. This is the subject of H. White; see *Metahistory*. For a succinct account connecting romantic nationalism with the "pan-" cultural movements (primarily pan-Slavism and pan-Aryanism), see Arendt, 222–66.

23. José Enrique Rodó, *Ariel*; see also González Echevarría, 17–32; and Ramos, 219–50.

24. Jorge Bocobo, in Quirino and Hilario, 299. Bocobo belonged to the very first generation of "*pensionados*": Filipino and Filipina recipients of US study grants, selected from a cross-section of regions throughout the archipelago and sponsored by the Philippine Commission under Governor General William Howard Taft in 1903. From 1917 until 1934 Bocobo served as the dean of the College of Law at the University of the Philippines (UP), after which he became the university president. During that period of time he shepherded the succeeding generations of Philippine presidents, officials, senators, and congressional representatives of the Philippines under the US insular government (1901–34), the Philippine Commonwealth (1935–46), and the Republic of the Philippines (post-1946)—most of whom graduated from the UP College of Law. At least three Philippine presidents passed through the UP College of Law under Bocobo: Carlos P. Garcia (1957–61), Diosdado Macapagal (1961–65), and Ferdinand Marcos (1965–86).

25. T. M. Kalaw's essay was first published as an editorial in the Spanish-language paper *Dietario Espiritual* (9 Sept. 1927).

26. Gonzalves's book provides an erudite and dexterous account of Bocobo's promotion of a national culture at the University of the Philippines; see 29–44.

27. See Homma, "Letter of the Commander-in-Chief of the Imperial Japanese Forces in the Philippines, addressed to His Excellency, Manuel L. Quezon, President of the Philippines, December 30, 1942."

28. For examples of Vargas's speeches on pan-East Asian solidarity, a "common East Asian race," and the historical destiny of the Co-Prosperity Sphere of Greater East Asia, see his selected speeches and statements in Malay, 161–223 (appendix B).

29. At the Greater East Asia Conference (held 5–6 Nov. 1943), Japan called together the leaders of Burma, Indonesia, India, and China as well as the Philippines, to officially sanction the creation of a Greater East Asia sphere defined by a common effort of these nations to "liberate the region from the yoke of British-American domination, and ensure their self-existence and self-defense" (*sic*) (see Chen). Prime Minister Hideki Tojo's words on Greater East Asia as the fulfilled promise of Oriental Enlightenment pick up exactly where the late nineteenth-century ilus-

trados left off: "A superior order of culture has existed in Greater East Asia from its very beginning. Especially the spiritual essence of the culture of Greater East Asia is the most sublime in the world. It is my belief that in the wide diffusion throughout the world of this culture of Greater East Asia by its further cultivation and refinement lies the salvation of mankind from the curse of materialistic civilization" (ibid.).

30. For earlier accounts of Artemio Ricarte's importance as a figure connecting the 1896 Philippine revolution with the inauguration of the Second Republic under imperial Japan, see Joaquin, *Question of Heroes*, 209–37; and Agoncillo, *Fateful Years*, 2: 917–19. For recent assessments of Ricarte and imperial Japan, see Ileto, "Wars with the US and Japan, and the Politics of History in the Philippines" (in Fujiwara and Nagano, 33–56); and Quibuyen, "Japan and America in the Filipino Nationalist Imagination" (in ibid., 106–31).

31. German legal scholar and jurist Carl Schmitt astutely analyzed the conspicuous eagerness of the United States to formally recognize newly independent republics like the Philippines in international organizations like the United Nations, along with its financial institutions like the World Bank and International Monetary Fund. See "El orden del mundo después de la segunda Guerra mundial," 19–36.

32. These refer, respectively, to Nick Joaquin's novel *The Woman Who Had Two Navels* (first published as a short story in 1952); *Portrait of the Artist As Filipino* (published in 1950); the psywar launched by CIA operative Edward Lansdale against the Hukbalahap (or *Hukbong Bayan Laban sa mga Hapon*, National Army Against the Japanese) rebellion in its postwar phase; and President Ramon Magsaysay, populist president sponsored and financed by the CIA. See Blum, 39–44.

Works Cited

Adib Majul, Cesar. *Mabini and the Philippine Revolution*. Quezon City: University of the Philippines Press, 1960. Print.

Agoncillo, Teodoro. *The Fateful Years: Japan's Adventure in the Philippines, 1941–1945*. 2 vols. Quezon City: R. P. Garcia, 1965. Print.

———. *Malolos: Crisis of the Republic*. Quezon City: University of the Philippines Press, 1997. Print.

Ahmad, Aijaz. *In Theory: Nations, Classes, Literatures (Radical Thinkers)*. London: Verso, 2008. Print.

Arendt, Hannah. *The Origins of Totalitarianism*. 1948. San Diego: Harcourt, Brace, Jovanovich, 1994. Print.

Blanco, John. "The Blood Compact: International Law and the State of Exception in the 1896 Filipino Revolution and the US Takeover of the Philippines." *Postcolonial Studies* 7:1 (2004): 27–48. Print.

———. *Frontier Constitutions: Christianity and Colonial Empire in the Nineteenth Century Philippines*. Berkeley: University of California Press, 2009. Print.

————. "Race as Praxis in the Philippines at the Turn of the Twentieth Century." *Southeast Asian Studies* (Kyoto) 49:3 (December 2011): 356–94. Print. Also available on web: http://kyoto-seas.org/2011/12/southeast-asian-studies-vol-49-no-3/. Web.

Blum, William. *Killing Hope: US Military and CIA Interventions Since World War II.* London: Zed Books, 2003. Print.

Bocobo, Jorge. "Filipino Contact With America." In Quirino, Eliseo, et al. eds. 290-304. Print.

Campomanes, Oscar, "1898 and the Nature of the New Empire." *Radical History Review* 73 (winter 1999): 130–44. Print.

Chen, C. Peter. "The Greater East Asia Conference 5 Nov 1943–6 Nov 1943." *World War II Database.* 4 Aug. 2014. Web.

Constantino, Renato. *Dissent and Counter-Consciousness.* Manila: Malaya Books, 1970. Print.

————. *The Philippines: (vol. 1): A Past Revisited.* Manila: Renato Constantino, 1975. Print.

De Bary, William Theodore, ed. *Sources of East Asian Tradition: The Modern Period.* Vol. 2. New York: Columbia University Press, 2008. Print.

De los Santos, Epifanio. "Cultura filipina." In *Trinidad H. Pardo de Tavera.* Manila: Impr. "Cultura Filipina," 1913. Print.

Espiritu, Augusto. *Five Faces of Exile: the Nation and Filipino Intellectuals.* Stanford, CA: Stanford University Press, 2005. Print.

Forés-Ganzon, Guadalupe, ed. *La Solidaridad.* 5 vols. Quezon City: University of the Philippines Press, 1967–73. Print.

Fradera, Josep. *Filipinas, la colonial más peculiar. La hacienda pública en la definición de la política colonial (1762–1868).* Madrid: Consejo Superior de Investigaciones Científicas, 2000. Print.

Furnivall, John. *Netherlands India: A Study of Plural Economy.* Cambridge: Cambridge University Press, 1939. Print.

González Echevarría, Roberto. *The Voice of the Masters: Writing and Authority in Modern Latin America.* Austin: University of Texas Press, 1985. Print.

Gonzalves, Theodore. *The Day the Dancers Stayed: Performing in the Filipino / American Diaspora.* Philadelphia, PA: Temple University Press, 2011. Print.

Hachiro, Arita. "The International Situation and Japan's Position." 1940. In *Sources of East Asian Tradition: The Modern Period,* vol. 2, ed. William Theodore De Bary, 622–23. New York: Columbia University Press, 2008. Print.

Hartendorp, A. V. H. *The Japanese Occupation of the Philippines.* 2 vols. Manila: Bookmark, 1967. Print.

Hau, Caroline Sy. "Privileging Roots and Routes: Filipino Intellectuals and the Contest over Epistemic Power and Authority." *Philippine Studies* 62.1 (2014): 29–65. Print.

————. "*Patria é intereses*: Reflections on the Origin and Changing Meanings of *Ilustrado*." *Philippine Studies* 59.1 (March 2011): 3–54. Print.

Hegel, G. W. F. *Lectures on the Philosophy of World History.* Trans. H. B. Nisbet. Cambridge: Cambridge University Press, 1975. Print.

Homma, Masaharu. "Letter of the Commander-in-Chief of the Imperial Japanese Forces in the Philippines, addressed to His Excellency, Manuel L. Quezon, President of the Philippines, December 30, 1942." Republic of the Philippines Presidential Museum and Library. Web.

Ileto, Reynaldo. "Orientalism and the Study of Philippine Politics." *Knowing America's Colony: A Hundred Years from the Philippine War.* Occasional Paper Series 13. Honolulu: Center for Philippine Studies, 1999. Print.

———. "Wars with the US and Japan, and the Politics of History in the Philippines." In *The Philippines and Japan in America's Shadow*, ed. Kiichi Fujiwara and Yoshiko Nagano, 33–56. Singapore: NUS Press, 2011. Print.

Joaquin, Nick. "The Filipino As Sajonista." In *Rediscovery: Essays on Philippine Life and Culture*, ed. Cynthia Nograles Lumbera and Teresita Gimenez Maceda, 219–35. Quezon City: National Bookstore, 1982. Print.

———. *Prose and Poems.* Manila: Graphic House, 1952. Print.

———. *A Question of Heroes.* Manila: National Bookstore, 1981. Print.

———. *Tropical Gothic.* Queensland: University of Queensland Press, 1972. Print.

———. *The Woman Who Had Two Navels.* Manila: Bookmark, 1991. Print.

Kalaw, Maximo. *The Development of Philippine Politics.* Manila: Solar, 1926. Print.

Kalaw, Teodoro M. "Americanization." In *Rediscovery: Essays on Philippine Life and Culture*, ed. Cynthia Nograles Lumbera and Teresita Gimenez Maceda, 155–58. Quezon City: National Bookstore, 1982. 155–58. Print.

Laurel, Jose. "Inaugural Address of President Jose P. Laurel, October 14, 1943." In *The Fateful Years: Japan's Adventure in the Philippines, 1941–1945*, ed. Teodoro Agoncillo, 2 vols., 1000–11 (appendix F). Quezon City: R. P. Garcia, 1965. Print.

———. "The Sophistication of Christ in the Orient." In *Thinking for Ourselves: A Collection of Representative Filipino Essays*, ed. Eliseo Quirino and Vicente Hilario, 64–76. Manila: Oriental Commercial Co., 1928. Print.

Lebbeus Redman, Wilfley, Pardo de Tavera, Trinidad H., et al. *The San José College case in the Supreme Court of the Philippine Islands: T. H. Pardo de Tavera, Louis M. Maus[and others] trustees of the College of San José, plaintiffs, versus the Holy Roman Apostolic Catholic Church, represented by the Most Reverend Archbishop of Manila[and others] defendants: brief for plaintiffs.* Manila: n.p., 1902. Print.

Lowe, Lisa. *Critical Terrains: French and British Orientalisms.* Ithaca: Cornell University Press, 1991. Print.

Lumbera, Cynthia Nograles, and Teresita Gimenez Maceda, eds. *Rediscovery: Essays on Philippine Life and Culture.* Quezon City: National Bookstore, 1982. Print.

Malay, Armando. *Occupied Philippines: The Role of Jorge B. Vargas During the Japanese Occupation.* Manila: Filipiniana Book Guild, 1967. Print.

McCoy, Alfred, ed. *An Anarchy of Families: State and Family in the Philippines.* Madison: University of Wisconsin Press, 1993. Print.

Mojares, Resil. *Brains of the Nation: Pedro Paterno, T. H. Pardo de Tavera, Isabelo de los Reyes, and the Production of Modern Knowledge.* Quezon City: Ateneo de Manila University Press, 2006. Print.

Morga, Antonio de. *Sucesos de las islas Filipinas*. 1609. Ed. and annot. José Rizal. Manila: National Historical Institute, 1993. Print.

Pardo de Tavera, Trinidad H. *The Character of Rizal*. Manila: Filatelica, 1918. Print.

———. "Conservation of the National Type." In *Thinking for Ourselves*. 330–46. Print.

———. "The Filipino Soul." *Thinking for Ourselves: A Collection of Representative Filipino Essays*, ed. Eliseo Quirino and Vicente Hilario, 170–88. Manila: Oriental Commercial Co., 1928. Print.

———. "The Heritage of Ignorance." In *Thinking for Ourselves: A Collection of Representative Filipino Essays*, ed. Eliseo Quirino and Vicente Hilario, 3–18. Manila: Oriental Commercial Co., 1928. Print.

———. "El legado del ignorantismo." In *Trindidad H. Pardo de Tavera*, ed. Epifanio de los Santos. Manila: Impr. 1913. Print.

Paredes, Ruby. "*Ilustrado* Legacy: The Pardo de Taveras of Manila." In *An Anarchy of Families: State and Family in the Philippines*, ed. Alfred McCoy, 347–80. Madison: University of Wisconsin Press, 1993. Print.

———. The *Ilustrado* and the Proconsul: Modeling a Colonial Dyad. Unpublished manuscript. Originally delivered at the "Vestiges of War Centennial Conference on the Philippine-American War." New York University Press (19–22 Feb. 1999). Print.

Pineda Tinio, María Teresa Trinidad. The Triumph of Tagalog and the Dominance of the Discourse on English: Language Politics in the Philippines during the American Colonial Period. PhD diss. National University of Singapore, 2009. Print.

Quezon, Manuel. "The Philippine Problem." In *Thinking for Ourselves: A Collection of Representative Filipino Essays*, ed. Eliseo Quirino and Vicente Hilario, 439–48. Manila: Oriental Commercial Co., 1928. Print.

Quibuyen, Floro. "Japan and America in the Filipino Nationalist Imagination: From Rizal to Ricarte." In *The Philippines and Japan in America's Shadow*, ed. Kiichi Fujiwara and Yoshiko Nagano, 106–31. Singapore: NUS Press, 2011. Print.

Quirino, Eliseo, and Vicente Hilario, eds. *Thinking for Ourselves: A Collection of Representative Filipino Essays*. Manila: Oriental Commercial Co., 1928. Print.

Rafael, Vicente. *The Promise of the Foreign: Nationalism and the Technics of Translation in the Spanish Philippines*. Durham, NC: Duke University Press, 2005. Print.

Rizal, José. *El filibusterismo*. https://itunes.apple.com/WebObjects/MZStore.woa/wa/viewBook?id=1B55416A335486 86EEC5397B66350DF8. 4 August 2014. Web.

———. "Filipinas dentro de cien años." In *La Solidaridad*, ed. Guadalupe Forés-Ganzon, 5 vols. Quezon City: University of the Philippines Press, 1967–73. Print.

———. *Reign of Greed*. Trans. Charles Derbyshire. Manila: Philippine Education Company, 1912. *Project Gutenberg*. 4 Aug. 2014. Web.

Rodó, José Enrique. *Ariel*. Valencia: Editorial Cervantes, 1920. *Project Gutenberg*. 4 Aug. 2014. Web.

Romualdez, Norberto. "Filipino Life and Culture." *Thinking for Ourselves: A Collection of Representative Filipino Essays*, ed. Eliseo Quirino and Vicente Hilario, 19–38. Manila: Oriental Commercial Co., 1928. Print.

Said, Edward. *Orientalism*. New York: Vintage, 1979. Print.

Sánchez, Luis Miguel Ángel. *El imperio en la vitrina. El colonialismo español en el Pacífico y la Exposición de Filipinas de 1887.* Madrid: Consejo Superior de Investigaciones Científicas, 2003. Print.

Schmitt, Carl. "El orden del mundo después de la Segunda Guerra Mundial." *Revista de Estudios Políticos* 122 (Mar. –Apr. 1962): 19–36. Print.

Thomas, Megan. *Orientalism, Propagandists, and* Ilustrados: *Filipino Scholarship and the End of Spanish Colonialism*. Minneapolis: University of Minnesota Press, 2012. Print.

Vargas, Jorge. *Address of Jorge B. Vargas, Chairman of the Philippine Executive Commission, on the Occasion of the Formal Inauguration of the KALIBAPI on Rizal Day, December 30, 1942.* Republic of the Philippines Presidential Museum and Library. Web.

———. "Selected Speeches and Statements." In *Occupied Philippines: The Role of Jorge B. Vargas During the Japanese Occupation*, Armando Malay, 161–223. Manila: Filipiniana Book Guild, 1967. Print.

White, Hayden. *Metahistory: The Historical Imagination in Nineteenth-Century Europe*. Baltimore, MD: Johns Hopkins University Press, 1973. Print.

PART II

Colonial Layerings, Imperial Crossings

4

Collaboration, Co-prosperity, and "Complete Independence"

Across the Pacific *(1942)*, *across Philippine Palimpsests*

VICTOR BASCARA

Why is it so difficult to speak of the relationship [of the
Philippines and the United States] in terms such as invasion,
resistance (so readily applied to the Japanese in World War
II), war, combat, colonialism, exploitation, discrimination?
—Reynaldo C. Ileto[1]

In posing this question in an essay about the Philippine-American
War (1899–1902[2]), Ileto parenthetically references Japanese Occupation during World War II as an instance implicitly comparable to US
pacification of the archipelago at the turn of the century. One might
immediately recall the spectacle of Japanese atrocities to answer Ileto's
question, but that would only reinforce Ileto's point about the politics of historical memory, of friendship and forgetting. To think that
the occupation and pacification of the Philippines by the Americans
was somehow carried out without brutalities or imperial acts called
"terrorism,"[3] as well as the counterinsurgent tactics such alleged acts
would inspire, is to have an inaccurate and perhaps wishful grasp of
what happened.[4] In contrast to Japan, "'Mother America' is owed a lifelong inner debt, or *utang na loób*, by the Filipino people she nurtured,"
Ileto observes.[5] From virtually the beginnings of US colonization of
the Philippines, the specter of Japan loomed as a possible successor
in the role of occupier.[6] If Spain was the residual colonial master and
the triumphant United States's regime was the dominant, then Japan
threatened to be the emergent force in the region to bring about a new
world order that did not sit well with American interests.[7]

Historical events, especially from late 1941 to mid-1945, appear to bear out the validity of this American anxiety. But until those events actually happened, beginning with the attack on Manila in late 1941, the subsequent invasion in the early months of 1942, and the horrific years of war and occupation that followed, the meaning of Japan in US colonial discourse about the Philippines was contentious and speculative. This chapter centers on a prominent example from popular US culture (John Huston's 1942 film *Across the Pacific* and its source material) as well as the discourse from hearings in the US Congress on the fate of the Philippines, c. 1919–39, to explore how US colonial discourse mobilized Japanese difference for coming to terms with the alignment of the Philippines and the United States during the colonial period.

Toward this objective, this chapter then considers the epistemology and tactics of collaboration and "amigo warfare," a generative term Ileto drew out from US counterinsurgency discourse during the Philippine-American War. In casting Japan as a threat to its mission in the Philippines, did the United States ironically end up making a compelling case for co-prosperity? Did US imperialism rely too heavily on the loyalty and gratitude of a population that may have had little reason to be faithful and thankful? The brutalities of World War II remobilized this triangulation. Prior to the outbreak of the Pacific War, such arguments risked being persuasive, even if—or probably because—they sometimes issued not only from the mouths of collaborators and spies, but also perhaps from pre-World War II US and Philippine political leaders attempting to codify and realize what was coming to be called "complete independence." While this analysis is not a history, its methodology attempts to draw out historical implications through analysis of selected period discourse that may be particularly symptomatic of ideological conditions. In this case, that discourse includes a 1941 short story serialized in *The Saturday Evening Post*, a 1942 Hollywood movie of that story starring Humphrey Bogart, and pertinent resonant moments from US congressional Hearings on the Philippines (c. 1919–39).

At issue then is the problem of loyalty for the project and implementation of empire—how loyalty is performed, read, and misread. Imperialism is premised on loyalty, and empires therefore ironically rely upon proliferations of surveillance. The ideal subject of colonialism is presumed to be the converted native, populations who genuflect not only in body but also in heart, mind, and soul. The colonized's faith in the colonizer and the colonizer's beliefs affirms the rectitude of the civilizing mission, and the colonized's resistance to those beliefs also betrays a fitness to be colonized in the first place. It is an irony of loyalty that it has historically demanded more rather than less surveillance.[8]

In appreciating the palimpsestic predicament of the Philippines, this chapter considers the figure of the spy, someone who strategically navigates between layers of those palimpsests through persuasive performances of loyalty, or even disloyalty. The telos of history can be found where loyalties are rewarded or punished. The steadfast are history's heroes, and the inconstant are vilified. For loyalty to be loyalty, it must operate independent of precise calculations of interest—including self-interest. Disregard for self-interest has been a hallmark of both the national hero and the terrorist. Consider the following from the 1902 testimony of the governor general of the Philippines William Howard Taft at a congressional hearing dealing with an insurgency that clearly resonates with the current War on Terror:

> Gov. Taft: . . . they are keeping them back from earning a living. They are keeping them back from their ordinary vocations. In the very province of Batangas itself the great majority desire peace and are only held there because of the system of terrorism of which I speak. Now, I say that warfare that depends upon terrorism and murder is a crime. That is all I have to say.
> Sen. Patterson: Is it because in your opinion the independence of the Philippine Islands has become hopeless that those who are contending for it are guilty of a crime?
> Gov. Taft: I think independence for the time has become hopeless.
> Sen. Patterson: And therefore those who are fighting for it are guilty of a crime?
> Gov. Taft: They are guilty of a crime in the method which they seek to attain it.[9]

The senatorial commission here gets Taft to articulate that his position is that fighting hopelessly for independence equals terrorism, equals a crime rather than war as such. By proceeding in violence with a lack of Taftian hope, the governor is in effect saying that these subjects are cast outside of reason, beyond the pale of modernity, thereby ironically demonstrating their fitness to be colonized or otherwise reconstructed after a regime change. The already underway program of US efforts in the archipelago then take on the character of upholding law against crime and defending civilization against terrorism.

Imperial Anxiety, or How Do You Say "F*** you" in Tagalog?

"Late in June, candidates arrive from every state in the Union . . . Alaska . . . the Philippines . . . the Army and National Guard—"[10] So begins the 1927 silent film *West Point*, starring the bankable William Haines and a charismatic young Joan Crawford. This explanatory title appears early on to set up the story of a brash young cadet (Haines) who eventually is transformed into a model officer. This geographic listing maps the reach of the domain of West Point and all it stands for; pedagogically, this title plots a *before* that will lead to an *after*. The *before* is one of "candidates" from the far-flung reaches of the nation and empire, while the presumed *after* of a West Point education is a commission as a second lieutenant in the US armed forces, possibly the Philippine Scouts branch of the US army, if that cadet hailed from the archipelago.[11]

Like many mechanisms of national and imperial culture, West Point produces proper subjects, as does *West Point*. Managing the risk of rebellion is structured into power, bearing out what Michel Foucault referred to as the "repressive hypothesis," and "perverse implantation,"[12] that is, that repression implies, identifies, and actually produces desire for resistance. There is certainly ample historical evidence that not "every state of the Union" or "the Philippines" has comfortably assented to compliance in the past. In the peaceful and prosperous days of 1927, such compliance may have come easier than in, say, the contentious times of 1861 or of 1899, but the fact of these histories of insurrection remains, even if somewhat repressed and otherwise reconstructed. New temptations and alliances may have emerged that test the capacity of the nation and the empire to inspire consensual allegiance. These then are the conditions of possibility for a military education in particular and of national/imperial subject formation in general. And so the listing of "every state of the Union . . . Alaska . . . the Philippines" may actually be useful for the empire to remember when considering the raw materials of the ideological work of officer training, especially if your local origins have been and perhaps still are imbued with resistance even if your presence seems to indicate perhaps the ultimate form of compliance through self-sacrifice.

In the case of 1899 and the onset of the Philippine-American War (or Philippine Insurrection), the exacerbation of that uncertainty found a name: "amigo warfare." In his generative work on "amigo warfare," Ileto makes the following speculation:

> Knowing more about the dynamics of amigo warfare, the ability to shift identities in changing contexts, could enlighten us about the whole issue of collaboration—collaboration not just during the war itself but throughout the whole period of colonial rule. It might even explain why Filipinos today seem to be so adept at handling tricky situations that demand shifting or multiple identities and commitments.[13]

Collaboration is a complicated and uncomfortable aspect of empire but historically it is indeed pervasive, a defining feature that makes an empire an empire, a complex manifestation of the consent of the colonized. Collaboration evidences a necessary malleability of the population to make them fit for colonization through their loyalty being able to shift to the (new) colonizer. Yet a malleable loyalty is not really loyalty at all. And the result is a colonized subject who may perform compliance, even in settings of extreme intimacy, while holding the potential for menace. In a resonant observation about military outcomes, Clausewitz observed that the

> result in war is never absolute. . . . The conquered State often sees in it only a passing evil, which may be repaired in after times by means of political combinations. How much this must modify the degree of tension, and the vigour of the efforts made, is evident in itself.[14]

These "after times" are our times, where the formerly colonized and conquered effect "repair," if not through "political combinations," then perhaps through micropolitics and microaggressions. And so an acerbic joke among US physicians inherits this history that goes something like the following: How do you say "fuck you" in Tagalog? Answer: "Yes, Doctor." The prospect of these tergiversations, whether of medical staff or of amigo warriors, potentially links critical agency with a residue of a buried history of collaboration, where, in Ileto's observations, collaboration is emblematic rather than deviant when that history is disinterred.

"What does it mean to bury the past?" asks Ileto, as he engages in the task of unearthing forgotten and otherwise misunderstood histories of US-Philippine "friendship."[15] More than two decades ago, Ileto had described this approach to recovered historical knowledge using the suggestive phrase "nonlinear emplotment" to challenge the then and still dominant project of "development," with the concomitant conceptions of Philippine national history that may echo aspects of US colonial conceptions of that history. Ileto plots that linearity as follows:

> Agoncillo's textbooks are considered exemplary in the nationalist tradition, but an examination of *all* modern history textbooks will reveal that they contain the following categories and chronological sequence: a Golden Age (pre-Hispanic society), the Fall (i.e., conquest by Spain in the sixteenth century), the Dark Age (seventeenth and eighteenth centuries), Economic and Social Development (nineteenth century), the Rise of Nationalist Consciousness (post-1872), the Birth of the Nation (1898), and either Suppressed Nationalism or Democratic Tutelage (post-1901, the U.S. Regime).[16]

To recognize nonlinear emplotment is to recognize incommensurable contradictions to this sequence, perhaps in the persistence of ideas and practices outside of modernization, as Ileto describes in his important history of nonsecular resistance, *Pasyon and Revolution*. To recognize the inheritance of these incommensurable contradictions to development is also to appreciate the dynamics of what Augusto Fauni Espiritu and Martin F. Manalansan IV have generatively termed "Philippine palimpsests."

The nonlinear, the palimpsestic, and even the contradictory can, I argue, be discerned at sites where contestation over divergent conceptions of destinies and development emerge. Collaborations then reveal the existence and stakes in Philippine palimpsests. Collaboration is a vexing notion to national development, especially when national development is understood as emerging from a colonized past. Such an emergence may be more paradigmatic than exceptional, as Benedict Anderson has implicitly contended.[17] Such real or imagined collaborations are with any of a number of putatively outside agents, whether Chinese merchants, Christian missionaries, Muslim proselytizers, American liberators-colonizers-liberators, Japanese co-prosperers-cum-occupiers, or anyone else who does not have a connection to the "Golden Age" of the archipelago imagined in national consciousness and perhaps intimated by archaeological discoveries such as the Laguna Copperplate Inscription (c. 900 CE).[18] The arrival at national independence then presumably means not only the end of empire but also the end of collaboration.[19] That is, the realization of nationhood presumably means arrival at a condition where desire for alternative futures has been eliminated, and therefore making nearly unthinkable incorporation into entities such as Spain, the United States, Japan, the Soviet bloc, the Vatican, Al Qaeda, neoliberal globalization, or anything else that might register as counter to interests that have come to be called national.

Undercover Little Brown Brother

We'll lose our preferential privileges in the United States,
and that will make some dislocations in our economy. But
freedom can't be bought for nothing. As it is, we are now no
more than a protectorate, a potential military stronghold
in the Far East. The United States will probably never set
us free, despite what they say. At the same time, we are not
allowed to make any commitments with our greatest friend
and nearest customer, Japan. We're between the devil and
the deep blue sea.
—Prof. Barca, economist, University of the Philippines
(c. June 1941)[20]

It should be noted that Dr. Barca is fictional, but what he says may not be so far off from the actual official, and strategic, words of Filipino leaders of that time and the years leading up to independence. Dr. Barca is also the villain of Carson's story, but, like many a good villain, his compelling complexity may reveal more about the actual state of things than the well-remembered virtues of a lantern-jawed hero fighting for truth, justice, and the American way.

In the June of 1927 of *West Point* or the June of 1941 of "Aloha Means Goodbye," The Philippine Islands were formally a part of the United States and had been for about a quarter century. Yet, as early as 1919, the US Congress was already holding committee hearings on "Philippine Independence," in what would eventually become the Tydings-McDuffie Act of 1934.[21] Along the way to the granting of independence in 1946, the phrase "Philippine Independence" in 1919 and 1924 would give way in 1930 to the more precise phrasing "the withdrawal of the sovereignty of the United States over the Philippine Islands and for the recognition of their independence, etc. [*sic*]." And by 1934 and 1939 the phrase "Complete Independence of the Philippine Islands" became the official way this idea was put into discourse. "Complete independence" was a phrase from the full title the 1934 Tydings-McDuffie Act, the law that would putatively dissolve the formal bonds between the United States and its colony, The Philippines, over the next twelve years—"an act to provide for the complete independence of the Philippine Islands" and so on. The phrases "Philippine independence" and sometimes "United States withdrawal" had been used in official government announcements and titles in the decade or more leading up to the passage of the act. Even as late as 1932 the phrase from the Hawes-Cutting bill (S. 3377) was "a bill to enable the people of the Philippine Islands to adopt a constitution and form a government." By 1934, the concept of "complete independence" emerged as the operative phrase. Between 1934 and 1946, World War II of course intervened. Yet, the timetable ended up not being disrupted, ultimately then appearing to keep to twelve-year plan that the 1934 act set up for "complete independence."

National and imperial culture, as Benedict Anderson and others theorists have asserted, inspire the allegiance and the sacrifice of those interpellated by national culture, from print culture to war memorials. Such allegiance and sacrifice are at their zenith when nationalism and imperialism seek to integrate and conspicuously celebrate those who bear markers of difference that have legitimated the inequalities that made a nation/empire materially and ideologically possible. But what happens when that national and imperial culture fails to generate that allegiance and sacrifice and instead inspires forms of resistance? The simple answer might seem to be decolonization. History may have turned out differently, and what we see is a decolonization deferred. And that deferral, I want to suggest, is tied to the all-too-familiar loss of an economically inflected conception of decolonization.[22] Not surprisingly, the entrance of the United States into World War II redrew political lines and economic interests. And the Cold War, as scholars like Jodi Kim and others have shown, only extended and dispersed these occlusions of the economic in the transition from the old to the new left.[23]

To grasp what this transition means it may be especially instructive to turn to those in the past who may have envisioned futures that did not come to pass. One such figure is the wartime collaborator, that intensely vilified bogeyperson who is perhaps the greatest anxiety for an empire fighting an imperial war, but who may also be a key asset of an anticolonial movement that, via conventional warfare, may be unable to effectively contend with its overwhelmingly powerful colonizer.[24] Indeed this kind of strategic nonalignment is what largely defined the thirdness of the Third World throughout the Cold War. But in the pre-Cold War moment, the Philippines gets situated in an earlier manifestation of a third space, that between the United States and Japan—or fourth space, if the residue of Spain is recognized—at a fifth column, in any case.

The potential for alignments with presumed enemies has been a familiar and effective strategy for the colonized and otherwise oppressed and exploited. This strategy led Malcolm X to assert that he was "desperate to join the Japanese Army"[25] or Muhammad Ali to famously refuse to fight the Viet Cong or Rev. Dr. Martin Luther King Jr. to say to CBS News that it "is amazing that so few Negroes have turned to Communism in the light of their desperate plight. I think it is one of the amazing developments of the twentieth century. How loyal the Negro has remained to America in sprite of his ling night of oppression and discrimination."[26] For the Philippines context under US colonial administration, historian Al McCoy describes how after the Japanese defeat of Russia in 1905 in the Ruso-Japanese War, the United States sought to cultivate an anti-Japanese sentiment in the Philippines.[27] Accordingly, performances of possible alignment with Japan could then be strategic for destabilizing the dominant empire's rule by gesturing toward the dominant one, as well as perhaps abiding by the residual one.

To come to terms with this configuration, the main cultural texts this paper proceeds from are (1) from summer 1941, Robert Carson's "Aloha Means Goodbye," a serialized suspenseful short story about the thwarting of a Japanese attempt to destroy Pearl Harbor with the help of collaborators, published in *The Saturday Evening Post* over five install-ments in June and July of 1941; (2) from late 1942, that story's adaptation as *Across the Pacific*, a 1942 film directed by John Huston and starring Humphrey Bogart; and (3) the pertinent official discourse of decolo-nization that Carson's and Huston's texts can be seen as a part of. The 1942 film, with its production and release that straddled attack on Pearl Harbor, changes the target from Pearl Harbor to another U.S. holding, namely, the Panama Canal. The film also changes the main collaborator to a Caucasian sociology professor, with a British accent and a Germanic name, on his way back to his job at the University of the Philippines; in the story, he is a Filipino economist on his way to Hawai'i to give a guest lecture at University of Hawai'i. The particular anxiety that the short story and the film manifest, and seek to manage, is, I argue, the anxiety concerning the alignment of Filipinos, especially the formally educated technocrats who would be—and historically have been—entrusted with shepherding a former colony into the emergent neoliberal globalization of the postcolonial, neocolonized world order.[28] That post-Cold War world order we now live in is one in which free trade agreements are negotiated in a spirit of creating what can be thought of as a global co-prosperity sphere of trans-oceanic partnerships. It could be argued that collaborators Dr. Barca (in Carson) and Dr. Lorenz (in Huston) may, for better or for worse, speak to unrealized goals of redistributed wealth and power after colonialism, if not necessarily the *means* of obtaining and directing that redistributed wealth and power—to Japanese capital-ists rather than US ones, and in any case, not necessarily to the masses, Filipino or otherwise.

In both the film and the serialized story, a key scene articulates the po-litical alignments that are being tested in the build-up to the Pacific War that had been raging for almost a year in the real world, but not yet reaching in the world of the film. The scene from the post-Pearl Harbor film is as follows, *Across the Pacific* (dir. John Huston, 1942) (0:17:32—0:18:18):

> Dr. Lorenz [Sidney Greenstreet]: I should enjoy listening to you two if you'll permit me.

Rick Leland [Humphrey Bogart]: You can referee.

Dr. Lorenz: Relationships between modern young Americans seem most peculiar to a man of my years. You give your lovemaking an assault-and-battery twist. Living so long in the Far East has perhaps given me a more or less Oriental view of things.

Alberta Marlow [Mary Astor]: We were discussing Philippine economics when we were so rudely interrupted.

Lorenz: My own field. Miss Marlowe was kind enough to listen to me.

Rick: They're going to be free in 1946, aren't they?

Lorenz: They are, provided America doesn't insist on fighting a war with Japan. It's my opinion however that that contingency is going to keep the Philippines from ever being free.

Alberta: Won't Japan gobble them up?

Rick: No offense but Japan or Canada or anybody else can have the Philippines as far as I'm concerned. It's hot in Manila.

Lorenz: It might be even hotter before long.

Alberta: Hot enough to go around in shorts? . . .

And now the scene from the serialized story published in *The Saturday Evening Post* in the summer of 1941:

"You were talking about Philippine economics before we were interrupted," Alberta reminded him.

"My own field," Doctor Barca said apologetically to Ricky. "Miss Marlow was kind enough to listen to me."

"You people are going to be free in 1946, aren't you?" Ricky said.

"I don't know. Are we?"

"Are you for it?"

"Definitely," Doctor Barca said, "providing America doesn't insist on fighting a war with Japan. But I'm afraid that contingency is going to keep us from ever being free. That and the stupidity and covetousness of some of our own people."

"Won't Japan gobble you up?"

"Why, if we're a good neighbor?"

"Aren't there a lot of economic problems involved?" Ricky said.

"We'll lose our preferential privileges in the United States, and that will make some dislocations in our economy. But freedom can't be bought for nothing. As it is, we are now no more than a protectorate, a potential military stronghold in the Far East. The United States will probably never set us free, despite what they say. At the same time, we are not allowed to make any commitments with our greatest friend and nearest customer, Japan. We're between the devil and the deep blue sea."

"Well," Ricky said, "no offense, but Japan, yourselves or anybody else can have you as far as I'm concerned. It's too hot in Manila."

The stakes and the tone may be rather different between the two versions, especially given who is speaking: a Filipino in Carson's story and a presumably European settler in Huston's film. There may even be a sense of wily irony on the part of Dr. Barca emerging through an attempted Socratic method persuading Rick: "I don't know. Are we?" and "Why, if we're a good neighbor?" The latter rhetorical question probably being a nod to the Good Neighbor Policy the United States adopted for Latin America at that time. Also he's changed from an economist to a sociologist (albeit an economic one), with all that we may infer from that. If we do the math, we can estimate that Dr. Barca, as a senior faculty member around 1941 would have been educated in the 1930s at the latest, and certainly would have come of age under US colonization. He is precisely the sort presumed to be formed by colonialism and rose to be one of the elites. Of course, he is fictional, but one might reasonably presume that his feasibility as a character depends upon parallels to possible perceptions of a colonial elite who came through, and perhaps also taught at, the University of the Philippines.[29]

What Dr. Barca also gets to the heart of is the predicament of insularity that *Downes v. Bidwell* (1901) made US empire constitutional, particularly the notion of the post-1898 new possessions as "foreign to the United States in a domestic sense," yet nevertheless under the plenary power of the United States. This idea arises in Barca (though not in Lorenz) as "not allowed to make any commitments with our greatest friend and nearest customer."

To grasp the historical and discursive field of these scenes, we can trace the discursive moves—particularly the sense of irony and even humor of the testifiers—spanning twenty years US congressional hearings on the (complete) independence of the Philippines, discourse that resonates with the Huston film and the Carson story. We might almost read these as a sort of "Dr. Barca goes to Washington." What follows are passages where the question of Japan emerges to illustrate how these politics of postcolonial alignment are put into discourse across different moments.

Monday, June 2, 1919

Sen. James Phelan (D-California):Do you mean to say that you have no fear of outside aggression in the event you are without protection of the United States or the league of nations?

[Hon.] Mr. [Manuel] Quezon [President of the Philippine Senate and Chairman of the Philippine Mission]: That is exactly what I mean.

Sen. Phelan: You have no fear of outside aggression?

Mr. Quezon: Yes, sir.

Sen. Phelan: Then, if aggression occurs you are in a position to resist it?

Mr. Quezon: I don't mean to say that. It would be too much for a Filipino to say that the Philippine Islands could withstand an attack from a first-class power now. We can't do it—not to-day anyway, nor I think the next 10 years or 15 years. Perhaps after that time we might be able to make it so hard to conquer the Philippines that no nation would care to do it. But we could not defend ourselves now, say, against Japan; but we do not believe that Japan has any desire to attack the Philippines . . .

Phelan: Now, what do you think about the possibility of Japan peacefully colonizing the Philippines as she is doing in California?

Mr. Quezon: Why, Senator, we can't prevent that, if Japan desires to do it . . . [30]

Quezon both plays on and assuages the concerns of the Americans about Japan, especially for a California senator worried about Japanese "colonizing" the Golden State, albeit "peacefully." The thrust of Quezon's remarks here point to a narrative of development that perhaps uncomfortably invokes a past of failed resistance to conquest by the United States, a failure that will not be repeated, after about a decade and a half of Philippine militarization and perhaps resistance by other means.

Five years later, Manuel Roxas continues this Congressional conversation, situating the Philippines betwixt two rival empires, rivals both militarily and commercially.

Monday, February 11, 1924

[Hon.] Mr. [Manuel] Roxas [Speaker of the House of Representatives
of the Philippine Islands]: The Japanese have known our country
ever since the sixteenth century. However, never since that time have
we had in our country more than 10,000 Japanese at one time. This
is explained by the fact that the Japanese people do not exhibit a
tendency to expand in the tropical zone. They cannot live or thrive in
a tropical country.

The failure to colonize Formosa, which the Japanese Government has
undertaken, exemplifies this truth . . .

Sen. William King (D-Utah): Then you have no apprehension, if you
received your independence, of any invasion by the Japanese?

Mr. Roxas: Absolutely not . . .

Mr. Willis: You mean, of course, industrial invasion. Military invasion is
another question, and we will come to that.

Sen. King: I take the position—and I think all those familiar with the
island will take the same position—that there is no danger of industrial or military invasion . . . [31]

Amidst familiar hypotheses about climatological fitness for settler
colonialism[32] is a telling distinction being made between "industrial
invasion" and "military invasion," with the latter being an overt assault
on sovereignty, while the former is ambiguous.

Six years later, in 1930, Roxas returns to Washington to testify again,
and he even more emphatically articulates harmonious Japan-Philip-
pines relations and the myth of the "Japanese menace":

Wednesday, January 15, 1930

[Hon.] Mr. [Manuel] Roxas [Speaker of the House of Representatives of the
Philippine Islands]: This statement would not be complete without reference
to the so-called Japanese menace to the independence of the Philippines
which imperialists continue to harp upon to the great embarrassment of both
the Government of the United States and Japan. The Filipinos, after a thorough consideration of that question, feel that no such fear of Japan need be en-
tertained. Japan is a nation that is showing a real desire for peace and a desire
to scrupulously maintain and respect the rights of other nations. Democracy
is fast gaining in that country; this is the best guarantee against imperialism.[33]

Two years later, the situating of Japan by advocates of complete Philippine independence makes that independence compelling, not despite but actually, in part, because of the Japan-Philippines-US relations.

Thursday, February 11, 1932

[Hon.] Clyde Tavenner [representing Philippine Civic Union]: The point is made that Japan is in favor of Philippine independence, so that she can go and take them. But I am convinced that Japan wants the United States to hold the Philippines, and to keep the flag flying there, so that if we get into trouble with Japan at any time, she can go over there and pull down the American flag, and make us send our fleet and our America boys there to fight her . . . I believe the day is come when Japan is going to say to you, "You taught us imperialism. Why is it worse for us to take Manchuria than it is for you to take the Philippines?"[34]

These pronouncements might now read as a recipe for appeasement, given the events of history. Yet the logic may be persuasive, given the hypocrisies and contradictions of empire, as well as the isolationist and antiwar ideas Tavenner's remarks articulate. (One might also hear resonance between the notion of "American boys" at the rise of fighting foreign wars in 1932 and "American boys" similarly mobilized thirty-eight years later, as articulated by Lyndon Johnson in his renunciation speech.)

Five years after the 1934 passage of the Tydings-McDuffie Act, attitudes toward Japan shift, as do military conditions. We hear again from Utah's Senator King, who participated in the Hearings back in 1924 also.

Thursday, February 23, 1939

Sen. King: It does seem to me that one important matter, though, which might be stressed—and I think it has been stressed—grows out of the fact that conditions in the Orient are somewhat different now from what they were in 1933, 1934, and 1935.

Mr. [Salvador] Araneta [former member of the Philippine Constitutional Assembly]: Exactly.

Sen. King: At that time some of us believed—I among that number—that Japan was entering upon an era of democratic development. I was mistaken. Certainly I would not want to turn you over, turn the

Filipinos over to be devoured by Japan. I wouldn't want, of course, to adopt any policy that might result in a conflict between the United States and Japan over the Philippines.[35]

So, what then does this mean for Dr. Barca and Dr. Lorenz? The answer may lie in the entrance of a curious figure in both the Carson story and the Huston film: a Filipino assassin who attempts to shoot these professors while the ship is docked (in NYC in the film and in Los Angeles in the story). The assassin fails to kill the professor; thwarted by Rick who uses that act to further perform to Barca/Lorenz that he is no friend to Philippine independence. The assassin is led away, presumably to be interrogated, tortured, and probably killed.

Given that the film was released in wartime, the assassin may come across as fairly unambiguous, as heroic and loyal to the US fight against Japan, a pawn, but a heroically sacrificed one. But given the complex process of decolonization that had begun well before the Philippines was colonized by the United States, this assassin may prove to be more difficult to reconcile neatly with the US cause. In neither the story nor the film does this character speak. One might want to ask this subaltern subject: On behalf of what future is he prepared to commit what can be understood as an act of war– an import-substitution economic future (in line with isolationist principles), or one of an export-oriented nature (in line with our current globalization)? Given that we see this assassin before Pearl Harbor, he might well have answered "complete independence," with all the promise and ambiguity that that entails.

Notes

1. Reynaldo Ileto, "The Philippine-American War: Friendship and Forgetting," 3.
2. The end date of the Philippine-American War is debatable, with some accounts of hostilities stretching out for a decade. Even the ambiguous ending of John Sayles's 2010 film *Amigo* may imply that the war, in various forms, persisted well after the overt pacification. Consider *Amigo* and *Avatar*. They are both movies about a recalcitrant population nevertheless attempting to cohabitate with an alien occupying force. A sympathetic protagonist struggles to make sense of the questionable project he finds himself to be a part of, and he feels a connection with one of the natives as well as with the native's way of life. Possible forms of collaboration ensue. In the marketing of John Sayles's admirable 2010 film *Amigo*, parallels to the current War

on Terror and the US occupations of Iraq and Afghanistan were presumed to be a selling point, especially perhaps for a presumed audience for an independent film. The film was not a box office success, which may perhaps point to its political and historical successes.

3. William Howard Taft explicitly uses the term "terrorism" in his 1904 testimony before a US congressional committee to describe the alleged conduct of the Filipino insurrections during the recently concluded war. See Henry Graff (ed.) *American Imperialism and the Philippine Insurrection (Testimony of the Times: Selections From Congressional Hearings)* (Boston: Little Brown, 1969), 96.

4. Ileto provides abundant evidence of the direct and indirect forms of violence that the occupation occasioned, from overt military actions to famines, disease, and agricultural devastation. This is, of course, not to say that Japanese occupation during World War II was not brutal also. On the pervasive brutality of the Pacific War, see John Dower, *War Without Mercy: Race and Power in the Pacific* War (New York: Pantheon, 1986).

5. Ileto, "Friendship and Forgetting," 3. For contemporary exploitations of these presumed Filipino traits in human trafficking, see Cindy C. Liou, Jeannie Choi, and Ziwei Hu, "Guestploitation: Examining Filipino Human-Trafficking Guest Worker Cases Through a Culturally Competent Practitioners Model," *AAPI Nexus* 11.1–2 (fall 2013): 57–80, 62.

6. See Al McCoy, *Policing America's Empire: The United States, The Philippines, and the Rise of the Surveillance State* (Madison: University of Wisconsin Press, 2009), 183–84. McCoy cites material expressing US efforts to look upon Japan with suspicion regarding the Philippines as early as 1905, soon after the Japanese defeat of Russia in the Ruso-Japanese War.

7. I borrow the dynamic of "Emergent, Dominant, and Residual" from Raymond Williams's *Marxism and Literature.*

8. For example, see McCoy, 8; and Vicente Rafael, *White Love*, 36–39, particularly regarding the uses of census-taking in the early US period.

9. Quoted in Graff, 96.

10. *West Point* (1927, dir. Walter Sedgwick). Ellipses in original.

11. The first West Point cadet from the Philippines, Vicente Lim, entered the USMA in 1910 and graduated in 1914 (https://en.wikipedia.org/wiki/Vicente_Lim#The_first_Filipino_graduate_of_West_Point). By the early 1970s, the Philippines had sent the largest number of foreign cadets. See K. Bruce Galloway and Robert Bowie Johnson Jr., *West Point: America's Power Fraternity* (New York: Simon and Schuster, 1973), 210–11. It should be noted that there is evidence of some recalcitrance even among the Philippine Scouts. See Richard Meixsel, "American exceptionalism in colonial forces?: The Philippine Scout mutiny of 1924," in *Colonial Armies in Southeast Asia*, ed. Karl Hack and Tobias Rettig (London: Routledge, 2006), 171–94.

12. Michel Foucault, *The History of Sexuality, Vol. 1.* 17–37.

13. Ileto, "Friendship and Forgetting," in Francia/Shaw, 7. Sarita See has persuasively applied Ileto's "amigo warfare" in her analyses of contemporary Filipino American

art and performance, particularly to appreciate the subversive cultural politics of comedians, such as Rex Navarrete.

14. Carl von Clausewitz, *On War*, book 1, chapter 1, 10, trans. Col. J. J. Graham, new and revised edition with an introduction and notes by Col. F. N. Maude, C.B. (late R.E.) vol. 1 (London Routledge & Kegan Paul, Ltd, 1962).

15. Ileto, 19.

16. Ileto, "Outline," 100.

17. The differences between the first and second editions of *Imagined Communities* may bear out this realization in Anderson's work. Anticolonial nationalisms go from being the "last wave" in the first edition to being arguably exemplary for all nationalisms. He does after all prominently use Rizal's *Noli* as an opening example of how national consciousness is manifested textually.

18. See Damon Woods, *The Philippines: A Global Studies Handbook* (Santa Barbara, CA: ABC-CLIO, 20067), 18–20.

19. The ending of the formal imperial era for the United States in the Philippines, is usually set at the conclusion of the Pacific War, an involvement that is a direct result of the wars waged four decades earlier. Conceptions of decolonization that were uniquely occasioned by the conditions of World War II, particularly those conceptions of decolonization that became visible through period discourse concerning US possessions coveted, and in some cases occupied, by Japan, as was the case with Guam and the Northern Marianas. See Keith Camacho, *Cultures of Commemoration: The Politics of War, Memory, and History in the Mariana Islands* (Honolulu: University of Hawai'i Press, 2011).

20. Robert Carson, "Aloha Means Goodbye," *Saturday Evening Post* (June and July 1941).

21. See H. Brett Melendy, "The Tydings McDuffie Act of 1934," in H. Kim, *Asian Americans and Congress* (Westport, CT: Greenwood Press, 1997), 283–308. Melendy offers an especially insightful analysis of the commercial interests (especially agricultural) that converged with political interests in the successful passage of the bill.

22. This loss is not unrelated to that which labor historian Michael Denning traces in his lament for that era's left organizing with the onset of the global antifascist struggle, also known as World War II. Michael Denning, *The Cultural Front* (1993).

23. Jodi Kim, *Ends of Empire: Asian American Cultural Politics and the Cold War* (Minneapolis: University of Minnesota Press, 2010), 8–9.

24. On the uncalculated if not incalculable Philippine losses during the US pacification of the archipelago, see Campomanes, "Casualty Figures of the American Soldier and the Other: Post-1898 Allegories of Imperial Nation-Building as 'Love and War'" in Luis Francia and Angel Velasco Shaw, *Vestiges of War* (New York: NYU Press, 1999), 134–62.

25. See George Lipsitz, "Desperate to join the Japanese Army," in *Perilous Memories*, ed. Fujitani, Yoneyama, and White.

26. Quotation transcribed at http://www.pbs.org/wgbh/amex/mlk/filmmore/pt.html, from the PBS American Experience documentary *Citizen King* (dir. Orlando Bagwell and Nolan Walker, 2004).

27. McCoy, *Policing America's Empire*. 183–84.

28. For a thoroughgoing critique of neoliberal globalization including but not limited to the Philippines, see Walden Bello, *Capitalism's Last Stand?: Deglobalization in the Age of Austerity* (London: Zed Books, 2013).

29. Examination of UP General Catalogs from the interwar era reveal a faculty composed of both Filipinos (for example, Conrado Benitez, PhD, "Professorial Lecturer on Economics") and some US transplants (for example, Mac H. Donaldson, PhD, "Professor of Economics") (c. 1922).

30. *Hearings Before The Committee on The Philippines, United States Senate and the Committee on Insular Affairs, House of Representatives, Held Jointly, June 2, 1919* (Washington, DC: Government Printing Office, 1919), 15.

31. *Hearings Before the Committee on Territories and Insular Possessions, United States Senate, 68th Congress, First Session on S. 912 (A Bill Providing for the Withdrawal of the United States from the Philippine Islands), February 11, 16, March 1 and 3, 1924* (Washington, DC: Government Printing Office, 1924), 10.

32. See also William Jennings Bryan's *On Imperialism* (1900), 76–77, where he states that "the white race will not live so near the equator," and draws on the example of Holland's experience in the sweltering Dutch East Indies (New York: Arno, 1970).

33. *Hearings Before the Committee on Territories and Insular Affairs, United States Senate, 71st Congress, Second Session on [Bills including] S. 3822 (A Bill to Provide for the Withdrawal of the Sovereignty of the United States over the Philippine Islands and for the Recognition of Their Independence, etc.), January 15, 20, February 3, 10, 17, 24, and March 10, 1930* (Washington, DC: Government Printing Office, 1930), 28.

34. *Hearings Before the Committee on Territories and Insular Affairs, United States Senate, 72nd Congress, First Session on S. 3377 (Hawes-Cutting Bill), A Bill Providing for the People of the Philippine Islands to Adopt a Constitution and Form a government for the Philippine Islands to Provide for the Independence of the Same and For Other Purposes), February 11 and 13, 1932* (Washington, DC: Government Printing Office, 1932), 52.

35. *Hearings Before the Committee on Territories and Insular Possessions, United States Senate, 76th Congress, First Session on S. 91028 (A Bill to Amend an Act Entitled "A Bill Providing for the People of the Philippine Islands to Adopt a Constitution and Form a government for the Philippine Islands to Provide for the Independence of the Same and For Other Purposes"), February 16 to March 15, 1939* (Washington, DC: Government Printing Office, 1939), 110–11.

5

A Wondrous World of Small Places

Childhood Education, US Colonial Biopolitics, and the Global Filipino

KIMBERLY ALIDIO

In this chapter, I argue for an expanded vocabulary with which to discuss US colonial power. I borrow from interdisciplinary theories of biopolitics, sovereignty, settler colonialism, and childhood to investigate the critical role of the early twentieth-century Filipino schoolchild to the generative and creative forms of US rule in the Philippines. Because I am invested in the many conversations that make up Filipino Studies, my analysis offers a possible way to link the global imaginary of historical US colonialism with the contemporary figure of the Global Filipino. This genealogy of a global space that set the terms of Filipino liberal, modern agency points to, I hope, further discussions of what sovereign liberation may look like: a deep, collective reevaluation of what constitutes Filipino life.

Global Imaginary and the Benevolent Assimilation Proclamation

"The earth is so vast and so full of wonderful things," states the *Filipino Teacher's Manual*, published in 1908. Counseling instructors in the American colonial public schools on how to teach geography to Filipino children, the *Manual* declares, "In studying the great picture of the world, which geography shows us, many new thoughts come to our minds and the power of imagination is increased as we try to form ideas of the various countries that we read about. The pupil's thought and imagination must be awakened."[1] This brief fragment of colonial pedagogy offers a glimpse of Filipino children's "education of desire" for the expansive possibilities of a global, even planetary, consciousness.[2]

The *Manual* shared a particularly colonial cosmopolitan orientation with related early twentieth-century educational texts, including English-language primers used in Philippine schools, American colonial teachers' reports, internationalist juvenile literature, and a small amount of Filipino schoolchildren's essays and letters published or available in the archives. The *Manual* guides the "native" Filipino teacher, soon to supplant Americans in nonsupervisory teaching positions in 1908, to direct the child to be a cosmopolitan learner: a discoverer of the world's oceans, land formations, climate variations, cultural diversity, and many countries.[3] In the process, the Filipino teacher refrains, as Tyson Lewis puts it, from "enforcing a sovereign decision . . . or performative control" upon the student.[4] In this scene of the Filipino teacher and pupil experiencing a concordant "awakening" of their own distinct capacities to reason, we can find the almost invisible hand of US colonial power. Military, economic, and political dominance marked the global space securing Filipino life, survival, and full capacity.

What does this short passage from the *Filipino Teacher's Manual* tell us about the US colonization of the Philippines (1898–1946) as a process of occupation enacting US sovereign power in place of Filipino national sovereignty? Educating Filipinos into a particular global imaginary was an important way in which the US colonial state worked as a disciplinary and biopolitical regime. In conversation with various interdisciplinary scholars of biopolitical administration and settler colonialism, I propose that US colonialism held sway over the Philippines by constituting Filipino life as the materialized sign of its sovereign power. Perhaps just as effectively as meting out deadly violence, US colonialism preserved Filipinos' biological survival and health on the level of the population. Throughout the twentieth century, the US colonial order promised a globalized future for the Philippines as a democratic and self-governing, independent nation through individual Filipinos' achievement of full subjecthood, reason, and incorporation into US-led geopolitical and economic regimes.

This was more than a rhetorical or ideological justification; it was also a critical exercise of colonial power: US colonial modernity in the Philippines governed Filipino life in a generative manner by characterizing it as perpetually emergent, on the levels of the individual and the collective, into self-regulation. In the colonial regime, Filipino ontological survival was based on the principle that full national sovereignty was impossible at the time of turn-of-the-century US military occupation. US sovereign power maintained that Filipino autonomous subjectivity was always subject to institutionalized conditions of punishment and associated with "bare life" and death.[5] Filipino national and biological life, under the sign of US colonial modernity, was to flourish sometime in the conditional, speculative future, and in an expansive global space shared by other self-determining nations and societies. As Achille Mbembe suggests, Western modernity was primarily a project of biopolitical sovereignty, rather than normative concepts of democracy and reason.[6] The US colonial state did not simply repress Filipino "resistance" but also worked to govern over and claim Filipino possession of an autonomous self and nationhood. US sovereignty over Filipinos became entangled with and reproduced Filipino's impulses for a continued existence.

In addition to the determining a biological level of existence, US colonial modernity managed cultural and political-economic forms of life, including Philippine nationalism. Late nineteenth-century Filipino liberal reformers and anticolonial revolutionaries declared the viability of the Filipino national subject, but with the arrival of the United States in 1898 in conjunction with Spanish American War, the Philippine nation's life remained insecure. US colonial occupation of the Philippines proceeded through clear domination of Filipino people exercised by the American military and civil governments. During the Philippine-American War (1899–1902) and in periods afterward, US practices of torture, mass imprisonment, and village depopulation produced large-scale death. The precarious life of the Philippine nation as the United States intervened in the Filipino anticolonial revolution was tied to the precarious lives of Filipinos who imagined themselves as fully sovereign and independent. In documented instances of direct repression and colonial control, the US military launched brutally violent campaigns against armed, militant Filipino nationalists. The civil government established top-down authority by passing the 1901 Sedition Act and the 1902 Brigandage Act criminalizing all expressions of Filipino nationalism and protecting US military aggression under the umbrella of just law.

In addition to these cases of brutal violence, American colonial power worked in more diffused, widespread and generative ways. The United States came as a guarantor, a protector of Filipino life, preceding aspirations for sovereign national power. The Benevolent Assimilation Proclamation, the 1898 declaration of United States sovereignty as a successor to Spanish political authority in the Philippines, infused colonial rule and military occupation with the notion of guaranteeing Filipino subjects "in their homes, in their employments, and in their personal and religious rights." The US military was to protect private property, or else give some payment when seizing it, and to open ports to international trade. While referring to Filipino nationalism in negative terms as dissent punishable by US military force, the Benevolent Assimilation Proclamation set the terms by which Filipinos were imagined to flourish as full subjects through reason, rights, and nationhood. The critical message in communicating the US colonial sovereignty was to include Filipinos in the "rights and liberties which is the heritage of free peoples," thereby dictating that all those "brought within the lawful rule" were to live and those beyond the law were subject to sociopolitical and biological death.[7] Since the mid-nineteenth-century, Filipino reformist and revolutionary movements were dynamically engaged with transnational and global modernity, particularly in Southeast Asian, Pacific, and Atlantic exchanges of liberal and revolutionary organizing.[8] US colonialism sought to make access to global connections into a technology of administrative rule by acting as exclusive gatekeeper of global modernity.

Simply, colonialism deployed discretionary power over subjected peoples' juridical and ontological conditions. In the process of dispossessing Filipino sovereignty, the United States practiced modes of inclusion and exclusion in such a way as to belie the tendency to see them as logics in fixed opposition to one another. The colonial state and cast the Philippines and other "unincorporated territories" as part of and yet apart from US polity. Formal political control of a multitude of Caribbean, Latin American, and Pacific territories meant that the United States maintained discretionary, colonial power to determine political status. As such, liberal democracy incorporated Filipinos, along with Kanaka Maoli, Chamorus, Puerto Ricans, and others, as colonial subjects placed oddly in relationship to the United States.[9] Beyond formal political colonialism, US biopolitical regimes expanded military and capitalist economic systems across the world, particularly in "small places" in Latin American and the Asian-Pacific regions, to institute development and modernization schemes in the Global South.

The global imaginary in which Filipinos and others were to be "assimilated" was a spatial and temporal arrangement quite apart from the US nation-state or American national identity.[10] Adapting the civilizationist global purview of classificatory human diversity and histories, the US colonial cosmopolitan vision viewed the world as a potentially liberal, inclusionary, modern, and multicultural empire. In a sense, the US-led geopolitical order expanded and adapted settler colonial logics of elimination and incorporation in an international projection of US settler colonial society.[11] Instead of being settled by Anglo-Americans or ruled exclusively by a US imperial state, the globalist version of settler colonialism would be nominally governed by the pursuit of each "small place" for maximal modern life. This is not to say that repressive, violent brutality was outmoded by biopolitical administration, but rather sustained by sovereign power over political, economic, cultural, and biological aspects of life possible within a global modern regime.

The productive, perversely life-giving power of US colonialism serves as a conundrum for those of us concerned with the genocidal effects of US militarization and counterinsurgency.[12] From the Philippine-American War of 1899 to post-2001 American military exercises, the Philippines has been shaped by the US global military complex, often termed by nationalists as "foreign imperialism." The long historical experience makes the US military regime no longer foreign as such to many nations and American colonies of the Asian-Pacific world.[13] In the post-Marcos dictatorship and post-US bases era, the US military can be seen as directly or indirectly acting in concert with the Philippine government to perform political and structural violence. Native American Studies scholars illuminate a way to understand both the life-securing and deadly nature of US colonial power by using the term "genocide" to think about how US settler colonialism secures the liberal, democratic settler society by incorporating and amalgamating Indigenous peoples and cultures, as well as eliminating and replacing them on stolen land.[14] A crucial understanding of US colonial regimes may require a close reading of various expressions of power used to govern subjects in all areas of society, political economy, and life.

Educational Biopolitics and Benevolent Assimilation

The Benevolent Assimilation Proclamation is notably focused on Filipino populations. Its statement of liberal individual rights foreshadows the administrative and disciplinary power exerted by US colonial social and political education programs. Promises of continuance and unprecedented thriving in the global modern sphere activated a host of institutions and individuals to perform the work of regulating and managing populations, sometimes directly on behalf of the colonial order but sometimes not.[15] During the Philippine-American War, the US military initiated efforts to teach Filipino children how to speak, read, and write English. Universal schooling was part of an American counterinsurgency operation.[16] At war's official end in 1902, the US civil government formally organized universal public schooling around the singular aim of childhood English language literacy. Throughout 1901, more than one thousand American teachers joined remaining US military personnel to train an estimated 150,000 school children.[17] The educative colonial regime operated on the productive friction between varied exertions of power: repressive domination and generative administration. Educational biopolitics notably involved the absence of a dominating, repressive colonial power and instead the guiding presence of teachers and, in the case of early twentieth-century Filipino children, the educative US colonial state.[18]

The purpose of English-language composition classes was to produce a "natural expression, in simple, clear English, of the child's own thought, not that of the teacher."[19] English-language lessons had a number of interrelated functions in the US colonial regime. By learning to write and read English, Filipino children gained rational self-determination to name their practical environment and declare intentional action. Secondly, schoolchildren came to self-realization through literacy by locating themselves in a particular geographical place, and in a specific temporal stage of "racial" history, development, and modernization. Lastly, students cast their awakening subjectivities from their local place outward to the imagined world. American colonial sovereignty defined and claimed each object lesson—language, locality, and globality—so that the Filipino schoolchild would claim each one, in turn, for her own.

English-language composition lessons were intimately tied with the subject of geography, particularly in exercises on composing letters to schoolchildren in other provinces and in the United States.[20] In 1905, Fernando Maglayo corresponded from Pangasinan, in northwest Luzon, with Forrest H. Reeder in Sherman, Texas, on the border with Oklahoma. In response to Reeder's questions about the Philippines, Maglayo provided a brief historical narrative, a list of agricultural products, and the names of fruits and trees. He proceeded to locate the topological features near his home province, noting that the neighboring mountainous city of Baguio "is cool nearly like your climate there [in] Tejas." Maglayo closes with further information on his social location: "Friend excuse me because I did not answer your letter sooner because I was busy to prepared the examination. Now I am 12 years old and I have two sisters. Now I am going to take a walk to the street and I closed now give my regard to your parents, sisters, brothers, cousins, friends [sic]. Yours truly."[21] Students were directed to write letters "made up of simple, direct statements, or questions" maximizing the exchange of information about natural resources, distances to trading capitals, customs, and climate. *The Filipino Teacher's Manual* suggested that "native" instructors familiarize themselves with "English-style" letters comprised of polite, succinct, and yet practical rhetoric. In contrast, Spanish-language letters presumably written by most educated Filipinos used too many adjectives and tended to insincerely flatter the recipient. However foreign and colonial the English language, it was taught by American teachers as a transparently descriptive rhetoric that would presumably "leave him [the Filipino child] free to put in any ideas of his own."[22] The educative US colonial regime exercised its power not by repressing Filipino thought and expression under linguistic conventions, but by deploying a communicative medium that generated Filipino "originality" and made it mobile in the English-speaking world.

As a colonial technology, English literacy would be used both to develop individual Filipino self-realization and preserve the life of local Filipino customs and culture.[23] The metropolitan language and publishing system were used in particular ways to get at the local colonial world, conveying to the colonized child both the global imaginary and her intimate surroundings. Americans who had taught in the Philippines wrote textbook primers used widely in provincial elementary and high schools for several decades. To provide English-language reading material for Filipino self-realization, primers such as the 1904 *Philippine Beginner's Book* sought to mirror the student's subjective experience and social world. The presumed sphere of the Filipino child included the natural and rural landscape of the pastoral tropics, family life, chores, play, the new public schools, and American teachers. It also included the child's local "heritage" of cultural myths, folk tales, and sayings, all translated into English, published in the United States and imported into Philippine schools. Through English-language primers, the US colonial system further anchored itself to native, local, provincial, and folk elements of a Filipino protonationalist selfhood. Revaluing the native and local was what invited Filipinos into participating in the colonial, global system.

While educating Filipino children in the desire for the global imaginary, the predominate concern of English literacy remained the student's embodied location. By including folktales and stories relating to "Malayan life" and the pastoral tropics, the *Third Insular Reader*, which went into three reprintings from 1905 to 1914, sought to connect Filipino children to their local cultural and social communities as well as to the "greater world." Colonial schooling directed the Filipino child to become attuned to her immediate surroundings. The student, at first, was to recognize and name ordinary objects around her, in addition to her own body. In geography class, she would draw a series of maps, starting with the roads connecting her homes to the neighborhood school, their town, province, archipelago, and, finally, nearby countries. Objects beyond her field of vision were then abstracted as image and word: if mountains can be seen in the distance, there would be other houses, towns, and children on those mountains. Further away were bodies of water, other countries, and capitals. From this regional knowledge base, the child would go on to study China and then the United States. The schoolchild found herself and her local place within the time-space coordinates of American colonial modernity: a panoramic, multicultural global space and a temporal mode of human civilizational, industrial, and democratic development. The particularly childish nature of the colonial geopolitical imaginary was the creative manipulation of scale, size, and distance so that each faraway place was made intimate while far enough to expand children's reasoning capacities. These creative capacities were essential to travel, migration, and the kinds of felt and flexible relationships within the US-led world.

Child Settlers and Colonial Futures

In the process of composing English-language descriptions of her practical environment, the schoolchild was an agent of remaking her local civil society into the telos of progress and development. More than two hundred miles south of Manila in Banton Island, public high school students in 1905 completed an assignment to write an English-language speech on social and political matters addressed to their class, their town, and "dear countrymen." [24] The students wrote about the promise of their cosmopolitan futures within the US colonial order. In his speech, V. F. Beltran highlights the opportunity to get a college degree in the United States through the scholarship, or *pensionado*, program, established two years before. He cites the chance to travel to St. Louis World's Fair of 1904 where a large number of Visayans were exhibited as "civilized natives" and their children attended a model school taught by a Filipina teacher.[25] Migration and global exchange both allow young Filipinos to invest in their sovereign ambitions. For many of the students, global forces filtered by US colonialism stimulate Filipinos' realization of their own political rights and national capacities. As Beltran explains, one of the object lessons offered by Americans is self-sufficiency: "While we remain quiet and prosperous under the United States flag, we must not fail how to learn the very interesting things that they teach us, that is, to govern ourselves." Close identification with outside world does not seem to result in a loss of identity, deracination, or alienation from place of origin. The new colonial order offers the world as a reflective surface. Beltran declares that colonial rule intends that "we might take more interest in our own aspirations."[26] Bantoan high school students identified their cosmopolitan futures with the US-led global imaginary. Filipino schoolchildren were the self-regulating subjects that would mark the new American world order as a constellation of autonomous, liberal democracies. Imperial sovereignty was expressed by the multitude of flourishing singularities.[27]

Other students wrote that changes in Banton since US colonial rule assured them of the capacity to follow their innermost desires with hard work and regular school attendance. Describing school programs of physical exercise and public health, Rufina Alma reports, "Not being sick causes the pupils to learn more because I think none of us wishes to miss even . . . a day or a half day of school without a great necessary for that is againts our selves [sic]."[28] On the whole, the students documented the newly normative, self-evident and possible in their lives. They presented practical logics of progress that they defined as industrialized modernity, rule of law, and moral perfection. By reading schoolchildren's papers as authorizing US colonial power over interwoven strands of biological, political, and cultural Filipino life, we may understand the diffused and generative nature of the colonial regime. In a statement of educational biopolitics, David P. Barrows, US colonial education administrator, asserted that Christianized peoples of lowland Luzon and the Visayan Islands, including Spanish- and Chinese-Filipino mestizos, possessed biological capacity and historical desire to flourish in the modern world.[29] In contrast were indigenous and Muslim people who were incompletely or entirely not under Spanish colonial rule: such populations were meant to disappear by decay and critical amalgamation into presumably stronger groups. Specific social locations, especially age and locality, carried Barrows' message. From the perspectives of their small island and their school experiences over the previous four years since the start of US colonial rule, Bantoan high school students educated their own communities on how Filipinos would persevere collectively under American and global power.

Filipino schoolchildren authored the new "cultural imaginaries" of US occupation, territorialization, and spatial relations.[30] To return to the *Filipino Teacher's Manual* that opened this chapter, I'm interested in the colonial discourses of Filipino schoolchildren awakening to their own reason, expression, and imagination. How might prohibited zones of decay, fantasies of substandard quality of life, and occulted backwardness activate such scenes of awakened capacities? Bantoan high school students illustrated the dystopia of life beyond the US colonial regime, a fantasized version of what Achille Mbembe identifies as "necropolitics," or the "creation of death-worlds."[31] In a speech he titled, "If the Philippines Had Been Independent," high school student Vicente Villavicencio speculated on the state of lawlessness without US governance: armed conflict, violence, and intimidation by "brigands" would escalate to threaten foreign investors and incite war with more powerful countries. Less benevolent colonization by Germany, France, England, Russia, or Japan would ensue, possibly closing off imported food and aid needed by a people presently lacking economic self-sufficiency. "Brigands," in American colonial law, included political dissidents and guerrilla insurgents. Accordingly, Villavicencio associated militant revolt against US sovereignty as impractical and, furthermore, deadly to Filipino existence.[32] While Filipino guerrillas insisted on their ability to outstaying the more militarily powerful occupying force, colonial "law and order" insisted that well-being, food, security, and a guaranteed future were possible with US sovereignty. Educated to embody the Filipino's collective future as "awakened" people, schoolchildren such as Villavicencio declared effectively, in English, that individual lives within a sovereign Philippines would be marked, at least in the present, by a vulnerable, bare existence.

Children came to the fore of Benevolent Assimilation and colonial biopolitics as a subpopulation made to be distinct from Filipino adults, in a way suggestive of settler colonial projects of institutionally isolating indigenous children for presumed reasons of rescue and civilization.[33] Many American colonial administrators, teachers, and travel writers highlighted the delightfully curious and responsive intelligence of Filipino children; some went further to describe how children's mental acuity faded into dull passivity once they entered puberty. Whether they were peasants or elites, "after a certain age without a start in their more pliable years, the mental soil became hard and difficult to cultivate."[34] Several Americans reported that Filipino "adults," including those over the age of fifteen, articulated their own demise by declaring that their "time" had passed. Later, in the interwar period, American colonial teacher and historian Austin Craig confirmed that grown-up Filipinos were as archaic as the horse-driver.

> The older generation was to be considered, but the laws of nature and nature's God have unalterably decreed that the future belongs to youth, and not to age. The product of the public schools now growing up are to be given the preference in public service, because they are best qualified for the present system. This is the law of progress, just as, however faithful, the *cochero* has to be replaced by the chauffeur when the automobile comes.[35]

The potential of the "race" that was found in the child predicted the natural but premature passing of the older generation, classified by the inability to speak English or disconnection from the US-led global imaginary. While marked for death by the "law of progress," Filipino adults did indeed continue to live through the American colonial period. Biopolitical administration located in the adult generation the "antagonisms" to the temporal narrative of colonial modernity.[36]

In this sense, children were positioned as settlers of US biopolitical colonialism, a separated-out population marked specifically for life. In this context, the 1901 US counterinsurgency campaign in Samar to "kill everyone over ten" was a fatal retribution against Filipino resistance in the form of depopulating an enemy population that nevertheless shared biopolitical concerns with colonial schooling: "awakening" and continued life through the reconstructed child.[37] Strictly speaking, Anglo-Americans in the Philippines did not pursue settler colonial practices of eliminating and amalgamating the indigenous and mestizo peoples, dispossessing them of land and sovereignty claims, and replacing existing societies with modern liberal democracies. Nor were Filipino children removed en masse from their parents and home communities or administratively targeted for rescue, as indigenous children were in North America and Australia.[38] Rather, the US biopolitical regime in the Philippines expressed sovereign power by holding sway over children's futures and their expressive communication of valuable life.

What was vital about Filipino children was their "natural curiosity" about the world around them. This quality undergirded colonized children's educability, made them take to the "transparent" medium of English, and trained them to be good reporters of local social conditions to global audiences. Childish curiosity was a primitive resource that could be activated for cosmopolitan learning. In early twentieth-century paternalist, civilizationalist racial discourses, all children possessed traits characteristic of their primitive developmental stage: impulse, passion, and rituals of play, as well as curiosity.[39] According to an American teacher, children in the Philippines had a distinctive childish and racialist primitivity: "It is among the younger generation that the promise lies. The little ones are bright and gentle and respectful, quite unlike the boisterous denizens of young America."[40] Filipino children were distinct from adult Filipinos, because the adult is categorically what the child promises to become: rational, self-directed, and sovereign. While the hierarchical difference between adult and child remained, Filipino adults were excluded from modern reason and sovereignty by colonial discourses infantilizing them as savage or semicivilized. The Manila branch of the racially segregated YMCA responsible for Filipino men's physical and spiritual health deemed the entire Filipino population "as a race . . . in the childhood of their development, . . . exhibit[ing] all the peculiarities, faults and virtues of a rapidly developing adolescent boy."[41] Furthermore, Filipino children differed from "boisterous" Anglo-American boys and young men by performing a distinctive childishness, attentively oriented toward American teachers and the world's wonders.

Given the many ways that childhood and racial primitivity were intertwined, educators and social scientists concurred with US colonial administrators that the precivilized/ preadult stage should be protected so that primitive traits of curiosity could be properly tapped. As suggested by a close reading of English-language primers published for the Philippines, the US colonial order claimed intimate knowledge with the Filipino child's external environment and interior subjectivity. To a greater extent than other US administrative, state-approved texts, school primers asserted this colonial cosmopolitan familiarity with a colonial population. Turn-of-the-twentieth-century US imperialist debates equivocated on whether the federal government could comprehend what anti-imperialist psychologist and philosopher William James called the "secrets of the Philippine soul" adequately enough to design colonial programs of democratic tutelage and capitalist development.[42] In contrast, colonial administrators confidently and pragmatically identified Filipino children's vital primitivity as the rightful domain of US knowledge. The ontological condition of Filipino childhood was a temporal period and also a political space of dependency delineated by US colonial power. Through their affective and incipiently rational qualities, Filipino children were both governed and incipiently self-governing subjects.[43]

The Global Filipino and the Neoliberal Present

The US-led global imaginary transmitted in the formal colonial regime in the Philippines preceded and presaged neoliberal globalization of the late twentieth century and our present time. This era of the Overseas

Filipino Worker (OFW) and, more generally, the Global Filipino can be traced backward through the discipline and management of Filipino subjects and populations into an imagined global sphere. Concepts of biopolitical colonial power and liberal settler colonialism may function as tools to continue conversations in Filipino Studies on several interrelated threads. This chapter's main concern of examining the multiple historical forms of US colonial sovereign power extends beyond Philippine postcolonial independence of 1946 to predominant global imaginary of the turn of the twentieth-first century. Neoliberalism advances a utopian global imaginary based on the belief that, to paraphrase David Harvey, market exchange within a fully integrated global economy constitutes the highest ethic of human activity. Sovereign reason organized to maximize prosperity, growth, and innovation also maximizes human connection across political, cultural, national, and economic divisions.[44] To illustrate, emotional, and commodity exchanges across the Filipino diaspora are inextricably and metonymically related in Filipino Canadian ethnographic narratives of choosing mass-produced products to pack into *balikbayan* boxes for consumption by family in the Philippines.[45] Utopian neoliberalism, similar to US colonialism in the Philippines, exercises biopolitical power over populations by reconstituting what it means to be human, free, and happy. The neoliberal argument posits that the Global Filipino is far from dehumanized or disempowered.

Diffused power characterizes late modern, democratic neoliberal societies, in which the state sovereignty is transformed both by the power of the economic market and by discourses of neoliberal individual actors who govern themselves in accordance with the market. Throughout the twentieth century to the present, the Philippines has been considered a viable nation and economy if it is part of the US-dominated global political economy. To maintain nation, family, and selfhood, the Filipino subject must reengineer herself into a global worker, accept training, and repackage her capacities and culture for the marketplace. Comparative advantage and global competitiveness amount to deadly regulation. To take advantage of neoliberal globalization's opportunities, Filipinos undertake training in globalized arrangements of flexible labor, transnational migration, and self-regulatory cross-cultural conduct. This disciplinary education is a central subject of Anna Guevarra's ethnography of Overseas Filipino

Workers, specifically women nurses and domestic workers exported outside the Philippines by a combination of Philippine state and private institutions. The ideal Great Filipino Worker is trained in techno-professional skills and cross-cultural communication and work styles, adaptable, and properly affective. In fashioning a genealogical link between the colonial Filipino child and the postcolonial Global Filipino, my intention is not to infantilize or sentimentalize the "care labor" of Filipina transnational workers. From Guevarra's analysis, we see that the affective, gendered, and cultural qualities that grant Filipino workers "added export value" in overseas labor markets are rationalized into techno-professional skills and sovereign, bottom-line management of kinship ties.[46]

The gendered and affective aspect of care labor does not negate or replace Filipina sovereign "dreaming in action." Neferti Tadiar refers to Filipino women's creative persistence within the framework of their heteropatriarchal commodification.

> In its idealized and therefore commodifiable form, [Filipina subjectivity] consists of practices of caring for others, of extending oneself to others, of serving and accommodating others. But even within that norm, it also consists of longing for better things, better worlds for oneself and for one's own and of bravely venturing out into the world with little or no guarantees of safety in search for new possibilities of life. Filipino subjectivity consists of those practices of dreaming in action that are indispensable to the work and commodity identity that Filipinas are called upon, *as Filipinas*, to perform.[47]

While the Global Filipina/o helps to fulfill basic human needs in the informal and formal service industries, she encounters commodified subjection. Still, Filipinas' capacity to engage with present-day concerns while speculating alternative and other worlds marks her global purview as one of humanist connection, generative of biological and political life. If indeed the Global Filipina has inherited such a role from US biopolitical colonialism and neoliberal globalization, she may use it to sustain life beyond what Tadiar calls the "norm" of her "Filipina subjectivity," namely, peoples and cultures marked for decay and death.

In the first place, sovereignty in the Filipino diaspora might reimagine the neoliberal representational scheme that manages and regulates women OFWs by casting them as either extremely vulnerable or supremely empowered. As Anna Guevarra notes, the Philippine state and private agencies exercise their own biopolitical administration by maintaining that OFWs, *by nature*, are not dehumanized objects, debased workers, sexually vulnerable, or robbed of creative free will. If properly trained to regulate their own behavior within a set of known risks of violence and death, OFWs will persevere in a heroic manner. Neoliberal discourse portrays the overseas worker as a full participant in Philippine national life, a rights-based individual, and as a privatized subject capable of "fighting back." In a documentary called "Empowered Filipina," sponsored by the Philippine Embassy in Abu Dhabi, Filipina businesswomen, health-care workers and domestics are shown to be vulnerable to labor and sexual abuse because they are perceived stereotypically as "immoral," disposable, and less than human. By including domestic workers, nightclub entertainers, and relatively disadvantaged Filipina workers in this discussion, the film provides a cross-class message resisting sexual and bodily violation. Perhaps not surprisingly, Filipina neoliberal agency requires replacing stereotypes of economic and sexual violability with postcolonial assets of professionalism, cosmopolitan education, and English-language literacy.[48] The effect is to participate in relegating some people marked by economic deprivation and sexual violability—some domestic, entertainment, and sex workers, for instance—beyond the norms of the valued humanity. Doing so misconstrues the many methodologies and epistemologies of how Filipinos persist creatively in the gray zones between informal and formal economies, for example, or more theoretically in the frictions of biopolitical regimes.

Conclusion: Sovereignty in the Diaspora

Creative capacities are essential for insight into colonialism in the past and for displacing present-day colonialism in all its forms. After all, US colonialism and neoliberal globalization have been quite creative in reproducing localized, ethnic, and national identities for the purpose of expressing sovereign power. The habits, inheritance, and effects that produce present-day colonialism, white supremacy, neoliberal globalization, and settler colonialism also maintain self-regulatory liberal, cosmopolitan identities. For example, the biopolitical idea of decolonization, especially in the diaspora, has been to create new methodologies based on a stable interior self. As Lily Mendoza has noted of the transnational *Sikolohiyang Pilipino* movement:

> Indigenization from within uses the indigenous culture as, at once, the starting point, source and basis of concepts, methods and theories. The goal is not merely to build upon exogenous constructs and indigenize their use and application. It is to develop its own analytical tools, instruments, and conceptual frameworks using the indigenous culture as the main reference point.[49]

The reclaimed selfhood reproduces the settler colonial practices that Scott Morgensen calls "turning native land and culture into an inheritance granting knowledge and ownership of themselves."[50] This centers the nonnative Filipino subject by displacing, celebrating and incorporating indigenous peoples. The objective and the method is a reorienting of the self in an imagined indigenous or nationalist space, in the space of the collective, transhistorical "we." Indigenization apparently directs the global Filipino's attention inward, away from the gaze and objects of the foreign, and beyond the confines of the present moment and political world. In this example, Filipinos are made to be complicit in the reproduction of biopolitical settler colonial power. Indigenization maximizes nonindigenous Filipino subjectivity by possessively incorporating the presumed "primitivity" or "precolonial" qualities of indigenous peoples of the Philippines in such a way as to displace indigenous people's inherent sovereignty claims against the Philippine state and nonindigenous Filipinos.[51]

Alternately, self-determination cannot be reduced to preserving Filipino liberal agency within a national or global space purporting to be inclusionary, modern, and democratic. While markedly different, the strategies of indigenization, on the one hand, and the pursuit of inclusion into modern rational polities, on the other, both inherit the effects of US biopolitical sovereignty. Stable formulations of a distinctive subjectivity and rootness in place are defined by regimes of Filipino life and death. To move beyond these regimes may denaturalize and transform the interdependent relationships forged from settler migration, militarization, and neoliberal economic power with others, including indigenous peoples, wherever Filipinos work and live.

Acknowledgments

Thanks to Karen Jania for her expert help in the University of Michigan Bentley Library Philippine Collection. Many thanks to those who engaged with earlier versions of this chapter at gatherings organized by the University of Illinois, Urbana-Champaign's Asian American Studies Department, and by the University of Michigan Philippine Study Group Association, particularly Augusto Espiritu, Moon-kie Jung, Martin Manalansan, Cynthia Marasigan, A. Naomi Paik, Martin Joseph Ponce, Debbie Reese, Sarita Echavez See, and Siobhan Somerville. For keeping me and my work going, I am grateful to kt shorb.

Notes

1. Theobald, *Filipino Teacher's Manual*, pp. 165, 167.
2. Stoler, *Race and the Education of Desire*.
3. Popkewitz, "The Reason of Reason."
4. Lewis, "Biopolitical Utopianism in Educational Theory," p. 695.
5. Agamben, *Homo sacer*.
6. Mbembe, "Necropolitics," p. 13; Foucault, *Society Must Be Defended*.
7. McKinley, "Benevolent Assimilation Proclamation"; McCoy, *Policing America's Empire*.
8. Blanco, *Frontier Constitutions*.
9. Burnett and Marshall, *Foreign in a Domestic Sense*.
10. Kramer, *Blood of Government*.
11. Morgensen, *Spaces Between Us*.
12. Rodriguez, *Suspended Apocalypse*; Shaw and Francia, *Vestiges of War*.
13. Camacho and Shigematsu, *Militarized Currents*.
14. Morgensen, *Spaces Between Us*.
15. McCoy and Scarano, *Colonial Crucible*; Anderson, *Colonial Pathologies*.
16. Racelis et al., *Bearers of Benevolence*; Khalili, "Gendered Practices of Counterinsurgency."
17. Racelis et al., *Bearers of Benevolence*, p. 4. Philippine Commission Report, 1901.
18. Lewis, "Biopolitical Utopianism in Educational Theory." For an argument on repressive domination, see Constantino, "Miseducation of the Filipino."
19. Theobald, *Filipino Teacher's Manual*, 123.
20. Newsom and Newsom, *Newsom Language Lessons*.
21. "A Little Filipino Boy's Letter"; "Filipino School Children." Spelling and grammatical errors preserved.
22. Theobald, *Filipino Teacher's Manual*, 119.
23. Theobald, *Filipino Teacher's Manual*; Blue et al., *Philippine Beginner's Book*; Gibbs, *Revised Insular Third Reader*; Rafael, *Promise of the Foreign*.

24. Beltran, "Progress."
25. Philippine Exposition Board, *Report*.
26. Beltran, "Progress."
27. Lewis, "Biopolitical Utopianism in Educational Theory" cites John Dewey and Hardt and Negri, *Empire*.
28. Alma, "Our School." Spelling and grammatical errors preserved.
29. Barrows, *Eighth Annual Report of the Director of Education*, p. 35; Barrows, *History of the Philippines*, p. 5.
30. Mbembe, "Necropolitics," 24–25.
31. Ibid., 40.
32. Villavicencio, "If the Philippines Had Been Independent."
33. Smith, *Conquest*; Jacobs, *White Mother to a Dark Race*.
34. McGovney, "Education in the Philippines"; Freer, *Philippine Experiences of An American Teacher*, pp. 275–77.
35. Letter from Austin Craig to Josephine Craig, 11 August 1927, excerpted in Racelis et al., *Bearers of Benevolence*, p. 242. See also John, *Philippine Saga*, pp. 114–15.
36. "[N]ew institutions of the [colonial] state call forth among the colonized new modes of resistance that are not, for all that, easily subsumed into modern categories." Lloyd, *Irish Times*, p. 5; Ileto, "Outlines of a Nonlinear Emplotment of Philippine History."
37. Borrinaga, *Balangiga Conflict Revisited*.
38. Wolfe, "Structure and Event"; Morgensen, *Spaces Between Us*; Smith, *Conquest*; Jacobs, *White Mother to a Dark Race*.
39. Morgensen, *Spaces Between Us*, p. 45; Bederman, *Manliness and Civilization*; Sánchez-Eppler, *Dependent States*; Steedman, *Strange Dislocations*.
40. Gilbert, *Great White Tribe of Filipinia*, 302.
41. Morrill, "Annual Report."
42. James, "Philippines Again," p. 161.
43. Sánchez-Eppler, *Dependent States*.
44. Harvey, *Brief History of Neoliberalism*.
45. *Balikbayan: Return to the Nation*.
46. Guevarra, *Marketing Dreams*.
47. Tadiar, "Filipinas 'Living in a Time of War,'" p. 377.
48. *Empowered Filipina*.
49. Mendoza, *Between the Homeland and Diaspora*, p. 47.
50. Morgensen, *Spaces Between Us*, p. 18.
51. These concluding thoughts are in conversation with Filipino Studies scholars' on settler colonialism and decolonization in the United States: Manalansan, *Global Divas*, pp. 123–24; See *Decolonized Eye*; Rodriguez, *Suspended Apocalypse*.

References

Agamben, Giorgio. *Homo sacer*. Stanford: Stanford University Press, 1998. Print.

Alma, Rufina. "Our School." 1905. Student's Papers, Frederick G. Behner papers, Bentley Historical Library, University of Michigan. Print.

Anderson, Warwick. *Colonial Pathologies*. Durham, NC: Duke University Press, 2006. Print.

Balikbayan: Return to the Nation. Dir. Dada Docot. 2011. University of British Columbia. Vimeo. Short video.

Barrows, David P. *Eighth Annual Report of the Director of Education*. Manila: Government Printing Office, 1908. Print.

——. *History of the Philippines*. New York: World Book, 1914. Print.

Bederman, Gail. *Manliness and Civilization*. Chicago: University of Chicago Press, 1995. Print.

Beltran, V. F. "Progress." 1905. Student's Papers, Frederick G. Behner Papers, Bentley Historical Library, University of Michigan. Print.

Blanco, John D. *Frontier Constitutions*. Berkeley: University of California Press, 2009. Print.

Blue, Helen Jacob, et al. *Philippine Beginner's Book*. New York: Macmillan, 1929. Print.

Borrinaga, Rolando O. *The Balangiga Conflict Revisited*. Quezon City, Philippines: New Day, 2003. Print.

Bruyneel, Kevin. *The Third Space of Sovereignty*. Minneapolis: University of Minnesota Press, 2007. Print.

Burnett, Christina Duffy, and Burke Marshall, eds. *Foreign in a Domestic Sense*. Durham, NC: Duke University Press, 2001. Print.

Camacho, Keith, and Setsu Shigematsu, *Militarized Currents*. Minneapolis: University of Minnesota Press, 2010. Print.

Constantino, Renato. "The Miseducation of the Filipino." 1968. In *Vestiges of War: The Philippine-American War and the Aftermath of an Imperial Dream 1899–1999*, ed. Angel Velasco Shaw and Luis Francia, 177–92. New York: New York University Press, 2002. Print.

Empowered Filipina: A Woman of Substance. Dir. Kamil Roxas. 2010. YouTube. Documentary.

"Filipino School Children: They Correspond with Pupil in School at Denison [Tex.]" *Dallas Morning News*. January 15, 1904: 4. Print.

Foucault, Michel. *Society Must Be Defended*. New York: Picador, 2004. Print.

Freer, William B. *The Philippine Experiences of an American Teacher*. New York: Scribner's, 1906. Print.

Gibbs, David. *Revised Insular Primer, Third Reader* New York: American Book Co., 1914. Print.

Gilbert, Paul T. *Great White Tribe in Filipinia*. Cincinnati: Jennings and Pye, 193. Print.

Guevarra, Anna Romina. *Marketing Dreams, Manufacturing Heroes*. New Brunswick, NJ: Rutgers University Press, 2010. Print.

Hardt, Michael, and Antonio Negri. *Empire*. Cambridge, MA: Harvard University Press, 2000. Print.

Harvey, David. *A Brief History of Neoliberalism*. London: Oxford University Press, 2005. Print.

Ileto, Reynaldo C. "Outlines of a Nonlinear Emplotment of Philippine History." In *The Politics of Culture in the Shadow of Capital*, ed. Lisa Lowe and David Lloyd, 98–131. Durham, NC: Duke University Press, 1997. Print.

Jacobs, Margaret D. *White Mother to a Dark Race*. Lincoln: University of Nebraska Press, 2009. Print.

James, William. "The Philippines Again." In *Essays, Comments, and Reviews*. Cambridge, MA: Harvard University Press, 1987. Originally published in *New York Evening Post*, Mar. 10, 1899: 4. Print.

Khalili, Laleh. "Gendered Practices of Counterinsurgency." *Review of International Studies* 37, no. 4 (Oct. 2011): 1471–91. Print.

Kramer, Paul. *Blood of Government*. Chapel Hill: University of North Carolina Press, 2005. Print.

Lewis, Tyson. "Biopolitical Utopianism in Educational Theory." *Educational Philosophy and Theory* 39, no. 7 (Dec. 2007): 683–702. Print.

"A Little Filipino Boy's Letter" *Dallas Morning News Magazine Supplement*. June 4, 1905: 6. Print.

Lloyd, David. *Irish Times*. Dublin: Field Day, 2008. Print.

Manalansan, Martin F. *Global Divas*. Durham, NC: Duke University Press, 2003. Print.

Mbembe, Achille, trans. Libby Meintjes, "Necropolitics" *Public Culture* 15, no. 1: 11–40. Print.

McCoy, Alfred W. *Policing America's Empire*. Madison: University of Wisconsin Press, 2009. Print.

McCoy, Alfred W., and Francisco A. Scarano, eds. *Colonial Crucible*. Madison: University of Wisconsin Press, 2009. Print.

McGovney, Dudley A. "Education in the Philippines." *New York Times*, February 1, 1903, p. 28. Print.

McKinley, William. "Benevolent Assimilation Proclamation." December 21, 1898. Print.

Mendoza, Lily S. *Between the Homeland and Diaspora*. New York: Routledge, 2002. Print.

Morgensen, Scott Lauria. *Spaces Between Us*. Minneapolis: University of Minnesota Press, 2011. Print.

Morrill, A. T. "Annual Report of the Foreign Secretaries of the International Committee, October 1, 1914 to September 30, 1915." Records of YMCA International Work in the Philippines. Kautz Family YMCA Archives. University of Minnesota. Print.

Newsom, Sidney C., and Lerona Payne Newsom. *Newsom Language Lessons*. Cambridge, MA: Athenaeum Press, Ginn and Company, 1904. Print.

Philippine Commission. *Report of the United States Philippine Commission to the Secretary of War for the period from December 1, 1900, to October 15, 1901*. Manila: Government Printing Office, 1901. Print.

Philippine Exposition Board. *Report of the Philippine Exposition Board in the U.S. for the Louisiana Purchase Exposition*. Washington, DC: Bureau of Insular Affairs, 1905. Print.

Popkewitz, Thomas. "The Reason of Reason: Cosmopolitanism and the Governing of Schooling." In *Dangerous Coagulations*, ed. Bernadette M. Baker and Katharina E. Heyning, 189–224. New York: Peter Lang, 2004. Print.

Racelis, Mary, et al., eds. *Bearers of Benevolence*. Pasig City, Philippines: Anvil, 2001. Print.

Rafael, Vicente L. *The Promise of the Foreign*. Durham, NC: Duke University Press. 2005. Print.

Rodriguez, Dylan. *Suspended Apocalypse*. Minneapolis: University of Minnesota Press, 2010. Print.

Sánchez-Eppler, Karen. *Dependent States*. Chicago: University of Chicago Press, 2005. Print.

See, Sarita Echavez. *Decolonized Eye*. Minneapolis: University of Minnesota Press, 2009. Print.

Shaw, Angel Velasco, and Luis Francia, eds. *Vestiges of War*. New York: New York University Press, 2002. Print.

Smith, Andrea. *Conquest*. Cambridge, MA: South End Press, 2005. Print.

Steedman, Carolyn. *Strange Dislocations*. Cambridge, MA: Harvard University Press, 1995. Print.

Stoler, Ann L. *Race and the Education of Desire*. Durham, NC, and London: Duke University Press, 1995. Print.

Tadiar, Neferti Xina M. "Filipinas 'Living in a Time of War.'" In *Pinay Power*, ed. Melinda L. de Jésus, 373–86. New York: Routledge, 2005. Print.

Theobald, Harry Couch. *Filipino Teacher's Manual*. New York: World Book, 1908.

Villavicencio, Vicente. "If the Philippines Had Been Independent." 1905 Student's Papers, Frederick G. Behner Papers, Bentley Historical Library, University of Michigan.

Wolfe, Patrick. "Structure and Event: Settler Colonialism and the Question of Genocide." In *Empire, Colony, Genocide*, ed. A. Dirk Moses, 102–32. Oxford: Berghahn, 2008. Print.

6

Ilustrado Transnationalism

Cross-Colonial Fields and Filipino Elites
at the Turn of the Twentieth Century

JULIAN GO

Introduction

In October of 1956, members and friends of Freedom House, founded in 1941 to serve as a "center advancing the goals of a free society," gathered in Washington, DC, to confer the organization's anniversary awards. Prior winners included President Dwight Eisenhower and Sir Winston Churchill. This time there were two awardees: Ramon Magsaysay, president of the Philippines, and Luis Muñoz Marín, governor of Puerto Rico. President Magsaysay was given the award for "teaching his people how to use their newly gained freedom to develop their greatest potentialities."[1] Muñoz Marín received the award from Walter Lipmman, who praised Puerto Rico for "finding its own way toward a very much better life" for its people.[2] Thus did the history of the Philippines and Puerto Rico converge. Their respective leaders (at least one of whom, Magsaysay, was a client of the Central Intelligence Agency) were conferred tokens of imperial loyalty by their imperial master, the United States.

This was not the first time that the histories of Puerto Rico and the Philippines crossed paths. For the first decades of the century, both had been subjected to direct US control as "unincorporated territories" of the United States, and both had been Spanish colonies before that. Nor was this the first time that a Filipino political leader stood alongside another political leader from another colony. Since 1907, ilustrados such as Benito Legarda, Manuel L. Quezon, and Pablo Ocampo among others sat in the halls of the US House of Representatives as resident commissioners alongside resident commissioners from Puerto Rico. One Puerto Rican commissioner had been Luis Muñoz Rivera, father of Luis Muñoz

Marin. And in the late nineteenth century, when the Philippines was still a Spanish colony, the Filipino ilustrados of the "propaganda movement" such as Rafael Del-Pan and Julio Llorente joined various political groups in Spain that included Puerto Ricans. Nor, finally, were Puerto Ricans the only other colonial peoples that Filipino leaders engaged. During the nineteenth century, ilustrado propagandists in Spain interacted not just with Puerto Rican elites but also with leading Cuban activists.

This chapter recovers some of these intraimperial cross-colonial interactions, with the aim of extending the scope of the existing historiography of the Philippines and hence, perhaps, deepening it. The premise is that the history of the Philippines is not just the history of a nation-state but also of Filipinos interacting with each other and others in transnational fields. The rich scholarship on the complexities of Philippine migration and the Filipino diaspora represents one strand of scholarship that illuminates such fields.[3] Work on Filipino writers and thinkers in the United States or on Jose Rizal's place within transnational anarchist movements in the late nineteenth century mark yet another strand.[4] The present chapter joins this literature. It offers a glance at the cross-colonial political conversations and interactions of leading Filipino elites during the late nineteenth and early twentieth centuries. This was a time when those elites crafted a new Philippine nationalism and mounted political campaigns against, and sometimes for, its two successive imperial masters: Spain and the United States. Along the way, they allied with their colonial counterparts even as they sometimes conflicted with them. The goal of this chapter is to examine some of these cross-colonial collaborations and conflicts in a preliminary and admittedly exploratory, rather than exhaustive, form. Let us begin in Madrid.

Cross-Colonial Propaganda

Most scholarship on Philippine nationalism includes some discussion of the "propagandists"—that is, the ilustrados who went to Spain in the late nineteenth century to study. These ilustrados imagined the Philippine nation in novel ways.[5] At the same time they organized and mobilized for reforms in the colony, hoping to influence policymakers in Spain directly. Their goals included political rights for Filipinos, equal to those held by Spaniards; the secularization of the parishes in the Philippines;

and making the Philippines an equal province within the Spanish system.[6] In pressing for these goals, the propagandists drew upon various influences and made numerous connections. Anderson's (2006) magisterial analysis illuminates how the likes of José Rizal and Isabelo de los Reyes were caught up in anarchist currents that connected them with Germans, Cubans, and Parisians—among others. But while Anderson highlights anarchist currents, there were other related organizations and political movements that warrant attention. Masonic associations are perhaps most notable. Freemasonry within the Spanish empire has a long history, extending back to Latin American nationalism in the eighteenth and early nineteenth centuries. Many Latin American leaders were associated with the Freemasons, not least Simón Bolivar. As Freemasonry was a secret association that offered space for free discourse, it had a natural affinity with anticolonial movements. Back in Manila, masonic groups had been founded by peninsular Spaniards, but these had barred Filipinos from participation. In Spain, Filipino students and thinkers forged their own masonic groups. And they used these groups to cultivate political networks and mount political campaigns.

One of the first known groups was founded in 1886 in Madrid. Known as La Logía Solidaridad, the founders included Ricardo Ayllon and the criollo Rafael Del-Pan (son of Jose Felipe del Pan, a Spanish resident of the Philippines who published *La Oceania Española* in Manila). The other key Filipino members were Evaristo Aguirre and Julio Llorente who had come to Spain as students at the University of Madrid (they had also been classmates of Jose Rizal at the Ateneo). But the Logia Solidaridad is not only notable for our purposes because of the Filipino members but also because other members were Cubans and Puerto Ricans. As of October 1886, at least ten members were from Cuba and two were from Puerto Rico (and another was from Martinique). Little is known about these individuals, but we do know that one of the founding Puerto Ricans was Herminio Diaz who would later, during US rule, become a leader in the Puerto Ricans' political party, the Federals (and later the Unionists).[7] Also notable is that this organization codified connections to the sprawling network of liberal Spaniards. One was Manuel Becerra. Becerra had been Grand Master of a Spanish-led masonic group the Gran Oriente de España; he is listed as signing the original charter of La Logía Solidaridad. Later Becerra would become the minister of colonies under the liberal regime of Mateo Sagasta (and would later have arguments with Jose Rizal over political reforms). La Logía Solidaridad also involved Miguel Morayta, who is listed as its honorary member. Morayta was likely one of the organization's prime movers.[8] A professor at the Universidad Central Madrid who taught Jose Rizal (and later served in the government of Spain's First Republic), Morayta was an active Spanish mason who became an ardent supporter of the propagandists. A few years after the founding of the *Logía Solidaridad,* Morayta would initiate the "Asociación Hispano-Filipino." The Association also included Jose Rizal, other propagandists and the soon-to-be-revolutionary Dominador Gomez.

Given this intraimperial, cross-colonial character of the organization, it is fitting that the Logía Solidaridad was meant not to just advance the interests of the Philippines but those of Cuba and Puerto Rico too.[9] As Aguirre explained to Jose Rizal in a letter, the Logía Solidaridad was meant to coordinate the colonies' demands for political rights and representation. They were supposed to work under the broad guidance of the famous Cuban-born activist Rafael M. de Labra. Labra had fought in Spain against slavery in the Antilles and by the end of the century had become a foremost voice in Madrid for the political autonomy of Cuba and Puerto Rico. With organizations like the Logía Solidaridad, Filipinos would become part of this larger movement for an overseas autonomous colonial sphere within the rubric of Spanish empire—or as Aguirre put it to Rizal, a "general ultra-marina autonomísta."[10]

The Logia Solidaridad is just one instance of cross-colonial efforts in which Filipinos participated. Even before 1886 when the Logia Solidaridad was founded, Graciano López Jaena had been actively organizing for Filipino causes and had done so within a wider cross-colonial field. We know that López Jaena was one of the first propagandists, to be later joined by Marcelo del Pilar and Jose Rizal, but it needs to be recalled that his early efforts were typically in concert with Cubans, Puerto Ricans, and others, putting the Philippines into a wider intraimperial frame. For instance, in 1883 he gave a speech at a banquet in Madrid, advancing his goal for Cuba, Puerto Rico, and the Philippines to be equally incorporated into the Spanish system. Present at the dinner were Spaniards as well as Cuban and Puerto Rican representatives, who also made speeches. In making his case for incorporation, López Jaena referred to

Spain as "Mother Spain" and Cuba and Puerto Rico as the Philippines' "amiable and beautiful sisters." There is also a sense in which López Jaena's efforts were global as well as cross-colonial. Present at the dinner were not just Spaniards and Spanish colonies but also Latin Americans, including representatives from the Republic of Mexico, Uruguay, and Paraguay. The dinner, after all, was under the umbrella of a nascent organization called the "Federación Hispano-Americana," an artistic, literary, and scientific group meant to unite Spaniards and Latin Americans.[11] Arguably, Morayta's "Asociación Hispano-Filipino" was partly modeled after the Federación Hispano-Americana.

Madrid was not the only scene of ilustrado activism, however.[12] In 1889, Marcelo del Pilar (who had recently arrived to Barcelona as the delegate of the Manila-based Comité de Propaganda) was among others who founded a new journal, *La Solidaridad,* in Barcelona in 1889. The journal was an important outlet for Filipino ilustrado politics: it involved Jose Rizal, Lopez Jaena, and numerous others and included contributions from the likes of Isabelo de los Reyes and Pedro Paterno. Miguel Morayta worked for the journal as well. Around the same time, Lopez Jaena helped formed a new masonic lodge in Barcelona, the Logia Revolución, which can be seen as the masonic arm of the journal. Other founders included Mariano Ponce, Jose Ma. Panganiban, and Marcelo del Pilar.[13]

This activity in Barcelona is renowned in the history of the Filipino propaganda movement, but it was not just Filipino. It was embedded in wider networks. While the *Solidaridad* journal was indeed manned by Filipinos, one of its founders was Celso Mir Deas, a Spanish editor of the Catalan newspaper *El Pueblo Soberano* (who would famously have a violent altercation with Antonio Luna). And it carried articles by the likes of Juan Jose Cañarte, a Cuban activist. Furthermore, while Schumacher calls *La Logia Revolución* "the first predominantly Filipino lodge,"[14] it also the case that the lodge served cross-colonial activity. The lodge itself included two Cubans: Juan Jose Cañarte, who contributed to the journal, and Justo Argudin. In addition, the lodge forged ties with Catalan activists. Catalonia at the time was a hotbed of cultural and political activity: Catalan leaders like Valenti Almirall, founder of *Diari Catala*, the first daily newspaper to be printed in Catalan, were helping to forge a new Catalan regional identity and questioning traditional relationships between Catalonia and Madrid. Just as Filipino propagandists initiated their campaigns, so were Catalan writers, thinkers, and politicians like Almirall calling for a unified Catalonia and administrative autonomy from Madrid.[15]

These Catalan activists mobilized through the press, cultural associations, and masonic organizations, and their efforts sometimes aligned with those of the ilustrados in Barcelona. Masonic activity reveals some of these alignments. Members of the Concordia Lodge no. 84, a branch of the Regional Lodge of Cataluña, attended banquets and meetings held by Filipino propagandists and reported on them in their periodical organ, *La Concordia*. One such Catalan, Luis Ballester, reported on a banquet held by Filipino propagandists in honor of Manual Labra and Miguel Morayta (who had recently founded the Hispano-Filipino Association) and expressed enthusiastic support of the Filipinos' cause. Hearing speeches by Mariano Ponce and Lopez Jaena, Ballester lamented the "shameful despotism" and "theocratic power" exercised over the Philippines by Madrid. He also affirmed his solidarity with the Filipinos' cause and referred to Morayta as the "father" of all the Filipinos and Catalans, who were Morayta's "sons." Lopez Jaena's speech in turn praised Cataluyña for being at the "forefront of progress" and insisted on everyone working together to heal "the whole social body." His words were met "with great applause."[16] In another meeting in 1890, Lopez Jaena implored Catalans to join the Philippines in its efforts to become an integral part of Spain rather than a subjugated colony and suggested that the Philippines offered a "vast market" for them to sell their cotton markets (this at a time when Catalan textile production had already become a major industry in Europe).[17]

Such banquets and meetings had outcomes besides speeches. In 1889, soon after its emergence, the Logia Revolución penned expositions and petitions to Mateo Sagasta, leader of the Spanish Liberal Party, and M. Becerra, the overseas minister. These called for the end to censorship in the Philippines, parliamentary representation in Madrid for Filipinos, and the end of administrative deportation in the Philippines. The authors of the exposition were listed as including Miguel Morayta, Galicano Apacible, C. Mir Deas, M. Ponce, Marcelo del Pilar, Lopez Jaena, and J. M. Jomapa. But it was also signed by at least twenty other masonic organizations besides Logia Revolución. While the identity of all the or-

[margin annotation: Solidarity important]

ganizations are not known, it is clear that many if not all of those listed were Catalan lodges like Avant no.149 and Concordia no. 84.[18]

The Catalan-Filipino connection may be deeper than has been conventionally acknowledged. In 1892, Jose Rizal founded La Liga Filipina in Manila. The goal was to unite the archipelago, support education, "fight violence and injustice," and "study and implement reforms" for the Philippines. The group included the likes of Andres Bonifacio and Juan Zulueta, and it was arguably modeled after the Catalans' organization, La Lliga de Catalyuña. The latter had been founded in 1887 by the prominent Catalan playwright Angel Guimerá and lawyer Joan Permanyer. Fighting for reforms in defense of Catalan identity, it included various other Catalan artists, lawyers, and thinkers (later including the famous Catalan architect Lluís Doménech)—the very sorts of artists and professionals whom Jose Rizal probably encountered during his previous trips to Barcelona. While we have no evidence from Rizal himself that he modeled La Liga Filipina after La Lliga de Catalyuña, we do know that a year after La Lliga de Catalyuña was founded, Rizal visited the Filipino ilustrados in Barcelona who had already been working with the Catalan movement. We also know that the Spanish term "liga" and its Catalan variant "lliga" was primarily used in the late nineteenth century in Catalyuña.[19]

There were limits to such cross-colonial solidarities however. Part of the problem was that the Philippines, though similar in some respects to Cuba, Puerto Rico, and Catalonia, occupied a different place in the Spanish empire than the others. This gave the Filipino elites political interests that differed from those of their colleagues. Unlike the others, for instance, the Philippines had long faced a Spanish colonial state operating through the distinct power of the friars. Furthermore, the Philippines was the only colony without representation in the Cortes.[20] Within the Spanish imperial hierarchy, it was on the lower—if not lowest—rung. Therefore, the propagandists' political demands for the secularization of the parishes or representation in Madrid were not echoed by Cubans and Puerto Ricans (even if they had been politely supported by them). The Catalans, too, had their distinct political projects, such as their first major one of defending the Catalan civil code against Madrileño intrusion.[21] These differences and more help explain why La Logia Solidaridad did not endure for long. Evaristo Aguirre intimated the future dissolution of Solidaridad in a letter to Jose Rizal soon after the lodge's establishment. While hoping for the best, he was skeptical that the alliance could effectively help them realize their goals.[22]

Revolutionary Circulations: Havana, Hong Kong, Paris, Manila

In short, while the Filipino propagandists allied at times with Cubans, Puerto Ricans, and Catalans, the alliances were never fully codified in a single political program. Cross-colonial solidarities took the form of discursive support for each others' campaigns, cross-colonial discussions or imaginative imitations and isomorphisms rather than sustained and concerted collaboration. Things were different during the Philippine revolution against Spain (1896–98). In this case, cross-colonial solidarity was at its strongest. While the revolution surely had its own internal logic—having to do with the distinct socioeconomic conditions of the archipelago, the impact of events like the 1872 execution of Mariano Gomez, Jose Burgos, and Jacinto Zamora (Filipino priests), and increasing repression by the colonial state—it is also the case that the Cubans' revolt helped fuel the fire.

As seen, by the time the Philippine revolution erupted in 1896, the Filipino propagandists had already made links with Cuban activists in Spain. They had been attuned to Cuba's situation: *La Solidaridad* not only carried articles from Cuban writers, it also tracked Cuban events and colonial legislation regarding Cuba. It also published commentary intimating parallels between Cuba and the Philippines. An article by Ferdinand Blumentritt in the journal even predicted parallel revolutions. Blumentritt noted the growth of educated Filipinos in the archipelago and in Spain, and he contended that there would come a time when they would either live at peace with Spain or fight for independence. Conjuring the memory of the Cubans' rebellion of the 1870s (which had led to abolition of slavery), he predicted:

In the latter event [of a Philippine revolution], they at least have the hope of obtaining by force, as the Cubans did, what Spain owes the Philippines: a guarantee of a free and honorable life to every loyal son of the nation, through reforms for assimilation, or make their country independent like she did with the Americas, or at least to die fighting in the field of battle for the welfare of their country, for the security of their homes and for personal dignity.[23]

[handwritten margin note: revolutions in other locations]

As the revolution finally spread beginning in 1896, such parallels were transformed into convergences. As Hagimoto (2010) demonstrates, the correspondence between Mariano Ponce and José Alberto Izquierdo helps us see these convergences. Ponce was a member of the Barcelona lodge Revolución that had included other Cubans before joining the Comité Revolucionario Filipino in Hong Kong. Izquierdo was a member of the Cuban community in Paris and had met Ponce in Madrid.[24] While in Hong Kong, Ponce praised the Cubans in his letters to Izquierdo. He also expressed their solidarity: "Since we have a common enemy, we Cubans and Filipinos should be in agreement. Do not forget that you are our older brothers and we are still new and inexperienced in these colossal labors, and therefore most in need of help, advice, and instructions. . . . Together we should smash our chains."[25] Ponce thus solicited information about the Cubans' efforts through Izquierdo. In turn, Izquierdo kept Ponce abreast of events while also serving as a mode of communication between the Filipinos and Cuban activists in the United States. Through Izquierdo, in fact, Ponce was able to connect with one of those Cuban activists directly. He wrote to Gonzalo de Quesada in New York to express his solidarity with the Cuban revolution and urge cooperation.

Cooperation made sense. The Spanish empire was a weakening entity at the time. Crushing one rebellion overseas was difficult enough; crushing two was even harder. This was predicted by Fernando Tarrida del Mármol, a Hispanic-Cuban intellectual, residing in Paris. In 1896 he published an article in *La Revue Blanche* contending that concurrent revolts in Cuba and the Philippines would deplete the Spanish imperial state of its coercive resources.[26] The Cuban and Filipino revolutionaries must have believed the same, for the Cuban exiles in the United States expressed desire to send material assistance to the Filipinos' efforts. The offer was reciprocated: Ponce expressed to Izquierdo that his colleagues in Manila planned to send troops to Havana to support the Cubans' effort.

While the transfer of troops never actually materialized, we do know that the Cuban revolution and the Philippine revolution were linked in other ways. For one, the Filipino revolutionaries were inspired and perhaps emboldened by events in Cuba. As the United States entered the Cuban fray and supported the Cuban revolution, for instance, this gave the Filipino junta in Hong Kong some hope.

They implored representatives of the United States in Hong Kong to help the Philippine revolution too:

> just as the Emperor Napoleon helped America in the war of separation from England, by whose aid the Americans attained independence, like assistance to be given the Cubans who are now fighting for independence—which protection and support the Filipinos now hope and pray may be granted them, because they in precisely the same position as the Cubans with their land drenched in blood.[27]

These attempts to curry American aid ended tragically (with the United States failing to help). But they nonetheless suggest that the Filipino revolutionaries envisioned the Cuban revolution as part of their history. ③ history

Also indicative is the fact that the Hong Kong junta in 1897, when commemorating the first anniversary of their revolution against Spain, offered a dedication to the 1897 Cuban revolution.[28] Back in Manila, the shared history was solidified further: Aguinaldo designed the new flag of the Philippine Republic, partly modeled after the Cubans' flag. The ④ flag colors, for instance, shared the same blue and red as Cuba's flag, and some have suggested that they were copied from the latter. In any case it shared the same general design: a triangle shape with stripes. This is a general design that the Puerto Rican flag also had, and the triangle shape can be traced to Masonic flags.[29] Furthermore, Aguinaldo oversaw the promulgation of the very first Philippine constitution, the constitution of the Republic of Biak-na-Bato. Written by Felix Ferrer and Isabelo ⑤ constitution Artacho, the constitution was copied directly from the Cuban constitution of Jimaguayú. The constitution was almost exactly the same. Much of it was verbatim. The only difference was that the Philippine constitution had four articles that formed the constitution's bill of rights that the Cuban constitution lacked.[30]

From Madrid to Washington

We now know that, despite these modalities of emulation of and inspiration from Cuba, the Philippines ended up in a very different situation. The Cubans overthrew Spanish rule and the United States recognized Cuban independence—with strings. The Philippines did not see the same fate; the resistance of Aguinaldo and his forces gave way to a painful and—for many Filipinos, a deadly—compliance. Unlike their Cuban counterparts, the Filipinos were not free. They faced a situation not unlike the one they had faced a decade earlier during Spanish rule. An external power ruled over them, and in order to at all realize their political goals, they had to struggle, strategize, and maneuver to within the limits the new empire imposed. Yet, they were not alone. The United States had allowed Cuba to remain nominally independent, but it had taken Puerto Rico, which, like the Philippines, would be declared an "unincorporated territory" of the US empire. In this context, Cubans would no longer be the only counterparts with whom to ally or emulate. Instead, Filipino elites also turned to their Puerto Rican counterparts, just as the propagandists in Madrid and Barcelona had done.

References to Cuba by Filipino politicians could still be found throughout the first two decades of US rule. Most Filipino statesmen in this period still maintained that they wanted eventual independence from the United States, so Cuban independence could still legitimately occupy their imaginary. The Nacionalista Party in 1910 thus petitioned the US secretary of war, J. M. Dickinson, when he visited the archipelago, for immediate independence, by saying "the Filipino people, who are ten times greater than Cuba in population, territory and resources, supporting themselves upon the rigorous logic of this altruistic action of America with respect to Cuba, consider themselves entitled to receive from the United States the same generous concession of INDEPENDENCE."[31] But knowing that the Americans would not grant independence over night, Filipino ilustrados had to look elsewhere than Cuba for political inspiration. Besides, some ilustrados did not want national independence and instead sought new ways to more effectively accommodate the new rulers. It is here where Puerto Rico again figured into their efforts (having disappeared temporarily from the ilustrados' consciousness during the revolution).

Consider the earliest and most important political group in US colonial politics during the early years of occupation: the political party known as the "Federal Party." First founded by Manila-based merchants, intellectuals, and professionals, most prominently Pardo de Tavera, the party was cultivated by US colonial officials as the party of peace. It eventually "spread like wildfire throughout the archipelago," according to official reports, and incorporated former revolutionaries who had laid down their arms and took their oaths to the United States.[32] Among them were Pedro Paterno, who had been active in Spain previously. The party was pro-American: not only did it proclaim loyalty to the United States; it also declared its hope that the Philippines would eventually be incorporated into the United States as a full-fledged state in the union.

The Federals' approach to US rule had its counterpart in Puerto Rico: there, in fact, most of the Puerto Rican elite welcomed US rule and proclaimed their interest in statehood in the union. The leading party in the first years of rule was also named the "Federal Party." The Federal Party had been, during Spanish rule, known as the "Autonomist Party," but it proclaimed itself "Federal" because it saw the United States as a federal system that continued the ideal of Spanish federalism and would thus incorporate foreign territories as equal states in the federal union. The party's platform stated:

> Upon meeting today, the old liberals conform their hopes and look for a name that corresponds to the methods and traditions of the federation [of the United States].And they want to be called the PARTIDO FEDERAL, because they continue believing in their autonomist ideal, and because there does not exist on the planet an autonomy so ample and so indestructible as that created when the patriarchs of the America of the North wrote their laws for its states and territories.[33]

But if the Federals of Puerto Rico and the Philippines had similar political platforms and a similar assimilative ideology (hoping for their respective colonies to be incorporated into the United States as states), they also shared a similar history. The Federals of Puerto Rico included Herminio Diaz who had been in lodges with Filipinos in Spain and Jose de Diego who had been in Barcelona. Furthermore, the newspaper of the Federals of Puerto Rico was called *La Democracia*; so too was the newspaper of the Filipino Federal Party. The parallels between the two parties are profound and were noted by the Puerto Rican Federals' newspaper *La Democracia*: "The Federal party in the Philippines, as in Puerto Rico, is made up of the greater capacities of the country and the richest men, representing the great majority of the Filipinos that were against the war, have accepted the change of nationality but with the aspiration of fighting until the

Philippines into a State in the American Union."[34] But the parallels are not accidental. The Federal Party of Puerto Rico was founded in late 1899, while the Filipino Federal party was founded a year later. The Filipinos in Manila were inspired by and thus copied their Caribbean colleagues. In fact, the Filipinos were directly copying their Caribbean colleagues. They had first named their party the "Autonomists" just as the Puerto Ricans' had done. Then, after their Puerto Rican counterparts changed their name to the Federal Party, so did they.[35]

While the Federal parties of the two colonies would each dissolve into other entities, Filipino and Puerto Rican elites continued to reference each other and at times forge solidarity. The possibilities for such solidarity and collaboration were strong. Both colonies occupied similar structural positions within the US imperial hierarchy (that is, both were "unincorporated," unlike Hawaii and Alaska). Furthermore, their respective leaders both spoke Spanish, and developments in communication like the telegraph permitted global discussion: Philippine newspapers received cables from Washington as well from China, London, Paris, and elsewhere. Perhaps most interestingly, too, both Puerto Rico and the Philippines had representatives in Washington who had routine face-to-face contact. Following the tradition of America's westward political expansion, each colony was allowed to send at least one "resident commissioner" to Washington, DC, to sit in Congress. Resident commissioners could not vote, but they could speak and participate in nonvoting activities of Congress. The first Philippine resident commissioners started in 1907: Benito Legarda and Pablo Ocampo. Manuel L. Quezon joined a couple of years later. Puerto Rico sent its first commissioner to Washington (Federico Degetau) in 1901. Later commissioners from Puerto Rico included Tulio Larringa and Luis Muñoz Rivera, prominent political leader and father of Luis Muñoz Marin. Residing together in Washington and sitting in Congress, Filipino and Puerto Rican leaders could confer, discuss, plan, and propagate together.

Cross-colonial collaboration subsequently came in a variety of forms. One was political borrowing. The Filipinos not only borrowed names of political parties from Puerto Rico, they also seized upon political developments there to advance their own political demands from Washington. In 1910, Resident Commissioners Manuel Quezon and Legarda wrote to President William H. Taft, former governor of the Philippines, complaining about the increasing "disappointment and dissatisfaction with the recent trend of [US] policy" in the Philippines. "Rightly or wrongly," they noted, "the Filipinos feel that progress along the lines of giving them increasing participation in the actual control of affairs has practically come to a stop." To remedy the situation they requested various reforms, one of which was the establishment of an upper legislative house, largely elected but also including appointees of Washington if necessary. Their model was legislation that Puerto Ricans had been demanding and which some US senators had been supporting. "We most strongly urge the establishment of such a body," they wrote, "which, in our judgment, should in the Philippines consist entirely of elective members, for reasons hereinafter set forth; but if this course be deemed inexpedient at this time, it should be provided, as in the case of Porto Rico [sic], that a certain proportion of its members should be appointed by the President of the United States." They continued, "No truer step in the development of the national policy above outlined could be taken than to give the Filipinos at last what is to be bestowed upon the inhabitants of Porto Rico—a proper separation of the different powers of government along the lines of enlightened statecraft."[36]

Another related instance of cross-colonial collaboration came in the form of solidarity rooted in common subjugation. Given that both Puerto Rico and the Philippines were both declared unincorporated territories, they could both bond based upon a discourse of oppression. When *La Correspondencia*, one of the Puerto Rican politicians' main newspapers, responded to Woodrow Wilson's claim that "self-government is not a thing" but a matter of "character," it declared, "The treaty of Paris [of 1898] says that the US congress will establish the rights and political status of the natives. It says nothing of the *character* of them. . . . No one spoke in Paris of the character of Filipinos and Puerto Ricans; no one asserted that the characteristics of both peoples should [determine] their rights."[37] A prominent Philippine newspaper, *The Philippine Review*, later carried an editorial that also scripted Puerto Rico and the Philippines as sharing similar subjugated positions. Complaining that US officials wielded too much power in the state, the editorial asserted, "This mockery of representative government exists in Porto Rico [sic] as well as the Philippines, and the bitter discontents which are everywhere and always the result of political arrangements of such character abound in both countries."[38]

While colonial subjugation served as one shared standpoint by which to forge cross-colonial solidarity, historical and ethnic identity served as another. As noted, many ilustrados had traveled to Spain in the late nineteenth century. Speaking Spanish and seeking equal rights and privileges as Peninsular Spaniards, they sometimes identified with Spain as their "mother Patria." They spoke much less of this at the turn of the century: the revolution against Spain and the politics of the Philippine-American War likely tempered open and persistent identification with Spain. But as the war waned, and as US rule wore on, certain sectors of the elite revived a pro-Spanish identity based upon shared language, history, and culture. In Puerto Rico, some political leaders looked back nostalgically to their political arrangements with Spain as more beneficial than with the United States. After all, Puerto Rico had had representation in the Spanish Cortes and, in 1898, was granted autonomous status with the empire. Hispanicism thus served as a political response to US rule. In the Philippines, Hispanicism was also summoned. One of the ilustrados' main Manila-based newspaper *El Renacimiento* carried reports on cultural events in Spain and published editorials extolling the virtues of Spanish culture.[39] New journals like *La Cultura Filipina* did the same. Later, in the 1910s, *Revista Filipina/Philippine Review* called for solidarity with Latin America, which included Cuba and Puerto Rico, on the basis of their Spanish heritage. It also used familial metaphors that had been common in late nineteenth-century Filipino-Spanish politics:

To Latin America:

We desire that we may all know each other.

Between you and us there is a bond of soul, heart, and tongue. It is for this reason that we greet you as a sister-race.

For some time you were, as we were, a province of Spain. But, as you did, to the noble love for Spain we preferred what is our own love: our love for our own country. And we parted as mother and son do part: never actually to separate, only to love each other as ever, only to make room for the unavoidable in nature: never to hate each other.

Thus, like Spain and Latin America, Cuba and Porto Rico [*sic*], Spain and the Philippines are now closer friends than ever they were before.[40]

Yet, as was the case during late Spanish rule, cross-colonial solidarity had limits. The limits arose in part from the structure of imperial policymaking itself. Congress had authority to pass laws for the two colonies, and in Congress there was always the fear that any legislation for one colony would serve as a precedent for the other. For instance, many Senators opposed legislation granting US citizenship to Puerto Ricans, not because they were against citizenship for Puerto Ricans, but because they were against citizenship for Filipinos. The idea of taking the Philippines as a colony had always been fraught with fear about incorporating an archipelago of "mongrols" and "savages" into the American body politic. Such fears were particularly pronounced in the US South and West. Of course, most American voters and policymakers classified both Filipinos and Puerto Ricans as racially inferior. But the Philippines, in the eyes of many in the metropole, was most threatening. Puerto Rico was seen as more Hispanic and more racially homogeneous than the Philippines (despite the large African American population), hence less of a threat to the American body politic.[41] In this context, as the elites pleaded and proposed for political reforms, they sometimes distanced themselves from each other in order to look more favorable than the other.

One instance of this occurred relatively early on, in 1902, when a bill came before the US Congress to change the position of Puerto Rican representative to Congress, at the time the "resident commissioner," into the position of "delegate." The latter position, while still not carrying voting rights, at least made the representative from Puerto Rico institutional similar to the already existing delegates from incorporated territories in the union (that is, the territories that would become states, like New Mexico and Oklahoma, which were not yet states). Amid Congressional debates on the matter, some Congressmen worried that this would set a precedent for the Philippines. In response, Federico Degetau, the Puerto Rican resident commissioner, drew sharp lines between Puerto Rico and the Philippines. He insisted such legislation would not serve as a precedent for the Philippines, on the grounds that the Philippines was a very different case. He pointed out that Puerto Rico and the Philippines had been treated very differently by Spain. While Puerto Rico had representation in Madrid, the Philippines had not. The implication, probably not lost on Degetau, was that Puerto Ricans were more deserving of delegate status. Degetau also pointed out that while Filipinos had revolted against US rule, Puerto Ricans had welcomed US rule from the outset: "When the generals of the American armies reached Porto Rico they found not an army that would interfere with them but a people unanimously disposed to receive them as the heralds of institutions that had been studied and loved in Puerto Rico for many years."[42] Again, the implication was that Puerto Ricans were more deserving, if not because they were putatively more American already. Later, Resident Commissioner Luis Muñoz Rivera intimated something similar in a debate over whether Puerto Ricans should be given US citizenship: "Our behavior during the past is a sufficient guarantee for our behavior in the future. Never a revolution there, in spite of our Latin blood; . . . never an attack against the majesty of law."[43]

The converse also occurred: Filipino politicians tried to distance themselves from Puerto Rico amidst their political efforts. For the Puerto Rican politicians did not always behave as the dutiful colonial subjects that Muñoz Rivera or Degetau had initially portrayed them to be. In 1909, the Puerto Rican House of Delegates led a protest against Washington's failure to grant them the political reforms they had been demanding (including an elective upper legislative house). The protest came in the form of legislative recalcitrance: the leading party in the House of Delegates, the Unionists, refused to pass an appropriations bill, which effectively put the finances of the colonial state on hold, thus tying the hands of the American officials at the top. American officials, not least President William H. Taft, were furious. A year later, Manuel Quezon and Benito Legarda seized upon the opportunity. In 1910, despite the Puerto Ricans' legislative recalcitrance, Secretary of War J. M. Dickinson proposed giving Puerto Rico an elective upper house. Quezon and Legarda insisted that the Philippines deserved the same thing. In a letter to Dickinson, they reiterated Dickinsons' proposal for Puerto Rico and insisted on its "applicability to the present situation of the Philippine Islands" on the grounds that the Filipinos expressed no "bad faith" and that there is "no real danger of the new legislature stopping the wheels of government." The suggestion, of course, was that the Puerto Rican legislature in fact had expressed "bad faith" by their legislative resistance.[44]

The attempts to differentiate rather than ally were unfortunate. There was no necessary reason for why the elites in the two colonies had to use each other as contrasting cases. Though it did make sense: as American policymakers often did everything they could to withhold political power from their colonial subjects, their colonial subjects in turn tried every discursive tactic they could to convince them otherwise, even if they involved pleas for distinction and differentiation from each other. This was a familiar imperial strategy, though perhaps unintentional, of divide and rule. In any case, it marked the horizon of limitation for cross-colonial collaboration in the US empire. It also reminds us that the cross-colonial fields in which Filipino ilustrados operated were not just fields of cooperation but also of competition and potential competition.[45]

Notes

1. "Magsaysay and Marin Will Receive Awards," *The Washington Post and Times Herald,* 27 Aug. 1956, p. 23.
2. "Exemplars of Freedom," *The Washington Post and Times Herald,* 12 Oct. 1956, p. 22.
3. M. F. Manalansan, *Global Divas: Filipino Gay Men in the Diaspora* (Durham, NC: Duke University Press Books, 2003).
4. A. F. Espiritu, *Five Faces of Exile: The Nation and Filipino American Intellectuals* (Stanford, CA: Stanford University Press, 2005); Benedict Anderson, *Under Three Flags: Anarchism and the Anti-Colonial Imagination* (New York: Verso, 2006). For a good discussion of recent work on the Philippine diaspora, see Vicente L. Rafael, "Reorientations: Notes on the Study of the Philippines in the United States," *Philippine Studies* 56, no. 4 (2008): 475–92.
5. Vicente L. Rafael, "Nationalism, Imagery, and the Filipino Intelligentsia in the Nineteenth Century," in *Discrepant Histories: Translocal Essays on Filipino Cultures,* ed. Vicente L. Rafael (Philadelphia, PA: Temple University Press, 1995).
6. Classic work on these ilustrados includes John N. Schumacher, The Filipino Nationalists' Propaganda Campaign in Europe, 1880–1895, PhD diss., Georgetown University, 1970); John N. Schumacher, *The Propaganda Movement 1880–1895* (Manila: Solidaridad, 1973); John N. Schumacher, *The Making of a Nation: Essays on Nineteenth-Century Filipino Nationalism* (Quezon City: Ateneo de Manila University Press, 1991). For more recent work, see Paul Kramer, *The Blood of Government: Race, Empire, the United States, & the Philippines* (Chapel Hill: University of North Carolina Press, 2006), pp. 35–86; R. B. Mojares, *Brains of the Nation: Pedro Paterno, The Pardo De Tavera, Isabelo De Los Reyes, and the Production of Modern Knowledge* (Quezon City: Ateneo De Manila University Press, 2006); and M. C. Thomas, "Isabelo De Los Reyes and the Philippine Contemporaries of La Solidaridad," *Philippine Studies* 54, no. 3 (2006).

7. "Logia Solidaridad, 1886," legajo 736, expediente 11, Centro Documental de la Memoria Histórica, Salamanca, Spain. See also M. Asuncion Ortiz de Andres, *Masoneria Y Democracia En El Siglo Xix: El Gran Oriente Español Y Su Proyección Político-Social (1888–1896)* (Madrid: Universidad Pontificia Comillas 1993), p. 273.

8. Schumacher, *Propaganda Movement 1880–1895*, p. 172.

9. Ortiz de Andres, *Masoneria Y Democracia En El Siglo Xix*, p. 273.

10. Aguirre to Rizal, quoted in Teodoro Kalaw, ed., *Epistolario Rizalino. Tomo Primero. 1877–1887* (Manila: Bureau of Printing, 1930), pp. 198–99. On Labra, see Ma. Dolores Domingo Acebron, *Rafael Maria De Labra: Cuba, Puerto Rico, Las Filipinas, Europa Y Marruecos En La Espana Del Sexenio Democratico Y La Restauración (1871–1918)* (Madrid: Consejo Superior de Investigaciones Cientificas, 2006).

11. See Graciano López Jaena, *Graciano López Jaena: Speeches, Articles and Letters*, trans. Encarnación Alzona and Teodoro Kalaw (Manila: National Historical Institute, 1994), pp. 23–25; and "Correo Nacional," in *Vanguardia*, 5 May 1883, p. 2896.

12. I am indebted to Gloria Cano of the Pompeu Fabra University for alerting me to the ilustrados' activities in Barcelona.

13. "Logia Revolución 1889," legajo 620, expediente 14, Centro Documental de la Memoria Histórica, Salamanca, Spain See also P. Sanchez Ferre, "La Masoneria Espanola Y El Conflicto Nacional Filipino," in *La Masonería En La España Del Siglo Xix: Il Symposium De Metodología Aplicada a La Historia De La Masonería Española, Salamanca, 2–5 De Julio De 1985*, ed. Junta de Castilla y León (Madrid: Consejería de Educación y Cultura, 1987), pp. 482–85.

14. Schumacher, *Making of a Nation*, p. 160.

15. A classic study of the Catalan movement is Isidre Molas, *Lliga Catalna: Un Estudi D'estasiología* (Barcelona: Edicions, 1972).

16. "En Familia," by Luis Ballester, in *La Concordia*, I, no. 4, Nov. 1888, pp. 30–31. Held in the Biblioteca Publica Arus, Barcleona, Spain.

17. "Despedida de Magalhaes Lima," *La Vanguardia*, 3 Oct. 1890. See also Sanchez Ferre, "La Masoneria Espanola Y El Conflicto Nacional Filipino," p. 488.

18. The lodges are listed in *La Concordia* II, no. 12, July 1889, pp. 95–96.

19. Quote is from Antonio Caulin Martinez "La masoneria en el entorno de la independencia filipina," p. 257, in *Sociabilidad fin de siglo: Espacios asociativos en torno a 1898*, ed. by Jean-Louis Guereña, Isidro Sánchez Sánchez, and Rafael Villena Espinosa (Cuenca: Ediciones de la Universidad de Castilla-La Mancha, 1999).

20. An article about the Philippines' comparably inferior status appeared in *La Solidaridad* II, no. 27, Mar. 1890, p. 123.

21. Siobhan Harty, "Lawyers, Codification, and the Origins of Catalan Nationalism, 1881–1901," *Law and History Review* 20, no. 2 (2002): 349–84.

22. Aguirre to Rizal, quoted in Kalaw, *Epistolario Rizalino. Tomo Primero. 1877–1887*, pp. 199.

23. *Solidaridad*, III, no. 47, 15 Jan. 1891, pp. 302–3.

24. Koichi Hagimoto, Between the Empires: Martí, Rizal and the Limits of Global Resistance, PhD diss., Department of Hispanic Languages and Literatures, University of Pittsburgh, 2010.

25. Hagimoto, "Between the Empires: Martí, Rizal and the Limits of Global Resistance," p. 37; orig. Mariano Ponce, *Cartas Sobre La Revolución* (Manila: Bureau of Printing, 1932), p. 29, my translation.

26. Paul Estrade, "El Acercamiento Filipino-Cubano En La Guerra Contra España (1896–1898)," in *El Caribe Y América Latina: El 98 En La Coyuntura Imperial*, eds. María Teresa Cortés Zavala, Consuelo Naranjo Orovio, and José Alfredo Uribe Salas, vol. II, p. 80 (Morelia: Instituto de Investigaciones Históricas, 1999).

27. "The Hong Kong Junta to the US Consul General, Hong Kong," Dorotéo Cortés, A. G. Medina, and Jose M. Basa, 29 Jan. 1897, quoted in R. M. Taylor, *The Philippine Insurrection against the United States*, 5 vols. (Pasay City, Philippines: Eugenio Lopez Foundation, 1971), vol. I, exhibit 22.

28. Estrade, "El Acercamiento Filipino-Cubano En La Guerra Contra España (1896–1898)," p. 84.

29. Manuel Quezon III offers the different interpretations of the origins of the flag on the website of the Philippine government's Office of Presidential Communications Development and Strategic Planning Office: http://pcdspo.gov.ph/2011/05/30/the-philippine-flag-belongs-to-a-family/ (accessed 6/26/12).

30. Joaquin G. Bernas, *A Historical and Juridical Study of the Philippine Bill of Rights* (Manila: Ateneo de Manila University Press, 1971); Joaquin G. Bernas, "Filipino Consciousness of Civil and Political Rights," *Philippine Studies* 25, no. 2 (1977): 163–85.

31. "Message to Hon. Jacob M. Dickinson, Popular Nacionalista League of the Philippines, Manila, August 29, 1910," Record Group 350, 364–124, United States National Archives, orig. cap.

32. United States Philippine Commission, *Report of the United States Philippine Commission to the Secretary of War for the Period from December 1, 1900 to October 15, 1901* (Washington, DC: Government Printing Office, 1901), I, p. 7; see also p. 165.

33. "Al Pueblo de Puerto Rico: Manifesto" in Eugenio (ed.) Fernández Méndez, *Antología Del Pensamiento Puertorriqueño (1900–1970)*, 2 vols. (Universidad de Puerto Rico, 1975), vol. 1, p. 46. More discussion of the Puerto Rican elites' ideology here can be found in Julian Go, *American Empire and the Politics of Meaning: Elite Political Cultures in the Philippines and Puerto Rico During U.S. Colonialism* (Durham, NC: Duke University Press, 2008).

34. "El partido federal . . . en Filipinas," *La Democracia*, 17 Apr. 1902, p. 3.

35. George A. Malcolm, *The Government of the Philippine Islands: Its Development and Fundamentals* (Rochester: The Lawyers Co-operative Publishing Company, 1916), p. 210.

36. Philippine Resident Commissioners (Quezon, Legarda) to President William H. Taft, 29 Mar. 1910, Papers of Manuel Quezon. Microfilm copy at Bentley Historical Library, Ann Arbor, MI.

37. "Otra Teoria," *La Correspondencia de Puerto Rico,* 9 Nov. 1910, p. 2.

38. *Philippine Review/Revista Filipina* 2, no. 1 (1917): 49.

39. For example, "Cultura Espanola," *El Renacimiento* (23 Mar. 1909). For an informative recent discussion of the newspaper *El Renacimiento,* see Gloria Cano, "Filipino Press Between Two Empires: *El Renacimiento,* a Newspaper with Too Much *Alma Filipina*," *Southeast Asian Studies* 49, no. 3 (2011).

40. *Philippine Review/Revista Filipina* 1, no. 1 (1916): 2. The editors called this sort of solidarity "Pan-American-Anglo-Hispanicism," because it also included the United States. "Instead of the West, as in olden days, we turn our eyes to the East, where lies our golden hope: America instead of Europe." To appeal to both Hispanic identity and US nationalism was surely novel at the time, but clearly it was meant as a gesture of friendship to the Filipinos' North American statesmen, like Senator Jones, who had been allying with Filipinos to grant them more autonomy. "It is there [in the United States] where our peaceful fights are being fought for the final definition of our political status, not by enemies, not by an inimical Congress, but by friends, for our friends they all are, all interested in the safer and more honorable legislation for the Philippines." They later mention explicitly the Jones Bill in the editorial. Finally, this was also a bid to join the new "Pan-American Union" which was in formation.

41. See Lanny Thompson, "The Imperial Republic: A Comparison of the Insular Territories under U.S. Dominion after 1898," *Pacific Historical Review* 71, no. 4 (2002).

42. Statement of Federico Degetau, *Hearings on H.R. 14083 Before the House Comm. On Insular Affairs,* 57th Congr. 1st Sess. 36 (1902), pp. 4–5.

43. Statement of Luis Muñoz Rivera, *Congressional Record,* 53, 5 May 1916, p. 7471.

44. Philippine Resident Commissioners to Secretary of War (Dickinson), 25 Apr. 1910, Papers of Manuel Quezon.

45. I am here applying the concept "field" from the work of Pierre Bourdieu; see, for instance, Pierre Bourdieu, *Homo Academicus* (Cambridge: Polity, 1988). See also Julian Go, "Global Fields and Imperial Forms: Field Theory and the British and American Empires," *Sociological Theory* 26, no. 3 (2008). Benedict Anderson's (2006) analysis of Jose Rizal and anarchism implicitly deploys the idea of a field—as in a gravitational field—when suggesting that the analysis is of "the gravitational force of anarchism between militant nationalisms on opposite sides of the planet," but Bourdieu's concept highlights competition as well as attraction. I am arguing that cross-colonial fields should be examined for both of these dimensions.

Works Cited

Anderson, Benedict. *Under Three Flags: Anarchism and the Anti-Colonial Imagination.* New York: Verso, 2006. Print.

Bernas, Joaquin G. "Filipino Consciousness of Civil and Political Rights." *Philippine Studies* 25, no. 2 (1977). Print.

――――. *A Historical and Juridical Study of the Philippine Bill of Rights*. Manila: Ateneo de Manila University Press, 1971. Print.

Bourdieu, Pierre. *Homo Academicus*. Cambridge: Polity, 1988. Print.

Cano, Gloria. "Filipino Press Between Two Empires: *El Renacimiento*, a Newspaper with Too Much *Alma Filipina*." *Southeast Asian Studies* 49, no. 3 (2011): 395–430. Print.

Domingo Acebron, Ma. Dolores. *Rafael Maria De Labra: Cuba, Puerto Rico, Las Filipinas, Europa Y Marruecos En La Espana Del Sexenio Democratico Y La Restauracion (1871–1918)* Madrid: Consejo Superior de Investigaciones Científicas, 2006. Print.

Espiritu, A. F. *Five Faces of Exile: The Nation and Filipino American Intellectuals*. Stanford, CA: Stanford University Press, 2005. Print.

Estrade, Paul. "El Acercamiento Filipino-Cubano En La Guerra Contra España (1896–1898)." In *El Caribe Y América Latina: El 98 En La Coyuntura Imperial*, ed. María Teresa Cortés Zavala, Consuelo Naranjo Orovio, and José Alfredo Uribe Salas, vol. II, 73–89. Morelia: Instituto de Investigaciones Históricas, 1999. Print.

Fernández Méndez, Eugenio, ed. *Antología Del Pensamiento Puertorriqueño (1900–1970)*. 2 vols. Universidad de Puerto Rico, 1975. Print.

Go, Julian. *American Empire and the Politics of Meaning: Elite Political Cultures in the Philippines and Puerto Rico During U.S. Colonialism*. Durham, NC: Duke University Press, 2008. Print.

――――. "Global Fields and Imperial Forms: Field Theory and the British and American Empires." *Sociological Theory* 26, no. 3 (2008): 201–29. Print.

Hagimoto, Koichi. Between the Empires: Martí, Rizal and the Limits of Global Resistance. PhD diss. University of Pittsburgh, 2010. Print.

Harty, Siobhan. "Lawyers, Codification, and the Origins of Catalan Nationalism, 1881–1901." *Law and History Review* 20, no. 2 (2002): 349–84. Print.

Kalaw, Teodoro, ed. *Epistolario Rizalino. Tomo Primero. 1877–1887.* Manila: Bureau of Printing, 1930. Print.

Kramer, Paul. *The Blood of Government: Race, Empire, the United States, & the Philippines*. Chapel Hill: University of North Carolina Press, 2006. Print.

López Jaena, Graciano. *Graciano López Jaena: Speeches, Articles and Letters*. Trans. Encarnación Alzona and Teodoro Kalaw. Manila: National Historical Institute, 1994. Print.

Malcolm, George A. *The Government of the Philippine Islands Its Development and Fundamentals*. 1916. Print.

Manalansan, M. F. *Global Divas: Filipino Gay Men in the Diaspora*. Durham, NC: Duke University Press, 2003. Print.

Mojares, R. B. *Brains of the Nation: Pedro Paterno, The Pardo De Tavera, Isabelo De Los Reyes, and the Production of Modern Knowledge*. Manila: Ateneo De Manila University Press, 2006. Print.

Molas, Isidre. *Lliga Catalna: Un Estudi D'estasiología*. Barcelona: Ediciones, 1972. Print.

Ortiz de Andres, M. Asuncion. *Masoneria Y Democracia En El Siglo Xix: El Gran Oriente Español Y Su Proyección Político-Social (1888–1896)*. Madrid: Universidad Pontificia Comillas, 1993. Print.

Ponce, Mariano. *Cartas Sobre La Revolución*. Manila: Bureau of Printing, 1932. Print.

Rafael, Vicente L. "Nationalism, Imagery, and the Filipino Intelligentsia in the Nineteenth Century." In *Discrepant Histories: Translocal Essays on Filipino Cultures*, ed. Vicente L. Rafael, 133–58. Philadelphia, PA: Temple University Press, 1995. Print.

———. "Reorientations: Notes on the Study of the Philippines in the United States." *Philippine Studies* 56, no. 4 (2008): 475–92. Print.

Sanchez Ferre, P. "La Masonería Española Y El Conflicto Nacional Filipino." In *La Masonería En La España Del Siglo Xix: Ii Symposium De Metodología Aplicada a La Historia De La Masonería Española, Salamanca, 2–5 De Julio De 1985*, ed. Junta de Castilla y León, 481–96. Madrid: Consejería de Educación y Cultura, 1987. Print.

Schumacher, John N. *The Filipino Nationalists' Propaganda Campaign in Europe, 1880–1895*. PhD diss. Georgetown University, 1970. Print.

———. *The Making of a Nation: Essays on Nineteenth-Century Filipino Nationalism*. Quezon City: Ateneo de Manila University Press, 1991. Print.

———. *The Propaganda Movement 1880–1895*. Manila: Solidaridad, 1973.

Taylor, R. M. *The Philippine Insurrection against the United States*. 5 vols. Pasay City, Philippines: Eugenio Lopez Foundation, 1971. Print.

Thomas, M. C. "Isabelo De Los Reyes and the Philippine Contemporaries of La Solidaridad." *Philippine Studies* 54, no. 3 (2006): 381–411. Print.

Thompson, Lanny. "The Imperial Republic: A Comparison of the Insular Territories Under U.S. Dominion after 1898." *Pacific Historical Review* 71, no. 4 (2002): 535–74.

United States Philippine Commission. *Report of the United States Philippine Commission to the Secretary of War for the Period from December 1, 1900 to October 15, 1901*. Washington, DC: Government Printing Office, 1901.

7

"Not Classifiable as Orientals or Caucasians or Negroes"

Filipino Racial Ontology and the Stalking Presence of the "Insane Filipino Soldier"

DYLAN RODRIGUEZ

Introduction: Reckoning with Casualty and Entanglement

THIS BOOK IS DEDICATED TO ALL THE INNOCENT
CASUALTIES, LIVING OR DEAD, OF A WAR THAT SHOULD
NEVER HAVE HAPPENED.
—Shaw and Francia, *Vestiges of War*

The 2002 anthology *Vestiges of War: The Philippine-American War and the Aftermath of an Imperial Dream, 1899–1999* opens with this solemn dedication, directing the reader's attention to a genealogy of death and trauma that is beyond either empirical reckoning or narrative/historical closure. It is to the defining morbidity and gravity of *Vestiges of War's* invocation of innocence and casualty, death and survival that I wish to return in this introductory framing, as a way to (1) locate *Philippine Palimpsests* within a contemporary political-intellectual continuity of Filipina/o responses to the distended genocidal logics of US empire; and (2) formally refocus a creative, critical, narrative energy on the conversations with casualty (not limited to the dead) that so often characterize the extra-academic and "nonscholarly" Filipina/o discourses that matter the most to many of us. The purpose here is to provide some political-intellectual traction for a long-term dialogue with Filipino casualty—its historicity, ghosts, and unaccounted suffering—that can permanently shadow and undercut the reified Philippine-American relation (and Filipino American identity) that has bloomed in the aftermath of a genocidal colonial conquest. I am ultimately concerned with the problem of whether and how Filipino racial being—what Denise da Silva calls the problematic of "raciality" (Silva)—is to be narrated, politicized, and inhabited as an unresolved (though no less constitutive) component of Filipino subjectivity more generally.

Consider the dispersals of affect and identification in which particular Filipino figures draw communal attention precisely because of how in their (imminent) absence they embody the historical surfaces of casualty and mortality: World War II veterans, *manongs*, individualized Philippine revolutionaries and nationalists, and martyrs of martial-law repression, for example, play a cohering, collective role in the making of Filipino (and Filipino American) political subjectivities, particularly as they offer a symbolic regime through which the apocalyptic formation of US coloniality can be temporally and geographically deferred (as a violence with a discrete beginning and end, occurring in a discrete and separable place) and somewhat rationally explained (as tragic colonialist phase, military mistake, set of rogue endeavors, and so on). Yet, if we are to be truthful about our *sensibility of the permanent damage done* by this irreparable contact with the American colonial nation-building project, we would probably have to admit that our primary reference points for historical casualty do not generally embrace an intimacy with those lost to the US military's genocidal sweep of multiple provinces in the decade following the Treaty of Paris.

The genocidal, cross-continental US racial colonial project reached one of its apotheosis points in the archipelago and has continued to inscribe its knowledges, violences, and (racial) ontologies on Filipinos across the so-called diaspora. It is necessary to track the origins of this racial-colonialist inscription in such mundane statements as the following, issued by the US-appointed provincial governor of Ilocos Norte in January 1902. Amplifying the increasingly common-sense notion that the people of the province—and the Philippines generally—were neither inherently "civilized" nor endowed with adequate mental capacity to absorb white racial modernity's political entitlements, the provincial governor reports:

> Popular election, which is an excellent system in civilized countries, where the rights of election and of vote are well known, where liberty is well understood, and the necessity for intelligence, and not force, recognized by the citizens, is rather premature in this province, where what

happens is just the opposite. I will not say that popular election is a bad system in this province; on the contrary, it is excellent for the people to learn its advantages as soon as possible: *but for this purpose it would be better not to allow the people, for some time to come at least, to elect the municipal officials, such as the president and vice-president,* who ought to be appointed after proper investigation of their character, their capacity, and their legal competency. (Beveridge 43; emphasis in original)

It is in one sense rather unsurprising that such rationalizations of American colonialist racial paternalism permeate Sen. Albert Beveridge's lengthy 1902 US congressional report "The Philippine Situation," a document that contains myriad summary statements from such US-appointed provincial administrators. As Reginald Horsman and others have duly noted, the civilizational discourse of latter nineteenth- and early twentieth-century American white supremacist statecraft is rife with such disqualifications of the white nation's racial subalterns, subhumans, and civil nonbeings (Horsman).

What is steadfastly remarkable in the case of the Philippines, however, is that such utterances emanated from *Filipino* subjects of American colonial statecraft with mind-numbing frequency, given the material conditions of contemporaneous, liquidation-based warfare surrounding this structure of "native" colonial complicity: here, it was one Governor Aguedo Agbayani who penned the statement of racial disqualification in the midst of a spreading US counterinsurgency against an anticolonialist guerilla movement. Put another way: in the heat of a US pacification campaign that historians agree was characterized by mass-based ecological and human destruction that extracted Philippine casualties numbering in at least the hundreds of thousands, it is stunningly easy to find Filipino appointees of the genocidal US colonialist state who were not only willing to accept the trappings of American governmental patronage, but were also capable of articulating political and ideological commitment to the very thesis of "civilization" that disqualified the majority of their (and the world's) people from recognition as inherently self-determining, rational, rightfully autonomous beings.

This archival moment signals one point of departure for the critical project of this chapter: What are we to make of Filipino raciality if its modern origins can be traced not only to the racial regime of the US colonial conquest, but also to "the Filipino's" selective *participation and delimited leadership* in fabricating her/his own racial assemblage, characterization, and state-endorsed "essence" as abject, uncivilized (if not "savage"), and in need of white supremacist colonial management? In this sense, the condition of Filipino subjection to US genocidal colonialism is not reducible to victimization or diasporic dispersal (Baldoz). What are the implications of considering modern Filipino racial ontology—formed in the genocidal US conquest—as constituted by *both* massive vulnerability to casualty and selective participation in the statecraft of colonial dominance?

Clearly, the work of conversing with Filipino casualty is about more than a reckoning with the wreckage of colonialist (mass) fatality and the lasting relations of military, economic, and political subjection wrought by the Progressive Era imperial project in which President William McKinley pronounced that "the mission of the United States [in the Philippines] is one of benevolent assimilation, substituting the mild sway of justice and right for arbitrary rule" (Aguinaldo and McKinley 83; Miller). The Filipino *entanglement* with, alongside, and in affirmation of the American nation-building project—including its colonialist and global hegemonies—is itself another rendition of "casualty" that carries its own violences, degradations, and complicities that disrupt the category of "innocence" initially advanced in the dedication from *Vestiges of War*. After all, the fullest conceptualization of casualty does not only address those who die and physiologically suffer; it also entails an apprehension of a broader apparatus of dominance—the racist state, military policy, colonial institution-building, compulsory cultural, economic, sexual, and economic regimes—into which the subjected peoples are absorbed: voluntarily, coercively, and everything in between.

The problem of entanglement raises fundamental questions about the ontological status of "the Filipino": in the crucible of the US colonialist conquest, we must ask whether and how the Filipino racial-colonial subject comes into existence and coheres as a recognized social being within the social categories, rhetorics, geographies, and epistemological structures of modern civilization and the racial nation-state. In what follows, I will revisit the problem of Filipino racial ontology by way of engaging the historical impasse that defines its emergence within (and lasting entanglement with) the US racial-colonial project. As the modern production of *human* being has always occurred within the categories, narratives, and (scientific, popular cultural, governmental, and other) discourses of *racial* being, the question of how Filipinos enter the realm of the racial-ontological has remained a vexing problem.

A short note on identification and terminology as I proceed: I use the term "Filipino" as a troubled placeholder rather than a normative category. Because my concern in this chapter is to address the problem of a racial ontology, I am embracing the productive critical possibilities that might emerge from engaging the actually existing, hegemonic structure of ethnonational (racial) identity—"Filipino"—that has been formed at the convergences of multiple global structures of colonial, national, and biopolitical power. "Filipino" is conceived here as an ontological vessel rather than a given identity category: it refers to a social identity constituted by the racial, gender, sexual, and nationalist logics of a Philippine modernity that is itself paradigmatically formed by a genocidal American racial colonialist modernity. Further, I reject the common rearticulations of Filipino subjectivity within contemporary multiculturalist discourses of diversity, in which the primary political project is to affirm the historical existence and agency of nonnormative and subaltern Filipinos (indigenous, queer, women, working class, politically left) within an otherwise reified (or at least underinterrogated) Philippine-American historical relation. I argue here that a strategic fixation on the dilemma of Filipino racial ontology may provide some useful critical tools for more radical and robust approaches to Filipino subjectivity (including feminist, queer, and indigenous methods) that productively disrupt those liberal, additive models of identity that do not lastingly confront the epochal violence of the US global project.

Filipino Racial Ontology

Filipino raciality—its sliding congruency with and disarticulation from the classificatory structures and political-cultural-scientific discourses of "race"—has always posed a vexing problem for the modern racial schema. There is no point in even attempting to address Filipino or Philippine raciality through definitive assertions of ethnographic distinctiveness or genealogical stock. Leon Wolff's confused anthropological meandering on this matter in the study *Little Brown Brothers* (1961) provides a primary taste of the dilemma posed by "Filipinos" to American racial modernity and its epistemological apparatus:

> The Filipinos themselves . . . remain something of an ethnological puzzle. Other than about forty thousand aboriginal Negritos, stunted in size and brain power, they are believed to be mainly descended from Malays who streamed into the islands from the South thousands of years ago. There is also some Chinese blood in the Filipino, for China has always been the archipelago's nearest civilized neighbor; and finally there are linguistic hints of a link with India and even Madagascar. As centuries passed, the taller intelligent Malays shoved the original Negritos deep into the mountainous hinterland. These Brown Malay men—not classifiable as Orientals or Caucasians or Negroes—average about five and a half feet tall and 125 pounds in weight. Racially there is no difference between the Mohammedan [sic] and Christian groups. (19–20)

The archive of Philippine responses to the white American racial schema further complicates the Filipino "ethnological puzzle." As a racial subject formation and political discourse sui generis, the very fabrication of the "Filipino" as a coherent racial being within the civil and governmental regimes of modernity was a task disparately undertaken by both male Philippine nationalist elites (positing Filipino racial compatibility with modern civilization) and the statecraft of the American colonialist project (premised on compulsory Filipino racial tutelage under US colonialist pedagogy and discipline). Despite their ostensible political opposition, both modalities of this racial discourse relied on the conceptual and ontological consolidation of a Filipino racial being that transcended (even if it did not actually obsolete) tribal, linguistic, and provincial differences. Both Philippine self-determination and American colonialism required the coherent racial existence of "the Filipino."

President Emilio Aguinaldo, in a momentous 1899 speech to the Philippine people, breathes official life into the Philippine nationalist racial project by tethering the possibility of self-determined Filipino subjectivity to the epistemic and governmental apparatuses of the rational modern subject:

> But remember that in order that our efforts may not be wasted, that our vows may be listened to, that our ends may be gained, it is indispensable that we adjust our actions to the rules of law and of right, learning to tri-

umph over our enemies and to conquer our own evil passions. (Schirmer and Shalom 21)

Though it has been insufficiently conceptualized as a densely *racial* social and cultural project, the contested production of "the Filipino" within colonialist modernity was inseparable from the political-intellectual drive toward nation-building and the discursive construction of sovereign (that is, capaciously self-determining and rational) Filipino subjectivity. These were the hallmarks of the petit bourgeois Philippine nationalist political opposition to the US colonial state and its cultural-military apparatus. Here, Aguinaldo contends that Filipino subjectivity must grapple with its own tendencies toward racial *affectability*—in Denise da Silva's terms, the racially degraded characteristic of having one's being determined by external and/or nonrational causes such as nature or (in Aguinaldo's terms) "passions"—and strive toward racial *transparency*—following Silva, the (inherently white, European, and Euroamerican) capacity for self-determination that derives from the existence of a rational "I," hallmarked in Aguinaldo's instance by the "rules of law and of right" (Silva).[1] Aguinaldo's proclamation of the grounds of Philippine independence is as much a racial telos as it is a national one.

Considered as such, the contested articulation of the Filipino *national* subject was fundamentally a set of arguments about whether and when a Filipino *racial* ontology would fully displace the subjection of a vulnerable *colonial* status that itself was undergoing massive, visceral revision within the traumatic movement from Spanish to American domination. The "national" articulated with the "racial," in tension with the "colonial." To come to terms with the lasting impact of this paradigmatic struggle to (racially) construct Filipino national-social being, we can consider how the turn of the twentieth-century forms the extended present tense within which Filipino racial ontology continues to be incubated, rationalized, and perplexed: while the post-1898 years revealed a "Filipino" undergoing its modern renovation as a national subjectivity that would definitively detribalize the Philippine archipelago (or perhaps, punitively tribalize and de-nationalize those ethno-religious groups that steadfastly resisted assimilation into either the US colonial or bourgeois Filipino nationalist regimes), this renovated Filipino never fully escaped its concrete entanglements with the genocide-oriented US national-imperial project (Kramer, *Blood of Government*).

The scale, temporal protraction, and extended ecological and physiological impact of the US colonialist conquest of the Philippines in the years following the Treaty of Paris—a period conventionally marked as that of the "Philippine-American War"—remain contested, due to a combination of archival insufficiency and a prevailing historiography that seems to studiously avoid recognition of the conquest as both culturally and biologically genocidal. To contextualize this criticism, we should be clear: we *do not and cannot* know, with any comprehensive precision or descriptive depth, the deforming and eviscerating effects of the US racial-colonial takeover during the turn of the twentieth century. While the conquest's direct and indirect (military/guerilla and civilian) fatalities, importation of communicable disease, strategic environmental destruction, disruption of indigenous cultural-economic practices and severing of extended familial genealogies, and mass-based killing are by now widely acknowledged in the existing historical literature, it is equally clear that even the most rigorous scholarly investigations cannot reconstruct an adequate accounting of what took place within the full sweep of the American invasion and occupation. (The best academic work can only illuminate the impact of the conquest on specific provincial areas, and even these have usually had to draw almost exclusively from archival US military reports and testimonials.) (See Kramer, *Blood of Government*; Miller; Francisco; Pomeroy; Agoncillo.)

I contend that this vacuum of historical comprehension constitutes more than an academic and intellectual conundrum: rather, it is the state of not knowing, the permanent condition of *bare familiarity* with the mind-boggling capacities of US racist and colonialist state violence and a lasting, ambivalent confrontation with the political willingness of the American nation-building project to actually deploy those capacities, that structure the problem of modern Filipino (racial) ontology.

Filipino subjectivity and social existence, which cannot be conceptualized outside of this fundamental entanglement with the genocidal capacity and political logic of the US social form, are permanently stalked by this condition of bare-familiarity with epoch-defining American racial-colonial violence. Here, I do not propose to offer a redemptive renarration of Filipino racial ontology that resolves—or even remotely comes to rational terms with—the permanent impasse we inhabit in relation to the historical foundations of the genocidal US colonial project. Instead, I am attempting to construct an alternative way to identify the modern "racial origin story" of the Filipino confrontation with the American genocidal colonial project that does not allow for easy resolutions, convenient narrative, and rhetorical closures, or compartmentalizing descriptions of the defining unknown that sits at the center of this vexed, century ongoing relation.

Historian Paul Kramer has compellingly outlined how the Filipino racial subjection to the US racist state and its colonialist distensions was distinct from the deadly North American discourses enmeshing Blacks and Indians. Refuting the often repeated and overly simplistic notion that the American racial conquest simplistically transported the foundational anti-Indian and anti-Black paradigms of US racist state violence to the Philippines, Kramer's study raises the complex question of whether and how Filipinos *actually inhabited (or failed to inhabit)* the vessels of raciality marked by the colonialist conquest's racialized military technologies and its racial appellations of "gugu" and "nigger."

> Rather than featuring the "projection" or "export" of preexisting [racial and imperial] formations, the war prompted, and was in turn fundamentally structured by, a process of racialization in which race-making and war-making were intimately connected [. . .].
>
> [W]ithin the Euro-American world, patterns of warfare were important markers of racial status: civilized people could be recognized in their civilized wars, savages in their guerilla ones. This interconnection meant that race-making and changing strategies and tactics moved together in a dark, violent spiral. (Kramer, *Blood of Government* 89–90)

Wolff's narration of the mythical opening shots in the Philippine-American War offers a particularly well-situated epistemic opening for explicating Kramer's critical historiographic intervention. If we are to appreciate Wolff's depiction, it is apparent that the US mandate of fatal disciplinary violence composes the military coalescence with Filipino soldiers, rather than contradicting it.

> At 8:30 p.m., February 4, 1899, Private William W. Grayson of Company B, 1st Nebraska Volunteers, was patrolling his regimental outpost near Santa Mesa, a desolate, scrubby suburb of Manila, in the Philippine Is-

lands . . . . In theory he and the Filipinos were allies in the war against Spain, but that conflict was over, for all practical purposes, and lately new tensions had been building up between the erstwhile friends. The patrol of which Grayson was a unit had orders, in fact, to shoot any Filipino soldier who might try to enter the neutral area which separated the two armies. (Wolff 9)

Drawing from US military accounts, Wolff further reveals the apparently normative and mundane presence of the vernaculars of anti-Black genocide in the white supremacist viscerality of the Philippine colonialist confrontation. (Civil Rights Congress; Vargas) According to Wolff, Private Grayson and one Private Miller confronted four Filipino "insurgents" on a dirt road near the San Juan Bridge in thus fateful night. His description of what transpired suggests both a historical parable and conceptual paradigm for our reflection on Filipino racial ontology:

> "*Halto, halto!*" snapped the native lieutenant. After a moment's deliberation, Grayson fired and dropped him. When two of the other natives sprang forward, Private Miller killed one and Grayson the other. Their marksmanship was astonishing; in total darkness they had wiped out three men with three bullets. They ran back to rejoin their patrol. "Line up, fellows," Grayson called out. "*The niggers are in here all through these yards.*" (9–10; emphasis added)

Here, it is worth amplifying Kramer's contention that white American soldiers' deployment of "nigger" on darker-skinned Philippine people eventually accumulated its own discursive and geographic specificity, to the point that periodic distinctions were drawn between "American niggers" and their Philippine counterparts (Kramer, *Blood of Government*, 127–30). However, what must not be lost in this necessary move toward historical and rhetorical nuance is that both discourses of "nigger" were/are genocidal in their logic (articulating notions of social neutralization/liquidation and physiological subjection/extermination), and (at least) protogenocidal in their enunciation.

While I will refrain from further summarizing Kramer's layered racial historiography here, there is no question that his work provides a crucial contextualization of the problem of racial ontology: once we account for the fact that Filipino raciality is not reducible to either a transposition or transculturation of the paradigmatic regimes of racist violence waged against Native and African descended peoples in the US mainland, how is it to be categorized or addressed as an object of our critical knowledge? More concretely, if we locate Filipino raciality within the distended present tense of a genocidal racial colonialist conquest, in which the US racist state reinvented itself in the archipelago within the policies, civilizational narratives, and on-the-ground practices of intensive physiological, ecological, and cultural extermination, is it possible to approach an intimacy with the lived experience of *nonbeing* that attaches itself to the racial colonial regime?

To clarify: by nonbeing, I am not suggesting that the subjects, survivors, opponents, and inheritors of racial colonialist regimes are not entirely expressive of their own insurgent forms of creativity, identity, political sovereignty, and collective action—rather, I am suggesting that the condition of raciality within racial colonialism always vacillates between labors of embodiment (activities that affirm one's humanity, even one's very visceral existence, within a material condition that is absolutely dehumanizing) and the systemic violence of physiological disintegration and disruption (a structuring of the surrounding world that constantly impugns one's bodily integrity and access to the things necessary for biological and cultural reproduction). There is a way to approach this dilemma that invites the company of an unexpected, voiceless group: the "insane Filipino soldiers" of the US colonial period.

"Insane Filipino Soldiers": The Status of Nonbeing

An adjoined group of historically ignored, seemingly tedious, and apparently insignificant documents from the sixtieth US Congress in 1908–9 raises an apparition of ontological crisis. House of Representatives Document No. 946, "Estimate for Care of Insane Filipino Soldiers, 1909," HR Document No 947, "Deficiency Estimate for Care of Insane Filipino Soldiers, 1908," and HR Document No. 1307, "Care of Insane Filipino Soldiers," are bare requests for monetary appropriations that amount to no more than six pages in total. Respectively submitted to the Committee on Appropriations and the Committee on Military Affairs, these records dryly denote the amount requested for the insane soldiers' care in the fiscal years of 1908–10 ($1,000, $3,000, and $1,500) while referencing the authorizing act of Congress (passed on May 11, 1908) that initially provided for such an appropriation. The rhetorical form of the requests is bare, impersonal, and bureaucratic:

> I have the honor to forward herewith, for transmission to Congress, a supplemental estimate of an appropriation of $3,000 required for the service of the fiscal year ending June 30, 1909, for the maintenance and treatment at asylums in the Philippine Islands of insane natives of the Philippine Islands cared for in such institutions conformably to the set approved May 11, 1908, making appropriations for the support of the Army for the fiscal year ending June 30, 1909.
> Very respectfully,
> ROBERT SHAW OLIVER
> Acting Secretary of War ("Estimate for Care of Insane Filipino Soldiers, 1909," 1)

The sparse details contained in these documents (and similar ones that followed in succession until at least 1920) ("Care of Insane Filipino Soldiers" [1920]) nonetheless invite historical scrutiny and deep reflection. HR Doc. No. 947 reveals that the appropriations are to be directed "for the care in the San Lazaro Hospital, Manila, of certain insane natives recently discharged from the Philippine Scouts on account of insanity" ("Deficiency Estimate for Care of Insane Filipino Soldiers, 1908" 2), while HR Doc. No. 946 references the original Congressional authorization of this clinical care in recounting:

> Hereafter the Secretary of War may, in his discretion, contract for the care, maintenance, and treatment of the insane natives of the Philippine Islands serving in the Army of the United States at any asylum in the Philippine Islands in all cases which he is now authorized by law to cause to be sent to the Government Hospital for the Insane in the District of Columbia." This legislation, it is supposed, is intended to provide for former Filipino soldiers who have become insane while in the military service and have been discharged there from on that account, or have become insane within a short time after leaving the service. ("Estimate for Care of Insane Filipino Soldiers, 1909" 2)

Aside from providing the crucial detail that these were in fact "natives" who served the US army, no further details regarding the insane Filipino soldiers are disclosed: their provincial origins are left unknown, their numbers are unspecified, the duration and quality of their clinical incarceration is not detailed, and the speculated or diagnosed causes of their insanity are left to silence. We have no idea how they were treated or medicated, and we cannot know the manner in which they were incarcerated in the asylum: Did they live in cells? Were they constantly locked? How were they punished for misbehavior? Did they ever again see loved ones or extended family members?

The insane Filipino soldier is *a simple matter of fact,* to be temporarily managed and eventually allowed to erode into the historical abyss. I should be honest in this moment: the ghosts of these allegedly insane Filipinos (presumably men) began to stalk me the moment I encountered these documents—or perhaps, they have been stalking us all along.

In his examination of the four-volume *Census of the Philippine Islands* (initiated in 1903, published in 1905) (Sanger, Ganett, and Olmsted), social historian Vicente Rafael is concerned with the US colonial project's incipient regime of representation, that is, the emerging discursive technologies through which the inherent discord and violence of colonization could be apprehended and reordered within the epistemological (and juridico-military) frameworks of an American white modernity. Importantly, Rafael illuminates how the seemingly menial task of collecting census data formed one of the rudimentary evaluative measures through which to calibrate Filipino readiness to assimilate into this modern (colonial) order. The census provided a racial colonial apparatus within which the Filipino's racial being could be abstracted, mapped, and quantified so as to demonstrate its relative capacity for the kind of rational thinking, bodily hygiene, and disciplined regimentation that was necessary for their eventual adaptation to the rigors of self-rule (Rafael 24).

The insane Filipino soldiers, whose existence escaped the otherwise massive data compilation of the *Census,*[2] are the scandalous nonpresence within the regime of white supremacist colonialist rationality. How might their nonbeing provide a method through which to imagine, narrate, or critically theorize the underside of what Rafael deftly calls the "white love" of the US colonial project of benevolent assimilation?

> White love holds out the promise of fathering, as it were, a "civilized peo-
> ple" capable in time of asserting its own character. But it also demands
> the indefinite submission to a program of discipline and reformation re-
> quiring the constant supervision of a sovereign master. (Rafael 23)

If it is true that "the reformation of natives as colonial subjects required
that they become visible and therefore accessible to those charged with
their supervision" (Rafael 23), what of those whose psychological profile, military linkage to the colonial racist state, and manifest mental/
emotional disordering (colonialism induced craziness) apparently
required their quarantining, medicalized treatment, and effective incarceration? How does the insane-excess of American racial colonialism
stalk the Filipino/American condition and call into being an *absolute
displacement* of subjectivity, historical sensibility, and political identity
that cannot be harnessed back into (that is, disciplined by) the relatively
coherent apparatuses of nationalism, diasporic identification, postcoloniality, or neoliberalism? Put differently, if we depart from Rafael's
understanding that "colonial supervision amounted to a powerful
form of surveillance, setting the limits of colonial identities within the
borders of the state" (23), we may find that there are geographical and
physiological sites—places, bodies, minds, states of being and nonbeing, being-there and being-absent—that sit just outside the surveillance
regime. These sites/people/absences not only pose a crisis for the ratio-
nalist objectives of the long historical American benevolence-dominion
over the Philippines, but also present an ontological dilemma that continues to structure Filipino social being.

What would be the consequences of accepting the possibility that the
condition—and barely traceable historical existence—of the insane Filipino soldiers actually represents a critical truth of Filipino (racial) ontology: that the ontological position of "the Filipino" is not fully addressed
by the categories of colonial racial chattel, indigenous subject/object of
conquest, resistant national(ist) subject, or transparent diasporic social
identity? If the purpose of ontology is to settle, with relative clarity, the
actual existence of things and the manner in which those things emerge
into coherent recognition as actually existing, and in this case as *socially
identifiable and legible* beings, then the nonbeing of the insane Filipino
soldier bridges ontology with evisceration.

The insane Filipino soldier is by definition outside the realm of rationality, yet he remains an evidentiary embodiment of Filipino interpellation by the US state; he cannot be assimilated into the colonial racial order, yet his "care" is specifically regimented by the stateside American legislature. This nonbeing cannot be situated within the ontological discourses of the emergent, overlapping regimes of modern raciality, benevolent assimilationist colonialism, or nationalist self-articulation. Filipino racial ontology, in this instance, remains structurally arrested by—thus always linked to—the remnants of the US racist state and its foundational colonialist violence. It is the nature of this bridging (ontology-evisceration) that energizes the apparition's stalking presence, and ultimately presents Filipino racial ontology as an unsettled problem rather than a coherent marking within the paradigmatic violences of racial modernity. Let us momentarily resist the impulse to resolve this problem, for the sake of allowing the stalking to effect a presence.

The Philippine Scouts and Indigenous Complicities

We must recognize at the outset that the "insane Filipino soldiers" of 1908 are misleadingly named. It is within the deceptiveness of their categorization that we might begin to access the historical conditions of their alleged mental disordering. These were not "Filipino soldiers" in the sense of being captured fighters from either a Philippine anticolonial revolutionary force (guerilla or otherwise) or a formalized Philippine military. Rather, this undifferentiated clinical/military category refers to an unnumbered, unnamed group from a peculiar auxiliary military formation called the Philippine Scouts. While the Scouts were Philippine in their nativity and provincial identification, *they were not soldiers fighting for either the self-determination of the Philippines or the indigenous autonomy of their provincial region or tribal group* (Linn; Woolard; Parker and Parrish; Marple; Ng; *Heritage of Valor; Philippine Scouts;* Franklin).

To the contrary, the Scouts were an invention of the US colonial project that drew from a recent history of military counterinsurgency strategies that exploited indigenous political conflicts for the strategic benefit of the colonial military's conquest and pacification objectives (which were themselves often conditioned by the imperatives of actual or incipient genocidal war making). Maj. Allen D. Marple, in a 1983 work titled *The Philippine Scouts: A Case Study in the Use of Indigenous Soldiers, Northern Luzon, the Philippine Islands, 1899*, straightforwardly situates the Scouts within a genealogy of indigenous military accomplices to American and European (genocidal) warfare that includes the Texas Rangers' exploitation of Mexican "guides and spies" during the Mexican War of the mid-nineteenth century, the US army's use of Pawnee Scouts during the Indian Wars (west of the Mississippi River) of the 1860s, and the British colonialist mobilization of African Scouts (including the Zulu Scouts in South Africa and the Elminas and Adansi Scouts in the West African theater) during the late nineteenth century. Marple notes that "it is no accident . . . that the US Army and other colonist armies carefully noted the success of the British Army in using indigenous scouts in their colonial armies around the world" (Marple 30). Making specific note of the American colonialist origins of the Philippine Scouts, Marple links the military strategies of the North American conquest to the Pacific one:

> Though much fighting was to take place over the next year until peace and amnesty were officially declared in May 1902, a cornerstone in the success of the revised American policy was implemented earlier in the war. As in a previous American war on foreign soil, the use and tactical integration of indigenous personnel and units into an American military field force demonstrated an appriopriate [*sic*] response to resolving the problems of an expeditionary force in alien territory. The origination of the Philippine Scouts during the Philippine Insurrection was quite identical to the use of Indian scouts during the American Indian Wars when a native force was raised and committed to battle under the colors of the United States Army. (47–48)

We must be careful to note that the formation of the Philippine Scouts took place within a *Philippine* genealogy of (intertribal and interprovincial) warfare as well. While these ostensibly "intra-Filipino" antagonisms were constituted by the Spanish and US colonialist relations of regional political differentiation (by way of strategic variations in political, economic, and military regime concentration), it is no less significant that these long-standing conflicts indicate the fundamental disunity of the very same Filipino subjectivity whose raciality was both under white supremacist scrutiny and in the midst of US colonialist discursive production. That is, the historical backdrop of the Philippine Scouts belies the allegation of a coherent Filipino subjectivity—and hence a Filipino racial ontology—by way of illuminating the violence of Philippine tribal and provincial differentiation. Brian McAllister Linn notes:

> The Philippine Scouts owed their origin to the irregular warriors raised from the Macabebes for service against guerillas in the swamps of central Luzon. Having served the Spanish for decades, the Macabebes were brutally persecuted by Aguinaldo's predominantly Tagalog supporters when the latter took over Pampanga province. On Samar, the Americans raised a scout unit from among the hemp merchant families who were losing both economic and political power as a result of insurgent exactions. By the end of the war, there were more than 15,000 Filipinos serving in officially recognized scout or constabulary units. (Linn 85)

Thus, the Scouts were not the duped or brainwashed subjects of American imperial propaganda who were somehow tricked into taking up arms against their presumptive "fellow Filipinos."

Rather, the US army's creation of the Philippine Scouts rearticulated and remobilized a longer-standing set of antagonisms between Philippine peoples that had already surfaced in similar form during the waning years of the Spanish colonial period. Elaborating the central role of the Macabebe tribe in the Scouts, Marple writes:

> Upon investigation, [First Lieutenant M.A. Batson] learned that the Macabebes had enlisted en masse with Spanish regiments fighting against the Tagalog revolutionaries during the Philippine Revolution in the late 1800's. For their loyalty to the Spanish, the Filipino revolutionaries imposed great cruelties upon the Macabebes—primarily because of intertribal hatreds and disloyalty to the revolutionary cause. The Macabebes anxiously awaited any opportunity to serve retribution on the Filipino revolutionaries.
>   ... Though both American generals feared their use. General Otis allowed Lieutenant Batson to devise a plan whereby under Batson's supervision, the Macabebes conducted boat exercises near their home driving out ladrones and revolutionaries. The experiment proved highly successful. In August [1899], Lieutenant Batson was allowed by General

> Otis to unofficially recruit, organize, and train one company of one hundred Macabebes. (71–72)

Another military scholar, in a 2006 article published by the US Army War College journal *Parameters*, affirms this portrayal by locating the Scouts within a longer account of "indigenous forces for counterinsurgency." Here, the writer's purpose is to place the tactics and strategies of the US military's War on Terror in a longer historical context of native collaborations with conquest and occupation:

> In particular, the Army recruited the Macabebes because the tribe had harbored a long-standing animosity for the Tagalogs, who constituted the majority of the insurgents. On Samar, the Americans organized a scout force with volunteers from hemp merchant families who opposed the guerrillas because they were losing influence as a result of insurgent actions. (Cassidy 49)

While suspicion of such accounts is appropriate given their almost exclusive reliance on US military sources and ideological alignment with American military objectives, it is worth noting that the existing historical delineation of the Scouts' political genealogy is consistent to a fault. Rather than wondering whether such work represents an accurate conveyance of the historical "truth" as such, perhaps we can read this scholarship as a body of *primary documents* offering a narrative of the US conquest that can be reread for the potential insight they provide to the problem of fabricating the modern Filipino ontology. Here, Kramer's examination of the spectacle of Philippine Scouts at the infamous 1904 St. Louis Exposition provides a useful critical lens:

> The [U.S. imperial] regime would have to manipulate Exposition conventions in order to make its case: that a pacified colony required men of reason and affairs, rather than soldiers, at its helm; that the rich resources of the Philippines demanded American investment and exploitation; and importantly, that the Filipino people, under the tutelage of American civilians and elite collaborators, were fundamentally assimilable to American "civilization." Model school-rooms, displays of agricultural export products, and marching Filipino Scouts and Constabularymen would convey the under-

lying messages of progress, economic development and the "civilization" of former hostiles and "primitives," a dynamic "process" compatible with larger fair aesthetics. (Kramer, "Making Concessions" 84–85)

Kramer's critical framing of the colonial project's racial-civilizational telos speaks to the cultural superstructure of racial ontology: in its hegemonic productions, the cultural articulation of "civilized" and/or actively "(self-)civilizing" raciality tends to require a relatively progressive, periodized marking of particular (and usually masculinized) racial beings' movement across modalities of existence, rationality, and social-intellectual capacity. The parading Philippine Scouts in the St. Louis Exposition are the glimmering refraction of their voiceless, forgotten counterparts in the Manila insane asylum. As racial-colonial spectacle, they purport to be the diametric opposite of—and obscuring presence over—the apparitional "insane Filipino Soldiers" in their performance of incipient Filipino modernity for the St. Louis audiences. Yet, the very condition of the Philippine Scouts' creation and the cultural method of their exploitation (by military scholars and St. Louis exhibitioners alike) leads us back to the ontological problem.

Conclusion: Stalking Casualty and Nonbeing

Here it is imperative to move from the realm of description to the realm of speculative and creative reflection: what must have been the lived experience of the Scouts, in their apparently effective complicity in the American colonialist conquest and political-military suppression of the archipelago, once they recognized that they were playing a strategically central role in the mind-bogglingly expedient and massively deadly extermination of Philippine independence struggle that resulted in objectively genocidal casualties, including direct and indirect fatalities of ordinary (nonguerilla, nonmilitarized) indigenous Philippine people? After all, it was certainly the case that the Macabebes and others eventually comprehended that the American conquest was singular and unprecedented in its violence and willingness to proliferate Philippine casualty, regardless of tribal affiliation of provincial loyalty.

It is here that we might return to Fanon. He writes, "Because it is a systematized negation of the other, a frenzied determination to deny the other any attribute of humanity, colonialism forces the colonized to constantly ask the question: 'Who am I in reality?'" (182). The insane Filipino soldier is among the first deaths of American multiculturalism in its emergent modern forms. Against the US racial colonial regime's dogged attempts to enact the Filipino's proctored inclusion in the trappings of white supremacist modernity and state-making, the apparition's answer to Fanon's colonial question is: *nothing.* The insane soldiers' coerced passage into the asylum, precisely *because* it is marked by historical silence and nonbeing, is evidence of the failure of American imperial democracy and the fundamental fraudulence of the ontological underpinnings of "the Filipino" as we have come to recognize (and inhabit) it. Here is an indication that the logic of white universalism, by its very nature breeds the physiological deterioration of racial antagonists, including those who intend to be included, empowered, assimilated, and, in this case, armed under the regime of American democracy and its governmentalities.

This is to neither ignore nor trivialize the forms of activist resistance, global advocacy, and social movement that have critically addressed US militarist, economic, and political/imperial hegemony over the archipelago since the turn of the twentieth century. Rather, it is to argue that such critical mobilizations are necessarily *incomplete* in their political-intellectual labor to the extent that they do not fully engage with the vexed racial ontology of the Filipino and attempt to sidestep or "resolve" this ontological problem rather than be stalked by it.

I should be clear on what I understand to be the political stakes of this stalking: the Filipino racial position, if its ontology is structurally disrupted, can be no less meaningfully inhabited, lived, and politicized in its *relationality* to other peoples' raciality and racial ontology. Thus, if Filipino raciality is to be an impactful political project rather than a dilemma to be definitively "resolved" or otherwise disavowed, it confronts life-or-death questions of racial affinity: with white supremacist being, racial chattel (non)being, indigenous and aboriginal being, and racial colonial being, among others. It is in this sense that the Filipino (in and beyond the United States) may be uniquely positioned to participate in the dismantling of post-civil rights multiculturalism and its "levelling rubric" (Wolfe 13) of race, ethnicity, and citizenship. If the problem to be addressed is not one of Filipino racial subjectivity or racial "identity," but rather one of racial relationality and affinity, the insane Filipino soldiers' stalking will serve us well, so long as we allow ourselves to be bothered and cajoled by their apparitional hovering.

It is appropriate to conclude this engagement with problem of Filipino racial ontology by openly valorizing those characteristically Filipino forms of knowledge production and pedagogical intimacy that stretch the limits of already cohered discursive fields (whether academic, religious, familial, activist, or otherwise). Reynaldo Ileto's methodological and epistemological example in the durable study *Pasyon and Revolution* provides an especially useful platform for this departure.

Ileto's project is to construct a social history—a "history from below"—that attempts to account for the idioms and discursive meaning of revolutionary anti-colonial movements to ordinary, non-elite Filipinos. He thus uses a breathtaking array of primary historical texts: "poems, songs, scattered autobiographies, confessions, prayers and folk sayings" (10). His primary focus is on the *pasyon* text as a vestibule for revolutionary thought and feeling, within which the narrative of Jesus Christ's death and resurrection became a discursive field through which the Philippine masses could think and imagine differently from the condition of colonialism. However, Ileto's departure from empiricist convention originates in his strategic fixation on the "factual errors" that proliferate in such vernacular texts' representation of historical events and conditions. It is in this tradition of Filipino disloyalty to the academic archive's "truth" that I am attempting to follow [...]: "When errors proliferate in a patterned manner, when rumors spread 'like wildfire,' when sources are biased in a consistent way we are in fact offered the opportunity to study the workings of the popular mind. This is applicable not only to 'folk' sources like riddles and epics but to works whose authors are known" (11).

From here Ileto suggests that a full engagement with "acts of compassion, weeping, and empathy" allows some access to historical experience—and of a popular historical narrative "truth"—that is otherwise obscured by positivist readings of such primary texts. Let us extrapolate Ileto's example so that we may fabricate a particular convening with casualty.

We might think here of the dissipated and often less-than-fully-coherent dialogues with myth, ancestry, the sacred, and the dead that make their way into the colonial afterlife of diasporic Filipino life worlds. Without overstating the case, it is safe to say that conversations with spirits, ghosts, and memories (particularly of those passed) are not merely spiritual rituals that have survived the onset of a Filipino (and American) modernity, but are also forms of sense-making, teaching, and historical (self-)narration that shape the material realities of everyday Filipino lives: such conversations influence how Filipinos work, play, eat, parent, consume, and collectively organize. As such, it may not only be worthwhile, but ethically necessary to generate critical theoretical work from within this realm, with an appreciation for how such dialogues are alive, material, and dynamic discursive formations that are open to creative interjections as well as scholarly critique. Here, I err on the side of interjection.

There is a typically colonialist racial tension at work in these forms of knowledge production, which both encompass and exceed the materiality of "haunting" that social theorist Avery Gordon has so perfectly articulated as "those singular yet repetitive instances when home becomes unfamiliar, when your bearings on the world lose direction, when the over-and-done-with comes alive, when what's been in your blind spot comes into view. Haunting raises specters, and it alters the experience of being in time, the way we separate the past, the present, and the future" (Gordon xvi). The Filipino excess that spills over Gordon's conception of haunting entails the manner in which specters and the over-and-done-with have never fully escaped the everyday purview—the "sociological imagination"—of Filipino modernity in the aftermath of US colonialism: put differently, there is a singular way that ghosts, the past, and memories of the dead have never quite reached Gordon's proverbial "blind spot," and are in fact central to the shaping of Filipino sociality and subjectivity. Yet, Gordon's notion remains incisively useful here because of the *selective* way in which Filipinos will allow themselves to be materially haunted. It is the *stalking* ghost, the apparition that is unacknowledged and seemingly imperceptible or insignificant, that concerns me here. The stalking ghost is the slippery, always-escaping factor in the formation of Filipino racial ontology.

Notes

1. See especially Silva's chapter 1, "Transparency Thesis," pp. 1–16.
2. While Volume III of the *Census* denotes the numbers of the "Civilized population returned as insane" in the various provinces on pp. 541–48, it makes no mention of the Filipino soldiers.

Works Cited

Agoncillo, Teodoro A. *History of the Filipino People.* Quezon City, Philippines: Garotech Pub, 1990.

Aguinaldo, Emilio, and William McKinley. *Communications Between the Executive Departments of the Government and Aguinaldo, Etc: Message from the President of the United States Transmitting, in Response to Resolution of the Senate of January 17, 1900, Copies of Communications between the Executive Departments of the Government and Aguinaldo or Other Persons Undertaking to Represent the People in Arms against the United States in the Philippine Islands, Together with Other Official Documents Relating to the Philippine Islands.* Washington, DC: Government Printing Office, 1900.

Baldoz, Rick. *The Third Asiatic Invasion: Empire and Migration in Filipino America, 1898–1946.* New York: New York University Press, 2011.

Beveridge, Albert J. *The Philippine Situation: Testimony and Statements of Witnesses, American and Foreign, Concerning: 1st. Conduct of Our Army. 2d. Reconcentration. 3d. Effect of Our Administration on the People. 4th. Filipino Self-Government and Effect of American Withdrawal. 5th. Foreign Testimony on Filipino Character and the Situation. 6th. Summary. June 23, 1902.—Ordered to Be Printed.* Washington, DC: Government Printing Office, 1902.

"Care of Insane Filipino Soldiers." Letter from the Secretary of the Treasury, Transmitting with a Copy of a Communication from the Secretary of War Submitting an Estimate of Appropriation for Care of Insane Filipino Soldiers. Washington, DC: Government Printing Office, 1909.

"Care of Insane Filipino Soldiers." Letter from the Secretary of the Treasury, Transmitting Supplemental Estimate of Appropriation Required by the War Department for the Care of Insane Filipino Soldiers, Fiscal Year 1920. May 24, 1920.—Referred to the Committee on Appropriations and Ordered to Be Printed. United States congressional serial set, serial set no. 7770. Washington, DC: Government Printing Office, 1920.

Cassidy, Robert M. "The Long Small War: Indigenous Forces for Counterinsurgency." *Parameters: Journal of the Us Army War College* 36.2 (2006): 47–62.

Civil Rights Congress. *We Charge Genocide.* New York: n.p., 1951.

"Deficiency Estimate for Care of Insane Filipino Soldiers, 1908." Letter from the Secretary of the Treasury, Transmitting a Copy of a Communication from the Acting Secretary of War Submitting an Estimate of Appropriation for Care of Insane Filipino Soldiers for the Fiscal Year Ended June 30, 1908. May 16, 1908.—Referred to the Committee on Appropriations and Ordered to Be Printed. United States congressional serial set, serial set no. 5375. Washington, DC: Government Printing Office, 1908.

"Estimate for Care of Insane Filipino Soldiers, 1909." Letter from the Secretary of the Treasury, Transmitting a Copy of a Communication from the Acting Secretary of War Submitting an Estimate of Appropriation for Care of Insane Filipino Soldiers for the Fiscal Year Ending June 30, 1909. May 16, 1908.—Referred to the Committee on Appropriations and Ordered to Be Printed. United States congressional serial set, serial set no. 5375. Washington, DC: Government Printing Office, 1908.

Fanon, Frantz. *The Wretched of the Earth*. Trans. Richard Philcox. New York: Grove Press, 2004.

Francisco, Luzviminda. "The First Vietnam: The Philippine-American War, 1899–1902." *Bulletin of Concerned Asian Scholars* 5.4 (1973): 2–16.

Franklin, Charles H. *History of the Philippine Scouts, 1899–1934*. Fort Humphreys, DC: Historical Section, Army War College, 1935.

Gordon, Avery. *Ghostly Matters: Haunting and the Sociological Imagination*. Minneapolis: University of Minnesota Press, 2008.

Heritage of Valor: A History of the Philippine Scouts, 100th Anniversary. Fort Sam Houston, TX: Fort Sam Houston Museum, 2001.

Horsman, Reginald. *Race and Manifest Destiny: The Origins of American Racial Anglo-Saxonism*. Cambridge, MA: Harvard University Press, 1981.

Kramer, Paul A. *The Blood of Government: Race, Empire, the United States, and the Philippines*. Chapel Hill: University of North Carolina Press, 2006.

———. "Making Concessions: Race and Empire Revisited at the Philippine Exposition, St. Louis, 1901–1905." *Radical History Review* 73 (1999): 74–114.

Linn, Brian McAllister. "The U.S. Army and Nation Building and Pacification in the Philippines." In *Armed Diplomacy: Two Centuries of American Campaigning, 5–7 August 2003*, 77–89. Fort Leavenworth, KS: Combat Studies Institute Press, 2003.

Marple, Allan D. *The Philippine Scouts: A Case Study in the Use of Indigenous Soldiers, Northern Luzon, the Philippine Islands, 1899*. Fort Leavenworth, KS: U.S. Army Command and General Staff College, 1983.

Miller, Stuart C. *Benevolent Assimilation: The American Conquest of the Philippines, 1899–1903*. New Haven, CT: Yale University Press, 1982.

Parker, Matthew A., and T. M. Parrish. The Philippine Scouts and the Practice of Counter-Insurgency in the Philippine-American War, 1899–1913. PhD diss. Baylor University, 2008.

The Philippine Scouts. Fort Sam Houston, TX: The Philippine Scouts Heritage Society, 1996.

"Philippine Scouts." *The Asian American Encyclopedia*. Ed. Franklin Ng. New York: Marshall Cavendish, 1995. 1220.

Pomeroy, William J. *American Neo-Colonialism: Its Emergence in the Philippines and Asia*. New York: International Publishers, 1970.

Rafael, Vicente L. *White Love: And Other Events in Filipino History*. Durham, NC: Duke University Press, 2000.

Sanger, Joseph P, Henry Gannett, and Victor H. Olmsted. *Census of the Philippine Islands: Taken Under the Direction of the Philippine Commission in the Year 1903, in Four Volumes*. Washington, DC: Government Printing Office, 1905. Bottom of Form

Schirmer, Daniel B., and Stephen R. Shalom. *The Philippines Reader: A History of Colonialism, Neocolonialism, Dictatorship, and Resistance*. Boston: South End Press, 1987.

Shaw, Angel V., and Luis Francia, eds. *Vestiges of War: The Philippine-American War and the Aftermath of an Imperial Dream, 1899–1999*. New York: New York University Press, 2002.

Silva, Denise F. *Toward a Global Idea of Race*. Minneapolis: University of Minnesota Press, 2007.

United States. Cong. *The Philippine Situation: Testimony and Statements of Witnesses, American and Foreign*. 57th Cong., 1st sess. Sen. Doc. 422. Washington, DC: Government Printing Office, 1902.

Vargas, João H. C. *Never Meant to Survive: Genocide and Utopias in Black Diaspora Communities*. Lanham, MD: Rowman & Littlefield Pub. Group, 2008.

Wolfe, Patrick. "After the Frontier: Separation and Absorption in US Indian Policy." *Settler Colonial Studies* 1.1 (2011): 13–51.

Wolff, Leon. *Little Brown Brother: How the United States Purchased and Pacified the Philippine Islands at the Century's Turn*. Garden City, NY: Doubleday, 1961.

Woolard, Jim R. *The Philippine Scouts: the Development of America's Colonial Army*. PhD diss. Columbus, 1975.

PART III

Nationalist Inscriptions

Blurrings and Erasures

8

Transnationalizing the History of the Chinese in the Philippines during the American Colonial Period

The Case of the Chinese Exclusion Act

RICHARD T. CHU

Introduction

A number of books have been written about the Chinese in the Philippines during or covering parts of the American colonial period (Tan; Jensen; Alejandrino; A. Wilson). However, such studies have mostly limited the examination of their history within the territorial boundaries of the Philippines. Since the Philippines was a US colony from 1898 to 1946, it makes sense to investigate to what extent US experience of its own "Chinaman" question in the metropole influenced US policies and treatment of the Chinese in the Philippines.[1] Taking inspiration from recent studies in Filipino/Filipino-American Studies that adopt a transnationalist framework in the study of the US empire (Kramer; Isaac; Go), this chapter aims to demonstrate how an examination of the interconnections between the history of the Chinese in the United States and that of the Chinese in the Philippines could lead to a better understanding of certain themes within the field, especially those that relate to identity, gender, race, empire, colonialism, and nationalism.[2]

In this chapter, the focus of interconnections between the center and the periphery is the Chinese Exclusion Act. The time frame investigated is from 1898 to 1903, that is, during the first five years of American colonial rule, and during which the Chinese Exclusion Act was officially applied to the Philippines. In terms of sources, reports and testimonies from the Schurman Commission and the different newspaper articles in Manila and in the United States will be utilized. Questions that this chapter seeks to answer include: What were the reasons for implementing such legislation in these two places? How were the reasons similar and different? More importantly, how does a transnational and comparative approach to answering these questions shed more light on the contradictions and tensions surrounding US racial politics and imperial ideology at the turn of the twentieth century? This chapter concludes with some suggestions on what other areas of inquiry can be explored using such an approach.

The Chinese Exclusion Act: A Comparison of the Arguments for Its Implementation in the United States and the Philippines

Reasons for the Implementation of the Chinese Exclusion Act in the United States: An Overview

The first significant wave of Chinese immigrants to arrive in the United States started around 1850, when large numbers of Chinese, mainly from the area surrounding the Pearl River Delta in the southern Chinese province of Guangdong, joined the Gold Rush in California. When the mines dried up, many shifted to work on the railroads and in agricultural farmlands. Toward the end of the nineteenth century, the Chinese could also be found in manufacturing, washing, domestic service, and other low-skilled occupations. Heavily concentrated in Hawaii and on the West Coast, their numbers expanded from a few thousand in the 1850s to as many as 107,000 in 1890. Women also came, but they only constituted a fraction of the total Chinese population.

Though welcomed initially, especially when considered as a panacea to the labor problem facing the United States after the abolition of slavery in the 1860s, the Chinese over time began to encounter discrimination—sometimes in the form of physical violence—against them, their families, their kin, and their co-workers. Various types of legislation were enacted to constrain or inhibit their movement, economic activity, and interaction with local white people. For instance, the Page Law of 1875 prohibited the importation of foreign women to work as prostitutes, but specifically targeted Chinese women, for fear that they would swell the number of settled Chinese families in the United States. Existing antimiscegenation laws at the time also prohibited intermarriages between whites and the Chinese. The most egregious legislation of all was the Chinese Exclusion Act of 1882, which barred Chinese laborers, both skilled and unskilled, from entering the United States for a period of ten years. In 1892, the Chinese Exclusion Act was renewed, and again in 1902. In 1904, it was extended indefinitely.[3]

What reasons lay behind the anti-Chinese sentiments of many Americans and the American government that culminated in the implementation of the Chinese Exclusion Act in the United States? Kurashige and Murray (96) summarized these reasons into categories of "race," "class," and "politics." In addition to these, I would add "gender."

Scholars who have used the "race" paradigm to explain the anti-Chinese movement in the United States point out that such xenophobia stemmed from a fear of the "yellow peril" or of the "yellow horde" invading the shores of the United States, bringing with it a race of people with their mysterious and dangerous practices that could destroy the social and moral fabric of American society. If allowed to stay, and worse, intermarry with American women, these people would dilute the racial purity of American society, producing a generation of "degenerate hybrids." Chinese men were also regarded as "sexual threats" to white women, as some white women had become prostitutes catering to the predominantly bachelor Chinese community. These women had also begun to practice the habit of opium smoking, causing them to lose their modesty, turn their sexual appetite approaching a "frenzied state," and stop being "pure, pious, domestic, and submissive" (Ahmad 58).

Those who use "class" to explain the enactment of the Chinese Exclusion Act argue that it was the threat provided by Chinese labor to white laborers and labor unions by driving down wages that propelled these disaffected workers and their unions to push for anti-Chinese laws. The refusal of the Chinese to join unions was also a reason for the anti-Chinese sentiment among them.[4] Calls for the limitation or prohibition of Chinese coolie labor were especially loudest during the economic depression that hit the United States in the late 1870s. Furthermore, the Chinese were viewed as "strangers" or "foreigners" who did not contribute to the economic welfare of the United States by not investing their money back into American soil, and instead sent as remittances to China.

An approach taken by Andrew Gyory points to "politics" as that engine that served to "fuel" and "steer" the United States toward excluding the Chinese. In other words, while anti-Chinese racist sentiment in the West Coast played a role in agitating for the control of Chinese labor, "(p)oliticians and national party leaders were the glue welding the active anti-Chinese racism of Westerners within the nascent anti-Chinese racism of other Americans" (257). To protect their political interests and advance their careers, politicians both in the West Coast and in Washington, DC, used the anti-Chinese sentiment prevalent among Americans and introduced the exclusion act as a way to gain popular support among their constituents.

While these paradigms of "race," "class," and "politics" explain convincingly why the Chinese Exclusion Act was implemented in the United States, another perspective—"gender"—can provide an additional layer of explanation. In the drive for imperialism in the latter part of the nineteenth century, during which the United States saw itself as a major player, the need for building up a stable society of strong and robust American men and pliant women was paramount (Hoganson 133–55). However, the presence of the Chinese in the United States could thwart this goal. For instance, the Chinese' habit of smoking opium was beginning to spread to the general American population. If left unchecked, this habit would deplete American men of their energies, thus creating a society of effete and "soft" men such as those of China. Some doctors wrote that American opium smokers would develop "Chinese" and feminine characteristics of "introspection, indifference, defeatism, and silence" (Ahmad 55). Consequently, the United States would become "weak" like China and be dominated by other world powers. Thus, issues of masculinity also influenced the logic of anti-Sinicism at the time.

From this general discussion of the different reasons for the implementation of the Chinese Exclusion Act in the United States, this chapter now turns to a discussion of the different reasons given for its implementation in the Philippines, as found in the different testimonies and questions given during the hearings conducted by the Schurman Commission and in various US and Philippine newspapers. This section also asks whether such reasons as they existed in the United States for the exclusion of the Chinese also existed in the Philippines, and that if there were variations, what factors could help explain such differences.

Reasons for the Exclusion of the Chinese in the Philippines:
The Schurman Commission

When the Americans took over the Philippines from Spain in 1898, they were at a loss as to how to deal with the heterogeneous population found in the Islands ("Chinaman Question" 5). One of the issues was how to deal with the thousands of Chinese living in the Philippines at the time.[5] In September of 1898, Major-General Elwell S. Otis, commander of the US Army in the Philippines, ordered the application of the Chinese Exclusion Act in the Philippines. However, the order was meant to be a temporary measure. In 1899, the US government sent the Schurman Commission to the Philippines to gather information about, among other things, the Chinese.[6] Arriving in early 1899, members of the commission spent several months interviewing various prominent people in Manila—ranging from foreign merchants, local residents, and Chinese merchants—and sought their opinions about the "Chinaman" question.

One of the arguments given by those opposed to the immigration of Chinese laborers to the Philippines that echoed one found in the United States was that Chinese labor competed with "native" labor. While in the United States "native" labor meant "white" labor, in the Philippines it pertained to the "indios" or "Filipinos."[7] Most of those who were of the opinion that Chinese laborers should be excluded agreed that the Chinese laborers in the Philippines, like those in the United States, were hardworking and thrifty, and who, through the wage-contract system, managed to enter the country and work for lower wages. But according to O. F. Williams, appointed acting American consul to the Philippines since 15 October 1897, the "Filipinos" felt very badly toward the system for "it (took) work away from them and (prevented) their receiving wages and gaining prosperity" (U.S. Philippine Commission 2: 252). Furthermore, to allow Chinese immigration would lead the Chinese to "swarm over" the Philippines and eventually spill over into the United States. Thus, the threat posed by Chinese laborers in the Philippines to "native" or "Filipino" labor was also a threat to "white" labor in the United States. While the Chinese Exclusion Act as it was applied in the United States had effectively stemmed the tide of Chinese immigration to the United States, a stream of Chinese immigrants could still manage to come in through the "back door." But by implementing the Chinese Exclusion Act in the Philippines the Chinese would be denied an alternative route to the United States. And move to the United States they would, for, as Williams declared, "America is looked upon as a heaven by them, and there is not anything that the Chinese would not do to get into America" (254).

Another reason that was given why Chinese laborers were undesirable was that they were unidentifiable, that is, as soon as they earned a "few dollars," they developed "into something else," that is, as a trader or merchant, as expressed in the testimony of Neil Macleod, and reiterated by Edwin H. Warner (U.S. Philippine Commission 2: 35; 198). Furthermore, O. F. Williams testified that the Chinese in the Philippines in general "simply hoarded what money they could earn . . . or what money they could spare from their earnings, and went back to China with it" (252), a sentiment similar to that provided by Edwin H. Warner (17). This image of the Chinese is reminiscent of the views expressed in the United States of the Chinese as "sojourners" or "foreigners" and not "settlers."

Those favoring the application of the Chinese exclusion laws in the Philippines also argued that, aside from laborers, merchants or traders should be excluded. For instance, William Daland, an American who had been in the Philippines for thirty years, professed that Chinese traders did not "enrich the country" and were "strong competitors against the better classes or more civilized" (U.S. Philippine Commission 2: 166–67).[8] And, like their ever-morphing laborer-counterpart, the Chinese merchant in the Philippines were also hard to locate or pinpoint, for they were of the "lower class," who went into "business transactions . . . [got] into trouble, . . . generally [ran] away and make a complete failure . . . [and] may have twenty names instead of one" (166).[9] Warner opined that even with a system of *cedulas* or certificates, it would be "very difficult" to identify the Chinese (201).

Another similar image being described between the Chinese in the United States and those in the Philippines was that they were "polygamists and heathens," in contrast to Filipinos who were "Christians as a rule" (U.S. Philippine Commission 2: 252). In particular, richer Chinese merchants would have more than one wife, sometimes as many as four (253), with one native wife in the Philippines and a "Chinese" wife in China (41).

Unlike those in the United States, however, the Chinese in the Philippines had had a long history of intermarrying with local women. The Chinese minister in Washington, DC, Wu Ting-fang, for example, in arguing against the application of the Chinese Exclusion Act in the Philippines, pointed out that "many of [the Chinese] were native born (in the Philippines) and intermingled by marriage with the Philippine races" (qtd. in Fonacier 9).

However, it was precisely this long practice of intermarrying with local women that some people opposed Chinese immigration to the Philippines. According to Charles Ilderton Barnes, an American businessman, this practice produced a society in which many natives of the Philippines had become, to some extent, "Chinese" (U.S. Philippine Commission 2: 187). While there was an opinion circulating that intermarriages with the Chinese might "improve" the native race, Barnes was of the opinion that the "mixing" of these two races did not produce a very satisfactory result," that is, the creation of a "Chinese mestizo" class (190). Most of those who testified viewed the Chinese mestizos with disfavor for the following reason: the leaders of the revolution against Spain and later on the fight versus the Americans were mostly "Chinese mestizos," including Emilio Aguinaldo, the president of the revolutionary Philippine government. For Warner, the Spanish policy of not allowing Chinese women to come to the Philippines had the unfortunate consequence of producing the "Chinese half-breeds" who were "causing all the trouble" (19). Macleod echoed the same sentiment a few days later when he testified that "[The Chinese] has a Tagalog wife here and his native wife at home. Some of them raise large families, and a great many of these families are among the insurrectos [insurgents]" (71).

Daland also called the Chinese mestizo the "worst class" of Philippine society, and the reason he gave was that "they have always been taken so; they are treacherous and unreliable, but they are smart; the touch of Chinese blood seems to make them more cunning" (U.S. Philippine Commission 2: 167).

R. W. Brown, an agent for a bank who had lived in the Philippines for twelve years, also regarded the Chinese mestizos as "very clever merchants" who were "very tricky," on whom one could not put much confidence in, and as citizens were of the "discontented" kind (U.S. Philippine Commission 2: 205). Carlos Palanca, a rich Chinese merchant who had lived in the Philippines for forty-three years, also had a low opinion of the Chinese mestizo. He described the Chinese mestizos as the "wealthiest Filipinos in the place," who obtained their wealth by charging usurious interest rates, but not having "very good intellects" (224).

The discussion on the Chinese mestizos thus rested on both racial and political issues. "Tainted" with Chinese blood, they had become the "worst class" in local society, assuming characteristics that made them untrustworthy, greedy, deceitful, and discontented. Politically, they made a "dangerous breed" that would continue fomenting trouble on American aspirations in the new colony.

A close examination of the questions and answers posed surrounding the Chinese mestizos shows that there was some misunderstanding on the definition of "mestizo." Under Spanish colonial rule, a mestizo was defined as a person whose father was Chinese or Chinese mestizo. Mestizos were considered indigenous subjects of Spain and not of China, and they had the same legal rights as the indios to participate in local government and changing their residence (Wickberg, "Chinese Mestizo," 64–65; *Chinese in Philippine Life* 31). Even after several generations, male and female descendants of Chinese paternal ancestors were considered mestizos (Wickberg, "Chinese Mestizo," 33; Robles 77).

However, when it came to first-generation Chinese mestizos, there seems to be a disagreement or confusion with regard to their identity. Under Spanish civil law, they were "mestizos," but how did people view them? To the Chinese father, he or she could be "Chinese," as can be gleaned from the testimony of Carlos Palanca. When asked to define who a mestizo was, he said, "in the commencement a Chinaman marries a Tagalo woman and they get children from that marriage, and their children marry in time and the descendants of that marriage are called mestizos" (U.S. Philippine Commission 2: 224).

Thus, Palanca's own son Engracio, whose mother was a Chinese mestiza, was to the eyes of his father, a "Chinese."[10] This makes sense, since Palanca, as pointed out earlier, was very critical of Chinese mestizos. But to him, these Chinese mestizos belonged to later generations, and who were descendants of intermarriages between Chinese mestizos.

In their report made after their investigations, the Schurman Commission stated that the Chinese in the Philippines had a long history of trade with "natives" of the Islands, and that they exerted great influence on the Philippine economy, especially in the realm of "commerce, industry, wealth, and production" (U.S. Philippine Commission 1: 152). They opined that the "chief reason for the prevailing and pronounced antipathy to the Chinese" was not due to the virtues or habits of the Chinese, but due to "labor competition" (154). Not only in labor did they offer competition, but also in commerce. For instance, they monopolized the tobacco industry and, in general, the wholesale and retail trade.

In concluding their report, the commission acknowledged the following: (1) there was Filipino hostility toward the Chinese, but that these varied from place to place; (2) Filipinos were less inclined to work than the Chinese; and (3) Chinese labor would be advantageous in developing some areas of commerce (for example, mining), and some areas in Luzon, Mindoro, Mindanao, and Palawan populated by "wild tribes" or those which were uninhabited. Thus, its recommendation to the president of the United States was for a careful consideration of the "question as to how, where, and for what purpose the Chinese should be allowed to enter the Archipelago" (159).

After the Schurman Commission submitted its report, it took several more months before the Chinese Exclusion Act was officially implemented in the Philippines. Hence, up until the end of 1901, the Otis proclamation continued to be the de facto law barring Chinese laborers from entering the country. On 29 April 1902, the US Congress extended the act in the United States and also approved its application in Hawaii and the Philippines. In the days, weeks, and months before and even after the implementation of the act in March of 1903, newspapers from both the United States and the Philippines published articles debating the pros and cons of extending this act to the colonies. What were the arguments some of these newspapers gave for supporting its implementation in the Philippines? Did these reasons echo those given for excluding the Chinese in the United States and those given during the Schurman Commission hearings?

Newspaper Articles and Reasons for the Exclusion of the Chinese in the Philippines

It seems that, for the most part, those who advocated for the application of the Exclusion Act in the Philippines reiterated some of the earlier fears pertaining to a Chinese "invasion" of the United States. For instance, the *Manila American* reported in an article "Congress has Disgruntled California" that some quarters in the United States were still unhappy with the application of the Chinese Exclusion Act in the Philippines because some of the changes that were made in the legislation were not enough to stop California from being "flooded with Asiatics." The detrimental effect that Chinese labor would also have on native labor was also cited. The *Washington Star* wrote that whatever had been decided in the United States should also be applied in the "recently acquired territory," since in the Philippines, there was

> popular objection to the Chinese quite as strong as that we find here at home. The Chinese are as cordially hated by the Filipinos as are the Spanish friars. To open the gates at Manila therefore would be as serious a mistake as to open them at San Francisco. There are disturbing factors enough in the archipelago without admitting within its borders a horde of people whose presence would work only injury to us and to themselves. (qtd. in "How the Papers")

Hence, reasons related to "race" and "class" were also operative in the arguments for the exclusion of the Chinese in the Philippines. In addition to these, "politics" played a role, in that the issue of whether to exclude the Chinese laborer was debated within the framework of the US quest in becoming a major global power. But herein lies the conundrum. On the one hand, the United States wanted to develop the Philippine countryside, having decided that the Philippines economy would be primarily based on agriculture. Thus, it would need manpower to farm the land and build the country's infrastructures, such as roads and railways, and the infusion of Chinese labor was seen as a solution to this labor problem. The development of the Philippine economy would also lead toward a better economic relationship with China. Hence, to exclude the Chinese from the Philippines would render the Philippine economy stagnant. On the other hand, it wanted to demonstrate to the Filipinos and other imperial powers that the United States was different from other colonial powers (that is, in the spirit of American exceptionalism), in that its conquest of the Philippines was to aid Filipinos achieve political, economic, and social progress, and to create a Philippine nation mainly for "Filipinos." As an article entitled "Some Light in the Philippines" which appeared in the *San Francisco Call* astutely framed it, the debate surrounding the "Chinese problem" in the Philippines was between those who viewed US annexation of the Philippines as a matter of "commerce and politics" and those who viewed it as a matter of "principle and interest," and that the issue could easily be resolved if people agreed on which purpose it was that the United States had annexed the Philippines.

The racial discourse as found in the Schurman Commission hearings to justify the exclusion of the Chinese was also found in the different newspapers. Yes, the Chinese were hardworking, while the Filipinos indolent. Furthermore, the *Manila American* stated that the Filipino, compared to the American, "is not a trustworthy laborer" ("Chinese Immigration"). However, in his report dated 1 October 1902, Taft wrote that to allow unlimited introduction of the Chinese into the Philippines "would be a great mistake," and that the objection of the Filipinos to such a course was "entirely logical and justified." He thus supported the limited immigration of the Chinese, saying:

> I do not think it would be just to the Filipinos, or a proper course for America in the development of this country, to do more than to . . . admit, upon reasonable restrictions, a certain limited number of skilled Chinese laborers, who may contribute to the construction of buildings and the making of other improvements, and who at the same time by their labor may communicate to Filipino apprentices the skill which the Filipinos so easily acquire. ("Governor Taft's Annual Report on the Islands")

As a solution to the problem that would result from the exclusion of Chinese laborers from the Philippines, some proposed that white laborers from the United States be imported. An article called "Railways: The Report" in the *San Francisco Call* stated that while it was true that Filipinos were "lazy" and "simple," in time their exposure to Americans would create in them a "new desire" that would "induce work." In other words, Filipinos, under American tutelage, would eventually become capable of achieving prosperity. An editorial dated 12 November 1900 from the *Washington Star* called for Americans to train the Filipinos into "effective workingmen." It ended by saying:

> The true American course is plain and straight. On the one side is (sic) present profit and future danger, wrecked land and a crushed people a record of shameful tyranny, as disgraceful as ever was written by Spain. On the other side will appear the growth of a people into prosperity and self-government, the discharge of a high trust for the benefit of civilization, a truly American demonstration of nation-making. Which shall it be? ("The Chinese in the Philippines")

However, some people found the idea of sending white laborers to the Philippines untenable. The different climatic conditions in the new colony were deemed too harsh for such men. Woodrow Wilson, in his five-volume work called *History of the American People*, wrote that "Caucasian laborers could not compete with the Chinese . . . who, with their yellow skin and debasing habits of life, seemed to them hardly fellow men at all, but evil spirits rather" (5: 185). The *Manila American* stated that the admission of Chinese to the Philippines would prevent the "white man (in the Philippines from being) injured" ("'Tis worth while to try"). Other races were also considered to replace the Chinese. For instance, the editor of the *Manila American*, G. O. Ziegenfuss, pointed out that the "colony of Moros, . . . can and do work, but cannot be depended upon" ("Editorial"). An article from the same newspaper dated 12 March 1902 mentioned that General Hughes, who had been assigned to the Philippines, testified before an "investigation committee" that white labor for the Philippines would be a "total failure" and that he favored the encouragement of "negro immigration" to supplant the gap in labor ("General Hughes"). A US official, Senator John T. Morgan of Alabama, had also proposed to the US president that black workers from the southern states be shipped to the Philippines as a way to solve the labor problem. However, the *Manila American* opposed the idea, pointing out that there were already blacks in the country, vestige of the Philippine-American War, who had defected, or who had decided to stay, and were "vagrants . . . [who] live off of the native women whom they terrorize into supporting them, and who are commonly called 'ladrones' [thieves] . . . worthless." The piece in the newspaper further stated:

> This land of mañana [tomorrow] is a paradise for the negro as a class, and he is working his graft for all there is in it. It has often been said by men of observation that the government at Washington made an awful blunder when it sent colored troops to the islands, and from the way in which a large majority of the discharged colored soldiers who remained in the islands have been conducting themselves, it is becoming plainer everyday that it was a blunder. ("Chinese Are Wanted")[11]

On 28 April 1903, the *Manila American* reported that the Civil Commission passed an act that effectively placed the law into effect. However, there was continued protest against the implementation of the Chinese Exclusion Act in the Philippines. One reason for opposing it was that American soldiers were asked to do the manual labor that Chinese labor could have performed. In an article entitled "Why Should American Soldiers Do Coolie's Work," we read that American soldiers were building the road in Lanao, Mindanao. The author of the article agreed that, since the war was supposed to be over, these soldiers could be required to perform noncombat or nonmilitary work, but "civil work" was not supposed to be equal to "manual labor." He went on to say that the reason why the American soldiers had to do the roadwork was that Filipinos were lazy, and that they considered themselves "to be equals and to have right to enjoy the blessing of personal liberty to the point of retarding the advancement of their country." These "quasi-brothers" were ungrateful to the Americans, for they questioned "our right . . . to civilize themselves, "and who deemed themselves "already fit to rank among independent nations of the world." Some of the American soldiers working on the road had become sick with cholera, and those who complained were court-martialed. The article continued to state that those Filipino soldiers who wore the American uniform and drew money from the government should relieve the Twenty-Eighth infantry, and that these Filipinos could be goaded or forced to do so "were we less concerned about wounding their pride." Even bribing them to work, by paying them three times the average wage, did not have any effect. The newspaper several months later printed an article called "Soldiers as Coolies" and the author pointed out that the decision by the War Department to "force" American soldiers to build roads in "Moro country" [that is, Mindanao] outraged many Americans, and that it was a disgrace to the United States that the administration:

> countenances the degradation of American manhood in the eyes of the world and place not only Americans but members of every other white race where savages can treat them with contempt. The soldiers who built the roads in Mindanao while the savages stood contemptuously by were considered by these uncouth fanatics as nothing more or less than coolies. And so long as white men are forced to perform a slave's duties in the Moro country they will be treated as slaves those people.

As we can see here, apart from "race," "class," and "politics," the perspective of "gender," in which US anxieties over projecting a masculinist image to both its colonial subjects and the outside world, also framed the debates surrounding the Chinese Exclusion Act in the Philippines.

Conclusion

This chapter is an attempt to compare and contrast the historical issues surrounding the "Chinaman" question in the Philippines and in the United States. Specifically, it focuses on the Chinese Exclusion Act and the arguments or reasons given by its proponents. One question this chapter sought to answer was: What were the similarities and differences between the arguments and reasons given for its implementation in the United States and those in the Philippines?

Naturally, any meaningful discussion in comparing the situation of the Chinese in the Philippines and the Chinese in the United States has to start with the obvious: the difference in the historical and geographical context in which the exclusion policies were applied. One main difference, for instance, was that, by the time the Chinese Exclusion Act was made operative indefinitely in the United States in 1902, several decades had already transpired in which the American public and the US government had had the chance to examine their "Chinaman" issue closely, to adjust and adapt their policies to the direction political, economic, and social winds of change blew, and to form their racialized view of the "Chinaman." In the case of the Philippines, the US government (both in the metropole and in the colony) did not have such luxury. Hence, the question of whether to allow laborers to enter the Philippines would persist for another decade or so. Another important difference was the fact that any decision made on the "Chinaman" question in the Philippines had to be measured against the civilizing project of the United States for its new colony as well as its quest to become an imperial power, albeit one that would showcase "American exceptionalism," as opposed to a mainly domestic issue or matter of national interest that framed the discussions of the Chinese in the United States. Furthermore, one has to take into account the longer history of the Chinese in the Philippines and their relationship with other Philippine ethnic groups.

The findings included in this chapter pertain to the reasons for excluding the Chinese in the Philippines and they are by no means exhaustive. Other sources, such as US congressional hearings or other newspapers, may reveal other reasons that could deepen or complicate those discussed herein. However, it is not within the scope of this chapter to include such sources. The main objective of this chapter is to demonstrate how paying attention to the interconnections between the historical experience of the Chinese in the Philippines and that of the Chinese elsewhere, and in this case, in the United States—an approach I broadly define as transnational and comparative—can lead us to broader perspectives, further insights, and new areas of research in our study of the history of the Chinese in the Philippines. In the course of examining the sources used in this chapter, I observed other facets of the "Chinaman" question in the Philippines that point to the transnational character of the issue. For instance, at the height of the discussions regarding the salience of implementing the Chinese Exclusion Act in the Philippines, a suggestion was made to learn from the British experience. An article reported that in British North Borneo, "Chinese cheap labor" had not "ruined" it. It further reported that in order to attract Chinese labor, the British allowed the Chinese to hold lands under perpetual lease, smoke opium, gamble, and to "follow other home customs to which American authorities would not dare give legal sanction" ("So British North Borneo"). Indeed, in its efforts to find solutions to its own "Chinaman" problem, the United States consulted the experiences of the Dutch, the British, and the Japanese in dealing with their own "Chinaman" problem, sending, for instance, delegations to Taiwan and British Malaya to examine how other imperial powers dealt with the opium question. A comparative study between the way the United States dealt with its Chinese colonial subjects and the way other European and the Japanese colonial powers did is one research area waiting to be explored and one that could lead to greater understandings of US history as well as that of Philippine history. Another suggested area of research requiring a transnational approach is to investigate how Americans returning to the United States from the Philippines helped influence the debate over policies governing the Chinese. A writer for *Manila American* pointed out that American soldiers returning from the Philippines were painting the conditions in the colony "in false colors" and hence giving "the people across the big pond the wrongest (*sic*) kind of wrong ideas of how matters really (were)" in the Philippines ("Let Us Work

Together"). As a consequence of this misinformation, the article called supporters of Chinese immigration to be vigilant in writing senators and congressmen in the United States to oppose the Chinese Exclusion Act. In sum, it is hoped that this chapter may convince the reader of the viability, importance, and productivity of using a transnational and comparative approach to the study of the history of the Chinese in the Philippines, particularly during the American colonial period.

Notes

1. Likewise, historical studies of the Chinese in the United States have not fully explored, if at all, how US experience of the Chinese question in the Philippines and other US colonial possessions might have affected US treatment of the Chinese in the metropole. However, it is not within the scope of this paper to undertake such project.

2. This chapter is part of a larger book project which aims to examine the interconnections between US experience of its Chinese immigrants and of the Chinese in the Philippines. The premise of the project is that a transnational and comparative approach to the study of certain events and issues involving the Chinese in both the metropole and the periphery would expand our understanding of the "Chinaman" questions the United States faced during its rise as an imperial power in the Pacific in the first half of the twentieth century. As mentioned, the focus of interconnections between the metropole and the periphery is on the Chinese Exclusion Act as applied in the Philippines. Other case studies to be investigated would be immigration laws, policies, and implementation; the construction of a "Chinatown" in Manila; the opium issue; prostitution; the boycott of Japanese goods in 1921; the Chinese labor question in both the United States and the Philippines; the Cable Act of 1921; and the lifting of the Chinese Exclusion Act in the United States in 1943.

3. Teachers, students, merchants, travelers, and diplomats were exempted, along with those who had already been living in the United States, provided they obtain special certificates known as Section 6 certificates that would allow them to come and go freely.

4. This, however, did not preclude the fact that Chinese laborers pressed for better working conditions, especially through the leaders of the Chinese community in the West Coast or through Chinese officials in the United States.

5. In 1899, the estimated number of Chinese residing in the Philippines was 40,000. In the census of 1903, the number was placed at 41,035, although other estimates put it at as many as 100,000 (Chu, *Chinese and Chinese Mestizos*, 291–92).

6. The commission, was headed by J. G. Shurman, hence its name. Other members were George Dewey, Charles Denby, and Dean C. Worcester.

7. Note that at the time when citizenship laws were just transitioning to nationalized ones, the term *indio*, a applied by the Spaniards to refer to the predominantly

Malay Christianized "natives," was still sometimes used, as seen in Neil Macleod's testimony (U.S. Philippine Commission 2: 35).

8. Benito Legarda, a prominent Filipino, shared Daland's view, and added that Chinese merchants were "dishonest" (U.S. Philippine Commission 2: 178).

9. Reacting to Daland's statement, one member of the commission commented that to exclude Chinese merchants would be "an exactly opposite idea from what we have at home" (U.S. Philippine Commission 2: 167).

10. Another "Chinese mestizo" who participated in the fight against the Spaniards and Americans, Mariano Limjap, was also considered "Chinese" when he tried to pass off as "mestizo" (Chu, "Rethinking," 55; Chu, *Chinese and Chinese Mestizos*, 248).

11. The article added that the wage that was going to be paid to the "negro" would not attract him, and that the Chinese was still the best type of labor for the country ("Chinese Are Wanted").

Works Cited

Ahmad, Diana L. "Opium Smoking, Anti-Chinese Attitudes, and the American Medical Community, 1850–1890." *American Nineteenth Century History* 1.2 (2000): 53–68. Print.

Alejandrino, Clark L. *A History of the 1902 Chinese Exclusion Act: American Colonial Transmission and Deterioration of Filipino-Chinese Relations*. Manila: Kaisa Para sa Kaunlaran, Inc., 2003. Print.

"Chinese Are Wanted, But No Negroes." *Manila American*. 10 Feb. 1903. Print.

"Chinese Immigration." *Manila American*. 24 Aug. 1903. Print.

"The Chinese in the Philippines." *Washington Star*. 12 Nov. 1901. Rpt. in Manila American, 28 Dec. 1901.

"Congress has Disgruntled California." *Manila American*. 2 May 1902. Print.

Chu, Richard T. *The Chinese and Chinese of Manila: Family, Identity, and Culture 1860s-1930s*. Leiden and Boston: Brill Publishing, 2010; Pasig City: Anvil Publishing, 2012. Print.

———. "The Chinaman Question: A Conundrum in U.S. Imperial Policy in the Pacific." *Kritika Kultura* 7 (2006): 8–25. Print.

———. "Rethinking the Chinese Mestizos of the Philippines." In *Beyond China: Migrating Identities*, ed. Yuanfang Shen and Penny Edwards, 44–74. Canberra: Centre for the Study of the Chinese Southern Diaspora, The Australian National University, 2002. Print.

"Editorial." *Manila American*. 22 Jan. 1902. Print.

Fonacier, Tomas S. "The Chinese Exclusion policy in the Philippines." *Social Sciences and Humanities Review* 14.1 (1949): 3–28. Print.

"General Hughes Advocates Negro Labor for Philippines." *Manila American*. 12 Mar. 1902. Print.

Go, Julian. *American Empire and the Politics of Meaning: Elite Political Cultures in the Philippines and Puerto Rico*. Durham, NC: Duke University Press, 2008. Print.

"Governor Taft's Annual Report on the Islands." *Manila American.* 9 Jan. 1903. Print.

Gyory, Andrew. *Closing the Gate: Race, Politics, and the Chinese Exclusion Act.* Chapel Hill: University of North Carolina Press, 1998. Print.

Hoganson, Kristin L. *Fighting for American Manhood: How Gender Politics Provoked the Spanish-American and Philippine-American War.* New Haven, CT: Yale University Press, 1998. Print.

"How the Papers View the Chinese Exclusion Law." *Manila American.* 15 Dec. 1901. Print.

Isaac, Allan P. *American Tropics: Articulating Filipino America.* Minneapolis: University of Minnesota Press, 2006. Print.

Jensen, Irene. *The Chinese in the Philippines during the American Regime, 1898–1946.* San Francisco: R and E Research Associates, 1975. Print.

Kramer, Paul. *The Blood of Government: Race, Empire, the United States, & the Philippines.* Chapel Hill: University of North Carolina Press, 2006. Print.

Kurashige, Lon, and Anne Yang Murray. *Major Problems in Asian American History: Documents and Essays.* Boston: Houghton and Mifflin, 2003. Print.

"Let Us Work Together." *Manila American.* 2 Sept. 1902. Print.

"Railways: The Report made by Expert; One Proposed Line is from Manila to Aparri; The Other Recommended is from Manila to Batangas; The Cost Price Estimates Based Upon Contract Chino labor as Natives Not Competent." *Manila American.* 23 Oct. 1902. Print.

Robles, Eliodoro G. *The Philippines in the Nineteenth Century.* Quezon City, Philippines: Malaya Books Inc., 1969. Print.

"So British North Borneo Is Not Ruined by Chinese Cheap Labor." *Manila American.* 15 Dec. 1901. Print.

"Soldiers as Coolies." *Manila American.* 11 Dec. 1903. Print.

"Some Light in the Philippines." *San Francisco Call.* Reprinted in *Manila American,* 9 May 1902. Print.

Tan, Antonio. *The Chinese in the Philippines, 1898–1935: A Study of Their National Awakening.* Quezon City: Garcia Publishing Co., 1972. Print.

"'Tis worth while to try." *Manila American.* 6 Aug. 1902. Print.

U.S. Philippine Commission. *Report of the Philippine Commission to the President,* 4 Vols. Washington, DC: Government Printing Office, 1899–1901. Print.

"Why Should Americans Do Coolie's Work?" *Manila American.* 28 Apr. 1903. Print.

Wickberg, Edgar Bernard. *The Chinese in Philippine life, 1850–1898.* 1965; rpt. Quezon City, Philippines: Ateneo de Manila University Press, 2000. Print.

———. "The Chinese Mestizo in Philippine History." *Journal of Southeast Asian History* 5.1 (1964): 62–100. Print.

Wilson, Andrew R. *Ambition and Identity: China and the Chinese in the Colonial Philippines.* Honolulu: University of Hawaii Press, 2004. Print.

Wilson, Woodrow. *History of the American People.* 5 vols. New York: Harper & Bros., 1902. Print.

9

Redressive Nationalisms, Queer Victimhood, and Japanese Duress

ROBERT DIAZ

Although Japan occupied the Philippines for less than three years, its effects continue to haunt the psyches of Filipinos in the diaspora. Among the images of death marches to Bataan, remnants of Manila's destruction during the war, and tales of soldiers' brutality to indigenous villagers, the victimization of *comfort women* and *japayukis* have indexed the harmful effects of Japanese incursion into the Philippine state. The term *comfort woman* (or *jugun ianfu*) refers to the more than two hundred thousand Asian women forcibly taken by the Japanese imperial army during the Pacific war. Aside from the Philippines, the military abducted women from Korea, Taiwan, Indonesia, Burma, China, and Thailand, in order to serve as their "sexual slaves" and as a way for the soldiers to have sanitary forms of release.[1] In response to their absence in the historical accounts of the war, the comfort women's movement mobilized in the early part of the 1990s. They collectively demanded that the Japanese government acknowledge and apologize for the atrocities perpetrated during colonialism, through symbolic and financial forms of redress. Their calls became especially more pressing as the number of women able to share their testimonies slowly dwindled with each passing day.

In the Philippine context, as the comfort women's movement became more public, films, television shows, and newspaper exposés began focusing on their plight. Oftentimes, these representations fetishized the women's experiences with violence and rape. Comfort women were seen as metonymic figures for national incapacity, most embodied through sensationalized scenes of Japanese-inflicted abuse. Feminists on the ground responded to such limited portrayals of comfort women by collecting testimonies from the *Lolas,* or grandmothers, as they were affectionately called. In her introduction to an anthology of such testimonies, Nelia Sancho asserts that most of the women she had spoken to did not see themselves as passive victims. She writes that "of the 14 years or more of support to the *Lolas*, we have seen survivors transform themselves from the 'victim' image to one who is empowered enough to articulate the call for a clear and unequivocal apology as well as legal compensation from the government" (15). Similarly, in her autobiography *Comfort Woman: A Filipina's Story of Prostitution and Slavery Under the Japanese Military*, Maria Henson invests equal energies in discussing her past as a peasant's daughter (fathered by one of the Spanish neocolonial landowners in her native province) and her life after the camp (working as a seamstress after her husband decides to leave her). By providing the full arc of her story before, during, and after abduction, Henson also foregrounds how her victimization under the Japanese military is part and parcel of the historical forms of patriarchy that Spanish, Japanese, and American colonial encounters effect.

Yet such efforts to articulate more nuanced narratives around *comfort women's* experiences stand in stark contrast to more commonly recycled stories that focus on their victimization and lack of agency. Such tropes coincided with the Philippine public's growing anxieties about Japanese political and economic clout after occupation. By the time the comfort women's movement started asserting their demands, the Philippine government had already established close economic ties with its former colonizer. From the 1970s onward, the Marcos regime had benefited financially from Japanese foreign investment, as it sought to rebuild and discipline the country's crippled infrastructure during martial law. The regime also encouraged the cultivation of various tourism industries, where Japan provided a steady stream of customers for the numerous red-light districts the government privately condoned but publicly disavowed. Japan also served as the recipient of entertainment labor shipped overseas, as part of the larger scheme by the Marcos government to streamline Filipino labor migration in order to become what Robyn Rodriguez defines as a "labor brokerage state." A majority of these entertainment jobs as overseas performing artists (OPAs) were being filled by Filipinas seeking a steady source of income abroad.

Filipina OPAs were then called *japayukis*. In common parlance, *japa-yuki* is synonymous with "sex worker," "prostitute," "guest relations officer" (GRO), "hostess," and "artist/performer." Although some of these women were indeed conscripted for sex work, majority of *japayukis* performed as hostesses, waitresses, singers, and dancers in Japanese nightclubs and bars. Some *japayukis* used their certification to find employment in markets outside of the entertainment industry, even if this entailed staying in Japan illegally. Others sought to find suitable spouses in order to stay indefinitely. In her study of *japayuki* representation, Nobue Suzuki highlights the similarly patriarchal ways that tabloids, films, and news media depicted Filipina women in the profession, through a very myopic lens of sexualization and victimhood. She writes that in movies like *Maricris Sioson*—which follows the travails of a Pinay, an overseas worker, who dies in Japan and is returned to her family with bruises and scars—the "historical and political-economic details were soon subsumed under the actual and fantasized practices of sex and prostitution" (443). These fantasies often imagined the *japayuki* as the quintessential sex worker and victim of Yakuza violence. Filipina *japayukis* embodied a contradiction; they were seen as either *bagong bayani*, or "new heroes," willing to sacrifice, or in some instances die to earn for their families in an age of global remittance dependency, or as women willing to undergo the constant threat of violence because of an irrepressible feminine materialism.

Such mainstream views about *japayukis* also affected foreign policy around their migration. In *Illicit Flirtations*, Rhacel Parrenas tracks how *japayukis* were labeled as "sex trafficked victims" by the US Department of State's *Trafficking in Persons Reports* (TIPs) immediately after September 11, 2001. With the prodding of the United States, the Philippines and Japan changed the certification processes for female entertainment laborers. The United States pushed for policies that required Japan-bound performers to take two years of training in various classes in the performing arts and to go through specific skills tests deemed useful for certification as entertainment laborers. This process was lengthy and costly, and it required the approval of "panels of experts" chosen by the government in order for the migrant's approval to move. Meant to stop human trafficking by legitimizing entertainment work, these new policies produced unequal standards for the certification of male and female labors. They have caused the number of Filipinas working in Japan to drastically decline.[2] Through Parrenas's detailed fieldwork, she also notes that these stricter requirements ended up furthering *japayuki* susceptibility to sex work rather than prevent it. Most of the women she interviewed mentioned being indebted to Philippine-based corporations responsible for completing their application process and placement. Such dependency, akin to being indentured to their Philippine contractors, drove some of the women to leave their employers and stay in Japan illegally.[3]

The contradictory representations of *comfort women* and *japayukis* serve as useful flashpoints for understanding how female victimhood has been imagined, particularly when such victimhood is coupled with anti-Japanese nationalism and demands for redress. Such representations foreground the significance of what I call redressive nationalisms in how certain figures, such as the victimized Filipina, have been portrayed from the 1970s onward. Redressive nationalisms involve the activation of patriotic sentiment and nationalistic zeal by linking such nationalistic fervor to symbolic and economic forms of redress. Redressive nationalisms also involve the circulation of heteronormative notions of victimhood, violence, and reparation, especially when these constructs are condoned, reproduced, and institutionalized by the nation-state. Redressive nationalisms are present in institutionalized strategies seemingly meant to enact reparation—monetary or otherwise—but in reality only further the consolidation of state power and expansion of transnational capital. Redressive nationalisms may even abject specific identities (often queer and transgressive) in the name of patriotism and reparation while attempting to address the violence done on these populations. In its heteronormative guises, redressive nationalisms deepens what Jasbir Puar has termed "homonationalism," or the national acceptance of particular queer subjects—often white, upwardly mobile, and male—at the expense of further marginalizing other queer subjects (brown bodies, immigrant bodies, terrorist bodies, and so on). Redressive nationalisms delineate which subjects are worthy of inclusion in the wholesale attempt to "repair" the broken postcolonial state.

Redressive nationalisms affect how the Philippines negotiates its complex and often unequal relationship with its former colonizer, at a time when Japan has shifted into the role of international business partner in an age of interlocking globalizations. Precisely because the Philippines has been unable to acknowledge the parallels between violent histories of colonial subjugation and the emerging realities of transnational capital's expansion, it has also been unable to adequately address the patriarchal and gendered assumptions that continue to haunt representations of Filipina victimhood under Japanese duress. In this regard, redressive nationalisms influence how Japanese colonialism and Filipina victimhood have been imagined, institutionalized, and understood as mutually related historical sites.

Given such political contexts, how might queer artists expose and critique redressive nationalism's visual, rhetorical, and grammatical strategies for articulating Filipina victimhood? Expanding on this question further, this chapter examines Gil Portes's *Markova, Comfort Gay* (2003) and Nick DeOcampo's *The Sex Warrior and the Samurai* (1996), two films that portray messy, episodic, and highly textured stories that queer the figure of the *comfort woman* and the *japayuki*. Set in the Philippines during Japanese occupation, *Markova, Comfort Gay* follows the life of Walter Dempster Jr., or Walterina Markova, and his four friends (Carmen, Sophie, Anita, and Minerva) as Japanese soldiers force them into "sexual slavery." Interpreting key moments of violence in the film, most evident in ritualized scenes of rape, I suggest that *Markova, Comfort Gay* challenges the very limited scripts female victimhood occupies, even as the film simultaneously shocks the audience with common homophobic images of *kabaklaan*. In the film, the *bakla* occupies the role of the comfort woman. Such a replacement produces a crisis of representation that presents the audience with a new set of paradigms for understanding female violence during colonization. *Sex Warriors and the Samurai* (1996) follows the life of Joann, a transgender *japayuki*, as she attempts to seek overseas employment in Japan. By refocusing on the queer *japayuki* as the victim of a growing overseas labor market, DeOcampo highlights how dominant representations of diasporic overseas contract work must intrinsically depend on strict notions of patronage, familial belonging, and nationalism, regardless of the victim's sexual identity.

Taken together, these films collectively gesture to the integral (and indeed, radical) relationship between "messiness" and "queerness." Writing about the parallels between queerness as mess, and mess as queerness, Martin Manalansan suggests that such a relationship "comes out of a critical reading of queer theory, popular culture, vernacular language, and everyday life. My use of queer and mess is not limited to bodies, objects, and desires but also relates to processes, behaviors, and situations. 'Queering' and 'messing up' are activities and actions as much as 'queer' and 'mess' can be about states/status, positions, identities, and orientations" (97). Such queer messiness, or messy queerness, can thus produce ways of being and knowing that "deviate from, resist, or run counter to the workings of normality" (97). In other words, queerness and messiness parallel each other precisely when they foreground how discomfort, dissonance, and disorder populate the critical frames and political yearnings of queer subjects that resist institutionalization, normalization, and co-optation. In this regard then, *Markova: Comfort Gay* and *Sex Warriors* deploy the political potentiality of queerness as mess as they unsettle well-known archives of Japanese inflicted violence, and as they present a queer-centric history of Japanese duress. Both films expose and also critique how the hegemonic representation of Filipina victimhood disciplines and delineates which subjects are worthy of such categorical and legal definitions, buttressed by redressive forms of nationalistic sentiment.

"If There's No Comfort Woman, Then What Do We Have?"

Markova, Comfort Gay was released in 2001 and garnered multiple awards for acting, directing, and screenplay locally and abroad. Perhaps to capitalize on a growing niche market, it was also screened in various LGBT-themed festivals in cities like San Francisco and Seattle. Not much has been written about Portes's work, even though it has received viewership abroad, and Dolphy Quizon, a well-known comedian in the Philippines, stars in it. A handful of reviews available online have criticized the film's representation of the *bakla* figure. Critics suggest that because it depicts gay subjects that are effeminate, campy, and prone to being seen through "inversion narratives," *Markova, Comfort Gay* does very little to challenge phobic assumptions about local gay representation.[4] Critics also suggest that the violence in the film is less believable to a public accustomed to seeing the effeminate *bakla* as desiring of sexual attention at all costs.[5]

Such critical apprehensions with the film's portrayal of *kabaklaan* are deeply rooted in the violence that Filipino/a sexual minorities continue to experience, encouraged by multiple forms of representation that make queerness legible only insofar as it conforms to tragic or comedic narratives and scripts. However, without discounting these concerns, this analysis moves away from the assumption that "screaming gay"— or what is often referred to in common parlance as the "parloristang" *bakla*[6]—serve no other political purpose but to demean *bakla* identities. As I have written elsewhere, such *bakla* representation can also enacting more capacious and class-transecting queer politics.[7] Such discomfort with *Markova's* version of *kabaklaan* may in fact privilege ways of interpreting the film that dictate the "right" type queer subject on screen, one that must be masculine, cosmopolitan, and upwardly mobile (of which Markova's character is not).

Yet *kabaklaan* can also gesture to the messiness of queer Filipino/a lives, in its affiliation with transgender identity, lower-class status, and affective promiscuity.[8] Focusing on the malleability of *bakla* in *Markova, Comfort Gay* enables us to see what political, theoretical, and historical questions such *kabklaan* opens up around our notions of anti-Japanese nationalism and redress.[9] If mainstream representations of comfort women have relied on particular assumptions about appropriate forms of Pinay femininities that signify victimhood, then the comfort gay messes up these assumptions by approximating the visual, grammatical, and rhetorical cues for making such victimized femininities legible in the first place. The comfort gay exposes the compositional nature of these femininities when tied to nationalism, violence, and redress.

Roland Tolentino has examined the political possibilities such approximations produce, through what he calls the act of queer "panggagaya." Placing *panggagaya* within specific historical context, he examines how Dolphy's portrayal of *kabaklaan* in Lino Brocka's *Ang Nanay Kong Tatay* (My father who is a mother)—as mimicry of masculine and feminine forms of domesticity—serve as a rich palimpsest by which to read Imelda and Ferdinand Marcos's manufactured domesticity during the time the film was released. As Tolentino writes:

The Marcoses, through some thirty years of conjugal dictatorship, disseminated images of their virile bodies embodying beauty and power where they become, in their minds, the "be all and end all" of power. Through national rituals that mark the spectacularization of their presidential bodies, the Marcoses have enforced a cultural grid to differentiate and hegemonize their bodily claim to power. Transvestism's spectacle operates by recoding the signifiers of the presidential bodies in its own gender, sexual and class based terms. This means that the transvestite's recoding of national codes also resignifies his desire to move beyond categories which impede, in actual material bases, the very limits of such transgression."

Tolentino's analysis serves as a useful departure point for my own analytical interests because it suggests that *kabaklaan's* potential for approximating malleable signifiers for masculinities and femininities can also challenge how such forms of embodiment are articulated, and sometimes even demanded, by institutions and state apparatuses. In a similar move, I would argue that *kabaklaan* in *Markova, Comfort Gay* recodes and redeploys the gendered and patriarchal tropes that have made the comfort woman a "woman" in the first place in order to unsettle how comfort women's bodies and lives have been imagined, and policed, within discourses of Japanese violence. If anything, the uncomfortable, problematic, and messy affective alignments of the female comfort woman and the comfort gay on screen offers us a rich space to queer patriarchal tropes of female identity, Japanese violence, and nationalistic zeal.

Markova, Comfort Gay immediately confronts the doubts about Markova's story, by beginning with the comfort gay's assertion that his story is real. We see Dempster waking up from a nightmare. He begins to wash his face in the morning, as his voice-over narrates, "Have you heard of comfort gay? This is the story of my life, one bad dream, a nightmare, but every bit as real." The assertion of authenticity works on multiple levels. On one level, Dempster confronts the difficulty of having the *bakla* be seen as a victim of abuse. Dempster must immediately demand inclusion in an archive of Japanese abuse that has already abjected the queer subject from it. On another level, and intimately related to the first, the film also follows the logic that the acquisition and production of truthful testimony is the primary mode for demanding and instituting redress on a global scale.[10] Comfort women's testimonies precisely depend on the state's acknowledgment of sexual abuse and violence as real, in order for any redress (psychic, legal, and monetary) to occur. Dempster thus must perform a narrative that already has specific historical meanings for the comfort women's movement. Strengthening this link further, a news segment about comfort women's "call for justice" encourages Dempster to tell his story in the first place. After seeing the exposé, and with some soul searching inside a Catholic church, Dempster contacts the reporter he sees in the documentary (Loren Legarda) in order to take part in this confessional ritual. Using Legarda as witness, Dempster joins the comfort women in their quest to be heard.

Yet the most seemingly obvious point in the movie also seems to be the most elusive: Markova is not a comfort "woman" at all. Shuttling between the names "Markova" and "Dempster" shows the film's crisis around the character's gender identity and sexuality. For instance, it is not clear which name stands in for whom, if Markova represents the "woman" who is abused and Dempster the "man" renarrating abuse. When Loren Legarda visits Dempster for the first and last time, she naively asks for Ma'am Markova or Mrs. Markova. When told of her absence, she calls attention to this lack angrily, "So . . . there isn't a Mrs. Markova here?" Dempster confirms that he is in fact not a comfort woman. She then restates her irritation, "So there also isn't any comfort woman? So, what do we have?" Dempster replies, "Comfort gay." The movie consistently registers the crisis of whether Dempster could be considered a victim of abuse, as a comfort gay.

As an attempt to normalize this crisis, *Markova, Comfort Gay* feminizes Dempster from the very beginning. During the first episodic flashback to his youth, Dempster sits on a swing with his female friends, admiring men playing basketball. His homophobic brother Bobby (Freddy Quizon) catches him and beats him up, demanding, "Remember this: be a man! Because you are a man, stupid!" Immediately after, Dempster is shown in his bedroom, refusing to follow these orders. He borrows his sister's clothing and makeup, and he admits that in doing so "the woman in me comes out." The makeup and the clothing function similarly to the comfort woman's narrative; they index Dempster or Walter's attempt at deciding a "truth" about his identity as they also index his "becoming" a woman. The penultimate proof of this transformation is Markova's being mistaken for a woman, which leads to her abuse. Japanese soldiers imprison Markova and her friends because they discover that the "female lounge dancers" they've courted (and had every intention of having sex with) are not women at all. Again the assertion of

Markova's maleness comes to the fore, as a Japanese soldier feels under her skirt and beats her up for being a man, before sending the group to a holding cell to perform sexual favors for Japanese troops. Violence in this movie indexes national identity. Aside from their outside clothing, violent acts are the only ways to differentiate characters sexually and racially from each other.

Markova, Comfort Gay seems to gesture toward the undecidability of gender precisely as these characters attempt to articulate an already lucid story about "female" abuse. Thus it constantly uses "woman" a site of contestation, highlighting the constitutive elements of female victimhood through the queer subject's dragging of Filipina identity under Japanese duress. Discussing the meaning of "realness" in *Paris Is Burning*, Judith Butler writes that "what determines the effect of realness is the ability to compel belief, to produce the naturalized effect" (129). As the drag performers approximate gender and racial norms in the ball circuit, they also produce a "morphological ideal that remains the standard which regulates the performance, but which no performance fully approximates" (129). In *Markova, Comfort Gay*, the "realness" of Markova's performance as a *comfort woman* challenges the legible ways in which "believability" becomes a defining concept for practicing nationalism and redress; Markova complicates the ways in which state discourses limit the "believability" of Japanese abuse around specific experiences of violence, and around specific victims of violence (so that it can only happen to women, and particular types of women). Indeed, even in Butler's formulation, the dragging of gender and racial norms paradoxically emphasizes the limits of performance to undo social constructs and their citational legacies. Thus, dragging another gender should not be seen as a self-creation that produces only contestation or even agency. Rather, gender and gender performativity are terms limited to a historicity by which they draw their meanings from. Thus the play on "woman" and "man" that Dempster or Markova performs is always already regulated by the heterosexist assumptions of the audience watching the film, and the ways the *bakla* is incompatible with the violated woman that narratives of female victimhood must enact on screen.

This performance can, however, mess these constraints up. What is most potent about *Markova, Comfort Gay* is that it uses heterosexist assumptions about queer desire to inevitably create what I would call a queer undoing of the very limited scripts "victimhood" occupies through and within the comfort woman's story. This queer undoing ushers in possibilities for disrupting citational forms and repeated attributes that have come to signify what "woman" means when represented under Japanese colonialism. Queerness disturbs, ruptures, undoes, destabilizes, and augments the already complicated representation of the woman as victim that these movies have traditionally relied on. Queerness exposes what Saidiya Hartman has called the "slipperiness" and "double edged" meaning of empathy, which scenes of subjection often call forth from the observer (19). Often staged to elicit rage and empathy, scenes of comfort women's abuse can also produce other complex emotions that range from empathy, horror, and even pleasure, rooted in the attempt to instill an anticolonial nationalist sentiment on the backs of a female victim's body by making this victim hypervisible as it simultaneously occludes her in order to privilege the viewer's sympathy.

In the most explicit example of this queer undoing, the movie repeatedly gestures to what makes the comfort woman figure most legible in any cinematic piece, violent scenes of rape. There are only two overtly anal-penetrative sex scenes depicted, and both are staged as rape. The first one occurs when the business partner of Dempster's brother abuses Dempster. Dempster is asked to run an errand for his brother, and he goes to the business partner's house to deliver a package. Instead of just receiving the package, his business partner seduces Dempster and then rapes him on the bed using a box of margarine as lubricant. The scene is incredibly violent, as Dempster is heard in the background shouting "huwag po" (please don't, in a respectful tone). Rather than being read as a moment of violence, however, this sexual act is seen in the film as initiating Dempster's "awakening" into queer sexuality. In what can be read as the movie's homophobic turn even as it seeks to "humanize" homosexuality, Dempster renarrates the rape as both painful and desirable: "I liked and didn't like it." Desire's articulation, its possibility, is jarring.

Rape in *Markova: Comfort Gay* possesses a new valence. Arguably the most violently graphic moment in the film, the second rape occurs in the stable as soldiers force Markova and her friends to perform multiple sexual acts. One of her friends yells "array" (meaning "ouch") while he is being raped, as he begs the Japanese abuser to stop. This moment is a literal restaging of the first rape scene. The young Dempster also utters this word and asks for reprieve as the camera pans away. What happens to the second rape scene then, when desire, not only of the rapist but also of the one being raped, is even alluded to? Rape in this movie possesses a new valence. The queerness of those being raped, their inability to be women in the first place, compels viewers to ask about victims' sexual desire, their yearning, and their pleasure. Does it matter that queer persons, as opposed to "passive women" are being raped? Might Markova and her friends desire the sexual acts they are being forced to perform? Uncomfortable as it is to think about rape in this light, *Markova, Comfort Gay* reroutes the phobic properties an audience might possess. It turns that phobic presence into a destabilizing force, one that can disturb the very narratives that have come to represent female identity in acts of rape. It problematizes how victimhood has become the key trope for reading Japanese scenes of terror and subjection in Philippine cinema after Japanese colonialism. Even though this scene of abjection is still phobic, produced through heteronormative representations of *bakla* figures as desiring their rape, it is also a restaging that is legibly fueled by the anxieties and resistance around the Japanese imperial project.

Markova and her friends get recast not merely as queer figures who are oppressed, but as Filipino citizens who have been able to both trouble narratives about female identity under duress and to "queer" Japan's own masculinity, which the Japanese soldiers represent. Interestingly, as the film progresses, one of Markova's friends becomes a revolutionary figure, luring Japanese soldiers into an alley by using her sexuality as a ruse, then stabbing them to death as revenge. I do not suggest of course that what Markova and her friends have done is necessarily liberatory, for their being exchangeable as sexual slaves with women points to just how tenuous "resistance" actually is. What I do suggest is that this moment of abuse can "deterritorialize" the limited allegories of "female identity" an audience is expecting, through the mingling of queerness with their symbolic valuations. In *Markova, Comfort Gay*, "woman" itself is called into crisis.

Queerness even seems to undo dominant narratives around Philippine liberation. As is expected with a movie set during Japanese colonialism, the US liberation gets portrayed as a moment when everyone is gaily celebrating all forms of freedom. Thus under US occupation, Markova can be her "true self." A scene where Markova dances in decadent clothing is punctuated by Anita's return from the market. Markova and Anita sing, "Happy days are here again!" They parade around the house, as they display the silky smoothness of the pantyhose that Anita was presumably only able to purchase because the United States has returned. The same pantyhose become a transitional object in the next scene. Before dancing gaily in front of an American audience, Markova strokes her legs and says: "How good it is . . . to feel like a real woman." In yet another instance of "freedom," Markova kisses a white solder. She then sees Carmen dressed as a man. Markova approaches and asks Carmen why she looks that way. Carmen responds that she has decided to return to the province in order to "forget the past, and try to change." Markova replies jokingly, "You bitch, you've never been uglier. It doesn't suit you." She further lectures Carmen on the virtues of finding one's true self.

The simplest and most obvious way to read this moment is to suggest that American liberation frees Markova from having to hide her queerness. She can now be herself. Surely this is what the movie tries to portray (since, as Carmen stands in for, it was "pretending" to be a woman that got them into trouble in the first place). However, while it is certain that the US "liberation" has always inherently been justified through the freeing of women and children, does it really intend to free queers? After the lecture, Carmen asks Markova whom she is kissing. Markova points to the white soldier. Carmen asks, "Does he know?" Markova's reply ultimately epitomizes the potency of queer undoing in *Markova, Comfort Gay*. Without a touch of irony and hesitation, with the most blatant naiveté, Markova insists, "of course."

Bakla Japayukis and the "Lure of the Yen"

While discussing the significance of homosexuality to his films, Nick DeOcampo notes that his primary goal is to shed light on the intimate relationships between sexuality and social struggle. DeOcampo suggests that in the Philippine context, the practicing of queer identity cannot be disassociated from experiences with economic hardship, since "a people's sexual life cannot be distanced from its economic-political-social-cultural well being" (395). He writes that these sexual economies acquired greater significance during the Marcos regime, "when poverty, sex tourism, media exploitation, political repression, economic collapse, and moral decay formed a nexus of historical determinants which endowed Philippine society with a disreputable image in general and gave the homosexual community an uphill battle in terms of recognition in particular" (396). Thus, the majority of his films reflect upon the linkages between gay identity and social strife, as he follows subjects that often see their class status as deeply influencing their queer identity. Aside from the need to elucidate the economic underpinnings of sexual repression, DeOcampo's oeuvre also sought to dismantle pervasive patriarchy. He reads this patriarchy as influencing gay representation. Thus, he wanted to move beyond depictions of gay persons that devolved into "slapstick comedies," or that resulted in a "repaired" subject who eventually married (396). Ultimately, his films belong to an archive of creative work that called for political change amid dictatorial rule. He gestured to his contemporaries Lino Brocka and Ishmael Bernal, since he saw them as comrades who sought to "extend the long tradition of struggle in the medium that has long been the tool of their country's oppression" (399).

These three overlapping themes—queer practices as being linked to social struggle, efforts to challenge patriarchy, and the activation of Philippine nationalism through demands for social equity—also saturate one of DeOcampo's last films, *Sex Warriors and the Samurai* (1996). The documentary begins by discussing the Philippines' multiple experiences with colonialism, and how Manila serves as the palimpsest for these changing colonial histories. Touring the ruins of the walled city Intramuros, DeOcampo laments, "Next to Manila Bay lies Intramuros. Once the imperial city of the Philippines, a cobweb of shadows is all that remain of the seven Cathedrals that once proclaimed our fate as God's Chosen people, the only Catholics in the orient. Intramuros was destroyed in a war between Japan and America, a war not of its own making" (DeOcampo 1996). The director's walk through the postcolonial metropolis is an effective metaphor for the retracing of and grappling with the effects of Spanish, Japanese, and American rule. As the site of war's aftermath, Intramuros indexes the literal violence of the imperial project on both the space and the population. These losses haunt and present themselves in the dark crevices of empire's ruins. At one point, he reflects with some irony: "In this ghost of a city, we are all creatures living under the shadows of the past." The choice to use Intramuros, and Manila in general, as an introduction to his film also indexes the ways in which narratives of desire, intimacies, and sexuality simultaneously coexist with narratives of empire building. Aside from being a tourist area, Intramuros and the spaces adjacent to it (such as Luneta Park, Malate, and Ermita) also serve as cruising spots, where queer intimacies, sexualities, and transactional relationships proliferate. Thus walking around Intramuros at night also poses the possibility of sex and other forms of pleasure seeking. These other possibilities highlight the parallels between colonial histories and histories of sexuality that have always existed within the Philippine context.

DeOcampo's film focuses on the effects of Japanese rule on the country and on the local government's acquiescence to Japanese economic power. Moving from Intramuros to the various red-light districts that dot Manila, the director reflects, "Today, the Japanese presence is stronger than ever. The closing of US bases here in 1991 opened the floodgates for a new Japanese invasion of our economy and social life, as if there had never been a cruel past. What disturbs me about these shifts in power is how readily our people have bowed to their new masters" (DeOcampo 1996). For DeOcampo, the red-light districts are painful reminders of Japanese capitalist expansion that just sought to continue where the American military project from the 1940s onward left off. The US naval bases and the Japanese red-light districts concretize the ways in which Filipinos have been utilized as sexual labor for their American *and* Japanese occupiers. The US bases, like the Japanese red-light districts that followed in Manila, provided sexual labor for women in cities such as Angeles and Olongapo.[11]

All these histories—sexual, economic, postcolonial, and national—then come together as DeOcampo interviews Joann, the *bakla japayuki* who goes through many hurdles in order to make it to Japan as a hostess. In terms of plot, *Sex Warriors and the Samurai* follows the typical representation of a *japayuki's* experiences. For example, *Joann's* desire to go to Japan as an entertainment laborer is portrayed in the film as deeply tied to her need to escape poverty and to aid her family financially. Joann is also primarily interpolated as a sex worker, similar to the ways in which the *japayuki* has been seen in movies and other cultural discourses. However, as viewers follow the grueling process Joann goes through more closely, in her attempts to be certified, they are also presented with representations of complicity, desire, and pleasure rarely associated with persons choosing to work in Japan. The audience sees a different side of hostess work through Joann, even though DeOcampo continually asserts how poverty forms the main impetus for her choices. Joann's retelling of her story, and the situations that DeOcampo chooses to highlight in the film, contradict even the director's own voice-overs that seek to frame how we are supposed to read the experience of being a queer *japayuki*. These contradictions highlight both the limits of the film, and its possibilities.

When we first meet Joann at one of the bars in Ermita, she is performing on stage, dancing and twirling with bravado. What follows is an interview with her. DeOcampo focuses on her face, as she sits on the counter smoking and wearing beautiful makeup, an elegantly shiny dress, and trendy glasses. She's tilting her head from side to side in a contemplative fashion, as she fans herself. After the director asks what type of work she does in Japan (*Anong ginagawa mo sa Japan?*), Joann obliges with a response. Her tone conveys a hint of playfulness and pride, as she narrates:

Syempre pag nasa Japan ka na kailangan mautak ka di ba? Kailangan gamitin mo ang utak mo. Ako kasi pag first day ko agad doon rumarampa agad ako eh, ang ginagawa ko talaga don pagdating na pagdating ko kunwari may yasami (day off kung tawagin) ako lalabas ako sa kalsada. Syempre magbibihis ako, magpapaganda ako, tatayo ako sa kanto. May mga car naman na dumadaan diyan hihitch ka ngayon, ngayon pag may kumagat na hitch, chicka may hada ka na.

(Of course when you are in Japan you have to be street-smart right? You have to use your brain. When it is my first day, I parade myself immediately, and what I really do when it is my day off is to go out onto the street. Of course I get dressed, and look very pretty. I stand on the corner. Cars will pass by, and I try to hitch. Now if someone bites, great, you have a blowjob coming.) (my translation)

To the regular viewer, Joann is simply retelling a story of sex work that is already legible (and as I have been arguing almost expected) when told by a *japayuki*. Yet as you observe her body language, the tone of her voice, and her posture in retelling her story, it becomes clear that Joann's narrative is also imbued with a sense of pride for being able to practice queerness *as* a *japayuki*. For example, her use of the verb "rumarampa," which DeOcampo does not translate in the subtitle, is particularly noteworthy. The root of this word is the noun *rampa*, which literally means a ramp or walkway. As a verb however, rampa (or the present perfect *rumarampa*) in swardspeak means to strut with confidence, to parade and show yours, and to "work" a given space in order to be noticed. The etymology of *rampa* in swardspeak comes from beauty pageants, since the ramp is the physical object the pageant contestants walk on as they go through the multiple challenges of the night. Thus, through her queer campiness, and queer sensibility, Joann is not merely recounting a moment of victimization because of her sex work, she is also renarrating a particular pleasure around the labor she performs. Similar to the beauty pageant queen that must defend or win her crown, Joann must win the admiration of her prospective client.

Joann's desire to be a *japayuki*—which involves the benefits of both payment and pleasure—is all but erased in DeOcampo's storytelling. Again, propelled by a seeming need to discuss queer sexuality through the lens of social struggle, DeOcampo frames our first encounter with Joann by saying, "Most *Japayukis* are women, much less is well known of groups of men who willingly take on the appearance of women, to satisfy the current Japanese taste for this sexual specialty. They have discovered a niche, in the yen market. Some Filipino gay men have even resorted to a sex change operation. Others have increased their income with artificial breasts." It is compelling that DeOcampo focuses on Joann's "willingness" as a mere result of the growing "niche" market for transgender hostesses. He immediately interpolates Joann's identity as gay, when in fact as one watches the documentary, Joann could easily be read as transgender, or, at the very least, as a transvestite *bakla*. Interestingly enough, the narrative that the director seeks to present hits road blocks in moments when his subjects state a "willingness" to be hostesses that do not easily fit narratives of coercion or force. Even as DeOcampo continually attempts to present Joann and her friends as "victims" of poverty, this narrative comes into tension with Joann's own words and performances of *bakla* camp and pleasure. These pleasures are often deeply connected to the ability to be queer in a way that departs from her life in the Philippines.

For example, in another scene, DeOcampo focuses on Joann and her friend as they gossip and give each other advice, on the travails of being a *japayuki*. The conversation occurs after both Joann and her friend have finished one of their certification classes. Joann turns to her friend, in order to ask for strategies for saving their earnings. In the process, both have a longer conversation about topics that range from dating Japanese boyfriends, to being treated as women in this relationship, to acquiring breasts. The conversation goes as follows:

> Friend: Are you happy? Do you enjoy yourself?
> (*Maligaya ka naman?*)
> Joann: Of course. You know how it is in Japan. When they see a gay man, they also want a girl. They [the Japanese] give everything. That's why many go to Japan. They like it there.
> (*Naman. Alam mo naman sa Japan pag gusto ng bakla, girl. Lahat ibibigay. Kaya nga maraming nagjajapan, feel nila doon eh.*)
> Joann: What do you do when you earn money from Japan?
> (*Paano kung nakakuha ka pera sa Japan, anong ginagawa mo?*)
> Friend: When I get tips in Japan, this is what I do. I budget and allocate everything already. Payments for extra baggage, for makeup, which we need for work. My salary is then allocated for my family.
> (*Pagnakakuha ako tip sa Japan, ganito ginagawa ko, nakabudget na iyan. Pagbayad bagahe, makeup, syempre kumakayod tayo Yung sahod ko nakatala na yan sa family.*)
> Joann: Do you live with your family?
> (*Magkasama kayo sa ahay*)
> Friend: Yeah, I give that to my mother. That's our budget at home.
> (*Oo binibigay ko yan sa mother ko, yan ang budget naming sa bahay.*)
> Joann: What happens to the money you give your mother? Do you see where it goes?
> (*Anong nangyayari sa binibigay mo sa mother mo may nakikita ka naman?*)
> Friend: Of course! For example, my house. Imagine! My house is 1.6 million pesos.
> (*Oo naman, like for example ang bahay ko. Imagine Tita ang bahay ko is 1.6 million pesos ha.*)
> Joann: Amazing.

(*Taray naman.*)

Friend: Of course, this is my eleventh trip.

(*Syempre pang eleven trips na eh.*)

Joann: If you can bring home Japan here, you would. Are your breasts
part of your savings? They're so big.

(*Kung puwede lang iuwi ang Japan dito iuuwi mo. Kasama ba dyan sa
ipon mo yung pinagawa mo sa suso mo, ang laki eh.*)

Friend: Of course. This is the technique. If you really want to earn
money in Japan, you need to have these. The cut depends on the doctor. It depends where he will have the silicone pass. I felt uneasiness
for two weeks. But after that it's fine.

(*Oo naman. Ito ang technique. Kung talagang gusto mo kumita sa
Japan kailangan mo magpagawa nito. Ang hiwa nito it depends sa doctor. Mga two week after the operation, uneasiness.*)

Joann: Yeah, it looks heavy.

(*Oo nga parang ang bigat.*)

Friend: But if you look at it, it looks like cleavage right?

(*Pero pag tiningnan mo para talagang cleavage di ba?*)

As one of the longest exchanges in the film, this conversation elucidates
the contradictions present in *Sex Warriors and the Samurai*. As a narrative of familial patronage, the conversations support DeOcampo's
constant lamentations that queer subjects are only accepted by their
families because of their value as sources of remittances and support.
Joann certainly supports this notion throughout the film, as she constantly suggests to other friends that her main goal is to support her
family. Through DeOcampo's own interviews with Joann's mother and
siblings, the former's family also corroborates this narrative. As Joann
asks at one point in the film, "what else are gays here for but to help our
families?" On the other hand, rather than see this type of patronage as
automatically negative, Joann's friend reads this patronage as an ability
to also shift the power dynamics that are commonly fixed in Filipino
families, by offering the queer subject a say in the affairs of the family
because of her financial leverage. Joann's friend is clearly less reticent in
seeing this patronage as only burdensome. Another typical stereotype
about Filipino hostesses that the conversation alludes to is the *japayuki*'s
desire to have relationships with Japanese men. Yet precisely because

both Joann and her friend are queer identified, this relationship takes on a new hue. For them, the relationship with Japanese men who are heterosexual and male, provide them with the way to read themselves as women, which they state in the conversation as "pa-girl."

Over and over again, the *bakla* subjects in DeOcampo's work see Japan as a space to practice queerness that they have not have been able to do so in the Philippines. Discussing a similar dynamic in her research on transgender *japayukis*, Rhacel Parrenas writes that transgender hostesses saw Japan as a "paraiso ng mga bakla," or paradise for the *bakla*. She notes that transgender *japayukis* "pursued work in Japan for adventure and the promise of romance. Interviewees described Japan as a much better place for transgender women to seek sexual relations with men, and they could walk the street free from harassment" (14). In other words, rather than see themselves as merely victims in the streets as sex workers, the transgender *japayukis* in Parrenas's research view their occupation and their trysts with clients as relationships. The point is not whether to argue if the *japayukis* have indeed been harassed on the street, but rather how the transgender *japayukis* have viewed the work they do, and how their queer identity and labor are intricately linked. Joann and her friend provide a useful example of how desire and pleasure for a heterosexual partner might actually possess multiple valences. In this instance we are provided with a much more complicated understanding of *bakla* that moves it outside of the identity "gay" even as DeOcampo as a director continually attempts to narrativize Joann's identity. Even though the conversation about acquiring breasts can be seen as a way for Joann's friend to emphasize entry into a different niche market in Japan, it also highlights a way for both to share experiences and advice about the pleasure of and desire for producing transactional relationships with their clients. In Parrenas's analysis, she recalls, "In the transgender community, we see the performance of bodily labor as a community effort when hostesses advice one another on surgical processes, recommend doctors, and share tips on nonsurgical forms of bodily alterations" (56). Thus, the sharing of information about surgeries and body alterations between transgender hostesses, rather than merely fostering "materialistic" goals for improvement, also foster belonging and community among both parties.

Local critics who have examined DeOcampo's films in the past have suggested that the director performs the same moralizing practices he goes against, by consistently seeing queer Filipinos as lacking any agency or will of their own (Tolentino 2001). For example, in his first film, *Oliver* he shows a gay man whose purpose in life is to perform in cabarets to support his family. Or, in *Revolutions Happen Like Refrains in a Song,* the coming-out narrative as a gay man serves as a palimpsest for a people's coming out of the Marcos regime. In these two films, DeOcampo often glances over the ways in which queer identities perform a politics of contestation precisely through their very embodiment of an inappropriate, uncontrollable, and excessive affect untranslatable through Westernized gazes. Precisely because he views homosexuality in the Philippines through the lens of poverty and political disenfranchisement, one could argue that DeOcampo limits the possible ways that Filipino queerness could be interpreted when it falls outside of these specific parameters. As Tolentino's reading of *Oliver* denotes, "DeOcampo's rhetoric eventually translates (homo)sexuality as a perversion of poverty so naturalized in Philippine society" (117). By focusing on economic and political hardship as the primary reason for any enactments of queer life, DeOcampo is susceptible to devaluing other motivations that exist around these performances.

In *Sex Warriors and the Samurai,* DeOcampo departs from previous work by choosing to highlight moments in the documentary where the queer subject's pleasure comes to the fore. Even as he attempts to moralize this pleasure, the film nonetheless highlights the paradox between Joann's own performances of queer desire, and the director's attempt to discipline this desire. I would argue that the paradox and the contradictions in the film are not merely a trite attempt at erasing these differences, but a gesturing to the complex narratives that Joann's embodiment of a transgender *jayapuki* creates. These contradictions highlight the fallacies that have limited *japayuki representation* as a whole. The film inevitably raises the specter of sexuality as challenging the limited iterations of the *japayuki* in the Filipino cultural imaginary. While the film gestures to traditional views of the *japayuki:* as possessing materialism that causes victimizations (because of poverty, in the hands of managers, and in interactions with the Japanese clients), it also subtends these stereotypes with a different reading of pleasures and motivations that surround being a queer *japayuki.*

Even the film's ending can be read as an attempt to challenge the limited notions of *japayukis* in cultural representation. The film ends with an image of Joann as a geisha, as she emerges from a group of half-naked, undulating men dancing to slow and sensual music. DeOcampo's voice-over then narrates that Joann has succeeded, and is now ready for export to Shinjuku, and the "land of the samurai." He then sutures this scene with another drag queer with a broken umbrella, which can signify a failed dream. There are multiple ways to read this ending. One way to read it would be to see the ways in which Joann's body, similar to the men around her, is ready to be fetishized for Western and Japanese gazes. DeOcampo supports this by saying in his discussion of Joann's readiness for export, similar to other Filipinos who have gone through certification to take part in the "flesh industry." On the other hand, one could also read this scene as a way to challenge both the normative iterations of masculinity and femininity that have policed the *japayuki's* body. The dancers and Joann highlight the malleability of these norms, by hyperbolizing specifically their key markers of both these constructs within the Philippine context (as either "hyperfeminine geisha," or "hypermasculine dancer"). Another way to read this scene is to see it as challenging even the viewer's limited understanding of the work that Joann performs, by attempting to undo the shame that *japayuki* labor has often elicited. Returning to Parrenas's research, she notes that the image of the geisha is a crucial one for *japayukis:* "Filipina hostesses like to view themselves as similar to geisha, or courtesans, perhaps to upgrade the image of their work in Japan, which is often dismissed by outsiders as nothing but prostitution" (31). In this regard, Joann's being a geisha reflects the multiple subjectivities that exist in *japayuki* labor. Her embodiment of the geisha, in itself, produces multiple readings of her subjectivity, and the desires and pleasure around being in this occupation. Rather than limit the film, then, DeOcampo's choice to end with Joann's performing as a geisha adds more layers to the queer subject's mimicking of a typical "female" narrative. Perhaps this is precisely DeOcampo's point. In ending the film with Joann as geisha, he gestures to the many possibilities that Joann's queerness offers, in expanding the limited ways in which *japayuki* embodiment is performed and ultimately enacted.

Victimhood and the Limits of Redress

In *Against Race*, Paul Gilroy cautions us against the overessentializing of victimhood in an age of redressive politics. He writes, "From Palestine to Bosnia, the image of the victim has become useful in all sorts of dubious maneuverings that can obscure the moral and political questions arising from the demands for justice. And yet, for all its pragmatic or strategic attractions, the role of victim has its drawbacks as the basis of any political identity" (113). In other words, the term "victim" can be a problematic coalitional position to occupy, even though it is an essential one when enacting demands for social justice. Gilroy's warning is especially relevant, as scholars in ethnic, postcolonial, and queer studies have convincingly argued that populations marginalized along gender, race, and sexuality have often possessed a precarious relationship to notions of victimhood; the state rarely addresses how specific marginalized persons have been negatively affected by its policies (Butler 1997, 2006; Brown 1995; Hartman 1997; Gilroy 2002). Providing a critique of redress as a process, Pablo De Greiff argues that one of the many problems with redress in its procedural form is that it can disaggregate specific types of victims and specific types of reparative methods. In the process of enacting redress on a case-by-case basis, the law tends to rank which victims and methods are more important than others (458). Even though De Greiff does not advocate that the state abandon processes of redress altogether, his examination unpacks the ways in which victims can be separated according to access to the courts (as some victims who are more educated and more economically mobile often fare better in getting redress), and according to the types of violence that they have experienced (as victims who the state defines as such are often the only ones awarded redress). Given all these factors, the difficulty around using victim as a coalitional term, especially when it is coupled with redress, is that the basis for who becomes eligible for such a label often relies on undertheorized, ahistorical, and unequal ideological frameworks that police the meaning of victimization itself.

Wendy Brown has also problematized the seemingly axiomatic linkages between victimhood and demands for justice, particularly when connected to minoritarian identity politics. She notes that minoritarian identity has often depended upon omnipresent affects of *resentment* and unquestioned attachments to "woundedness." In the attempts by antiracist politics to be legible in the eyes of the state, minoritarian identity turns to "woundedness," which "installs its pain over its unredeemed history in the very foundation of its political claim, in its demand for recognition as identity" (74). Brown raises a significant question about the ways in which minoritarian subjects attempt to challenge injustice through articulations of pain, at the expense of wholly being defined by that pain.

Collectively, these scholars raise important questions regarding the complications that arise when state governments and nongovernmental organizations rearticulate victimhood for their own purposes.[12] In the case of *comfort women*, the most troubling effects of these policies can be traced to how the women have renarrated their own victimization to appease the state's limited interpretation of their experiences. As You-Me Park writes, in their response to former Japanese Prime Minister Nakasone's statement that comfort women could not be considered "victims" since they were "paid" as "prostitutes," the Korean government and various NGOs "took it upon themselves to speak for former comfort women by echoing the patriarchal assumptions of Japanese officials. National sentiments were provoked and exploited in casting former comfort women as young (the age of the comfort women was a big issue of contention, as if it would have been all right if the Japanese Imperial army had the decency to conscript only women over 18 years of age) and virginal (again, the assumption seems to be that it would have been better if only they took women who were sexually active, and, thus, 'impure')" (205). The egregious assumption here is that being a comfort woman can only describe certain people and not others. Someone who is young and virginal can be ascribed to this victimized positionality while someone who is considered a "prostitute," and, thus, someone who is already tainted, polluted, and "used" cannot. The experiences of female victimhood and violence certainly run the gamut of possible narratives deserving of redress. The virginal woman and the sex worker are both worthy of comfort women's redress. As Park's example shows, the attempt to elicit national shame for what Japan has done to the national population—by equating the rape of the comfort woman with the rape of its people—also simultaneously makes some women more dispensable than others in this national-legislative-affective framework.[13]

In an interview published soon after *Markova, Comfort Gay's* release, Walter Dempster (the character that Markova was based on) mentions Maria Henson's discomfort when Dempster discussed his abduction with her. In response, Henson questioned whether Markova could be seen as a victim of the comfort women system, both because of his sexuality, and his affective comportment when discussing his past. He writes:

> And you know when Korina Sanchez [television announcer] interviewed me, she put Nana Rosa [famous Philippine comfort woman who has led the fight for acknowledgement, apology and reparations] with me. And do you know what Nana Rosa said? "Oh, I don't believe these gays. If the Japanese soldiers found out that he was man, they would kill him." And I said, "How do you know? Did you see what the Japanese did to us? You were not there. The Japanese just raped us." And Korina said, "When I interview Nana Rosa, she is crying. But when I interview Walter, he keeps on laughing." I said, "Why should I cry? That was way back. It's bygone now. There is nothing to cry for. Past is past. Why should I cry? I'm just happy I'm alive.

This exchange embodies the many tensions that this work seeks to unpack and ultimately challenge. Henson and Sanchez doubt Dempster's authenticity as a comfort gay because of two specific assumptions: (1) that *bakla* identities cannot be victims of rape, since that would entail the queering of the rapist's sexuality (so, it would have been more "believable" if Markova would have been killed upon the discovery of her "maleness"); and (2) that specific expectations of affective output police the grounds of authentic retelling (so that crying is the only authentic means in which a comfort woman can articulate her story). These assumptions are all the more egregious, since they are reiterated by another victim of Japanese violence, and the news representative, both of whom are supposed to feel affinity with Markova's calls for redress. This exchange registers the need to challenge the normative assumptions about Japanese violence and the ways in which this violence has been represented. These assumptions police not only narratives that do not conform to the gendered expectations of the appropriate victim, they also ultimately discipline what types of violence count as worthy of redress.[14] These assumptions are deeply powerful, as the popular representations of *comfort women* also bleed into specific laws, juridical enactments, and redressive acknowledgments by the state.

Similar to the comfort woman, the *japayuki* is also a vexed figure, as state and popular discourses have defined what this figure means in our diasporic imaginaries. Returning to Parrenas, she suggests that: "the binary categories we currently have for thinking about the migration of Filipina hostesses—either free subject (migrant) or enslaved subject (trafficked person)—fail to capture the complex dynamics of coercion and choice that embody their labor migration and experiences." In response to these limited dualities, Parrenas advocates for a theoretical project that both acknowledges *japayuki* agency, as it unpacks the constraints that impede their social life. Although *Sex Warriors* does not forward a direct solution to the limited ways in which *japayukis* have been systemically and pejoratively represented, it nonetheless offers new paradigms for understanding *japayuki* labor through the experiences of queer Filipinos. In so doing, the film also raises complex questions about desire and complicity that begins to chip away at these entrenched assumptions.

What does it mean to allegorize narratives of abuse, resistance, and the demands for social justice by deploying a particular figuration of victimized female identity? Comfort women and *japayukis* serve as cultural markers of the ways in which contradictory notions of gender, sexuality, and victimhood are resignified in diasporic imaginaries. By examining two films that specifically queer these figures, we begin to see how a queer undoing exposes the tenuousness and proscriptive characteristics of the gendered assumptions around them. This analysis ultimately reflects on the performative force of redressive nationalism in order to chart a new archive of Filipino colonial history rarely studied within Asian American, Filipino, and Queer Studies. The specificities and aftermaths of Japanese colonialism in the Philippines have yet to be fully explored with similar theoretical depth in these disciplinary formations. This is a curious oversight given that central to the transnationalizing of Filipino studies has been the analysis of multiple forms of empire building and their effects on diasporic memory. Resituating our critical gaze, my analysis thus seeks to encourage new scholarship in this brief but rich historical period in order to ask what ghosts of Japanese colonialisms continue to haunt us, and to what effects. Providing new flashpoints into diasporic nationalisms, I also produce new archives of queer experiences and representational practices that hopefully enrich our understanding of the ways in which Filipino queer subjectivities are produced locally and globally. *Markova* and *Sex Warriors* deploy *bakla* representation in very powerful ways, in order to interrogate the linkages between victimhood and nationalistic redress.

Notes

1. For a detailed history of "sexual slavery" during the war, and of the *comfort women's* movement from the 1990s onward, see *Legacies of the Comfort Women of World War II* (Stetz and Oh 2001); *True Stories of the Korean Comfort Women* (Howard 1995); and *Japan's Comfort Women: Sexual Slavery and Prostitution during World War II and US Occupation* (Tanaka 2002). For a collection of informed and critical essays on the topic, see a special issue of *Positions: Asia Critique* (5.1) on the topic of "Comfort Women: Colonialism, War and Sex" (Choi 1997).

2. The funds for these certification courses, and for the processing of travel documents, were provided by management agencies in the Philippines who in a sense "found" the jobs and processed all the paperwork for the *japayuki*. The latter would then have to pay all of these expenditures back through her income, even though this income was unequally distributed between the club owners, the managers, and the Filipina workers. Thus, this grueling process presented a bleak reality for *japayukis*; indentured servitude to their Philippine promoters, managers, and agents actually made them more susceptible to coercion for sex work outside of the purview of the clubs that they worked in.

3. Parennas writes that the "universal imposition of American moral principles regarding trafficking fails to solve the conditions of trafficking for Filipina migrant entertainers in Japan. Instead, TVPA exacerbates their condition of trafficking by leaving the entertainers more vulnerable to indenture" (137). This is made more egregious by the fact that, as Parrenas argues in her most recent work *Illicit Flirtations* (2011), there is no empirical evidence to suggest that majority of *japayukis* are either trafficked or perform sex work in Japanese bars as a primarily function of their work. In fact, Parennas notes that the labor the women did practices what she calls "illicit flirtations," or enactments of playfulness that mask extremely effective survival tactics for negotiating the sexuality that the women had to perform at the various clubs they had worked in.

4. The historian Nicanor Tiongson links such portrayals of *kabaklan* to his discomfort with Quizon being named a National Artist in 2009. In an op-ed piece discussing why Quizon would never be a National Artist, he writes that "The two icons he created for film and TV—the screaming gay and the happy-go-lucky poor man—have, in the majority of his movies, equated gayness with abnormality and mindless frivolity on the one hand, and romanticized or deodorized poverty on the other." Inquirer http://opinion.inquirer.net/32218/scapegoat-for-suspended-national-artist-process

5. In a more thoughtful review of the film, Jacqui Sahashe observes that as an oxymoronic term, "comfort gay" conflates two experiences of violence, that of the gay subject who's path to self-discovery is punctuated by moments of abuse perpetrated by

his homophobic brother, and that of the comfort woman, who's abduction and rape under Japanese military oppression signify the need for reparation and redress. The term denotes seemingly contradictory identities that Markova embodies as she articulates the details of her past. In his review of the film, Jacqui Sadashige notes, "For as much as the film offers glimpses of Filipino history—ranging from the American military presence to the rise of popular comic acts—it is equally invested in the search for individual gay identity" (1337).

6. This term comes from the assumption that the loud, effeminate *bakla* is of a lower-class status and thus works at a beauty parlor. For more of the common representations of this figure in local contexts, see *Ladlad: An Anthology of Gay Writing* (Garcia and Remoto 1994).

7. In *Global Divas* (2003), Manalansan provides a thorough critique of the limitations of this classed reading of *bakla* identity. Recently, in his research on *bakla* drag performance in the *Amazing Show*, William Peterson also summarizes these debates about *bakla* identity quite succinctly. Patterson also notes that "while the *bakla* may be predisposed to 'become' a woman externally, because the inner soul is female, the way in which this is accomplished and performed is driven by a larger, external transnational imaginary" (601). See *Theatre Journal* (63.4 [2011])

8. See "The Limits of Bakla and Gay: Feminist Readings of *My Husband's Lover*, *Vice Ganda*, and *Charice Pempengco*" (40.3 [2015]).

9. See "Transgendered Women in the Philippines," *International Journal of Transgenderism* 10.2 (2007).

10. As Martin Manalansan notes in his analysis of Portes's other queer film *Miguel/Michelle*, the undertheorized concept of "readership" or "spectatorship" in Western "gay cinema" tends to devalue the complex identificatory processes that can occur between the figure on screen and the audience watching, even though "the so-called unsuspecting public and the nameless hordes of disembodied eyes in dark screening rooms are in fact culturally knowledgeable bodies and lives that actively engage with and interpret the ideas and images on the screen" (37).

11. For a detailed analysis of various processes of reparations or redress, and their relationship to testimony, see *The Handbook of Reparations* (Greiff 2010).

12. This link between US and Japanese imperialisms then inspire DeOcampo's anti-Japanese rhetoric and nationalism, which he signals by including his own family into the documentary's narrative. Aside from scenes of Intramuros and red-light districts, *Sex Warriors* begins with a discussion of how his father Emilio had avenged DeOcampo's grandfather, who was beheaded by the Japanese. Emilio joined the guerilla movement. His inclusion in the documentary is no small matter. Roland Tolentino suggests that traditionally, the inclusion of the postcolonial documentarian in film is a key political move, given that "self-representation becomes a juncture for a representation of the postcolonial subject, that, in turn, becomes a juncture for a representation of the postcolonial nation" (85).

13. Historically, the parameters that dictate who to accept as victims and who to abject—and the tensions around collective as opposed to private reparation—stem

from Japan's being able to pursue limited definition of "reparation" as process after the war. Historians note that contrary to Germany, for instance, which had its post-war reparations defined for it by the United States and other Allied nations, Japan was able to define what process it would pursue when enacting monetary redress for those it occupied during the war. Thus, rather than a cause difficulties for Japan, reparation became an economic means for the country to rebuild and continue as-serting itself through the spread of transnational capital. Reparation, in this regard, could be equated with economic investment. Utilizing juridical and monetary reparation for its own purposes, Japan was able to establish itself as the key source of transnational investment that those the country previously colonized would then depend on after the war. Japan's form of reparation was not about addressing past violence but about expanding its economic hold on previously occupied nations. This policy allowed Japan to disavow any form of monetary reparations to victims, since victims themselves were not a consideration in the political equation for enacting redress. For an incisive essay on Japanese attempts at reparation imme-diately after the war, see *War Guilt and World Politics After World War II* (Berger 2012). Berger's chapter entitled "Japan: The Model Impenitent" especially discusses the historical underpinnings of the Japanese difference in reparation models. Won Soon Park's article, "Japanese Reparations Policies and the Comfort Women Ques-tion" also specifically discusses Japan's reparation policies specifically in relation-ship to the comfort woman's movement. See *positions: asia critique* (5.1 [1997]).

14. Some comfort women have had to emphasize particular elements of their story and exaggerate parts of their experiences so that their plight would be acknowl-edged by those who would advance their reparative causes. For example, while conducting interviews with Korean comfort women, Kim Gibson voices anger at the realization that the comfort women had already learned to practice emphasiz-ing which parts of their story to tell for most effect, given the types of organiza-tions that have visited them, and the money they received from them: "Each of the grandmas I interviewed preferred to start out citing her age at time of capture and then move directly to the initial period of bondage. Each wanted to tell me immediately about 'how many soldiers a day,' the medical examination, the ve-nereal diseases, her menstruation, fees for services, and more than anything else, about the particular sadism of the soldiers, recruiters, and managers. Each infor-mant was convinced that she knew what I wanted. They all had experience and could give me the information I sought. It was also quite obvious that they had learned to adjust their stories for maximum political impact. The 'formula' was firmly established" (259). Aside from the violence of a past history that is being retold, one is witnessing the violence of policing *how* a story is retold around the limited parameters that dictate the definitions of a clearly legible victim worthy of redress. Governments and nongovernmental organizations, although they meant well, also enacted a moralistic tone about sexuality and were only concerned with the women because they could mine the moment of their violence for their own political and sensationalist purposes.

Works Cited

Brocka, L. (Director). (1978). *Ang Nanay Kong Tatay*. Manila: Lotus Films.

Brown, W. (1995). *States of Injury: Power and Freedom in Late Modernity*. Princeton, NJ: Princeton University Press.

Butler, J. (1993). *Bodies That Matter: On the Discursive Limits of "Sex."* New York: Routledge Press.

De Greiff, P. (2010). Justice and Reparations. In Pablo De Greiff (ed.), *The Handbook of Reparations* (451–77). New York: Oxford University Press.

DeOcampo, N. (Director). (1983). *Oliver*.

———. (1993). Homosexuality as Dissent/Cinema as Subversion: Articulating Gay Consciousness in the Philippines. *Queer Looks: Perspectives on Lesbian and Gay Film and Video*. Martha G., John Greyser, and Pratibha Parmar (eds). New York: Routledge Press.

———. (Director). (1987). *Revolutions Happen Like Refrains in a Song*.

———. (Director). (1996). *The Sex Warriors and the Samurai*. London: Formation Films.

Diaz, R. (2015). Limits of *Bakla* and Gay: Feminist Readings of *My Husband's Lover, Vice Ganda*, and *Charice Pempengco. Signs* 40.3: 721–45.

Gilroy, P. (2002). *Against Race: Imagining Political Culture Beyond the Color Line*. Cambridge, MA: Harvard University Press.

Hartman, S. (1997). *Scenes of Subjection: Terror, Slavery, and Self-Making in Nineteenth-Century America*. New York: Oxford University Press.

Henson, M. (1999). *Comfort Woman: A Filipina's Story of Prostitution and Slavery Under the Japanese Military*. Lanham, MD: Rowman & Littlefield Publishers.

Livingston, J. (Director). (1990). *Paris Is Burning*. Los Angeles: Miramax.

Manalansan, M. (2003). *Global Divas: Filipino Gay Men in the Diaspora*. Durham, NC: Duke University Press.

———. (2014). The Stuff of Archives: Mess, Migration, and Queer Lives. *Radical History Review* 120: 94–107.

Park, You-Me. (2000). Comforting the Nation: 'Comfort Women,' the Politics of Apology and the Workings of Gender. *Interventions* 2.2: 199–211.

Parrenas, R. (2008). *The Force of Domesticity: Filipina Migrants and Globalization*. New York: New York University Press.

———. (2011). *Illicit Flirtations: Labor, Migration, and Sex Trafficking in Tokyo*. Stanford, CA: Stanford University Press.

Portes, G. (Director). (2000). *Markova, Comfort Gay*. Manila: RVQ Productions.

Suzuki, N. (2011). *Japayuki*, or, Spectacles for the Transnational Middle Class. *Positions* 19.2: 439–62.

Tiongson, N. (2012, July 8). Scapegoat for Suspended National Artists Process? *Philippine Daily Inquirer*. Retrieved from http://opinion.inquirer.net/32218/scapegoat-for-suspended-national-artist-process.

Tolentino, R. (2000). Transvestites and Transgressions: Panggagaya in Philippine Gay Cinema. *Journal of Homosexuality* 39.3–4: 325–37.

———. (2001). *National/Transnational: Subject Formation and Media in and on The Philippines*. Manila: Ateneo De Manila Press.

10

Decolonizing Manila-Men and St. Maló, Louisiana

A Queer Postcolonial Asian American Critique

KALE BANTIGUE FAJARDO

What is now called "St. Maló" or "Bayou St. Maló" in St. Bernard Parish in the state of Louisiana is part of the ancestral lands and waters of the United Houma Nation. (See Figure 10.1.) Approximately seventeen thousand tribal citizens reside within their territory located along the southeastern coast of Louisiana. According to the Houma Nation, "Within this area, distinct tribal communities are situated among the interwoven bayous and canals where Houmas traditionally earned a living."[1] Because the US federal government (including the Bureau of Indian Affairs) does not recognize the Houma nation as a sovereign indigenous nation, the Houma are denied expanded political and cultural sovereignty. From an anticolonial and antiracist perspective, it is clear that the bayous and lands in and around St. Maló are first and foremost indigenous territories currently inhabited by indigenous Houma.[2]

Louisiana can also be read as a part of the "Black Atlantic"[3] or the "Black Queer Atlantic,"[4] part of a queer and/or African diasporic and oceanic world, connected through spaces, places, and cities of the historic Atlantic and Caribbean slave trade and plantation system. In this geography St. Maló was a site of African diasporic resistance and decolonization. The bayou area is named after Juan St. Maló or Jean St. Maló, an African man who escaped plantation slavery to lead a group of other formerly enslaved Africans in an armed struggle against colonial-settler Spaniards in the early 1780s.[5] St. Maló (the man) used Lake Borgne and connected bayous as waterways from which to strike against colonial slave owners. Spanish authorities executed St. Maló by hanging in 1784.[6]

FIGURE 10.1. Map of Louisiana highlighting St. Bernard Parish. St. Maló is located on Lake Borgne shoreline between Shell Beach and The Biloxi State Wildlife Management Area in St. Bernard Parish.

St. Maló waters are also connected to the Pacific Ocean and Philippine seas, as St. Maló is also the site of one of the first Indio/Malay villages in the Americas. As a result of community-based historian Marina Espina's *Filipinos in Louisiana,*[7] St. Maló (the site) became a better-known and at times heralded location in Asian American and Filipino/a American Studies. By historicizing Indios/Filipinos in Louisiana, Espina's scholarship helped to map an alternative geographic arrival point or temporal moment of mobility and settlement for Asians in the Americas; that is, as an alternative to the California or West Coast models of Asian American Studies.[8] St. Maló, however, is not simply a novel geography through which to promote a particular kind of ethnic/racial/nationalist identity politics; for example, focusing narrowly on the fact that Filipinos were the "first Asians in the Americas," a point that E.

San Juan made in the early 1990s.[9] As Omise'eke N. Tinsley suggests in "Black Atlantic, Queer Atlantic," the sea obscures origins, so my interests lie less in proving which group of Asians were in the Americas first, but more with how St. Mal ó can potentially intervene in Asian American Studies, Filipino/a American Studies, and masculinity studies through a postcolonial, queer, and Filipino/a diasporic approach.

In the field of Asian American Studies, scholars such as Gary Okihiro and Stephen Sumida, for example, address the historical presence and literary significance of "Manila-men" in Louisiana in their respective works *Common Ground: Reimagining American History* and "East of California."[10] Both scholars stress different regions and states of the United States as sites of alternative Asian American histories and literature, resulting in a decentering of what Okihiro describes as an East (Coast)/West (Coast) hegemonic binary or what Sumida calls the dominant "Californic" paradigm in Asian American Studies. While their critiques are important, both scholars (in the works previously cited) still stress analyses of Asian/Asian American spaces, places, and regions within the boundaries of the United States as a nation-state, rather than highlighting transoceanic or transnational connections. Keeping this point in mind, St. Mal ó is not only an alternative "Asian American" site in the United States, but St. Mal ó can also be linked, for example, to a larger Indio/a or Filipino/a diaspora (in the past and present) that includes geographies and oceanographies in the broader Western Hemisphere and other continents of the world.[11]

This chapter dialogues with scholar Sarita See's notion of *region as sites of power/knowledge accumulation* in the Foucauldian and Saidian senses of power/knowledge.[12] That is, Said theorized that European scholars, colonial officials, travelers, and political leaders produced scholarship and discourse that "Othered" Arabs and "the Orient" (Middle East) enabling and maintaining European colonial rule in the region. Foucault theorized a similar point about discourse and its relationship to subject formations, but addressed, for example, European psychiatric discourse and the construction of "deviants." While See investigates US American colonial power/knowledge institutionalized in the US Midwest, for example, at the University of Michigan (Ann Arbor) where See previously taught and where a vast archive of US colonial materials are stored, my chapter reveals how the US American south and in particular, Louisiana, are also regional and local coordinates where US colonial knowledge production related to Indios from Las Filipinas also developed. To illustrate this, I show how Lafcadio Hearn's well-known essay, "St. Maló: A Lacustrine Village in Louisiana" is a prime example of US orientalist, primitivist, and gothic knowledge-production written and published *prior* to the Spanish-American-Cuban-American-Philippine-American Wars and the US occupation of the Philippines in 1898. While Asian Americanists may be more familiar with orientalist and primitivist images of indigenous peoples from the Philippines through spectacles such as the 1904 St. Louis World's Fair (upriver from New Orleans) where Filipino/as were displayed in a zoo-like setting, Hearn's St. Maló essay illustrates a slightly earlier, geographically and thematically connected narrative of US American orientalism and primitivism targeting Filipino/as. Hearn's travel or ethnographic vignette also attempts to discursively naturalize what I call a "colonial/ orientalist/ ethnographic/ and gothic optics" (and at some narrative moments: erotics) where Hearn's vision and writing as a developing orientalist (he later expanded his orientalist and primitivist writings by writing about East Asian and Caribbean locations)[13] contain homoerotic and homosocial interest, attraction, and repulsion to and from the Malay sailors and fishermen who lived in St. Maló at the time of journey. In this chapter, I closely read Hearn's travel account and the accompanying magazine sketches, and I pay special attention to tropes of geography, race, and gender.

In December 2008, I traveled to St. Maló (by air) from Minneapolis, Minnesota, (where I currently live) to New Orleans and reached YCloskey, a present-day village in St. Bernard Parish geographically situated closest to historical St. Maló by automobile. During this first field trip, my goal was to conduct preliminary research by (re)tracing Lafcadio Hearn's journey as best as I could by car, in order to develop a sense of the lay of the land and water. In January 2010, I again flew to New Orleans, but this time, I also chartered a fishing-boat based in YCloskey. My objective in 2010 was to (re)examine Hearn's "voyage," this time via water, in order to improve my understanding of Hearn's optics and narrative in his St. Maló essay. In 2010, I talked further with contemporary residents in YCloskey, to learn about local knowledge regarding historical St. Maló; relevant hydro-spaces such as Lake Borgne and the Gulf; and contemporary issues affecting the area (for example, community-building efforts post-Hurricane Katrina that devastated the area in 2005). In 2010, I also conducted archival and historical research at the Historical New Orleans Collection at the Williams Research Center in the French Quarter of New Orleans.

Based in New York and published by Harper and Brothers (1857–1916) *Harper's Weekly* ("*A Journal of Civilization*") was a publication that featured domestic and international news, fiction, essays, and humor. *Harper's Weekly* published Hearn's St. Maló essay in 1883. Lafcadio Hearn is the author of this essay, but his name does not appear as a byline. Additionally, although this influential essay is used but not directly cited in community-based historian Marina Espina's book, *Filipinos in Louisiana*, published in 1988, I read Hearn's account as a significant piece of evidence that partially enables Espina to argue that indigenous sailors from Las Filipinas jumped ship in Acapulco, Mexico, later migrating to and settling in New Orleans (then a Spanish port city) in the 1700s. Espina uses the specific date of 1763 to mark the migration and settlement, but this is a contested date.[14]

Distributed on March 31, 1883, Hearn's St. Maló essay was the second essay featured in the *Harper's Weekly* on that date. According to Hearn, his main purpose for taking a boat to St. Maló was so that he could learn more about the "oriental settlement" and its curious inhabitants, and afterward write a journalistic or quasi-ethnographic report. The other purpose was to give the *Harper's Weekly* artist, J. O. Davidson, a "novel subject [for] artistic study."[15] In this spirit, *The Times-Democrat* (a newspaper in New Orleans) chartered an Italian lugger (a type of sailboat) for their "strange voyage" to the "unexplored region of Lake Borgne." They cast off and begin their lacustrine journey at the "Spanish Fort," sailing northeastwardly across Lake Pontchartrain (of Hurricane Katrina fame, which overflowed with Gulf waters and eventually flooded New Orleans and nearby parishes) to find "a certain strange settlement of Malay fishermen—Tagalas from the Philippine Islands,"[16] which Hearn says has been there for almost fifty years. Emphasizing St. Maló's remoteness, Hearn writes that "the place of their lacustrine village is not precisely mentioned upon maps,"[17] and until recently, "the world ignored . . . their amphibious existence."[18] Pressing this point, Hearn writes that the US mail service "has never found its way thither."[19] Through a trope that intertwines deviancy ("strange-ness"), geographic distance, and cultural and economic marginality, Hearn suggests that he and Davidson, like other European "explorers" before them, are on a masculinist colonial big lake adventure, sailing away from known (European) civilization into unchartered and yet-to-be-discovered waters.

Through the term "amphibious," Hearn also introduces the supposed primitive racial embodiment of the Malay sailors and fishermen in a time where evolutionary biology and racist anthropology reigned supreme. In an intertextually connected novel entitled, *Chita: A Memory of Last Island*,[20] published in 1889, six years after Hearn's St. Maló essay, a story about a French Creole child found and saved during the terrible hurricane of August 10, 1857, and who was later adopted by a Spanish couple living on a Gulf Island off of the Louisiana coast, Hearn writes of the primitive natural environment of this area:

> There are regions of Louisiana coast whose aspect seems not of the present, but of the immemorial past of that epoch when low flat reaches to primordial continent first arose into form above a Silurian Sea. . . . [T]he general appearance of [the] marsh verdure is vague enough, as it ranges away towards the sand, to convey the idea of amphibious vegetation,— a primitive flora as yet undecided whether to retain marine habits and forms, or to assume terrestrial ones . . . [21]

Here, Hearn writes of Louisiana as an ultra-anachronistic place, evoking a prehistoric past where lands and waters shifted. Louisiana here is temporal-frontier, strange and paradoxical, literally submerged in or by the past. The amphibian flora's hybridity and in-between-ness also echoes Hearn's earlier writing about the so-called wild and amphibious St. Maló Malays who sustained themselves through a half-land, half-aquatic livelihood of fishing, which Hearn suggests is a primitive human condition.

In a move toward the dramatic, Hearn relays a rumor and writes that Italian luggermen (sailors) had heard of a "ghastly 'Chinese' colony in the reedy swamps south of Lake Borgne."[22] The Italians heard that "orientals" lived there in "peace and harmony without the presence of a single woman, but finally had managed to import an oblique-eyed beauty from beyond the Yellow Sea."[23] As a result of the "oriental" woman's presence, for the first time supposedly the St. Maló residents began to quarrel, "provoking much shedding of blood."[24] Seeking peace, wise elders supposedly "sentenc[ed] the woman to be hewn in pieces and flung to the alligators of the bayou."[25] Hearn acknowledges this may or may not have happened, but through his opening lines and the horrific tale, Hearn further underscores St. Maló's strange geography, race, class, and gender practices. That is, he emphasizes St. Maló's fishermen's deviant homosociality due to the fact that St. Maló was an overwhelming majority-male village, which did not fit into dominant heteronormative or heterosexual ways of living. The possible violence resulting from an "oriental" woman entering the bayou-space suggests further that an all-male world is supposedly unnatural and indeed unhealthy, possibly producing violence. Thus, location, race, class, gender, and sexuality (axes of difference) are co-constitutive, discursively producing Indios or Malays as ultrastrange, deviant, exotic, and primitive.

Hearn continues the voyage and narrative to St. Maló, emphasizing the colors and sites he sees on Lake Borgne: "the greenish-yellow of the reeds chang[ing] into misty blue . . . all water and sky, motionless blue and . . . lazulite."[26] He highlights a lighthouse that has "a piano . . . for girls to play . . . comfortably furnished rooms, and a good library."[27] Their lugger sails through the Rigolets, (a narrow water passageway leading to Lake Borgne), and they pass Fort Pike at night. In the darkness, boatmen and passengers hear a "moaning that seamen hear far inland while dreaming at home of phantom seas."[28] Hearn's report shifts from the familiar sounds, sites, and pleasures of familiar white southern US American society, as the narrative moves from the comforting colors of misty blue and lazulite; imaginaries of girls playing piano; and white folks reading in a respectable library toward an unfamiliar maritime zone signified by deep moaning sounds in the dark. The lighthouse serves as a metonym for white Southern civility, modernity, and heteronormative and reproductive domesticity.

Lake Borgne in the aforementioned passage is an unfamiliar and potentially unsafe waterway—not peaceful, predictable, or manageable (the more traditional understanding and writing of lakes), but rather, a body of water akin to a scary sea, frightening in its depth, unpredictability, and illegibility—symbolically oceanic in a Freudian sense (that is, the oceanic to Freud was part of the primitive ego).[29] The sea draws beachcombers, swimmers, or sailors with its soothing rhythms and sounds, like infants drawn to their mothers, yet the sea can also overwhelm and destroy, as illustrated by the Indian Ocean earthquake and tsunami (2004), Hurricane Katrina (2005), the more recent Japanese earthquake and tsunami (2011), among other oceanic disturbances and disasters from around the world. In Freudian psychoanalytical theory, the child (usually male with Freud), does not want to be engulfed by an oceanic femininity or maternity. Instead, he desires bodily integrity and a clear sense of self.

By stressing the "deep moaning" sounds heard in the dark, Hearn's St. Maló essay also suggests a gothic orientation. That is, waters are simultaneously picturesque and monstrous, lovely, yet menacing . . . until we learn that the moaning is "only a mighty chorus of frogs, innumerable millions of frogs, chanting in the darkness over unnumbered leagues of swamp and lagoon."[30] Indeed, having finally reached the *eastern side* of the Rigolets, the once calm blue waters are explicitly described as a dangerous sea. (Recall Said's analysis of how "East" and "West" are constructed in orientalist discourse.) Their boat is lost in the danger zone temporarily, but they eventually find the mouth of a bayou that leads to the village of St. Maló.

When Hearn and Davidson arrive at the Malay settlement, Hearn writes of the "odd" boats near a makeshift wharf and the "stilt houses" built in a "Manila style." The two white men also notice the different colors and numerous animals present, noting: green banks, green water, and green fungi on the wooden houses, and lots of gray mud, "pitted with hoof-prints of hogs . . . [and] sometimes alligator prints . . . "[31] (See Figure 10.2.) Hearn writes that a pig is missing and loose and there are pathetic-looking fowl at Saint Maló too. There are also mosquitoes, sand flies, fleas, spiders, woodworms, wood ticks, water hens, plover, snakes, and even possible wildcats, otters, muskrats, minks, raccoons, rabbits, buzzards, and the occasional bald eagle! Hearn's narrative again reiterates that the two white male "voyagers" are emphatically far-removed from supposedly civilized white US American society, now seeing firsthand a supposedly primitive multicolored and dark frontier, a muddy vortex of a village swirling with strangeness, exotica, environmental hazards, and beasts.[32] In Hearn's arrival scene at St. Maló, he describes it in the following way: "We reached Saint Maló upon a leaden-colored day, and the scenery its gray ghastliness recalled to us the weird landscape painted with words by Edgar Poe—*Silence: a Fragment.*" Here, Hearn explicitly reveals his fondness for Edgar Allan Poe's gothic stories. Hearn chose "The Raven" as his self-styled nickname, after Poe's famous poem.[33]

FIGURE 10.2. "The Lacustrine Village of Saint Malo, Louisiana," *Harper's Weekly,*
March 31, 1883, p. 196.

To understand Poe's influence on Hearn, it is necessary to address Poe's
short story here, "A Descent into the Maelstrom,"[34] as Poe's short story and
Hearn's novella *Chita* both address the power, beauty, and horrors of the sea.
While "A Descent into the Maelstrom" is about a sea-vortex off of the coast
of Norway, *Chita* is about a destructive hurricane in the Gulf. Hearn and Poe
write about landscapes and seascapes in similar ways. For example, writing
about the island close to where the Nordic maelstrom unpredictably emerges,
Poe writes, "There was visible a small bleak-looking island. . . . About two
miles nearer the land, arose another of smaller size, hideously craggy and
barren, and encompassed at various intervals by a cluster of dark rocks."[35] If
we read this description next to Hearn's St. Maló arrival scene, we can see that
both authors emphasize the ghastliness and hideousness of unfamiliar land-
and-seascapes, in order to potentially provoke fear, suspense, or revulsion in
the reader, standard gothic narrative maneuvers.

Further developing this trope of geographic marginality and strange-
ness, Hearn appears to have traveled by boat, in order to perhaps further
heighten the imagined primitive time-space of the "strange Malay settle-

ment." That is, Hearn perhaps chose *not* to travel part way to St. Bernard Parish by rail, which by this time extended east of New Orleans. Trains and also steamboats were key modes of transportation in Louisiana used to move sugar cane and other valuable commodities.[36] While it is unclear if passengers were allowed on this particular railway, it is historically documented that New Orleans was an industrialized Gulf-and-Mississippi River-city and trains and tracks ran east to St. Bernard Parish in 1883. Rather than discussing industrialization or telling readers of these technological and transportation developments, which he does in his novella, *Chita*, Hearn instead reinforces (at specific points in his essay) the popular trope of touristic travel through the picturesque, a common aesthetic strategy in European-based travelogues of the nineteenth century, which travelers writing about the United States also deployed when describing or promoting new travel destinations in the relatively young, yet continually and problematically expanding settler-colonial nation of the United States. As Thomas Ruys Smith argues when describing the lower Mississippi River, for example, a popular destination in the antebellum South, travelers and writers frequently relied on the trope of the picturesque, even as Mississippi River towns and cities were significantly industrializing.[37]

In Hearn's orientalist colonial ethnographic and gothic cartography, the Rigolets (the narrow passageway that Hearn and Davidson traveled on before arriving on Lake Borgne) represent the dividing line that separates the West from the East, the space that marks the differences between white civility and social calmness (for example, waters were calm on one side) and colorful brown incivility and chaos (a "turbulent sea" and a subtropical jungle scene on the other side). This narrative repeats the binary between the "West" and "East" and the West's supposed superiority as postcolonial literary critic Edward Said theorized.[38] As Hearn moves eastward, away from New Orleans, toward St. Maló, the racial and cultural gaps grow wider for the crew and passengers, as well as for the white bourgeois reading public who may have chosen to identify with or were discursively interpellated.

Now in St. Maló, Hearn continues to explicitly articulate the connection between the strange geography, strange race, and strange gender that exist among the residents of St. Maló. He writes, "Such is the land: its human inhabitants are not less strange, wild, picturesque."[39] Below, I quote Hearn at length to document and reveal how he imagines "primitive race" through bodily difference—skin color, facial features, and hair types of Malays from the Philippines. Hearn writes:

> Most of them are cinnamon-colored men; a few are glossily yellow. . . . [T] heir features are irregular without being repulsive; some have the cheek-bones very prominent, and the eyes of several are set slightly aslant. The hair is generally intensely black and straight, but with some individuals it is curly and browner. In Manila there are several varieties of the Malay race, and these Louisiana settlers represents more than one type. None of them appeared tall; the greater number were undersized, but all well knit and supple as freshwater eels. Their hands and feet were small; their movements quick and easy, but sailorly likewise, as of men accustomed to walk up on rocking decks in rough weather.[40]

In this narrative unit, Hearn signals an ethnographic and homoerotic curiosity with and/or attraction to the "strange, wild, and picturesque" Malay sailors and fishermen. "Well knit and supple as freshwater eels" suggests a physical admiration of the Manila-men as Hearn's optics zooms in on the muscularity and softness of Malay bodies, and notably, through a phallic symbol—eels. Indeed, it is almost as if Hearn himself touched or stroked these attractive watermen in order to satisfy his ethnographic and erotic curiosity, expressing what postcolonial feminist scholar Anne McClintock calls "porno-tropics" in *Imperial Leather.*[41] McClintock theorizes that porno-tropics are sexualized tropes of European colonialism that eroticize and seek to sexually and politically conquer natives, while simultaneously inscribing tropical geographies as similarly exotic and hypersexual.

Hearn's eroticized ethnographic admiration in his St. Maló essay contradicts a later, yet absolutely connected, description of Malay men in Hearn's story, *Chita* (1888). Describing the aftermath of the flood resulting from a hurricane, Hearn writes about two Malay men named Valentino and Juan who Hearn imagines discovering a drowned white woman of high society, a victim of a destructive hurricane and flood in 1856. Hearn writes, "Over her heart you will find it, Valentino—the locket held by that fine Swiss chain of woven hair—*Caya manan!* [sic]. And it is not your quadroon bondmaid, sweet lady, who now disrobes you so roughly; those Malay hands are *less deft* than hers,—but she slumbers very far away from you, and man not be aroused from her sleep. '*Na quita mo! Dalaga!—na quita maganda!*' . . . Juan, the fastenings of those diamond ear-drops are much too complicated for your peon fingers: tear them out!—Dispense, *chulita!*"[42] (Emphasis mine.)

In this passage, the white woman is dead and still delicate, defenseless against brown Malay men and their wandering hands. The white lady's female quadroon servant is not there to protect her from brown savages. Malay men are inscribed as racially, sexually, and socially obscene–looters and buzzards who steal money and jewelry from corpses, inappropriately touching victims, including fine white southern belles. Hearn writes of the Malay men as bayou and Gulf pirates who steal, loot, and perhaps even suffer from necrophilia, as Hearn imagines the Malay men expressing sexual desires for the dead. The racialized and classed gender and sexuality of Malay men in *Chita* foreshadows later discourses of Filipino migrant men in the early twentieth century who many white US Americans believed were hypersexual, socially inappropriate and even disgusting.[43] Hearn's contradictory, yet complementary, narratives about Malay men can, therefore, be read as part of his orientalist colonial ethnographic and gothic optics where desire, attraction, intrigue, repulsion, and grotesquery interweave.

Additionally, Hearn's emphasis on the Malay's "sailorly" demeanor (in the long quote from his St. Maló essay) can also be read as narrative strategy to further mark Indio/Malay strangeness vis-à-vis what I would call "terrestrial normativity." Maritime studies scholars such as Allan Sekula and Marcus Rediker make a similar point in their analyses of working-class (usually white or black) sailors. Social observers and commentators in the seventeenth and eighteenth centuries historically constructed these sailors as deviant and marginal because of their different or socially queer maritime ways of living, working, speaking, moving, and dressing. Recall too that Rediker and Sekula's sailors were usually on all-male or majority male ships.[44]

Toward the end of his report, Hearn discusses at great length the gambling at the Malay settlement. Although mentioning that the St. Maló men are polite (they always say "Buenas Noches") and they don't drink alcohol while gambling, Hearn sums up the social scene at St. Maló as "grotesque."[45] (See Figure 10.3, bottom gambling scene.) In this sketch Donaldson depicts the brown Malay fishermen and sailors in a large group, an all-male pack

FIGURE 10.3. "Gambling at Saint Malo," *Harper's Weekly,* March 31, 1883, p. 197.

dangerously lurking in the shadows, participating in unproductive games of chance (that is, unproductive in that gambling is not part of capitalist production and profit). The Malay men's brown-ness is accentuated by the time of the gambling (evening), which makes the men appear darker. This point is evident if the Malay men gambling sketch is compared to the sketches of two white men (top of Figure 10.3). While these figures are sketched in-dividually, presumably in daylight, where their whiteness becomes more apparent, in contrast, Donaldson draws the Malay men as in anonymous shadows (especially the Malay men in the back of the sketch), a silhouetted brown "horde" suggesting their supposed collective racial primitiveness, in-distinguishability, and danger.[46]

In the contemporary art world, African American feminist artist Kara Walker provocatively (re)engages shadows and silhouettes of African Americans in the context of racist nineteenth-century media (such as *Harper's Weekly*) and institutionalized white supremacy and plantation slavery more broadly in the US American South. Like Malay fishermen and sailors, white writers and artists often depicted African Americans in the US South as socially indistinguishable and primitive, more sil-houette or cartoon, not fully human or fully man or woman. Walker's artwork reanimates black silhouettes and shadows (often silhouettes of black females, but black males too) through large "cut outs" that rehisto-ricizes slavery, the plantation, race, white supremacy, desire, and shame. In telling a different history or story through the cut-outs, Walker sug-gests that her art "ha[s] to do with exchanges of power, attempts to steal power away from others."[47] Walker's understanding of shadows, sil-houettes, and race and racism in the nineteenth-century US American South inform my interpretation of Malay gambling in Hearn's narrative and Malay shadows and silhouettes in Donaldson's sketch.

Moreover, Hearn and Donaldson's focus on degenerate, lazy, and un-productive Asian male gambling is broadly connected to how pundits and writers depicted "frontiersmen" more generally, especially those liv-ing or working on the Mississippi River and in the bayous.[48] Donaldson's sketch also echoes and reinforces notions of Yellow or Brown Peril, as Hearn describes the scene as "grotesque" and the Chinese Exclusion Act became law in 1882, one year before *Harper's Weekly* published Hearn's St. Maló essay. This sketch is, therefore, not simply about the figure of the unproductive or socially deviant frontiersman or waterman, but rather, when more fully contextualized, the sketch is symbolic of orien-talism and anti-Asian sentiments that were prevalent in dominant white societies in the United States during the nineteenth century.

To close his St. Maló essay, Hearn relays additional information about the settlement and its residents, briefly discussing the few mestizos who live in the village; how justice is handled when disputes arise; and the fact that no furniture exists in the village. Hearn and Davidson stay long enough to watch a gorgeous Lake Borgne sunset and then return to New Orleans by boat.

I turn now to the first set of sketches by Donaldson that depict the indigenous Indio/Malay/Filipino houses found at the St. Maló settlement, architectural structures usually called "bahay na nipa" (in English: house made of palm leaves [and bamboo],) or "bahay kubo" (in English: the cube-shaped house [or hut.]) Historically, these indigenous Indio/Filipino structures (usually elevated above the ground) were designed to protect indigenous people who lived in the lowlands from streams and rivers, which regularly overflow and also from "the tropical ground, [which] crawls with insects, mosquitoes and rats and exudes heat and dampness."[49] The structure's slatted bamboo floors and woven bamboo or nipa walls also allow air to circulate freely, an important feature of indigenous Southeast Asian tropical architecture. Before Spanish and US American colonialisms in the archipelago, bahay na nipa were also used as temporary houses, part of the "kaingin" method of rice cultivation where areas of woodland were burned and which created fertile compost for growing rice. Lowland Filipinos built bahay na nipa then typically moved on, allowing the soil to regenerate. In a precolonial indigenous agricultural and social context, native peoples saw temporary dwelling such as bahay na nipa as more comfortable and desirable, compared to permanent houses built with materials such as stone or concrete, which were either unavailable (via the landscape or new technology) at this point in time.

With Spanish colonialism in the archipelago beginning in the 16th Century, architecture and gender changed significantly and the bahay kubo lost some of its social desirability. Scholar Cristina Blanc-Stanton notes that in a Spanish colonial context in the Visayas, "a man's honor and prestige [was] tied to the defense of house, land, and family, which constitute[d] the base of his social standing, in the community."[50] She argues that house, land, and family became increasingly important in the Visayas during the Spanish colonial period because the Spaniards imposed a colonial architecture that they built to strengthen their political authority. According to Blanc-Stanton, "The symbols of authority . . . were the stone churches and houses, a sharp contrast to the indigenous wooden forts and bamboo houses."[51] During the US occupation of the Philippines, US Americans also imposed a European-based architectural style–one they deemed as "modern"—which they viewed as superior to native Filipino architecture.[52] Visually interpreted alongside these European/American colonial devaluations of indigenous Indio/Filipino architecture, David's sketches of St. Maló bayou architecture (although not made of the traditional nipa or bamboo)—in conjunction with Hearn's written report–makes a similar orientalist or primitivist gesture to render Malays as inferior subjects precisely through Eurocentric notions of proper, "modern," or "civilized" architecture and dwelling. (Recall too the emphasis on the light house.)

In the second set of sketches Hearn and Davidson continue to focus on primitive domesticity and dwelling, which is connected to the history of Europeans and white US Americans feminizing Asian men and masculinities. Although as I previously mentioned, sometimes whites described Malays or Filipinos as hypermasculine, precisely through hyper(hetero)sexuality (which I addressed in the novella *Chita*), in the context of US orientalism, as a general trend, Asians or "orientals" were or are often feminized, so at times, Malays and Filipinos are also included in this kind of gendering. In the middle sketch entitled, "Bits of St. Maló Scenery" (that includes multiple bahay kubo in Figure 10.3), the caption at the bottom reads "vegetable garden" and tattered laundry hangs out to dry. The garden, laundry, and outdoor oven (the latter is located in center in between the two sketches of white men, also in Figure 10.3) seek to highlight St. Maló's *primitive queer homosociality* (that is, it is in the context of heteronormativity and heterosexuality, the absence of women signals a profound social abnormality) and the way in which indigenous Manila-men must perhaps unnaturally (or perhaps naturally) do "women's work" in their homosocial, all-male village.

Instead of reading these sketches through this European and white colonial optics, we can instead engage a postcolonial, queer, and Filipino/a rereading by drawing on indigenous psycho-socio concepts such as *kapwa* (togetherness) and *pakikiisa* (striving for oneness), first theorized by Virgilio Enriquez as core indigenous Filipino concepts and codes of conduct in his theoretical framework on "Sikolohiyang Pilipino" (Filipino/a Psychology.)[53] The bread oven, laundry, and garden are strongly symbolic of these indigenous psycho-social concepts, as each potentially contribute to the overall well being of the collective or settlement. In other words, these important spaces of everyday practices of Filipino homosocial domesticity—baking, washing clothes, and growing food—are interpretable as signs of social interdependency, solidarity, unity, and homosocial male/masculine caring that are critical to how Filipino/a personhood, including how Filipino masculinities and manhood are partially constructed.

Conclusion

Like the Philippines, many waters, histories, and literatures flow in and through Louisiana's complex system of hydrologies. Bayous, lakes, and rivers, plus the oceanic space of the Gulf of Mexico hold submerged or submarine histories.[54] Listing "[the] great enemies of our [Philippine or Filipino] textual heritage," Gina Apostol in her recent novel, *The Revolution According to Raymundo Mata* (2009), includes, "*Fires, Insects, and Worms, plus Wars and Typhoons*"[55] after "*kleptos*" [who steal books and materials from libraries and archives]" as the primary perpetrators (emphasis by italics are Apostol's; emphasis through underlining is mine). As Apostol's novel addresses, many Philippine texts have been destroyed, fragmented, flooded, liquidated, stolen, and/or relocated to colonial archives, and many are also lost further in layers of linguistic and cultural translations. In Louisiana, a parallel historical and present reality exists in terms of how water and weather can affect or damage texts and histories, as well as how multiple regimes of colonial power/knowledge (French, Spanish, and US American) palimpsestically linger in and haunt Louisiana (in a similar way that the Philippines is haunted.) Although completely forgotten or metaphorically washed away in official histories of Louisiana, presented, for example, at the French Quarter Visitor Center,[56] part of the Jean Lafitte National Historical Park and Preserve, under US National Park Service, or ethnographically distorted or misunderstood in essays like Hearn's, historical evidence documents that Indios from the present-day Philippines undoubtedly lived and worked in St. Maló, Louisiana before the US occupation of the Philippines in 1898, a key historical flashpoint in Philippine/Filipino/a American Studies.

When "Captain Billy" (a pseudonym for the local Canary Islander American fishing guide who took me to St. Maló by boat in 2010) and I finally approach St. Maló after a few hours of checking out Lake Borgne, he gives me a friendly warning, seemingly not wanting me to be disappointed upon arrival. "There's nothing there," Captain Billy says. (See Figure 10.4.) At first glance I see what looks to be a small island with

FIGURE 10.4. *Yet, there remained something there.* St. Maló, Louisiana, January 2010. Photo credit: Kale Bantigue Fajardo.

bushes, weeds, small trees, and a little beach. St. Maló is perhaps lonesome, but not ghastly. After quietly looking at the site longer, a village of watermen emerges.

Morenos, a few mestizos, and an African man (noted in Hearn's essay) maneuver boats and *bangkas* (canoes) tending nets, much like fishermen still do in some parts of the present-day Philippines and Louisiana gulf, despite the encroachment of industrial fishing, typhoons, hurricanes, and oil spills. At one of the bigger houses close to shore, I hear fishermen and boatmen talking, arguing, and laughing in their wabi-sabi, elegantly weathered wooden home. In the distance, a fisherman paddles his bangka, alone with his thoughts. At another house, outside: a man looks after his chickens, while inside, his companion looks at an old family photograph. A man sitting under a tree, having just finished a letter to his sweetheart in Manila, begins to compose a poem for his lover in New Orleans. And in a boat stored in a shady spot, two brothers take a siesta because they rose early that morning before dawn, to help in the baking of bread for their *kuyas, tios,* and amigos (older brothers, uncles, and friends.)

Captain Billy was half right. On that sunny January day in 2010, the Indio/Malay fishing village at St. Maló was long gone. *Yet, there was something there.* If as Apostol writes our textual and, hence, linguistic, historical, cultural heritages are important to engage, but also in peril, and if as I have attempted to show here the colonial archive is profoundly limited, but nevertheless useful in illustrating the cultural politics of colonial knowledge, and secondly, if the colonial archive is consistently distorted and indeed racist, then sometimes we must *literally revisit and rewrite* sites and spaces of "nothingness," or loss, not for the grand project of recreating or naturalizing a utopic indigenous past, but to participate in the powerful act of imagining or reimagining alternative realities and world-views. This is our intellectual and creative challenge: to produce alternative tropes and narratives, humbly, yet persistently striving to contribute to Philippine and/or Filipino/a diasporic textual and cultural heritages.[57]

Notes

1. http://www.unitedhoumanation.org/
2. On the importance of addressing indigeneity and present realities of colonialism for Native peoples, especially in the context of queer/postcolonial/diaspora studies, see Andrea Smith, "Queer Theory and Native Studies: The Heteronormativity of Settler Colonialism," *GLQ: A Journal of Lesbian and Gay Studies* 16.1–2 (2010): 42–68.
3. Paul Gilroy, *Black Atlantic: Modernity and Double Consciousness* (Cambridge, MA: Harvard University Press, 1993).
4. Omise'eke Natasha Tinsley, "Black Atlantic, Queer Atlantic: Queer Imaginings of the Middle Passage" *GLQ: A Journal of Lesbian and Gay Studies* 14.2–3 (2008): 191–215.
5. "Juan San Malo," *A Dictionary of Louisiana Biography,* vol. II (1988), 714.
6. Ibid.
7. Marina Espina, *Filipinos in Louisiana* (New Orleans: A.F. Laborde and Sons, 1988).
8. Stephen H. Sumida, "East of California: Points of Origin in Asian American Studies," *Journal of Asian American Studies* 1.1 (1998): 83–100.
9. E. San Juan, "Configuring the Filipino Diaspora in the United States," *Diaspora: A Journal of Transnational Studies* 3.2 (1994): 117–33.
10. Gary Okihiro, *Common Ground: Reimagining American History* (Princeton, NJ: Princeton University Press, 2001); Stephen H. Sumida, "East of California: Points of Origin in Asian American Studies," *Journal of Asian American Studies* 1.1 (1998): 83–100.
11. For discussions of how Manila-men helped to forge multiple transoceanic connections around the world, see for example, Evelyn Hu-DeHart, "Latin America in Asia-Pacific Perspective," in *What's in a Rim? Critical Perspectives on the Pacific*

Region Idea, ed. Arif Dirlik, 251–82. (Lanham, MD: Rowman and Littlefield Publishers, 1998); "Asian American Studies as Global Studies," paper presented at *Re/Siting Asian American Studies: Connecting Critical Approaches in the Field*, Rutgers University, February 19, 2010; and Kale Bantigue Fajardo, "Race of the Century" in *Filipino Crosscurrents: Oceanographies of Seafaring, Masculinities, and Globalization* (Minneapolis: University of Minnesota Press, 2011).

12. Sarita See, "Hair Lines: Filipino American Art and the Uses of Abstraction," paper presented at *Re/Siting Asian American Studies: Connecting Critical Approaches in the Field*, Rutgers University, February 19, 2010; Edward Said, *Orientalism* (New York: Vintage / First Vintage Books Edition, 1979); and Michel Foucault, *Power/Knowledge: Selected Interviews and Other Writings, 1972–1977* (New York: Vintage, 1980).

13. See, for example, Lafcadio Hearn, "Some Chinese Ghosts," "Two Years in the French West Indies," and "Youma: The Story of a West-Indian Slave," all in *Lafcadio Hearn: American Writings*, 1–74, 149–542, 543–614 (New York: Literary Classics of the US, 2009).

14. Espina does cite Hearn in an academic essay, "Filipinos in New Orleans," *The Proceedings of the Louisiana Academy of Sciences*, vol. XXXVII (1974), 117–21. On the controversies surrounding the 1763 arrival date, Espina's research, and the "politics of origins" in Asian American Studies, see Malcolm H. Churchill, "Louisiana History and Early Filipino Settlement: Searching for the Story," *Bulletin of the American Historical Collection* 27.3 (1999): 25–48; Floro L. Mercene, *Manila Men in the New World: Filipino Migration to Mexico and the Americas from the Sixteenth Century* (Quezon City: University of the Philippines Press, 2007); and Theodore Gonzalves, "Opposing 'Origins,'" paper presented at Association for Asian American Studies Conference, New Orleans LA, May 18–21, 2011.

15. Lafcadio Hearn, "Saint Malô: A Lacustrine Village in Louisiana," in *Lafcadio Hearn: American Writings*, 731 (New York: Literary Classics of the United States, 2009).

16. Ibid., 730.

17. Ibid.

18. Ibid.

19. Ibid., 731.

20. Lafcadio Hearn, "Chita: A Memory of Last Island," in *Lafcadio Hearn: American Writings* (New York: Literary Classics of the United States, 2009).

21. Ibid., 98.

22. Hearn, "Saint Malô," 731.

23. Ibid.

24. Ibid.

25. Ibid.

26. Ibid.

27. Ibid., 732.

28. Ibid.

29. Sigmund Freud, *Civilization and its Discontents* (Eastford, CT: Martino Books, 1930/2010).

30. Hearn, "Saint Malô," 732.

31. Ibid., 734.

32. See James Cameron (Director and Writer), *Avatar*. Twentieth Century Fox Film Corporation, 2009; and http://www.imdb.com/title/tt0499549/locations.

33. Nina H. Kinnard, *Lafcadio Hearn* (New York: D. Appleton and Company, 1912), 71; Edgar Allan Poe, *The Raven* (Boston: Northeastern University Press, 1986).

34. Edgar Allan Poe, "A Descent into the Maelstrom," in *Great Tales of Horror* by Edgar Allan Poe, 98–114 (New York: Bantam Books, 1964).

35. Ibid., 99.

36. Merl E. Reed, *New Orleans and the Railroads: The Struggle for Commercial Empire, 1830–1860* (Baton Rouge: Louisiana State University Press for the Louisiana Historical Association, 1966).

37. Thomas Ruys Smith, "Europeans on this 'Foul Stream,'" in *River of Dreams: Imagining the Mississippi Before Mark Twain*, by Thomas Ruys Smith, 79–110 (Baton Rouge: Louisiana State University Press, 2007).

38. Edward Said, *Orientalism* (New York: Vintage, 1979).

39. Hearn, "Saint Maló," 735.

40. Ibid.

41. Anne McClintock, *Imperial Leather: Race, Gender, and Sexuality in Colonial Conquest* (New York: Routledge, 1995).

42. Hearn, *Chita*, 96.

43. See, for example, Linda España Maram, *Creating Masculinity in Los Angeles's Little Manila: Working-Class Filipinos and Popular Culture in the United States* (New York: Columbia University Press, 2006); and Carlos Bulosan, *America is in the Heart* (Seattle: University of Washington Press, 1977).

44. Allan Sekula, *Fish Story* (Dusseldorf: Richter Verlag, 1995); Marcus Rediker, *Between the Devil and the Deep Blue Sea: Merchant Seamen, Pirates, and the Anglo-American Maritime World, 1700–1750* (Cambridge: Cambridge University Press, 1987).

45. Hearn, "Saint Maló," 742.

46. See Kara Walker, *My Complement, My Enemy, My Oppressor, My Love*. Exhibit at Walker Art Center, Minneapolis, MN, February 17-May 13, 2007; and Hamza Walker, "Kara Walker: Cut it Out," *NKA: Journal of Contemporary African Art Now*. 11/12 (fall/winter 2000)

47. Kara Walker in Sollins, Susan, Exec Producer. *Art21: Art in the 21st Century*. DVD, PBS Home Video Dist, 2003.

48. Thomas Ruys Smith, "Jackson and the 'Half-Horse, Half Alligators,'" in *River of Dreams: Imagining the Mississippi Before Mark Twain*, by Thomas Ruys Smith, 45–78 (Baton Rouge: Louisiana State University Press, 2007).

49. Fernando N. Zialcita and Martin I. Tinio, "It All Started With the Bahay Kubo," in *Philippine Ancestral Houses*, by Fernando N. Zialcita and Martin I. Tinio, Jr., 6 (Quezon City: GCF Books, 2006).

50. Cristina Blanc-Szanton, "Collision of Cultures: Historical Reformulations of Gender in the Lowland Visayas, Philippines," in *Power and Difference: Gender in Island Southeast Asia*, ed. Jane Monning Atkinson and Shelly Errington, 347 (1990).

51. Ibid., 363.

52. Thomas S. Hines, "The Imperial Façade: Daniel H. Burnham and American Architectural Planning in the Philippines," *Pacific Historical Review* 41.1: 33–53.

53. Virgilio G. Enriquez, *Sikolohiyang Pilipino: From Colonial to Liberation Psychology: The Philippine Experience* (Diliman, Quezon City: University of the Philippines Press, 1992).

54. On submerged histories and the sea, see Edourd Glissant, *Caribbean Discourse: Selected Essays* (Charlottesville: University of Virginia Press, 1999). For a queer Black feminist perspective on submerged histories and the sea, see Omise'eke Natasha Tinsley, "Black Atlantic, Queer Atlantic: Queer Imaginings of the Middle Passage," *GLQ: A Journal of Lesbian and Gay Studies* 14.2–3 (2008): 191–215.

55. Gina Apostol, *The Revolution According to Raymundo Mata*, 15 (Pasig City: Anvil, 2009).

56. I examined the Louisiana historical exhibit at the French Quarter Visitor Center during my ethnographic field trip to New Orleans in 2008.

57. On the idea of revisiting or traveling to important cultural sites and rewriting or reimagining histories, see Saidiya Hartman, "Venus in Two Acts," *Small Axe* 26, 12.2 (June 2008): 1–14; *Lose Your Mother: A Journey Along the Atlantic Slave Route* (New York: Farrar, Straus and Giroux, 2007); and Omise'eke Natasha Tinsley, *Water, Shoulders, Into the Black Pacific* (forthcoming), a queer black historical novel that reimagines the queer histories of female shipbuilders of color in Richmond, California, during World War II.

PART IV

The Filipino Body in Time and Space

11

Pinoy Posteriority

MARTIN JOSEPH PONCE

This chapter endeavors to further Filipino Studies' engagements with the politics of gender and sexuality by analyzing two novels—Ricardo Ramos's *Flipping* (1998) and Han Ong's *The Disinherited* (2004)—through the frames of racialized and neocolonial queer positionalities and temporalities.[1] Part of the larger field of contemporary queer diasporic Filipino literature whose authors include Noël Alumit, Jessica Hagedorn, Joseph Legaspi, R. Zamora Linmark, Bino Realuyo, Nice Rodriguez, and Joel B. Tan, among others, these two texts pose serious challenges to some of the political values espoused by Filipino Studies scholarship as a result of the prominence accorded to the critical frameworks of empire and diaspora during the past two decades. These analytics have productively explored the legacies of Spanish and US colonialisms in the Philippines and their influences on migration to and social life in the United States and elsewhere. Premised on critiques of colonialism, imperialism, assimilation, marginalization, patriarchy, dictatorship, and capitalist globalization, this work has tended to privilege discourses, actors, and institutions that advance anticolonial, antiracist, antisexist, and anticapitalist movements, while noting the impossibility of pure oppositionality.

What do we do, then, with literary texts whose queer protagonists do *not* abide by such values and tenets? Napoleon Ramos in *Flipping* is an unabashedly antiblack, Filipino "bottom" living in 1970s San Francisco who single-mindedly attempts to secure a white American "top" for a husband. Pitik Sindit in *The Disinherited* is a fifteen-year-old erotic dancer living in 1990s Manila who similarly seeks a wealthy white American man to ferry him away from his impoverished, isolated life to an idealized America. While we might denigrate these characters' aspirations as identifications with dominant whiteness or as tactical strategies for acquiring some degree of power within highly stratified social constraints, the texts' satirical, subversive stances toward political pieties preempt absolute denunciations of the characters.

Indeed, Ramos and Ong seem to be irreverently playing with the image of the Asian/American male in US popular discourse as feminized, foreign, and ineffectual (Eng and Hom; Fung). To be sure, there is a long history of perceiving Filipino males as *hyper*sexual—from the US colonial period at the turn of the century, through the early decades of working-class labor migration, through the notorious "*Blu's Hanging* controversy" and the Andrew Cunanan "shooting spree" in the late 1990s—that complicates the conflation of Filipino and Asian genders and sexualities (Chuh 31–57; Isaac xvi–xxv, 126; Koshy 91–131; Takaki 327–35). Nonetheless, *Flipping* and *The Disinherited* engage the politics of sexuality through the association between the two, the former through ample (ironic) references to Filipinos as "Orientals," the latter through references to the Philippines as a "Third World" country analogous to Thailand and its sex tourist economy. By juxtaposing a novel set predominantly in the United States next to one set mostly in the Philippines, my queer diasporic analysis explores the continuities and differences that structure these racial-sexual figurations and desires. Not only are Napoleon Ramos and Pitik Sindit patently uninvested in reasserting a masculinist posture; they seemingly subordinate themselves to racial and neocolonial hierarchies—though not without acquiring or grasping for a certain kind of power via that self-subordination. How, then, might we read novels whose queer characters' desires are attached to sources of dominant power that highly circumscribe, if not obliterate, the very conditions of their lives? As Judith Butler phrases it in a philosophical register, "What does it mean to embrace the very form of power—regulation, prohibition, suppression—that threatens one with dissolution in an effort, precisely, to persist in one's own existence?" (9). Or, as Juana María Rodríguez asks while urging us to "learn to read submission and service differently" in "relation to both sex and sociality" (338), "how do we begin to make sense of our politically incorrect erotic desires? More to the point, what kind of sense is even desirable or possible?" (342).

Sketching the parameters of what I'm calling "Pinoy posteriority" constitutes my attempt to make sense of these queer literary inscriptions as something other than manifestations of political backwardness that drags on the progressive vanguard's strenuous efforts to alleviate social oppression.[2] Drawing on posteriority's temporal, spatial, hierarchical, and corporeal dimensions (belated, behind, inferior, backside), the phrase intends to signify across various registers of meaning that link political positioning (ideological regressiveness), sexual positioning ("bottoming"), and social positioning (subordinate status).[3] These layers of significance are meant to resonate with scholarship on queer temporalities, for example, with Elizabeth Freeman's call to attend to the ways that "the gaps and fissures in the 'modern' get displaced backward into a hypersexualized or desexualized 'premodern'" (Introduction 160), or with Heather Love's considerations of "feeling backward" and "risking abjection" (30). These resonances get amplified in relation to tropes of "development" since racial, colonial, and sexual others have historically been categorized along evolutionary lines distinguishing primitives from moderns, arrested (queer) developers from developed (heterosexual) adults, underdeveloped or developing from overdeveloped or post-industrial economies (Eng 4–15; Hoad; Tadiar 37–149). That the language of being behind the times so neatly links up with both neocolonial and neoliberal notions of political and economic underdevelopment *and* globalized and racialized visions of abjected homo-sex positions compels us to theorize the connections among the political, economic, and sexual as not merely metaphorical or mimetic, but also as embodied and enacted in everyday experience and sustained through superstition and stereotype.

Syncing with the queer of color and postcolonial critiques of these developmental models, I thus also use "Pinoy posteriority" as a methodological approach to these intertwined positionings that does not a priori discipline the queer Filipino subject into a properly "progressive" or "modern" actor but seeks to comprehend its figuration, location, and desires vis-à-vis the structural and affective forces that constitute it. This speculation explores the kinds of knowledges that are produced when we adopt what Nguyen Tan Hoang calls "gay Asian bottomhood as a hermeneutic" (*View* 24)—"a view from the bottom" (21), he elaborates, "that complicates the links between the passive position and Oriental passivity" and "undermines normative sexual, gender, and racial and standards" (2). *Flipping* and *The Disinherited* not only resist the equation of power with "top as dominant and active" (7), but even more perversely focus on characters who flaunt the orientalized abjected bottom in hopes of establishing a long-lasting relationship with a white American man. From the viewpoint of a heterosexist cultural politics that sees getting penetrated by a white body as antithetical to the project of Asian remasculinization, Napoleon and Pitik are, of course, worthy only of consummate disdain. But even from the perspective of a liberal politics of gay toleration, these characters' promiscuity, self-objectification, and desire for American whiteness run the risk of reinforcing "negative" stereotypes about racialized gay men as sex-hungry, lacking in self-esteem, courting disease and disaster in the profligate deployments of their sexualities. Neither moral opprobrium, rescue mission, nor rationalization, the analytic of Pinoy posteriority focuses on the unstable symbolics that accrue to and are read off of embodied sexual practices, while examining those symbolics within and against the temporalizing frame of world-historical queer progression. This approach resists the conventional assignment of power (domination/submission) and affect (pride/shame) to both the corporeal and temporal frames of posteriority, while at the same time refusing to capitulate to a cultural relativist stance that precludes any mode of political critique.

In this light, I interpret Napoleon's and Pitik's sexual practices and attitudes not merely as deplorable effects of colonialism, imperialism, racialization, and globalization, nor as naïve collusions with oppressive institutions, but as provocative occasions to explore the pleasures and powers of racialized "bottomhood" in connection with queer temporalities. Even as the novels deconstruct normative ideals of white gayness as the endpoints of modern gay development, they also desist from substituting a more multicultural, inclusive, or "Filipino" queer culture in the former's stead. The novels produce necessary critiques of social hierarchies within racialized queer spaces but do not or cannot reimagine historically material queer Filipino identities as somehow transcending the forms of their subjection. It is these irresolutions that enable us to perceive the political ambiguities that inhere in a Filipino Studies which takes queer sex, gender, and sexuality as its points of entry, not its belated afterthoughts.

Ass-backwards: Lust and Loathing in San Francisco

Hovering somewhere between gay pulp and lit porn, *Flipping* is narrated retrospectively, from the vantage point of the early 1990s, through Napoleon's flippant voice (until the final three chapters). Though partly a coming-of-age story, the novel is organized more around episodic sex scenes and sexual relationships than the evolution of plot or identity. Aside from the incestuous fellatio he performed on his half-brother Solomon and his nephew Felipe when they were teenagers, Napoleon's sexcapades are consistently framed by racial difference and power, and he takes wicked delight in reinscribing stereotypes around race, age, anatomy, and sex roles. For example, his desire "for the [white] bearded-daddy type" is linked to the notion that "hair on the face and body is very masculine," whereas "smooth-skinned Orientals . . . seem like giggly teenagers, no matter how old we get" (17). In Napoleon's mind, these bodily characteristics entail authentic genders and definite sex positions: "Real men sprout hair, and we smooth, soft ones should kneel and worship their hairinesses" (49). To worship, for Napoleon, is to be on the oral and anal receiving end of sex.

Although the novel focuses primarily on Filipino-white eroticisms, it does devote discrete chapters to Napoleon's encounters with a group of Chicano men in San Francisco ("The Spanish Conquests") and a darkskinned, presumably Middle Eastern, Muslim man that he works for in Palo Alto ("Ravished by a Pasha"). In true Napoleonic fashion, the narrator recurs to stereotypical grammars when describing his sexual exploits, classifying the well-endowed Miguel, who has a Chicana girlfriend, as "the perfect little macho" (64) for only penetrating Napoleon; Miguel's cousin Manuel as "gay" though not a "'joto' or 'maricón'" (60); and Miguel's younger brother Pablo, a.k.a. "Pablita," as "queerer even than me" for being racially indiscriminate in his homoerotic desires (61). Similarly, Napoleon recurs to orientalist tropes when describing his boss Mohammed ("I heard that some Moslems specialize in fucking sweet young things" [65]), noting the "thick (and very bushy) rug" that burns his skin during sex (67), the "nice Oriental carpet in [Mohammed's] office" (68), and the man's authoritative demeanor (though he does pay Napoleon $25 a pop for his additional services).

These deviations into cross-color sex acts notwithstanding, *Flipping* reserves its most trenchant satire for Filipino-white (mis)perceptions and relationships. While hierarchies might be "sexy" and constitutive of erotic fantasy and practice as queer scholars often argue, *Flipping* reveals the decidedly *fantastical* nature of Napoleon's desires. The novel deconstructs stereotypical racial and sexual symbology not by bringing forth a prouder, more politicized Pinoy who encourages Napoleon to get over his erotic investment in whiteness, but by allowing the racial fantasy to implode. Neither of his white "husbands," Martin or Alan, that is, maintain their positions on top. When he starts screwing Martin, for instance, Napoleon is "amazed that he permitted it" and "still more amazed when I realized he liked it. Shocked and appalled, dearie! I thought I had a daddy, a butch, hairy husband, but he turned out to be a bearded lady with moist (hairy) thighs and a hungry hole" (74). Napoleon's expectations of Martin's successor, Alan, sour just as quickly. Though he thinks he "now had a real stud in Alan" (74), he soon discovers that "Alan was butch only in my fantasies" (75). Napoleon eventually finds out that Alan has not only been getting "black-topped" by a janitor at work, but has also been using an enormous black dildo at home. Napoleon's feeling of betrayal is not due to the "extra-marital" affair but to the fact "that he had fooled me into thinking he was a total top" (86). Although "Alan [had] seemed so butch, as well as *so* white," Napoleon concludes that "he wasn't all man" (82). Through these reversals, Napoleon discovers that his beliefs in the divine order of things have been shaken up: "I thought that God had decreed that Orientals are passive and Occidentals were put into the world with cocks to satisfy us, but I'd been learning that masculine white men liked to be passive too" (115).

For Napoleon, versatility and reciprocity are precisely *not* what he wants. During an argument, Alan tries to enlighten Napoleon about the virtues of US gay culture: "This is the 1970s," he says, "you can be a top sometimes and a bottom others" (90). "We can be equals," he goes on to say. "You don't have to always service me and jack yourself off" (92)—to which Napoleon thinks to himself, "*No darling, we're not going to be equals. I'm going to be the boss, and you're going to beg for whatever you get*" (92). Rejecting Alan's proposal of equality, Napoleon assumes the dominant position of "master," takes control of when and how they have sex, but still insists on seeking "a 100% man, not another queen, like myself" (95–96). To his dismay, Napoleon even performs the role of master in bondage-and-domination play with Martin and other white men. Despite ample evidence that 100 percent men are "hard to find" (95), Napoleon remains committed to his bottomhood and perplexed by the sexual ideology of equality.

That Napoleon refuses to acquiesce to what the novel describes (albeit in passing) as an emerging gay ethos of equality and reciprocity in the Bay Area of the 1970s and clings instead to his racialized position of bottomhood in the face of a crumbling idealized whiteness constitutes part of the contradictory discourse of Pinoy posteriority. He scorns what Alan Sinfield delineates as the "dominant metropolitan ideology," which holds "that the most suitable partner, gay or straight, will be of similar age, class, and race to oneself" (59). Sinfield notes "the emergence of egalitarian relations as a sign of progress" and suggests, following David Halperin, that "modern homosexuality is [based on] the opportunity to transcend hierarchy": "Homosexual relations cease to be compulsorily structured by a polarization of identities and roles" (59). But if it is no longer necessary to abide by social hierarchies, is there not, in effect, a compulsory mandate to *abolish* them—rhetorically, if not always in practice—in order to participate in "modern homosexuality"? Within this context, Napoleon's desires come off as resolutely unmodern, a sign of political regression. "Ass upturned, like I've so often been throughout my life" (11), as he describes himself on the first page of the novel, Napoleon's politics are ass-backwards. Rather than assert a full-frontal attack against Asian emasculation, he prefers a bottoms-up approach. Paradoxically, his yearning for a perfect white top to fill his eager brown bottom is precisely the sexual stance through which he challenges the prevailing teleology of romantic egalitarianism.

Napoleon's self-ascribed bottomhood, however, applies solely to his relation to whiteness. At one point, he directly conflates desire for and identification with whiteness through sex: "I wanted people to see that I was white inside, and I took a lot of white cocks inside of me trying to prove it. They left milk behind. It still didn't make me white. Even though by that period I was giving some back, I was still trying to *be* a white boy, not just to have white boys" (120). While this conflation of desire and identification may not be unusual within the discourse of interracial gay sex, it also seems implicitly linked to Napoleon's virulent antiblack racism. What Napoleon finds appalling is not only that his white partners flip over into bottoms, but that "they were bottoms who liked big, black cocks shoved up their hairy white asses" (47). It is incomprehensible and reprehensible to him that white men could view both Asians and blacks as equally attractive since he thinks the latter's only redeeming quality is the alleged size of their penises (47).

What accounts for Napoleon's attraction to whiteness and his aversion to blackness? The "Publisher's Preface" describes how "*Flipping* became a controversial book" even "before its release" (3), particularly due to "Napoleon's attitudes about black people" (4). "Sensitive readers" are forewarned about these "deeply disturbing" passages (4), and Napoleon himself is diagnosed "as [a] victim of racist acts" who "identifies more with his oppressors than he does with the oppressed": "The vivid scenes of humiliation that the child, Napoleon, endures in school haunt *Flipping*'s narrative like a deeply repressed memory" (5).

The preface is referring to two scenes of racially motivated sexual degradation in Napoleon's past. The first takes place while he was "growing up [as] the only Pinoy around" in Virginia as a prepubescent boy (24). When one of the boys "read[s] that Pinoys eat dog" (24), the Chinese epithets hurled at Napoleon give way to an ultimatum: he can either eat his roasted dog Fido, or perform oral sex on the boys. Napoleon chooses the latter, finishing off "six boys in less than five minutes" (25). The following year, while living in Florida, he is similarly subjected to sexual domination after being called "'gook' every day until after Easter" (27). During that holiday season, a bully learns "about Filipino crucifixions" from a newspaper, and a group of older boys strip Napoleon, tie him to a cross, and urinate on him (27). Rather than incite anger or hatred, these moments of early racialized sexploitation lead to his identification with the "white boys" whom he "revered as gods" (31), as the preface suggests. In the same chapter that he's mock-crucified and pissed on, Napoleon recalls trying "to bleach [his] skin" (31).

Contrary to the preface, however, his reverence toward whiteness is only tenuously connected to his revulsion toward blackness. It is not as though Napoleon picks up his racism from the white characters in the novel. In fact, in response to Napoleon's profuse use of the N-word, Alan states, "You know I don't like that word" (88). Napoleon's racism seems to be an effect of his belief in the inflexibility of desire: gay men should only perform one sex role (top or bottom) and orient their desires toward just one "race."[4]

The publisher's psychologizing of Napoleon's racism not only individual-izes his "political incorrectness," but also renders his "unaware[ness]" of his offensiveness as a form of false consciousness that might be demystified—if not by him, then *over time*. Napoleon's narration is followed by a chapter told by his nephew Felipe that is set during his uncle's funeral (Napoleon dies of AIDS-related complications). The novel's sequencing implies a developmen-tal mode of temporality in which political consciousness-raising increases from one generation to the next—but only insofar as Felipe rejects what he calls "the stereotype of Filipino passivity" (165). "Progress is America's most important product," he states. "In two generations my family has gone from being colonized to servicing white men to being serviced by them—not the fall of the white man. His turning over. Still fucking us over but eager to get fucked. Durable brown dick burrowing up the ass of the empire that is no more" (154). Predictably, Felipe contests white racism and imperialism by flipping the script, declaring his status as a "macho Flip" who penetrates but does not get penetrated by others: "Better to be thought of as a tight-ass. Hard body, hard cock, hard ass" (161). Though he is willing to let "white men, white women, brown men, brown women" suck him off (155), when it comes to blacks, he's more ambivalent: "I'm probably something of a racist, but a lot less so than the rest of my family. I have fucked a few black men and a few have sucked me off. I don't loathe them the way my dad and my uncle did. . . . I'm not repelled, but I'm also not attracted" (155). Felipe, then, is sorta gay, sorta racist, but at least not a bottom "servicing white men."

Given this intergenerational temporality, does *Flipping* leave no vi-able space for the likes of a Napoleon? Despite the evident fun the novel has with displaying Napoleon's rampant bottom pleasures, do his racial fantasies and racist fulminations ultimately consign him to political pos-teriority? As I will suggest in my consideration of the two myths inserted toward the end of the novel, the answer is basically yes. But allow me to indulge in the queer temporal technique of delay and deferral and turn first to *The Disinherited* so that Napoleon's and Pitik's fairy tales can be compared in the conclusion.

Bottoms-up: Romance and Rescue in Manila

Han Ong's second novel *The Disinherited* follows in the trail blazed by his earlier *Fixer Chao* (2001) but trains its satirical sights on the

Philippines rather than New York City. Told through third-person narration, *The Disinherited* describes the forty-four-year-old protagonist Roger Caracera's return from the United States to Manila at the death of his father Jesus Caracera. Uprooted as a teenager and brought by his father to San Francisco, the "dark star" (6) Roger spent his youth engaged in "compulsory delinquency" to compensate for "his schooling and his churchgoing" (16) in the Philippines, later turning to sex with women as part of his rebellion, and winding up two decades later as an adjunct creative-writing teacher at Columbia University. The estranged youngest son is summoned back to the Philippines for the reading of Jesus's will—only to find out, to his astonishment and horror, that his sugar mogul of a patriarch has bequeathed him $500,000. The will explains that the large sum accorded to Roger arises not out of favoritism but to *"help him repair this fundamental inadequacy"* of being ill-equipped to engage the business of life (45).

Disdainful of the Caracera family's class arrogance and ill-begotten wealth (they own a deteriorating sugar plantation in Negros), Roger endeavors to rid himself of the money as quickly and anonymously as possible, as much to spite his family as to wallow in the "pleasure of degradation" that he takes in being an "utter failure" as a writer and more ambitiously as a Caracera (15). He first attempts to repay the debt that he feels his father owes to the mistreated workers in Negros by distributing the money to them. Failing that, he decides to sponsor and coach Donnie Osmond Magulay, a defiant, wary, rising teenage tennis star from humble origins, whom Roger eventually sends to Nick Bollettieri's tennis academy in the United States.

Roger's most concerted efforts at disbursing his inheritance, however, revolve around Pitik Sindit. Years before, Roger had received from his Uncle Eustacio $60,000, which he managed to fritter away in two years. Although he at first thought that the money was transferred from one outcast to another, then later "as a vote of confidence from one gay man to another" (which saddens him since he thinks "that he had taken the money under false pretenses, not being gay" [77]), Roger discovers during his trip to the Philippines that the money was originally intended for Pitik Sindit but redirected to himself in order to protect the family's good name. But Roger's righteous indignation at what he believes is the family's homophobic treatment of Eustacio gets complicated when he learns that Pitik Sindit "turned out to be not a man, not even a young man, but a boy" (141). Though the deceased Uncle Eustacio's intentions toward the boy remain "a complete mystery" throughout the novel (243), and though Pitik barely recalls the man who left him the money, the entry of Roger into Pitik's life gives rise to a host of ethical ambiguities that force us to confront disconcerting questions around age, race, national, and class differences.

In keeping with the analytical view from the bottom, consider the scene when Roger first sees Pitik. Halfway through the novel, Roger tracks down the fifteen-year-old erotic dancer at Madame Sonia's private "House of Beauty and Pain" where a group of foreign white men eagerly await, with plastic containers in their laps, the appearance of Pitik as Blueboy. Roger describes the boy's "moves [as] substandard, not even meeting the minimum requirement for graceless seduction" (151). To Roger, Pitik looks "like an acolyte—trying out moves memorized from a guidebook" (151). Roger soon learns that Blueboy's "ass was the new and—to judge by the men's redoubled efforts—long-awaited attraction" (151). The repulsed/bemused spectator surmises that it is precisely the "undevelopedness of the boy's body and especially the tentativeness and ineptitude of his routine" that serve not as "obstacles [to be] overcome" but as "the very direct routes to the men's desires" (153). Roger's observations imply that Pitik's appeal derives neither from his embodiment of the expert erotic dancer (he is evidently no "macho dancer") nor of the demure "Oriental" stereotype alone. Rather, it is the simultaneous familiar but failed Western approximations (dancing to ABBA in a blue speedo) and "native" submission (once the speedo is discarded) that produce Pitik's attractiveness as a brown youth. The graceless, mechanical dance steps provide crucial reminders that Pitik, for all his cheeks-massaging sensuality, is, at bottom, just a boy.

While this description of Pitik's allure—a performance of earnest artifice, as it were—may accord with the conventions of rice queen tourism, Roger's subsequent query raises the issue of Pitik's own consciousness:

The boy, it was clear, was aware of his expert hold on the audience. He'd been stroking his cheeks for what seemed like an eternity. The music had changed and still he was waxing both buttocks with his palms, turning this way for one end of the audience, that way for the other, this way that

way, again and again. What could he find to think about all the time that
his head was between his legs, near the ground? (153)

What indeed might be running through the boy's head, besides a rush of
blood, face down, bottom up?

Numerous scholars of international gay sex tourism and of gaysian
representation in magazines, guide books, porn videos, websites, and
memoirs have noted the ways that these practices and media construct
and proliferate hierarchical relations of power between West and East,
white and colored, older and younger, wealthy and poor, developed and
underdeveloped by recurring to homo-orientalist topoi of passivity, androgyny, youthfulness, innocence, and charm (see, for example, Boone;
Hagland; Han; Nguyen "Resurrection"; Waitt and Markwell). But what
about the queer Asian youth himself? Discussing the media coverage
of so-called pederasty and pedophilia in Pagsanjan, Philippines, during the filming of *Apocalypse Now* (1979), Greta Ai-Yu Niu notes the
"erasure of the sexuality of those who are designated 'minors', denying
their subject status and rendering them voiceless to describe the range
of dangers and pleasures they may experience" (92). In her analysis of
the construction of the Caribbean "native"—"fetishized as sexual other
at the inauguration of imperialism, now recolonized by white gay capital
through tourism" (68–69)—M. Jacqui Alexander similarly asserts that
the "'queer fetishized native' . . . is made to remain silent within this local
economy in order to be appropriately consumed. . . . [T]his fetish cannot
live and breathe, ideologically that is, for purposes other than the foreign
or the sexual, nor is he permitted to travel" (70). Eng-Beng Lim echoes
these sentiments in his recent exploration of the white man/native boy
dyad across transnational Asian contexts, noting that historically "the
silent native boys [in Western homo-orientalist literature and art] are
represented either as a curiosity, mystery, or source of fascination, their
discursive absence or silence marked by their anonymous faces etched
on paintings and photographs" (5). Shifting critical attention away from
the "compulsory love for the white man" (72), Lim proceeds to ask, "But
what of the Asian boy? Is he always to be the white man's fetish or symp-
tom, the one who is a point of critical interest insofar as he triggers the
white man's complex of defenses and reactions in a racialized state of
mind? . . . What would it mean then to engage the native boy as 'Asian

American,' 'Asian diasporic,' and/or 'postcolonial' in a queer, national, and transnational context?" (143).

Ong's engagement with the queer postcolonial Asian boy in *The Disinherited* is multivalent insofar as Pitik/Blueboy is not, in the end, permitted to travel, but neither is he entirely stripped of agency or incentive. First propositioned and de-virginized at age seven through the mediation of Madame Sonia, Pitik has been dancing and occasionally having sex with "particular fan[s]" for eight years by the novel's present (201). Though he has acquired a long list of admirers, his desires are specific: he goes out only with "foreigners," not Filipinos like the forgettable Uncle Eustacio, and he wants to be "beloved by . . . a Handsome American" who will take him to the promised land (220). As enticements, Pitik augments his youth and androgyny by administering skin cleansers and whiteners and by avoiding manual exertion to "[retard] the onset of roughness and musculature" (199–200). Perhaps most tellingly, he adopts the stage name "Blueboy" from the title of a US porn magazine. Initially humbled that Madame Sonia would group him with the "clean-cut collegiate white boys," "who were, to him, far superior," he eventually concludes that "he was the star. He was the good dancer who made the men lose control" (197). At the climax of Pitik's dance routine, Madame Sonia pours the men's ejaculate, cup by cup, down his backside. In Pitik's mind, foreign adult men are driven to the Philippines not by depravity but by his desirability: "There was something in this country which held them. Sometimes, they called this pull 'love.' In the case of the men Pitik had come across, *Pitik* was the factor" (255).

Pitik's efforts are portrayed not as those of a mercenary callboy willing to wallow in semen for the chance at a new life but of an incorrigible romantic. Dubbing Roger Caracera "Cary Grant" while the man trails the boy to determine where he works, Pitik imagines that Roger's disguise is meant "to obscure his great love for the boy" (204). Even when he finds out that Roger is not gay and isn't sexually attracted to boys (208, 285), Pitik repeatedly interprets Roger's acts toward him—particularly, "buying" him from Madame Sonia and trying to wrest him away from the American Mr. Feingold—as signs of the man's affection. Pitik wants to be treated neither as a "charity" case (216) nor as Roger's "son" when the man enrolls him in St. Jude Catholic school (247). And Pitik goes so far as to concoct scenarios in his mind where Roger might be a "latent homosexual" (245) who simply needs to refocus his "wash of passion" for the Philippines onto himself (256). In short, Pitik wants Roger's money and solicitude "as a measure of Cary Grant's love, nothing less" (220).

What does Pitik think about, then, with his head tucked between his legs? Spatial dislocation and self-division: "He could be dancing in front of dreary, anonymous men, his head bent groundward," while "his soul and heart [are] swaddled in the comforts of his imagined America" (220). And honored distinction: "He wanted America as part of a package that would include, first and foremost, a beloved, a lover who, understanding what he deserved, gave it to him, gave him America, thereby broadcasting his specialness to the world: he had been singled out of an entire nation of hopefuls" (215).

By the yardstick of most progressive politics, Pitik fails miserably; he is the embodiment of embarrassment. His desire for a white wealthy American lover seems to conspire with the neocolonial forces that make gay sex tourism possible and desirable. Can we, though, read Pitik's posterior positionality otherwise? Part of that contextualization, I would argue, needs to account for both international sex tourism and Filipino queerphobia. Poverty does partly explain why the boy engages in sex work. When Roger visits Pitik and his mother in the slum area of Bambang, "He was left with a lingering impression of what Blueboy was trying to gyrate his skinny ass out of" (187). But poverty only partially informs Pitik's fantasies of escape. While Roger tries to extricate Pitik and his mother from their dismal shantytown—setting them up in a middle-class apartment, procuring for them official ID's, teaching them how to use a bank account, enrolling Pitik at St. Jude's: all of which the boy stonily, grudgingly accepts—Pitik himself identifies queerphobia as the root cause of his ambitions.

The novel shifts narrative point of view in part four, hones in on Pitik's perspective, and describes the "special ridicule" he receives at school for being the only student with "days-off privileges" (193). His male classmates mock his exaggerated "sensitivity," putting "their hands to their foreheads and their chests in a pantomime of feminine bereavement, like penitent churchwomen" (193). Pitik endures these effeminaphobic pantomimes with the stoicism and solitude of Job (194). Near the end of the novel, Roger reads an essay on the story of Jonah swallowed by the whale that the boy had written at St. Jude's: "By enduring this signal, novel hardship," Pitik writes, Jonah "had become extraordinary, living into legend" (364).

Pitik thus views his transformation into Blueboy not as a capitulation to sexploitation and objectification but as a means of overcoming the hazards of queerphobia and as a step toward legendary status. As secret revenge against the humiliations suffered at the hands of his peers and neighbors, Pitik faithfully believes that genuine American love will save him:

> As in a fairy tale where evil people had only a momentary reign over the heroine before she delivered, by escaping, the final satisfying come-uppance, he too would show up the teachers, his classmates, his stupid neighbors who were mock-squeamish at the sight of him and his mother. He too would take flight in a carriage, in this instance, a Philippine Air Lines plane that would deliver him abroad to live with a foreigner. This prince would be a white man, one of Pitik's fans so besotted with the boy that he had to have Pitik by his side. . . . Everyone in his old life would finally see him, Pitik, magically princesslike. (199)

This focus on queerphobic hardship, isolation, and "bullying," complicates the usual reasons provided for youth sex work: foreign tourism, military occupation, poverty, and putative "cultural norms" that condone child sex work with parental approval (for example, *Pom Pom*; Zafft and Tidball). While the gay tourist website *Utopia Asia* declares that "Filipino gays are usually fully integrated into their extended families and live in a society that is generally tolerant and inclusive of GLBT" people ("Travel and Resources: Philippines"), *The Disinherited* shows that such statements are optimistic at best.

Here, then, we enter the fraught terrain that scholars of both queer sex tourism abroad and queer sexual asylum in Western countries confront from opposite ends of analysis (on the latter, see Epps et al.; Luibhéid and Cantú). On the one hand, the "Third World" is seen as relatively less tolerant toward nonnormative genders and sexualities than the "First World," while simultaneously serving as a notorious sexual playground for Westerners' "illicit" desires. On the other hand, the West's progressive freedoms and protections are predicated on homonormative moral prohibitions against desires and liaisons that do not adhere to the "modern" ideal of "egalitarian relations" that are "exclusive, lifelong, companionate, romantic, and mutual" (Sinfield 59).

The white American self-identified "lover of boys" Mr. Feingold, who courts Pitik, voices some of these contradictory ascriptions. He declares to Roger: "In a few respects, America is not the First World. . . . It has its backward aspects too" (282). In response, Roger articulates the normative position toward cross-age, interracial relations, loathing the "mismatch" between Feingold and Pitik—a "contrast [that] spoke not of a custodial, protective union but rather of the relationship between master and slave, . . . between hunter and prey" (286–87). Roger damns Feingold for being so "clearly" American, "prosperous, oblivious," and "giant," while Pitik is "so junior, unformed, unprotected, so eager to be swept up" (287).

And yet, Roger characteristically changes his mind about Feingold later when he realizes that the most emotion he (Roger) can summon for Pitik is pity, not love. Three times Feingold comes to Roger's upscale Makati apartment, where Pitik has gone after leaving the American, pleading for the boy's return. Feingold explains that he had "abandoned" his closeted life in Altadena, California, waiting for his father to die so "he could finally pursue his dream and flee for more tolerant locales, such as Thailand and the Philippines" (321). Again, Feingold echoes his notion that America is "backward" compared to Southeast Asia when it comes to man-boy relationships. While Feingold's treatment of Pitik in public vacillates between fawning patron and corrective grammar instructor, Ong hints that his "generosity" comes with strings attached. Previously, Feingold had refused to hand Pitik over to Roger, "dragging along the boy, who was suddenly seen to be unhappy. Perhaps the boy's pants were uncomfortable, for his walk looked obstructed, hemorrhoidal" (286). Despite himself and this indication that Pitik's bottoming is discomforting, Roger later relaxes his "initial moral outrage at Feingold's 'tendencies'" due to the man's "emotionalism, his easy tears and willingness to humiliate himself by naked pleading" (322). This wet "badge of shaming love" transforms Feingold's "pederasty" in Roger's view "into something more forgivable" (322).

Whatever we might make of Feingold's weepy supplications and Roger's relenting attitude, it is evident that what *Pitik* wants is the whole package: love, money, a handsome white American man, and America itself. In the end, however, Roger leaves Pitik in his apartment, returns to New York, and discovers six months later, when he comes back to the Philippines, that Pitik is dead. Several weeks after Roger's departure, Pitik had located the residence of one of Roger's aunts, planted himself in front of the gate, and screamed at passing cars, upbraiding the family for keeping them apart. Two days later, rumors proliferate of the boy's murder or suicide and the botched police investigation.

Postscript: On Filipino Fairy Tales

The queer protagonists of *Flipping* and *The Disinherited* both die. To paraphrase Ana Castillo, to those "for whom there is no kindness in their hearts for [young men] who ha[ve] enjoyed life" (33) or tried to enjoy life—especially if that enjoyment partakes of willing bottomhood— these deaths may come as satisfying conclusions. But interpreting the novels in this way reads them as morality tales: Napoleon and Pitik get their due comeuppance, as *The Disinherited*'s narrator might say, shutting down any alternative knowledges generated by their desires. To reframe my opening concerns by recurring to the least likely diasporic Filipino writer to enter a discussion of Pinoy posteriority, consider these words from Carey McWilliams's introduction to the 1973 reissue of Carlos Bulosan's *America Is in the Heart* (1946): "One of the best ways to view and understand a society is to see it from the bottom looking up. To be sure, the underview is incomplete. Bottom dogs see, know, and learn a lot but their perspective is limited. But they see more, I have come to believe, than those who occupy the middle and upper reaches; their view is less inhibited, less circumscribed" (xx). Whereas Bulosan's "underview" focuses on colonial, racial, class, and heterosexual exploitations, Ramos and Ong thread those issues with explicit same-sex content in postwar US and Philippine contexts. What do these "less inhibited" perspectives "from the bottom looking up" enable us to see?

Resuming my deferred discussion of *Flipping*, the novel unexpectedly includes two fairy tales that embrace the Pinoy bottom. The first, placed between Napoleon's and Felipe's narratives, appears to be a sort of allegory of AIDS in which the "young Filipino-American queen" Anggo escapes the evil spirit feeding on human flesh in San Francisco by fleeing to Mindanao where he is protected by Amtulao, the hung and horny Filipino warrior (145). Anggo's happiness contrasts directly with Napoleon's failure to fulfill his fantasy: "Anggo could not believe that he had finally found a husband. He was even more surprised that he could be in love with a Filipino, and a dark one from the primitive south at that. But there he was, a jungle princess in an enchanted jungle principality. . . . Their life together was a tropical, homosexual idyll" (152). In the second fairy tale that closes the book, the sky god brings together Hudhud, a transgendered cross-dresser who's been locked up in a tower by his sultan father, and Bantugan, a warrior who shows more interest in war than girls. Again, the effeminate *bakla* and the masculine warrior live together in harmony.

Though both tales affirm the Pinoy bottom while reinscribing gender difference, they do so by setting the stories in the Philippines, largely removing the complications of racial difference, and extricating the characters from historical time and placing them in mythical time. As the author Ricardo Ramos himself puts it, "Anggo and Hudhud live happily ever after, because that is how fairy tales end. Nate [Napoleon] and Felipe live in a real world, a real multiethnic San Francisco Bay Area. They get a lot of what they value as pleasure, much of it from white people, but don't inhabit fairy tales" (qtd. in Murray 124). It is as though gay bottomhood is possible and joyous, uncompromised by the social vectors and vexations of racial hierarchy, only within the realm of the Filipino fairy tale.

In contrast to these mythic happy endings, *The Disinherited* abruptly terminates Pitik's embarrassing desires and behaviors. While critical of rescue tales and fairy tales, sexploitation and queerphobia alike, *The Disinherited* can entertain Pitik's relentless aspirations for only so long before transforming his romantic longings—"Love, love, love. In this way, he was truly his age. He was a fifteen-year-old boy, blue with pining" (204)—into heartless, wordless accusations. In the final two pages, Pitik gets to fulfill part of his wish: he ends up appearing, to Roger's eyes, in the World War II film *Fiesta of the Damned* that was being shot while Roger was in the Philippines. Pitik's filmic specter, materializing as "the dead boy's twin," haunts Roger's New York movie-going experience (368). In this regard, Pitik is transported to America but only insofar as his "princesslike" qualities are transmuted into ghostly "implacable" hatred (368). Partly the product of Roger's guilty conscience and partly the novel's critique of American savior stories (*Fiesta of the Damned* portrays MacArthur's "liberation" of the Philippines from Japanese occupation), Pitik's variable presence in the film compels Roger to return to the theater again and again. What haunts Roger and makes "a mockery of the movie" is not a queer, romantic Pitik but a hopeless, hateful one (369). The only Pitik that can, as the concluding sentence puts it, "finally [be] beloved and courted and welcome[d]" by the masochistic Roger in America is this "unsmiling," vengeful figure (369). The Filipino fairy and the tale of his overcoming ridicule and alienation are no more, replaced by a joyless, silent, unblinking apparition. Thus does the novel's political critique return us to the more familiar emotional terrain of revenge—a boy's coy smiles, upturned cheeks, and ardent love effectively and decisively disappeared from view.

Given Napoleon's and Pitik's untimely deaths, we might ask whether Pinoy posteriority has anything worthwhile to bequeath to posterity. The scholarship on queer temporalities has taught us to be wary of relegating bygone events and emotions, acts and affects, to the dustbin of oblivion since they have an uncanny way of returning to haunt the present and future (a notion that Pitik's movie-ghost seems to literalize). The novels' irresolutions notwithstanding, rather than read Napoleon and Pitik as either "anachronisms" of a modernizing queer global culture or as "vestigial aspects" of racial/"Third World" homosexualities, to borrow from Martin Manalansan (18), I would view their desires, practices, and fantasies as contradictory attempts to endure, if not dismantle, the hazards of white supremacy, queerphobia, and poverty. In this respect, these figures deserve less denunciation than understanding.[5]

Instead of taking their deaths, recuperated through myth or spectral retribution, as the final word, I think it's necessary to throw the onus back onto the reader. To find Napoleon and Pitik, at some visceral level, detestable or pitiable for their investments in whiteness, Americanness, butchness, and prosperity and their revulsion toward blackness and Filipinoness is to recognize through that recoil the stark ways that those attributes continue to be valued and devalued. As Bobby Benedicto writes, "Recognition of the involvement and complicity of the subject in the very hierarchies and limits that oppress him requires a rethinking of resistance, a movement away from the exteriorization of oppressors toward a reflexive challenge, a radical reassessment of self-conception" (305). Reframed in this context, condemning Napoleon and Pitik can only take place from a political and epistemic position of superiority, a high-minded knowingness that disavows our own internalizations of these de/valuations. Is the progressive move merely to invert those attributes, substituting "sticky rice" for "rice queen," same-age for cross-age relations, equality for hierarchy? If we wish that they had pursued alternate routes, that their passionate desires were directed elsewhere, then we need to not only reflexively reassess our own self-conceptions but also work toward rendering those alternatives viable and desirable. In the meantime, so long as the social hierarchies delimiting the horizons of racialized and neocolonized queers persist, we can expect the Napoleons and Pitiks to go on their fairy ways.

Notes

Many thanks to the feedback I received at the 2009 American Studies Association meeting, the 2011 Critical Ethnic Studies conference, and the 2012 Disorientations Working Group at the Institute for Research on Women at Rutgers University, where parts of this chapter were first presented.

1. There is scant scholarly criticism on these novels. For brief considerations of *Flipping* and *The Disinherited*, see Murray and Nubla, respectively.

2. My analysis heeds Bobby Benedicto's caution against "the dismissal of individuals who actively identify with notions such as the 'global gay' as victims of a kind of false consciousness promulgated by Western media and global capital" (275), since such dismissals render "the global gay-identified men in the developing world as dupes of U.S. hegemony, stripped of agency" (279). In other words, critiques of the "global gay" image and its supposed world-homogenizing effects wind up positing a local, "authentic" version of non-Western sexuality that the "native" (in Benedicto's case, the contemporary, upper-class, mobile, gay Filipino) is supposed to adhere to and champion over and against the commodified trappings and seductions of Western models of gayness.

3. Darieck Scott analogously theorizes the "bottom" in a black cultural context "to signify the nadir of a hierarchy (a political position possibly abject) and as a sexual position: the one involving coercion and historical and present realities of conquest, enslavement, domination, cruelty, torture, and the like; the other, consent/play referencing the elements of the former" (164). For other considerations of black bottomhood, debasement, abjection, masochism, and the like, see Freeman *Time* 137–70; Reid-Pharr 99–149; and Stockton.

4. I suspect as well that Ramos hyperexaggerates Napoleon's racism in order to make this taboo topic a matter of public discussion. Without forgiving Napoleon's anti-blackness, Ramos is nonetheless quite right that cross-color representation within the realm of queer US cultural production is fairly rare. As his narrator puts it, "The whites mix with the blacks and the whites mix with the yellow-brown, but the blacks and the yellow-brown don't mix" (88).

5. One reviewer of *The Disinherited* claims that Pitik's "first scene, at a sex club in a Manila slum, is disgusting in the extreme, even as it strains credulity" (James).

Works Cited

Alexander, M. Jacqui. *Pedagogies of Crossing: Meditations on Feminism, Sexual Politics, Memory, and the Sacred*. Durham, NC: Duke University Press, 2005. Print.

Benedicto, Bobby. "Desiring Sameness: Globalization, Agency, and the Filipino Gay Imaginary." *Journal of Homosexuality* 55.2 (2008): 274–311. Print.

Boone, Joseph A. "Vacation Cruises; or, The Homoerotics of Orientalism." *PMLA* 110.1 (1995): 89–107. Print.

Butler, Judith. *The Psychic Life of Power: Theories in Subjection*. Stanford, CA: Stanford University Press, 1997. Print.

Castillo, Ana. *So Far From God*. New York: Plume, 1993. Print.

Chuh, Kandice. *Imagine Otherwise: On Asian Americanist Critique*. Durham, NC: Duke University Press, 2003. Print.

Eng, David L. *Racial Castration: Managing Masculinity in Asian America*. Durham, NC: Duke University Press, 2001. Print.

Eng, David L., and Alice Y. Hom, eds. *Q & A: Queer in Asian America*. Philadelphia, PA: Temple University Press, 1998. Print.

Epps, Bradley S., Keja Valens, and González B. Johnson. *Passing Lines: Sexuality and Immigration*. Cambridge, MA: Harvard University, David Rockefeller Center for Latin American Studies, 2005. Print.

Freeman, Elizabeth. Introduction. *Queer Temporalities*. Spec. issue of *GLQ: A Journal of Lesbian and Gay Studies* 13.2–3 (2007): 159–76. Print.

———. *Time Binds: Queer Temporalities, Queer Histories*. Durham, NC: Duke University Press, 2010. Print.

Fung, Richard. "Looking for My Penis: The Eroticized Asian in Gay Video Porn." In *Asian American Sexualities*, ed. Russell Leong, 181–98. New York: Routledge, 1996. Print.

Hagland, Paul EeNam Park. "'Undressing the Oriental Boy': The Gay Asian in the Social Imaginary of the White Gay Male." In *Looking Queer: Body Image and Identity in Lesbian, Bisexual, Gay, and Transgender Communities*, ed. Dawn Atkins, 277–93. New York: Haworth Press, 1998. Print.

Han, Chong-suk. "Sexy Like a Girl and Horny Like a Boy: Contemporary Gay 'Western' Narratives About Gay Asian Men." *Critical Sociology* 34.6 (2008): 829–50. Print.

Hoad, Neville. "Arrested Development or the Queerness of Savages: Resisting Evolutionary Narratives of Difference." *Postcolonial Studies* 3.2 (2000): 133–58. Print.

Isaac, Allan Punzalan. *American Tropics: Articulating Filipino America*. Minneapolis: University of Minnesota Press, 2006. Print.

James, Jamie. "A Strange Magic." Rev. of *The Disinherited*, by Han Ong. *Time,* 13 Sept. 2004. Web. 22 Mar. 2012.

Koshy, Susan. *Sexual Naturalization: Asian Americans and Miscegenation*. Stanford, CA: Stanford University Press, 2004. Print.

Lim, Eng-Beng. *Brown Boys and Rice Queens: Spellbinding Performance in the Asias*. New York: New York University Press, 2014. Print.

Love, Heather. *Feeling Backward: Loss and the Politics of Queer History*. Cambridge, MA: Harvard University Press, 2007. Print.

Luibhéid, Eithne and Lionel Cantú Jr., eds. *Queer Migrations: Sexuality, US Citizenship and Border Crossings*. Minnesota: University of Minnesota Press, 2005. Print.

Manalansan, Martin F., IV. *Global Divas: Filipino Gay Men in the Diaspora*. Durham, NC: Duke University Press, 2003. Print.

McWilliams, Carey. Introduction. *America Is in the Heart*. By Carlos Bulosan. 1946. Seattle: University of Washington Press, 1973. Print.

Murray, Stephen O. "Representations of Desires in Some Recent Gay Asian-American Writings." *Journal of Homosexuality* 45.1 (2003): 111–42.

Nguyen Tan Hoang. "The Resurrection of Brandon Lee: The Making of a Gay Asian American Porn Star." In *Porn Studies*, ed. Linda Williams, 223–70. Durham, NC: Duke University Press, 2004.

———. *A View from the Bottom: Asian American Masculinity and Sexual Representation*. Durham, NC: Duke University Press, 2014. Print.

Niu, Greta Ai-Yu. "'Easy Money in Male Prostitution': An Imperialist *Apocalypse Now* in the Philippines." *Continuum: Journal of Media & Cultural Studies* 14.1 (2000): 91–106. Print.

Nubla, Gladys. "Innocence and the Child of Sex Tourism in Filipino/American Literature and Culture." *Rocky Mountain Review* 63.2 (2009): 233–40. Print.

Ong, Han. *The Disinherited*. New York: Farrar, Straus and Giroux, 2004. Print.

Pom Pom: Child and Youth Prostitution in the Philippines. Quezon City: Health Action Information Network, 1987. Print.

Ramos, Ricardo. *Flipping*. Bangkok and Oakland, CA: Floating Lotus, 1998. Print.

Reid-Pharr, Robert F. *Black Gay Man*. New York: New York University Press, 2001. Print.

Rodriguez, Juana Maria. "Queer Sociality and Other Sexual Fantasies." *GLQ: A Journal of Lesbian and Gay Studies* 17.2–3 (2011): 331–48. Print.

Scott, Darieck. *Extravagant Abjection: Blackness, Power, and Sexuality in the African American Literary Imagination*. New York: New York University Press, 2010. Print.

Sinfield, Alan. *On Sexuality and Power*. New York: Columbia University Press, 2004. Print.

Stockton, Kathryn Bond. *Beautiful Bottom, Beautiful Shame: Where "Black" Meets "Queer."* Durham, NC: Duke University Press, 2006. Print.

Tadiar, Neferti Xina M. *Fantasy-Production: Sexual Economies and Other Philippine Consequences for the New World Order*. Hong Kong: Hong Kong University Press, 2003. Print.

Takaki, Ronald. *Strangers from a Different Shore: A History of Asian Americans*. Rev. ed. Boston: Little, Brown, 1998. Print.

"Travel and Resources: Philippines." *Utopia Asia*, n.d. Web. 21 Mar. 2012.

Waitt, Gordon, and Kevin Markwell. *Gay Tourism: Culture and Context*. New York: Haworth Hospitality Press, 2006. Print.

Zafft, Carmen R., and Sriyani Tidball. "A Survey of Child Sex Tourism in the Philippines." Second Annual Interdisciplinary Conference on Human Trafficking, University of Nebraska, Lincoln, 2010. Print.

12

The Case of Felicidad Ocampo

A Palimpsest of Transpacific Feminism

DENISE CRUZ

By the mid-1930s, Filipina author Felicidad Ocampo had earned her place as one of the men and women featured in the ninth volume of Zoilo M. Galang's *Encyclopedia of the Philippines.* Devoted to the "Builders of the New Philippines," the volume's subtitle alluded to the recent establishment of the Philippine Commonwealth (1935) and the islands' eventual transition to full independence from the United States.[1] As one of the noteworthy Filipinas and Filipinos who were part of this tribute, Ocampo was a logical choice. After all, she was a woman who had "seen much, lived much, and studied much" (Junius II: 59), for she had traveled and worked in the United States, participated in study programs at US universities, and published a number of romance novels. Born in 1900 in Iriga, Camarines Sur, she initially moved abroad as a student in the mid-1920s (reportedly to study law at Columbia University). Brief accounts situate her in varied locations and professions in the 1920s and 1930s; she was a social worker in Northern California, a nurse working with Native American populations in Washington State, a lawyer in Nevada, and a screen writer in Los Angeles (Junius II: Galang, "With Our Writers"). Ocampo's novels drew upon these experiences, and in less than a decade she wrote at least five romances published in the Philippines and the United States. All of them explore various aspects of what I call transpacific feminism, a term that describes the complex processes of how Filipinas responded to multiple imperial and national transitions.[2] Yet despite her inclusion in the encyclopedia's who's-who list, and even though she was one of the most prolific transpacific Filipina writers of her time, the name Felicidad Ocampo would eventually be forgotten, and she would disappear from critical memory in both countries.

In this chapter I present the case of Felicidad Ocampo to model a palimpsestic approach to the archive. In the following analysis, which draws together elements of Ocampo's biography, her strategies of representation, and her feminist claims, I am inspired by the multiple meanings of the word *palimpsest*, which refers to a textual object, scraped off and written over, and, in its verb form, describes the act of turning something into a palimpsest. In these dual forms, *palimpsest* describes, on the one hand, an archive of texts themselves as objects of study—and the continued value of searching for what has gone unstudied or unacknowledged—and, on the other hand, how we critically read these texts. Thus in addition to stressing the value of what the archive offers in terms of its ability to document new realms of knowledge, history, and culture, the metaphor of the palimpsest also emphasizes how we can use the archive and what it illuminates to reconfigure and rewrite the very ways in which we approach literary texts and authorial strategies.[3] A palimpsestic methodology is one that includes recovery, reworking, and reconsideration. For my purposes, such acts of research and reading are crucial to feminist critical practice not only because they include women who have been excluded or forgotten in dominant narratives of Filipina/o history and culture, but also because they reconsider the gendered patterns that have determined our scholarship. The palimpsestic methodology employed below therefore first contends that both transpacific Filipina women and literature were essential to the workings of nationalism and feminism in the early twentieth-century Philippines. But I also argue that this transpacific Filipina's texts offer opportunities to read Filipina/o and Filipina/o American cultural production as intricately connected to the histories of other people of color in the United States.

In previously published work, I have recovered unstudied works of literature and print culture in order to recognize the importance of Filipina women to transpacific geopolitics from the early to mid-twentieth century.[4] In the Philippines, the US occupation (1898–1946) saw the simultaneous emergence of literature in English, movements advocating for independence and women's suffrage, and a persistent fascination with the transpacific Filipina. In the pages of literary magazines, novels, and newspapers, Filipina and Filipino authors responded to increasing numbers of women who quickly matriculated through the new

US-sponsored public university system, traveled to the United States for graduate degree or study-abroad programs, and returned to enter the workforce as professors, doctors, nurses, teachers, and lawyers. Celebrated and reviled, versions of new Filipinas abounded in Philippine texts, from the university coed who was portrayed as easily swayed by her exposure to US education and American popular culture, to the liberated new woman who was the icon of the suffrage movement.[5]

Felicidad Ocampo devoted much of her literary career to imagining these modern girls and new women. She published her first romance novels, *The Lonesome Cabin* (1931) and *The Brown Maiden* (1932) in the United States. A few years later, she began writing serial romances for the journal, *The Philippine Forum,* a monthly periodical based out of Manila, which ran during the initial years of the Philippine Commonwealth and was supervised by the nation's foremost Filipino intellectuals.[6] For these audiences, Ocampo constructed a wide variety of women: a young girl from the rural Pacific Northwest who dreams of life in the big city (*The Lonesome Cabin*); a Filipina who foregoes her elite status in the Philippines to marry a white American *(The Brown Maiden)*; an Irish and Spanish-American mestiza who is a successful lawyer and becomes a congresswoman (*Portia*); an orphan born in the Philippines to white American parents, then raised as a Filipina mestiza and destined to become a doctor (*The Woman Doctor*).[7] On a scale of representational diversity alone, these women present an extraordinary range. Even in all their variety, they are all nevertheless linked by a recurring interest in conflicts between careers and domesticity, a repeated emphasis on anxieties related to motherhood, and a fascination with crossing boundaries of nation, race, class, and gender. Ocampo uses recurring literary strategies to facilitate this exploration, including her complicated representation of mixed-race female characters, or plots that feature women who become involved in close, intimate relationships with immigrant and working-class people.

Despite her productivity as a writer, Ocampo dropped into obscurity for reasons that stemmed not only from the subject matter and aesthetics of the works themselves but also from the publishing climate in both countries.[8] Leopoldo Yabes, one of the first scholars of Philippine literature in English, dismissed her novels in favor of others produced by authors whom he viewed as more aesthetically talented (Yabes). Writing for the *Commonwealth Advocate*, the reviewer Junius II offered a more measured assessment. On the one hand, the review "Brown Maiden Writes" acknowledges Ocampo's importance as one of only a handful of Filipina and Filipino authors publishing in the United States. On the other hand, the article also recognizes the unsteadiness of her work, and the review points to characteristics that diminished their value as "entertaining little tale[s]" that are "clean and moral" (Junius II, 59). But the reviewer also uses Ocampo's case as a means of harshly critiquing the insular literary marketplace in the Philippines, an unfortunate situation that he attributes not to lack of interest on the part of the readers but rather the "indifference" and "apathy of local publishers and booksellers" (60). As a result, the review contends that Ocampo's achievements have remained unknown:

> Little has been said and written about the only Filipino woman writer whose books have been found acceptable for filming. It would be a safe wager to bet that a very small per cent [*sic*] of the Filipinos have ever heard of her. But the people of the Philippines can hardly be blamed for that; the neglect lies rather with the booksellers and publishers in Manila who have failed to call attention to what is being published in and about the Philippines. (59–60)

Though this article takes to task Manila's literary marketplace for relegating authors like Ocampo to obscurity, the content of Ocampo's texts themselves would have made them controversial reading material. Even though Ocampo intended her work to be both entertaining and readable (her genre of choice is, after all, the popular romance), she also used this form to broach some of the most charged issues of her time, from women's rights to race prejudice, from immigration to interethnic and transpacific conflicts, and from mixed-race marriage to the legalization of absolute divorce. Webbed together, these dynamics of publishing, the aesthetics of the texts, the romance form as a genre, and their subject matter further influenced Ocampo's fate.

Presenting and reconsidering a new palimpsest of transpacific Filipina feminism, I return to Ocampo's work to address the oft-mentioned scarcity of texts that account for Filipina experience, especially during the twentieth century. Scholars of transpacific Philippine and Filipina/o

American history have long wrestled with the limitations of the archive. In the United States, migration patterns and immigration restrictions led to numbers of Filipina migrant women that were significantly smaller than their male counterparts. But recent scholarship has illuminated the importance of another group of Filipinas who were also present in the United States, those who like Ocampo were *pensionadas*, students who were funded by the US government or participated in special programs of study.[9] Critics such as Catherine Ceniza Choy and Dawn Mabalon have filled in the historical contours of various forms of Filipina migration during the early twentieth century.[10] Their work intersects with significant recovery efforts by their colleagues in the Philippines, including Thelma Kintanar, Christina Pantoja Hidalgo, Edna Zapanta Manlapaz, and the Ateneo Library of Women's Writings (ALIWW), housed at Ateneo de Manila University, and their focus on accounting for and analyzing the vibrant literary production of Filipinas throughout the twentieth century.

Alongside the objective of archival recovery, however, I also offer a palimpsestic approach to the particularities of Ocampo's texts. Although my interests lie primarily in representations of femininity in a sampling of Ocampo's novels, the analysis also centers on her manipulation of other crossings, including the interaction between an author and her constructed audience, and representational strategies that respond to a complicated network of transpacific politics, race and class relations in the United States, and women's movements in both countries. Drawing upon a rich critical history that has analyzed nineteenth- and twentieth-century writers of color and their use of constructions of race and class to undermine and subvert gendered formations, my discussion centers on Ocampo's crafting of women who form relationships that transgress boundaries, and on her strategic constructions of female characters in ways that carefully broach tumultuous subject matter with her Philippine and American readership.[11] I focus on two novels—the *Lonesome Cabin*, published in the United States in 1931, and *Portia: A Novel*, published serially in the Philippines in from 1936 to 1937. In the first section, I argue that Ocampo responds to tensions among raced and classed communities in the United States; these interethnic and transpacific relations complicate Ocampo's feminist claims. In the last section, I move across the Pacific, to examine how Ocampo must recast the terms of these arguments for a readership in Manila, especially at the height of women's suffrage debates in the Philippines. My recovery and reconsideration of Felicidad Ocampo and her work, then, ultimately offers palimpsests that further contextualize the uneven and difficult imperial histories of race, gender, class, and nation, and compel us to rethink how transpacific Filipinas imagined themselves and other women amid these dynamics.

Ocampo's publication of her novels in the United States was a remarkable feat, especially because during the early twentieth century even accessing the market was extremely difficult for Filipina and Filipino authors. Across the Pacific, writers of Philippine literature in English benefited from a climate that actively encouraged literary production, from the development of university writing programs, to the creation and circulation of literary journals, to formal and informal networks of authors. The publishing situation for Filipinas and Filipinos in the United States was far different, for these men and women often published in small journals dedicated to the expatriate or immigrant community. Working in isolation, they rarely published in book format, and those who were fortunate enough to do so struggled to gain any sort of critical acclaim or financial success.[12]

Moreover, the 1920s and 1930s were not easy years to be a Filipina or Filipino in the United States. In addition to the limited publishing market, Ocampo also had to work against the rising tides of public anxieties surrounding the presence of Filipino and other migrant laborers. Negotiating this politically unstable climate, her US-published novel *The Lonesome Cabin* counters the dominant discourse of benevolent US empire—the notion that the occupation of the Philippines was rooted in altruistic, moral imperatives that would benefit the islands. Drawing upon mutual histories of exclusion and racism experienced by marginalized peoples, Ocampo used the form of the popular romance to consider the opportunities created for rural American and immigrant women, who discover that working in US cities offers them a potential escape route from normative definitions of gender. Yet Ocampo's novels are also important precisely because of their ambiguous treatment of these trajectories, and she presents a woman's exploration of professional and domestic options as no easy task. Thus even though Ocampo's romances end with the requisite marriage between the heroine and the man she loves, these conclusions are rife with uncertainty. Ocampo's version of the popular romance, then, defies the very resolution that is at the heart of the genre's structure.

The Lonesome Cabin tracks a young woman's move from the country to the city. Betty Conrad, the novel's main character, dreams of a life that will take her beyond the porch of her mother's boarding house in a rural part of the Pacific Northwest. She begins the novel confined to the place where she lives and works, and the narrator describes her as a sheltered young woman who has never set eyes on a cityscape, much less traveled across an ocean (28). "Let me take care of myself for awhile," she urges one of her admirers, "I have never been able to live my own life yet. You know what I mean; I have never been free. I am not unhappy, but I want to do something, not very big but something different than just to be a housewife. Something that is worthy to think about, something useful" (17). Betty's life changes completely when she meets a boarder, Arnold Grimm, who secretly falls in love with her and is determined to work behind the scenes to ensure her success. The Conrads relocate to the un-named city nearby, where Betty becomes a secretary, quickly advances in her career, and entertains the dueling affections of her supervisor, Charles Logan, and the lovesick Arnold. These interactions with rich businessmen lead to fantasies that center not merely on romance, love, and marriage, but also include the kind of material life that marrying these men might lead to, the "rare treat of after dinner coffee," and car rides on a gentle summer night (44). Ocampo complicates this plot of upward class mobility with the introduction of Christina Krause, who immediately becomes Betty's professional and romantic rival. Christina's "Spanish jealousy" (52) at first manifests itself innocuously. She is stern and critical of Betty in the workplace, but once Betty clearly emerges as both men's love interest, Christina decides to plot her revenge by wooing Charles. Consumed by her jealousy and passion, Krause is so committed to "play[ing] the game well" (81) that she is eventually unable to control its outcome. In one last, desperate attempt to secure Charles' affections, Christina steals company bonds, frames Betty, and finally, consumed by guilt, falls into a "stupor" (119), and confesses to her crimes.

The Lonesome Cabin, to some extent, does valorize the freedom that comes with city life, education, and a career. But in this novel, a working woman's experience, though perhaps offering a life of financial independence, is not glamorous or easy but rather filled with constant turmoil, difficulty, and anxiety. Moreover, the text indicates that the dangers of singlehood are race and class-based, for it is working-class ethnic women like Christina Krause who are physically damaged by the difficulties of this life. Fueling the plot's more dramatic twists and turns, Christina is completely unlike the other characters because she is the only one who is ethnically marked. The text describes her as a beautiful, striking young woman with German and Spanish heritage. "You are almost foreign, Miss Krause," observes Arnold Grimm at their first meeting (32). This equivocation parallels other referential asides that illuminate Christina's conspicuous yet disarming status as an ethnic other. The novel signals her foreignness not only through her German last name and black hair and eyes, but more importantly through emotions and actions that the text attributes to her racial mixture.

Christina's combination of race-based characteristics serves conflicting purposes in the novel. Two overlapping histories of racial mixture—race relations in the United States and imperialism in the Philippines—ripple through all of Ocampo's novels, especially in her often perplexing construction of mixed-race women, who sometimes appear to be threatening and at others are presented with sympathy and even admiration. A mestiza would have been read very differently in the Philippines, where racial mixture did not carry the same implications as miscegenation in the United States. This dynamic is perhaps best illustrated by the fact that the terms *Filipino* and *Filipina*, in their twentieth-century nationalist formations, connoted something completely different during the years of Spanish rule. Similar to *creole*, *Filipina/o* described people of Spanish descent who were born in the colony.[13] At the turn of the twentieth century, the meaning of this term began to shift alongside developments in Philippine nationalism, and Filipina/o would eventually describe not just Spanish creoles but also came to encompass a larger group of people who were once classed as mestiza/o, *india/o*, *moro* (those who were Muslim), or *infieles* (those of animist beliefs). In part because of the long history of intermarriage in the Philippines, many of Spanish mestiza/o elite were part of a land-owning and powerful class.

The fraught representation of Christina Krause registers the dual contexts of Spanish and US empires in the Philippines, as well as an influx of new women entering the workforce in both countries. Overlaying these historical and cultural influences onto the characterization of Christina, *The Lonesome Cabin* crafts a woman whose combination of Spanish and Southern European traits fuels her extraordinary success in her professional life. Christina, the narrator explains, was "the product of a curious marriage; when her father was touring Spain he met the pretty daughter of a Spanish captain and eloped with her; she had the qualities of both, the Yankee shrewdness and capacity that made her a capable stenographer, complicated by occasional outcroppings of Southern Europe, furious bursts of temper, slow and smoldering vindictiveness, and a passionate nature" (38). Christina's mixture is both advantageous and potentially insidious, for part of her effectiveness in the workplace also stems from her "curious" blending of Spanish and Southern European backgrounds. She is associated with neither farm nor factory, and for much of the text, she is extraordinarily successful and moves through the professional world adeptly. Her productivity, however, also promises to be transformative in potentially dangerous ways, for she "proceeded to change the entire office routine with the thoroughness of a Mexican revolutionary president" (57). Christina's Spanish ancestry ties her to the vestiges of the Spanish elite class in the Philippines, yet her position as a stenographer resonates with the many Filipinas who were graduating from universities, rapidly entering the workforce, and effecting an important shift in class and gendered dynamics in urban centers such as Manila. She thus embodies the anxieties that arose from a transition in class-consciousness, as an elite aristocracy contended with the emergence of a new middle class.

In the above description of Christina as similar to a "Mexican revolutionary president," Ocampo also reveals her awareness of a turbulent political environment in the United States, especially for Southern European, Filipino, and Mexican migrants. Her position in the Pacific Northwest exposed her, without question, to substantial racial tensions that were exacerbated by the rapidly growing presence of migrant Filipino laborers on the West Coast.[14] She defers some of these conflicts onto an alternate ethnically marked body, yet one that does not completely escape anti-immigrant sentiment. Krause's last name ties her to Germans and Southern Europeans, whose large numbers in the United States had also become a cause of concern and led to the legislation of quotas to limit immigration from eastern and southern Europe.[15] Moreover, what appears to be a passing reference to Mexico would have been more notable to a 1930s reader conscious of the increase of Mexican people moving into the United States after the revolution.

The employ of a racially mixed character is also itself a literary strategy. Christina's racial mixture is central to Ocampo's version of a particular form of the romance and its focus on the tragic circumstances of ethnic female characters. Her mixed-race heritage becomes her tragic flaw, and her demise in the novel extends and complicates more familiar constructions of mixed-race characters in United States and Philippine literature, such as the tragic mulatta of African American texts, the traitorous mestiza Malintzín/Malinche in Latina/o and Chicana/o literature, and the doomed María Clara of Philippine nationalist literature. Although these representations of mixed-race women serve a broad range of purposes in literary and cultural production, they point to the ways in which mixed bodies exemplify the permeability of boundaries that define race, nation, and gender. In works of African American literature, the tragic mulatta, as a woman who represents both racial and sexual transgressions, opposes—and thus also often shores up— contrasting definitions of bourgeois femininity (Carby; Goyal; Tate). While the tragic mulatta sometimes serves as an embodiment of the evils of racial injustice and systemic oppression of women, her fate arises not only from these evils but also from her flawed, racially mixed body. As a corresponding symbol of women who confound normative (and often male-orchestrated nationalism), Malintzín, the native woman who supposedly became Hernando Cortes's lover and interpreter, is a figure whose racial mixture represents nationalist and sexual betrayal (Alcalá; Alarcón; Cutter). And María Clara, who originated in Jose Rizal's novel *Noli Me Tangere* (1898), was by the 1930s a cultural phenomenon in the Philippines, a woman who had become a vestige of the lingering traces of traditional Spanish femininity.[16] These prototypes are all rooted in the mixed-race woman's incarnation of a failed commitment to the nation and her transgression of the boundaries that would define a national or ethnic community. Ocampo's characterization of Christina similarly highlights the mestiza as a fascinating yet also threatening combination.

To be sure, Christina's vilification in the novel, at least at first, stems from the racial crucible that leads to her supposedly uncontrollable emotions. Ocampo also uses Christina's character as a means of examining the potential shortcomings of a young woman's desire to be, as Betty terms it, "independent," to have a career, some experience of life in the city, and to live on her own. At the same time, this representation is also steeped in ambiguity, primarily stemming from Betty, who as the novel's center-of-consciousness sympathizes with her rival. I argue that this ambiguity ultimately reveals the complexities of the text's feminist claims, as Christina's plot evolves into a cautionary tale for the novel's white female protagonist. Containing Christina's behavior, the novel projects two different futures for women who essentially have very similar desires. The white female protagonist is the romance's victorious heroine, while the ethnically marked character suffers and is punished. The tragedy of Christina Krause thus serves to also manage this volatile combination, and to sanction a woman who is too ambitious, too desiring, and too indiscriminating.

The vilification of Christina thus shifts in its final pages to a story of a woman whose dogged pursuit of heterosexual love and partnership leads to insanity. Her fall into madness begins with her failed relationship with Charles, continues with her attempt to frame her rival, and culminates in her transformation into a "wicked woman" (119). Her insanity is at first manifested in extreme paranoia, for as she confides to Betty, "I am afraid to sleep, I am always seeing something. I doze for a little, and when I waken [sic] there are people in the room. They stand around the bed and talk about me" (118). In the novel's closing pages, Christina's rants begin to focus on her pregnancy as contributing to her madness. "I wanted [Charles] for myself," she confesses, "and for the sake of the baby which is to be born in the near future. I tried everything to prevent it, but it was too late, and it was the cause of my illness" (119). The pronoun "it" here encompasses many turns of events—including her failed desire and the failed plot to implicate Betty—but "it" most importantly refers to the baby. This shocking revelation leads immediately to Christina's final moment in the text; afterward, "then she went into a stupor" (119).

Haunted by the memory of Christina's damaged psyche, Betty ends up marrying, but she only does so after intense bouts of anxiety, spurred by the frightening prospects of pregnancy and motherhood. These new realities shift marriage, in Betty's mind, from romantic "vision" of wedded bliss into a future that instead "loomed large, almost menacing" (124). Betty's interaction with Christina has taught her, according to the narrator, an important lesson that links marriage to physical and mental degradation, the "law of compensation, that for every joy one pays in suffering; women who married went down into the valley of death for children" (124). The narrator then emphasizes the link between childbirth and the destruction of young women's bodies: "One must love and be loved very tenderly to pay for that. The scale must balance, and there were other things; women grew old, and age was not always lovely. This very maternity was fatal to beauty. Visions of childbearing women with sagging breasts, and relaxed bodies, came to her. That was part of the price" (124). Betty reaches her decision to marry Arnold, then, only after she recognizes "the risk that all women took, with her eyes open" (127). Amid the trepidation surrounding marriage and motherhood in the novel's closing pages, the seeming stability and safe harbor offered in text's final lines seems too naïve. "Looking into his steady eyes," the narrator offers, "she knew that she was safe. She would never wither for him" (127). These final lines not only contradict the psychological anguish that plagues Betty in the previous pages, but their confidence in a woman's ability to stave off the inevitable also clearly describes an impossibility.

In *The Lonesome Cabin,* Ocampo's female characters wrestle with the uncertainties of personal desire, which is often at odds with the ramifications of choosing between professional and more traditional options for women's lives. This fraught exploration of transpacific feminism is further complicated by the overlap of transitions in the United States and the Philippines, as both contended with imperial and national developments that were significantly altering the cultural landscape. In both nations, these changeovers coincided with momentum for women's rights, the growth of educational and career opportunities, and the corresponding repercussions in the lives of women. Employing the sentimentality of the popular romance, Ocampo uses this genre in ways that allow both her mixed-race and white female characters to express emotions and ambitions that are a threat to the order of traditional, elite domesticity, and womanhood in both countries. Christina's success in her career and her uncontrollable ambition thus leads to her undoing, and Betty's desire for independence and her paralyzing fear of motherhood predicts a darker future that belies the engagement that concludes the novel. The oblique representation of Betty Conrad and Christina Krause, characters that embody both the hope for and potential threat of new constructs of femininity, thus imagines a woman's place in the world as vexed and uncertain.

Ocampo extends her tenuous engagement with transpacific feminism in her Philippine publication *Portia*, a novel that takes up some of the most controversial topics in Manila public and print discourse. The novel begins in Reno, Nevada, a location already recognized by the 1930s as a place where couples from all over the world, after establishing a Nevada residency, could obtain quick and easy divorces.[17] In the novel's opening, Ocampo's narrator connects the city known to many as "nothing but a divorce colony" (August 1936, 73) to the novel's production in the Philippines. "Reno," observes the narrator, "is situated on an island of the sea of matrimony, parted in the middle by the Truckee River, which flows from the reef of many causes to the harbor of renewed hopes and possibly more trouble. The tides come in the Southern Pacific and are untied the same way" (73). In these opening lines, Ocampo employs a language of islands and oceans to identify Reno as a cultural locale that is remarkable, a site where marriage is no longer deemed sacrosanct. Her figurative language also draws a map that links this desert landscape to archipelagos in the South Pacific. Imagining unlikely connections between the "divorce colony" of Reno and the former US colony of the Philippines, the text merges the waters of the Truckee River with the unseen harbors and tides of the Pacific. This metaphor figures Reno as a transpacific site, imaginatively tied to the readers in Manila who hold the pages of *The Philippine Forum* in their hands.

The Philippine Forum's inaugural issue appeared in December 1935, only about a month after the formal establishment of the Philippine commonwealth, an act that occurred after more than three decades of US occupation. The editors marked this occasion with an introduction to their readers and a formal statement of the magazine's objectives. The brief articles "Our Greetings" and "Our Purpose" deftly limn the complexities of not only a country in transition but also a dual readership that would have included English-literate elites in the Philippines and American expatriates. Brimming with pride, the editors praise their new nation and its people, yet also recognize the "government and people of the United States through whose generosity unequalled in the annals of colonization the establishment of the Philippine Commonwealth has been made possible" ("Our Greetings," 14). The first issue clearly links the achievement of a key goal for Philippine nationalism to the very emergence of the periodical itself, which the editors "hope[d] . . . may in time become the Nation's monthly" (Our Purpose, 13). "This magazine," they claim, "will seek to reflect dynamic Filipinism and impress Filipino dynamism on public affairs. It will be a vehicle for the free expression of their thoughts and views on different problems. . . . It will be a staunch defender of the rights and liberties of the people. It will do its full part to advance progress" (13). The *Forum's* two-year run included articles on politics, government, and education, as well as brief book reviews and editorials. Contributing authors were both Filipina/o and American. Felicidad Ocampo was one of only a few women on the editorial staff; she also published the periodical's only works of serial fiction.

For the editors and readers of *The Philippine Forum*, the women's movement was part of the periodical's dedication to furthering progress and advocating for greater civil liberties. From 1935 to 1937, the battle over women's suffrage in the Philippines intensified. While the women's vote was on the negotiating table during the establishment of the commonwealth, suffrage for Filipinas was ultimately excluded from the first constitution. Instead, constitutional convention delegates decided to defer the question of women's suffrage until April 1937, when eligible Filipinas where briefly enfranchised in order to participate in a plebiscite that determined whether suffrage would pass. The January 1937 issue of *The Philippine Forum* featured an editorial that championed the women's vote and urged its readers to take part in the campaign. Arguing that "democracy shall become more meaningful when this shall be a government of women as well as men," the *Forum* urged their readers to mobilize: "Liberal men and women have an obligation to the present generation and to posterity. . . . Apathetic women should redouble their effort and energy. Men should cooperate to make the plebiscite on woman suffrage a success" ("Woman Suffrage," 12). Alongside these overt statements of support, the editors also included Ocampo's *Portia*, and they were "glad that the first novel to appear in this magazine should come from a Filipino woman writer" ("Miss Felicidad"). The novel's serial run in the *Forum*—beginning in August 1936 and ending in April 1937, the same month that more than four hundred thousand Filipinas voted in favor of women's suffrage—overlapped with the culmination of this debate.

The correspondence between Ocampo's romance and the arc of progress toward the women's vote, however, is more than just temporal. Indeed, the subject matter of *Portia* is fitting for a readership that, while reading through each installment of the romance, would also be cognizant of the ebb and flow of undercurrents in the suffrage debate. Extracted from the context of its publication in *The Philippine Forum*, the novel's plot, its setting, and its heroine might seem to have little to do with transpacific feminism. Yet even though Reno might initially seem geographically and culturally far afield from Manila, Ocampo's opening lines also illuminate the significance of divorce in the Philippines, especially given the context of women's suffrage debates of the 1930s. Even today, the question of absolute divorce for reasons other than adultery remains a hotly debated issue in the Philippines. In 1936 divorce was becoming especially important because of larger shifts surrounding Filipina femininity in urban centers such as Manila. Many who opposed suffrage saw divorce as inextricably attached to the women's vote, part of a troubling spectrum of women who seemed uninterested in marriage and family.

During suffrage debates, opponents raised the specter of more liberal divorce laws in the United States as a prototype of the dangers of women's liberation. The people of the Philippines should consider, noted delegate Escareal, "America as an example, for it is the country to which our suffragettes refer in order to reinforce their point of view. What is the situation there? What is the mental attitude of all American women? Many American women do not care if they get separated from their husbands. In fact, once in a while, they get a divorce and a brand-new husband, as they get a brand-new automobile" (Constitutional Convention). Although the passage of Act 2710 during the US occupation (1917) meant that Filipina and Filipinos could obtain a divorce on the grounds of adultery, people like Escareal pointed to divorce as part of a continuum that included Filipinas graduating from universities, greater numbers of women in the workforce, and women's suffrage.[18] Such portraits of American women as callously and freely substituting one man for another were critical to arguments that viewed divorce in the Philippines as the horrifying end of the nation's prophesied moral devolution.

How did Ocampo choose to navigate these rough political waters? Avoiding a direct treatment of women's liberation and divorce in the Philippines, Ocampo instead shifts the stage and carefully approaches the construction of the novel's central protagonist; she relocates both the novel's setting and its heroine right into the eye of the storm, a location that itself would have evoked the above sentiments expressed by Escareal. In contrast to the callous American woman who discards one man in favor of another (and the novel certainly does feature white women who do so), Patricia Flynn weighs the repercussions of marriage and divorce with a weary heart. As a divorce attorney in Reno, she is astonished by how quickly and easily men and women decide to end their marriages, and she initially claims that she would prefer to not marry at all. She is nevertheless committed to the goal of becoming a successful divorce lawyer, especially because she follows in the footsteps of her father, a divorce attorney who is so successful that goes by the nickname, "The Great Divide." As a woman who, for much of the novel, is committed to her career above all else, Patricia Flynn's character would have resonated with readers well aware of the controversies about young working women in the Philippines.

Like the earlier presentation of Christina Krause in *The Lonesome Cabin*, *Portia* also links Flynn's racial mixture to her flouting of gendered constraints, as her location in the United States and her implied connections to Filipina femininity provide a method for representing an ambitious young career woman for a Manila readership. In addition to linking the Philippines to Reno through the languages of tides, oceans, islands, and colonies, Ocampo uses racial mixture and religious affinities to code her main character as evocative of Filipina femininity. Unlike Christina Krause, Patricia is clearly the novel's heroine. Her racial mixture recalls potential connections that draw together the Philippines, Spain, and Ireland. The text constructs these associations by evoking first the importance of Catholicism and its importance to these three countries; second, the status of Irish and Filipina/o people in the United States; and third, the elite status of Spanish mestiza/os in the Philippines. Patricia has "dark hair" and "beautiful blue eyes," which had "belong[ed] to the Flynn family way back in Ireland for generations; but the shape of her face and her complexion, the brow and eyelashes, her red lips and appealing smile, she had gotten from her Spanish-Californian mother" (August 1936, 74). The phrase "Spanish-Californian" would have been a crucial distinction for Ocampo's Philippine audience, as Patricia's Spanish heritage would have registered to readers of *The Philippine Forum* as a tie to an elite aristocracy.

Ocampo's mixed-race heroine is a prototype of elite women's independence, but she nevertheless also maintains that this potential career arc cannot be idealized. Instead, the gendered hierarchy of the legal and political world constantly thwarts Patricia's efforts at establishing a career. These difficulties stem not from her ineptitude or lack of experience, but rather the circumstances surrounding her: a world controlled by men and their limited notions of femininity. The narrator often emphasizes Patricia's incredible beauty; she is remarkable, more attractive than any "front line chorus girl or any movie star in Hollywood" (October 1936, 80). When she attempts to counter a rival lawyer's assertion that she won her first case because the judge is partial to pretty young women, Patricia attempts to prove him wrong by camouflaging herself in "cheap tread" heavy stockings and "flat-heeled buckle oxfords" (80). This effort is immediately a failure, and "the most beautiful woman in Reno, in fact the most beautiful woman in the legal world, showed up looking like a caricature on the most important day of her life" (81–82). But Patricia fails not because of how ridiculous her costume is (or the idea that she has to go to these extraordinary lengths to prove her intelligence and skill), but rather because, as she finds out, the game itself is rigged. Despite her efforts to win this legal battle on intelligence and skill alone, Patricia loses because the opposing counsel for the case unscrupulously steals evidence and pays off witnesses.

While Ocampo imagines a woman who transgresses the gendered bounds of the professional world, she nevertheless also maintains that women will find these boundaries increasingly difficult to overcome. Disenchanted with the legal world, Patricia wearily transitions into a career in politics. Ocampo represents this decision as a feminist venture; Patricia runs for US Congress after being convinced to do so by the League of Women Voters, and her victory is a moment of revenge, as the other contender is the same lawyer to whom she loses earlier in the novel. She soon realizes that Washington, DC's political world is similarly frustrating and even more infantilizing than any Nevada court-room. As the youngest representative on the hill, she becomes known among her male peers as the "Baby Congresswoman." Her work in the legislature conflicts with her constant invitations to teas and dinners, and the pressure to dress appropriately and conform to the social codes of Washington (so much so that she has to hire a social secretary just to manage this part of her career). She soon becomes especially "tired of the idiotic smile on women's faces, tired of their chatter, their artificial manners talk [*sic*], their pretensions" (April 1937, 73). Again and again, Patricia's efforts to find success in law and politics are upended by men who dismiss her intelligence and skill, socialites who try to convince her to marry, and the difficult overlap of political and domestic life.

Patricia's difficulties highlight Ocampo's awareness of a Philippine reading audience that was battling with increasing cultural anxieties about Filipina career women who seemed, according to news com-mentary, completely uninterested in upholding traditional notions of bourgeois home life, marriage, and femininity. Given her experience as a divorce attorney, it is no surprise that Patricia has a cynical view of marriage. She firmly "believed that career vs. marriage wouldn't work. And it would never work, except in the very rarest cases where the wife is almost a super-woman, and since she was not, she was afraid to take a chance" (August 1936, 74). However, Patricia also waffles back and forth, and her uncertainty becomes a central conflict of the novel, as she rel-ishes attention from men and is clearly in love with her best friend, yet constantly convinces herself that she must approach any potential in-tersection of marriage and career life as rationally as possible. She tries to think out the options "coolly and from all angles" (September 1936, 79), but in the end she fails to come to a resolution. Ocampo constructs a heroine who approaches this weighty decision with as much care as possible, one who eventually decides to marry but only with great trepidation and after much convincing. Ultimately, she decides that the life of a congresswoman may not be for her. Her increasing disillu-sion is matched by her developing interest in marriage as a substitute: "when the session adjourns she will marry Daniel Caraway and be just a woman, even if she has to come back to finish her term, she'll have Dan always to console her. She saw her failure as a Congresswoman, she saw failure assailed big, strong, brainy men who had already won fame and knew every steps [*sic*] of the way" (April 1937, 63). Patricia's turn to marriage progresses in this heartrending way, as she gradually becomes more and more discouraged by the restrictions of the professional world and begins to consciously accept the plot of marriage and romance. The final pages of Ocampo's novel even shift the text's narrative center, which moves from a perspective that focuses Patricia to one that zeroes in on her aunt. Patricia's last comments about marriage remain uncertain and filled with trepidation. When her bridesmaid asks, "Don't you want to get married?", the nervous bride can't even finish her reply: "I wanted to, and yet I don't know—" (April 1937, 83). These final moments are the culmination of a text that, like *The Lonesome Cabin*, is persistently ambivalent about marriage, even though the novel's heroine agrees to this fate.

Offering a version of transpacific feminism that centers on uncertainty and the lack of resolution, Ocampo theorizes the fraught dynamics of women's liberation, the complex emotions that arise from merging of a woman's desire for a career, and the ambiguity that accompanies them. Each installment of *Portia* meditates on the tremendous challenges a woman encounters as she attempts to fulfill desires and ambitions that conflict with models of femininity, from the ambitious young career woman, to the successful female politician and trailblazer, to the future wife and mother. In the end, there is no easy confluence of these professional and domestic forms. The serial romance serves to illuminate these struggles, and Ocampo's novel offers a play-by-play of the rise and fall of a career woman's difficulties, an ebb and flow that coincided with the unfolding of the suffrage debate on a broader political and cultural stage. The uneasiness that marks this engagement with feminism reveals the complexities of enacting the "more meaningful" democracy that was hopefully envisioned by the editors in January 1937. Rather, the novel is a reminder that achieving large-scale changes in the lives of women will not be so simple, and that the accomplishment of the women's vote would serve as only the beginning of a worthy yet arduous process.

In *The Lonesome Cabin*, *Portia*, and her other published romances, Ocampo explores a central question: What place will the modern working woman have in the future of the Philippines and the United States? In the end, Ocampo's novels do not offer a simple answer to this query, nor do they present a romanticized solution that would effortlessly weave together the threads of transpacific feminism, marriage, and motherhood. Instead, they offer palimpsests that are not readily deciphered, that resist a singular interpretation. These texts demonstrate how one Filipina author wrestled with transpacific feminism in all its complexities, and in ways that addressed both Philippine and US audiences. Their crossings of race, nation, and class also attest to the importance of reading Filipina/o and Filipina/o American history in conversation with those of other marginalized and oppressed peoples. These texts, then, draw attention to how the contexts of early twentieth-century Filipina and Filipino literature and culture are mutually informed rather than isolated. The recovery, rereading, and reconsideration prompted by Ocampo's novels thus provide opportunities to rethink twentieth-century US-Philippine relations in ways that extend beyond the novels' particulars. Indeed, the case of Felicidad Ocampo emphasizes how early twentieth-century Filipinas, so often represented as an undocumented absence, were dynamically engaging the most pressing issues of their time.

Notes

1. This ten-year transitional period would eventually be interrupted by the Japanese occupation.
2. In my previous work, I used "transpacific femininities" to describe a broader constellation of representational strategies, cultural discourse, and authorial practices that, while still focused on the importance of transpacific Filipina women, did not necessarily espouse feminist politics.
3. Postcolonial Studies scholars who have been especially influential to these concluding thoughts include Guha; Stoler; and Burton.
4. My first book, *Transpacific Femininities: The Making of the Modern Filipina*, analyzed connections between the rise of Philippine print culture in English and the emergence of new classes of transpacific women during the early twentieth century.
5. The recurring cultural appearances of these transpacific Filipinas were connected to the global rise of modern female figures in India, Hong Kong, China, and Japan. See Weinbaum et al., *Modern Girl Around the World*.
6. The masthead for the journal includes prominent Filipino figures, such as Maximo Kalaw, Camilo Osias, and Francisco Benitez.
7. Ocampo only published two installments of *A Woman Doctor*, as the periodical ended publication before the novel's run was completed.
8. See chapter 3 of Cruz.
9. See Espiritu and Choy for a discussion of these educational opportunities and their history.

10. In addition to work by the scholars mentioned, see the recovery of texts authored by Filipinas, including Buell; Monrayo; and Panlilio.

11. As I discuss below, I read Ocampo's work alongside constructions in ethnic American (especially African American and Chicana/o) and Philippine literature. My analysis of Ocampo's authorial strategies is greatly influenced by Viet Thanh Nguyen's discussion of resistance, accommodation, and Asian American authorship in *Race and Resistance*.

12. Notable exceptions during this period include Jose García Villa and Carlos Bulosan. For other recent work that focuses on this early period, see Ponce.

13. See Anderson, 227–63; Kramer, 35–86; and Rafael, 19–51.

14. See Ngai; Parennas; Volpp; España-Maram; and Baldoz.

15. These tensions would ultimately have direct repercussions on debates over Philippine independence. Ultimately, legislation for Philippine independence would not be passed in the United States until it was attached to limitations on Philippine immigration. See Ngai.

16. For readings of María Clara, see Arrizón; Cruz; Rafael, "Language, Identity"; Rafael, *The Promise of the Foreign*; and Roces.

17. While couples might have been able to obtain these divorces, they would not have been recognized as legal in the Philippines. See Pamfilo.

18. This act was repealed during the Japanese occupation, and in 1943 Executive Order 141 allowed for divorce on nine grounds (Pamfilo, 422–23).

Works Cited

Alarcón, Norma. "Traddutora, Traditora: A Paradigmatic Figure of Chicana Feminism." *Cultural Critique* 13 (fall 1989): 57–87. Print.

Alcalá, Rita Cano. "From Chingada to Chingona: La Malinche Redefined or, a Long Line of Hermanas." *Aztlán* 26, no. 2 (fall 2001): 31–61. Print.

Anderson, Benedict R. O'G. *The Spectre of Comparisons: Nationalism, Southeast Asia, and the World*. London: Verso, 1998. Print.

Arrizón, Alicia. *Queering Mestizaje: Transculturation and Performance*, 119–53. Ann Arbor: University of Michigan Press, 2006. Print.

Baldoz, Rick. *The Third Asiatic Invasion: Empire and Migration in Filipino America, 1898–1946*. New York: New York University Press, 2011. Print.

Buell, Evangeline Canonizado. *Twenty-Five Chickens and a Pig for a Bride*. San Francisco: T'boli, 2006. Print.

Burton, Antoinette. *Dwelling in the Archive: Women Writing House, Home, and History in Late Colonial India*. Oxford: Oxford University Press, 2003. Print.

Carby, Hazel. *Reconstructing Womanhood: The Emergence of the Afro-American Woman Novelist*. New York: Oxford University Press, 1987. Print.

Choy, Catherine Ceniza. *Empire of Care: Nursing and Migration in Filipino American History*. Durham, NC: Duke University Press, 2003. Print.

———. "A Filipino Woman in America: The Life and Work of Encarnacion Alzona." *Genre: Forms of Discourse and Culture* 39, no. 3 (fall 2006): 127–40. Print.

Constitutional Convention Record: Manila, Philippines 4, no. 78 (October 31, 1934), 534. Print.

Cruz, Denise. *Transpacific Femininities: The Making of the Modern Filipina.* Durham, NC: Duke University Press, 2012. Print.

Cutter, Martha. "Malinche's Legacy: Translation, Betrayal, and Interlingualism in Chicano/a Literature." *Arizona Quarterly: A Journal of American Literature, Culture, and Theory* 66, no. 1 (spring 2010): 1–33. Print.

España-Maram, Linda. *Creating Masculinity in Los Angeles's Little Manila, 1920s-1950s: Working-Class Filipinos and Popular Culture.* New York: Columbia University Press, 2006. Print.

Espiritu, Augusto Fauni. *Five Faces of Exile: The Nation and Filipino American Intellectuals.* Stanford, CA: Stanford University Press, 2005. Print.

Galang, Zoilo M., ed. "Ocampo, Felicidad V." *Encyclopedia of the Philippines*, vol. 9, 445–46. Manila: Philippine Education Company, 1936. Print.

Goyal, Yogita. *Romance, Diaspora, and Black Atlantic Literature.* Cambridge: Cambridge University Press, 2010. Print.

"Greetings." *The Philippine Forum,* December 1935, 13. Print.

Guha, Ranajit. "The Prose of Counter-Insurgency." In *Culture, Power, History: A Reader in Contemporary Social Theory,* ed. Nicholas Dirks, Geoff Eley, and Sherry Ortner, 336–71. Princeton, NJ: Princeton University Press, 1994. Print.

Hidalgo, Cristina Pantoja. *Filipino Woman Writing: Home and Exile in the Autobiographical Narratives of Ten Writers.* Manila: Ateneo de Manila University Press, 1994. Print.

———. *A Gentle Subversion: Essays on Philippine Fiction in English.* Quezon City: University of the Philippines Press, 1998. Print.

———. *Over a Cup of Ginger Tea: Conversations on the Literary Narratives of Filipino Women.* Diliman, Quezon City: University of the Philippines Press, 2006. Print.

Junius II. "Brown Maiden Writes." *The Commonwealth Advocate* 1, no. 10 (October–November 1935): 59–60. Print.

Kintanar, Thelma. *Women Reading: Feminist Perspectives on Philippine Literary Texts.* Diliman, Quezon City: University of the Philippines Press, 1992. Print.

Kramer, Paul. *The Blood of Government: Race, Empire, the United States, and the Philippines.* Chapel Hill: University of North Carolina Press, 2006. Print.

Mabalon, Dawn, and Rico Reyes. *Filipinos in Stockton.* Charleston, SC: Arcadia Publishing, 2008.

Manlapaz, Edna Zapanta. "Filipino Women Writers in English." *World Englishes* 23, no. 1 (2004): 183–90. Print.

———. "Literature in English by Filipino Women." *Feminist Studies* 26, no. 1 (2000): 187–200. Print.

"Miss Felicidad V. Ocampo." *The Philippine Forum,* August 1936, 4. Print.

Monrayo, Angeles. *Tomorrow's Memories: A Diary, 1924–1928.* Honolulu: University of Hawai'i Press, 2003. Print.

Ngai, Mae M. *Impossible Subjects: Illegal Aliens and the Making of Modern America.* Princeton, NJ: Princeton University Press, 2004. Print.

Nguyen, Viet Thanh. *Race and Resistance: Literature and Politics in Asian America.* New York: Oxford University Press, 2002. Print.

Ocampo, Felicidad V. *The Lonesome Cabin.* Boston: Meador, 1931. Print.

———. *The Brown Maiden.* Boston: Meador, 1932. Print.

———. *Portia: A Novel. The Philippine Forum,* August 1936 to April 1937. Print.

———. *The Woman Doctor. The Philippine Forum,* May–June 1937 to July 1937. Print.

"Our Purpose." *The Philippine Forum,* December 1935, 13–14. Print.

Pamfilo, Floralie M. "Ending Marital Inequities and Revisiting the Issues on Divorce: Should it Finally Be Allowed in the Philippines?" *Ateneo Law Journal* 52 (2007): 418–62. Print.

Panlilio, Yay. *The Crucible: An Autobiography by "Colonel Yay," Filipina American Guerrilla.* 1950. Reprinted with an introduction and notes by Denise Cruz. New Brunswick, NJ: Rutgers University Press, 2009. Print.

Parreñas, Rhacel Salazar. "White Trash Meets the 'Little Brown Monkeys': The Taxi Dance Hall as a Site of Interracial and Gender Alliances between White Working Class Women and Filipino Immigrant Men in the 1920s and 30s." *Amerasia Journal* 24, no. 2 (1998): 115–34. Print.

Ponce, Martin Joseph. *Beyond the Nation: Diasporic Filipino Literature and Queer Reading.* New York: New York University Press, 2012.

Rafael, Vicente. "Language, Identity, and Gender in Rizal's *Noli.*" *Review of Indonesian and Malaysian Affairs* 18 (winter 1984): 110–40. Print.

———. *The Promise of the Foreign: Nationalism and the Technics of Translation in the Spanish Philippines.* Durham, NC: Duke University Press, 2005. Print.

Roces, Mina. "Is the Suffragist an American Colonial Construct? Defining 'the Filipino Woman' in the Colonial Philippines." *Women's Suffrage in Asia: Gender, Nationalism, and Democracy,* ed. Louise Edwards and Mina Roces, 24–58. London: Routledge Curzon, 2004. Print.

———. "Women in Philippine Politics and Society." *Mixed Blessing: The Impact of the American Colonial Experience on Politics and Society in the Philippines,* ed. Hazel M. McFerson, 159–84. Westport, CT: Greenwood Press, 2002. Print.

Stoler, Ann Laura. *Along the Archival Grain: Epistemic Anxieties and Colonial Common Sense.* Princeton, NJ: Princeton University Press, 2009. Print.

Tate, Claudia. *Domestic Allegories of Political Desire: The Black Heroine's Text at the Turn of the Century.* New York: Oxford University Press, 1992. Print.

Weinbaum, Alys Eve, et al., eds. *The Modern Girl Around the World: Consumption, Modernity, and Globalization.* Durham, NC, and London: Duke University Press, 2008. Print.

"Woman Suffrage." *The Philippine Forum* 2, January 1937, 12. Print.

Yabes, Leopoldo Y. "The Filipino Novel in English." *Herald Mid-Week Magazine,* September 10, 1941. Print.

13

Hair Lines

Filipino American Art and the Uses of Abstraction

SARITA ECHAVEZ SEE

Contemporary Filipino American artists deploy abstraction as a way to parody both the primitivizing Orientalism of the natural history museum and the exoticizing Orientalism of the art world. Using degradable materials such as soap, erasers, and her own hair to create geometrical lines, patterns, and shapes, the sculptor Reanne Estrada has turned away from illusion and the figural representation of the racialized body as the basis for producing racial art and instead tactically has turned to the formal and the abstract. Such tactics counter the imperial and Orientalist politics of visuality by politicizing the form and medium rather than the thematic content of art. Such tactics also constitute a refusal of a false alternative—that artists of color need produce true or authentic depictions of their communities—and instead propose decolonizing approaches to racial art.

Five years after the publication of Rudyard Kipling's poem "The White Man's Burden: The United States and the Philippines," about twenty million people visited the 1904 World's Fair in St. Louis, Missouri. With more than a thousand live Filipinos on display, the Philippine Exhibit was the fair's most popular attraction. But the spectacular nature of this imperial spectacle has occluded the fact that in 1904 guerilla warfare against the Americans was still ongoing in the Philippine countryside even though the United States had declared the Philippine American War officially over in 1902.[1] The visual display of Filipinos temporally as well as ideologically coincides with the military conquest of the Philippines, a brutal and brutally forgotten war that scholars recently have described as genocidal according to even the most conservative definitions of genocide.[2] Thus, the idea that empire is tightly bound up with vision holds true for Filipinos arguably more so than for any other colonized subjects of the United States. What are some of the consequences of the unique intimacy of this relation between empire and vision in the Philippine example?

This chapter first addresses the contemporary display of timeless Filipino savagery in the American natural history museum, which serves as a useful allegory for the possessive accumulation subtending imperial knowledge, before turning to a discussion of contemporary artists' responses to this history of narrating Filipinos out of history and out of culture. Countering the imperial museum's framing of bodies and artifacts as evidence of a fundamental Filipino lack of history, Filipino American artists have turned away from illusion and from the figural representation of the body as the basis for producing racial art. Highly conscious of the oscillation between hypervisibility and invisibility that has structured Filipino American postcoloniality, artists instead tactically have retreated from the gaze in ways that politicize the form rather than the content of racial art.[3] Such decolonizing tactics enjoin the critic not only to comment on the history and the stakes of contemporary Filipino American art but also to configure history *as stakes*.[4]

Located in Ann Arbor, the University of Michigan's Museum of Natural History is one of three repositories for the university's massive collection on the Philippines. Over 135,000 people visit the museum every year, including twenty thousand school children in groups.[5] Completed in 1928, the gray, four-story building houses a small, dimly lit display on the Philippines tucked away in a corner of the top floor.[6] Climbing up the staircase from the ground floor, the visitor glimpses the very big and very small fossils inhabiting the "Hall of Evolution" on the second floor, and then the feathery and leathery skins of "Michigan wildlife" suspended behind glass on the third floor. A display case devoted to extinct animals stands on the landing between the third and fourth floors. The stretched, parched skins of various nonexistent creatures thus form the prelude to the fourth floor, which displays a series of Native American dioramas followed by the glittering rocks and minerals in the "Geology" room and then finally the tiny Philippine exhibit in a corner of the "Anthropology" room. The logics of extinction and petrification are thoroughly enmeshed with that of primitivism. In ways reminiscent of the spatiality of the 1904 World's Fair, Filipinos are demarcated from the indigenous peoples of the Americas, yet primitiveness flows through the entire floor.

Note how subtly primitivism is built into the very architecture of the fourth floor. The curved shape of the "Anthropology" room—calling to

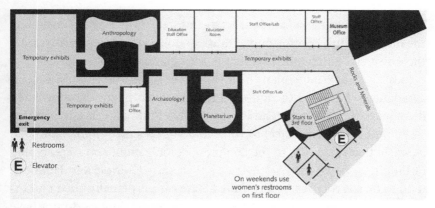

FIGURE 13.1. Floor plan of fourth floor of the University of Michigan's Exhibit Museum of Natural History. Image credit: John Klausmeyer.

mind a kidney or a digestive tract—marks it off from the rectilinearity of the previous rooms (see Figure 13.1). Its wood fixtures and furnishings contribute to a basic theme of roundness and brownness, which together evoke a sense of the organic and the seamless and thus reinforce the idea of the primitive. Only the apertures of the exhibit cases are rectilinear and white, thus declaring that *this is the way to see into the display* and to make sense of the people and objects on show. A hodgepodge of things greets the eye: a large ceramic urn, human teeth, spears, bracelets, and burial items. Alongside late nineteenth-century photographs of gun-toting University of Michigan faculty and students conducting zoological research in the Philippines, these artifacts narrate the daily life of the eternal primitive. These artifacts are visually accessible behind "transparent but impregnable partitions."[7] The visiting schoolchildren know that they are not allowed to touch. They get the message: Look but don't touch. Indeed, the act of "seeing into" the display enables the replacement of the tactile by the visual.

In a sense what actually is on display is the museum's inability to do anything other than simply possess its Philippine connection. The massive size of the actual collection stands in striking contrast to the smallness of the exhibit. It is, simply put, a cache. Moreover, the spatial, architectural, and textual features of the museum's top floor indicates that the museum is at a loss as to how to narrativize and locate the Philippines, especially regarding the university's relation to the Philippines and American imperialism. Indeed, the museum is invested in *not* telling the history of this relationship because to do so would require revealing the university's direct involvement in the colonization of America's first colony in Asia. Producing its own version of America's "confession and avoidance syndrome," the museum tellingly lacks historiography when it comes to the Philippines and instead tells a Philippine lack of history.[8]

Filipinos are thus subject to what could be called a *primitivizing Orientalism* that is specific to the conquest, colonization, and stereotyping of Filipinos.[9] Whereas East Asians, particularly Chinese and Japanese, tend to be stereotyped in the United States as perpetually alien and inassimilable because they have too much culture, Filipinos do not have enough culture. In marked contrast with the excess culture attributed to East Asians, Filipinos are associated with excess embodiment, which can be traced to phenomena such as the display of live Filipinos in a World's Fair more than a century ago and the display of a university's collection today. The recent exhibition *The Third Mind: American Artists Contemplate Asia, 1860–1989* in New York City is a useful contemporary example of the continuing potency in the mainstream art world of this division between the primitive Asian who innately lacks culture and thus offers nothing of aesthetic value and the decadent Asian whose excess culture, on the one hand, subtends permanent racial outsider status for East Asian Americans and, on the other hand, serves as aesthetic inspiration for white American artists, especially those associated with modernism. Given this legacy and predicament, contemporary Filipino American artists have had very little space in which to maneuver should they wish to enter the mainstream art world, let alone counter this history of displaying Filipino savagery. Perhaps unsurprisingly, instead of producing illusionist or figural representational works that seek to show the true Filipino, artists like Reanne Estrada have retreated from the gaze and have become known for works that do not want to be known.[10] It is not the content of art that these artists have sought to politicize, but rather form, and in so doing they have given the critic rich opportunities to reflect on the stakes and conditions of racial art and postcolonial representation in the United States.

Since the mid-1990s the sculptor Reanne Estrada has developed a body of work both as a solo artist and as a member of the feminist Filipina art collective known as Mail Order Brides (M.O.B.). Based in California, she is cofounder of an independent consultancy that designs and develops politically progressive, media-based projects that, for example, foster sustainable forms of community leadership in ghettoized neighborhoods. In sharp contrast with the defined goals of her consultancy and the satirical didacticism of M.O.B.'s critique of the current-day trade in Asian women, Estrada's solo art is quiet and understated. Her solo work features simple, stark geometrical shapes made of degradable, everyday material like packing tape, hair, soap, and erasers.[11] Estrada says that her work is "very physical, very analog."[12] For example, for *Tenuous (tentatively titled)* she painstakingly cuts and shapes polypropylene packing tape into lucent sculptures whose clean sharp lines and florets belie the stickiness of the material (see Figures 13.2–3). In her soap series, she lines soap bars with strands of her own hair (see Figure 13.4). The title *II. One Thousand, One Hundred Eight* refers to the astounding number of hairs, from her own naturally curly mop, that she has coaxed into perfectly straight lines marking a mirrored pair of Ivory soap bars. In her erasers series, she laboriously inks circular gray patterns onto erasers, which in *General Tri-Corn (6)* look like they have sprouted either delicate flowers or disgusting mold (see Figure 13.5).

Estrada works and reworks the ideas of misrecognition, decay, and erasure, a process that constitutes an elaborate retreat from the gaze. She claims that her work is about everyday objects passing for art. But it is a process that can be reversed as soon as one starts using the objects— erasers, soap—for their everyday function. They start to disintegrate and decompose.[13] There is a satirical quality to her erasers series wherein the eraser is marked by the very materials whose markings it is meant to eliminate. According to Estrada, the "agents of their eradication" are also the objects of eradication. She also describes her work as "process-intensive high-relief drawing or low-relief sculpture" that exist "between two and three dimensions" and that "shift between drawing and sculpture." In her hands, "solid three-dimensional things" are transformed into "delicate line drawings."[14] Indeed, in the photograph of *One Thousand*, the deep vertical shadow between the soap bars laterally bisects the whole work and indicates that it is a three-dimensional sculpture rather than a two-dimensional drawing.

This elaborate retreat from the gaze achieves several interventions in the politics of the imperial display of the nonwhite body. *One Thousand* is bi-

FIGURE 13.2. Reanne Estrada, *Tenuous (tentatively titled)*, 2005, polypropylene packing tape on painted wall, dimensions variable, as shown 7.5 x 15 ft. Installation view of *Cut*, Lizabeth Oliveria Gallery, Los Angeles, CA.

sected horizontally by an eerily reconstituted hairline, calling up feelings of simultaneous disgust and pleasure in the viewer. For hair does not belong on soap. Hair defiles soap. The viewer recoils from such a combination of materials even as Estrada makes formally beautiful what is materially abject. Looking more closely at the lettered outlines of the "Ivory" brand in *One Thousand*, we see that Estrada's choice of soap works as a metaphor for the crucial role of racist discourses and policies about sanitation, hygiene, and purity in the maintenance of colonial order.[15] Faintly marked as it is, the soap unmistakably spells out a word that clearly symbolizes the whiteness of colonial law and of aesthetic value. If "ivory" denotes whiteness, it also denotes beauty. The soap series thus recalls the infamous turn-of-the-century cartoons that depict President William McKinley and the new colonial subjects of the Philippines. On the cover of the recent and important collection *The Forbidden Book: The Philippine American War in Political Cartoons* edited by Abe Ignacio et al., the dirty little Filipino must be scrubbed clean by the benevolent white slightly exasperated father-figure.

Estrada also pulls off a thoroughgoing parody of the natural history museum. Encased in a shadowbox sitting atop a pedestal, the soap bars

FIGURE 13.3. Detail from *Tenuous (tentatively titled)*, 2001–6, polypropylene packing tape on painted wall, 10 x 12 ft.

of *One Thousand* mimic the museum's message "Look but don't touch" even as their everyday function calls for them to be touched, picked up, and handled. Moreover, if the protocols of the imperial museum generally require the realist or even literal representation of the Filipino in the form of dioramas, photographs, and human remains, Estrada's work obediently if ironically follows those protocols. The soap is lined, after all, by the hair of the Filipina. The adhesive packing tape picks up her skin. Although at first glance *One Thousand* and *Tenuous* would seem to have nothing to do with either the real or the realist representation of the Filipino, Estrada's clean, sparse lines turn out to be mimicking not only two-dimensionality but also the museum's hyperembodiment of the Filipino. It looks like there is no Filipino, but in fact s/he literally is there. It becomes clearer as to why Estrada calls *Tenuous* an "extended self-portrait": "While making *Tenuous (tentatively titled),* my skin adheres to the tape, embedding and 'encoding' my genetic material within its translucent 'skin' and resulting in a kind of verifiable artist signature."[16] Together these acts of ironized mimicry render visible the racialized processes of primitivizing Orientalism.

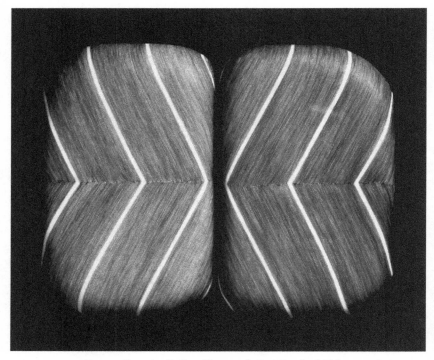

FIGURE 13.4. Reanne Estrada, *II. One Thousand, One Hundred Eight*, 1998, hair on Ivory soap in shadowbox on terry-cloth-covered pedestal, 37 x 10 x 11 in.

Moreover, by turning her hair into a line, Estrada indicates that she is conducting a powerful parody of multiculturalism in the contemporary art world. This particular literalization of the artist's signature involves the transformation of (literal) ethnic content into (abstract) artistic form. Moreover, it imitates the abstract lines and shapes associated with Minimal art. This is a double parody. Firstly, her work exemplifies that undertaken by artists of color—Allan DeSouza and Paul Pfeiffer leap to mind—to reject the multiculturalist demand to produce an ethnic content that can be made easily intelligible and consumable by the viewer. In retreating from the gaze, Estrada turns away from illusion and from the representation of external, recognizable reality, especially the figural representation of the racialized body, as the basis for producing and evaluating racial art. Her minimalist shapes and use of degradable materials propose counterintuitive ways to think about identity as a politics of evading, rather than securing, visibility and legibility. This constitutes

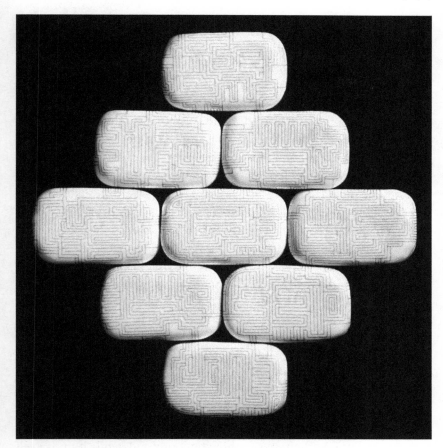

FIGURE 13.5. *General Tri-Corn (6)*, 2003, ink on erasers, 4.5 x 4.5 x .5 in.

a refusal of a false alternative, a refusal of the mandate to produce verisimilitude and images of the real, true, or ideal Filipino. At the same time, it must be said that Estrada's and other artists' of color retreat from the gaze indicates the severity and success of the political right's backlash against oppositional art by sexual and/or racial minority artists beginning in the 1980s of Ronald Reagan's America.[17]

Secondly, the simple act of transforming a hair into a line reveals the complex workings of Orientalism in the art world. The appeal of Estrada's soap series has to do with its stark spare elegance. They are cunning transpositions of Frank Stella's "black paintings," which "incorporated symmetrical series of thin white stripes that replicated the canvas shape when seen against their black backgrounds" and thus exemplify Stella's turn from abstract expressionism to minimalism.[18] In short, they constitute sustained mimicry and even mockery of high modernism. At stake here is yet another indictment of the terms of entrance into the (white) art world. Inclusion in the art world would seem to demand the form or appearance of modernist abstraction. If Estrada is critiquing the art world's multiculturalist assumption that realism rather than abstraction should be the basis for evaluating racial art, then she also is critiquing the corollary assumption: only real (white) artists make real (modernist, abstract) art.

However, as the 2009 exhibition "The Third Mind: American Artists Contemplate Asia" so extravagantly and so haphazardly shows, the spare elegance of high modernism is to be traced to the Far East or, more accurately, to the Orientalism of American artists inspired by particular religious and philosophical traditions in China and Japan.[19] In short, Estrada's *One Thousand, One Hundred Eight* parodies the Orientalist roots of America's modernist aesthetic. Indeed, the interplay between two forms of Orientalism would seem to be at the heart of the modernist aesthetic. If certain aspects of American modernism can be traced not to East Asia but to the Orientalist idea of East Asia as a site of ancient and excessive culture, the Philippines would seem to offer no such idea or culture. Entirely excluded from "The Third Mind," the Philippines figures yet again as nonpresence. Exemplary of primitivizing Orientalism, the Philippines figures as nothing but body and, while it finds itself on display in the natural history museum, it has no such place in "The Third Mind." Let me underscore what is at stake: my point is emphatically not that "The Third Mind" is politically incorrect or unwilling to include all the countries of Asia, but rather that it reveals the intra-Asian dimension of American Orientalism. In juxtaposition with the natural history museum, the art exhibition serves as an example of the interplay between, on the one hand, a primitivizing Orientalism associated with peoples who are subhuman because they have no culture and, on the other hand, an Orientalism associated with peoples who are inhuman because they have too much culture. Thus, Estrada's work shows the complementarity between the racial politics of the art world and those of the natural history museum. Both venues ideologically dictate that Filipinos are innately incapable of making art.

Given this legacy and context, we can see how very little space there has been for Filipino American artists to maneuver in. The artist's use of figural or illusionist representation risks repeating the imperial mandate of fixing bodies in visibility, exemplified by the primivitizing Orientalism of the anthropological museum. At the same time, the artist's turn to abstraction risks double unintelligibility. For example, *One Thousand* could be interpreted as "not Filipino enough" for viewers invested in mimetic forms of racial art.[20] On the other hand, it could be interpreted as "not white enough" or "not (East) Asian enough" for viewers invested in the Eurocentrism of the art world. These are the conditions under which Filipino American artists like Estrada work.

The exceptionally wily and circuitous nature of Estrada's art thus comes as no surprise. Her art trains us not to *look for* illusionist, representational works that configure the Filipino as content. She trains us rather to *look at* the medium, materiality, and form of postcolonial subjectivity. She uses abstract, nonmimetic shape such that "content" recedes as the mode in which Filipino postcoloniality gets represented. Moreover, we are made to look at and not touch what is touched everyday. Unable to touch that which is ordinarily touchable, we also are asked to contemplate the oscillation between two-dimensionality and three-dimensionality, and in so doing we find ourselves considering the content of form. It is crucial to understand that Estrada *uses* abstraction. Abstraction in her work is a practice that lets one see the shape of things, but it also lets one hide things. Through the practice of abstraction, Estrada ensures that there are no easily recognizable or legible signs of identity in her work, and by wrenching identity away from the regime of the visible, she successfully politicizes perception. Perception becomes an unreliable adjudicator of racial difference and racism. It does not yield evidence so easily or directly. It does not precede knowledge but rather shapes knowledge. Rather than shoring up the colonial aesthetic, Estrada insists on producing abstract work that *looks* apolitical. This is an act of infinitival, rather than infinite, meaning production, which relies on relentlessly indirect, circuitous methods. This practice of abstraction entails techniques of camouflage and trickery, wherein the postcolonial artist uses stolen signs from the dominant culture both for and to other purposes.

In his scholarship on the Philippine American War, the historian Reynaldo Ileto has pointed out that Filipinos developed ways of feigning friendship, playing dead, and hiding and waiting. What the Americans derogatorily called "amigo warfare" denotes a Filipino style of resistance, which relied on decentralization from town centers as well as a bicultural mode of living in the towns—friends and collaborators to the Americans during the day and enemies during the night. Ileto speculates that this history "might even explain why Filipinos today seem to be so adept at handling tricky situations that demand shifting or multiple identifications and commitments" (7). But it was "illegal to remember the war," as Ileto baldly puts it.[21] In the encounter with the violence of imperial forgetting, Filipinos have turned to shape-shifting of many kinds. But these sorts of resistance tactics do not lend themselves to memorialization. Such strategies and identities do not lend themselves to history or, more precisely, to historical representation as content.

Yet in their circuitous ways, Estrada and other Filipino American artists nonetheless lead us to an understanding of the relation between race, the aesthetic, and empire. They have understood the historical relation of abstraction to the *real*. As scholars of nineteenth-century American culture like Jenine Dallal have shown, the idea of empire is abstracted from the materiality of conquest and reduced to concepts that can be debated rhetorically in nineteenth-century continental expansionism and early twentieth-century transoceanic expansionism. Indeed, Dallal argues that the expansionist aesthetic became possible only through its detachment from imperial politics and practice: "Aesthetic form ... [is] inscribed by diverse imperial idioms, and [is] set free not *from* but *by way of* these ideological moorings."[22] In 1899 as the conquest of the Philippines was underway, the philosopher William James succinctly described the relation between rhetorical abstraction and what was called "expansionism" in nineteenth-century America:

> The worst vice that an oration or any other expression of human nature can have is abstractness. Abstractness means empty simplicity, non-reference to features essential to the case. Of all the carnivals of emptiness and abstractness that the world has seen, our national discussions over the Philippine policy probably bear away the palm. The arch abstractionists have been the promoters of expansion; and of them all Governor Roosevelt now writes himself down as the very chief. The empty abstractions had unrestricted right of way—unfitness, anarchy, clean sweep, no entanglement, no parley,

unconditional surrender, supremacy of the flag; then indeed good government, Christian civilization, freedom, brotherly protection, kind offices, all
that the heart of man or people can desire. The crime of which we accuse
Governor Roosevelt's party is that of treating an intensely living and concrete situation by a set of bald and hollow abstractions.[23]

Describing abstraction as a "crime," James scathingly condemns the utter
commitment of the "promoters of expansion" to "empty abstractions."
Contemporary artists like Estrada can be said to satirically mimic the
"arch abstractionists" who shaped American colonialism. Thus, the rep-
etition of aesthetic abstraction reveals the historical process of imperial
abstraction. Abstraction emerges as an artistic practice that configures
history as stakes.

What then of the critic? The function of the critic is to repeat the
work of the artist such that history is allowed to emerge and so that the
artist is not doomed to repeat the imperial mandate of fixing bodies in
visibility. Estrada laboriously slices, reassembles, and presents everyday
material in ways that reveal the historical processes of empire and race.
We can see how Estrada parodies both the anthropological museum's
fetishization of Filipino lack of culture and the art world's fetishization
of (East) Asian hyperculture. We can see how the Filipino is rendered
hypervisible in the former and invisible in the latter. In other words, the
artist creates labor where there was none and in so doing accords value
where there was none.

So too must the critic.

Notes

1. The career of Rudyard Kipling's poem "The White Man's Burden: The United States
   and the Philippines" may be said to serve as the literary counterpart to this act of
   visual occlusion. While guerilla warfare against the Americans was ongoing in the
   Philippines, Doubleday published a collection of Kipling's poetry *Collected Verse of
   Rudyard Kipling* that not only excised the poem's subtitle "The United States and the
   Philippines" but also wrongly categorized the poem under the subheading "Service
   Songs—South African War." See *Collected Verse of Rudyard Kipling* (Garden City,
   NY: Doubleday Page, 1911), 215–71. By contrast, in 1940 Doubleday published another
   collection of Kipling's poetry *Rudyard Kipling's Verse: Definitive Edition* that included
   the original subtitle, perhaps not coincidentally in the year that the Japanese expelled

the Americans from the Philippines. See *Rudyard Kipling's Verse, Definitive Edition* (Garden City, NY: Doubleday Page, 1940), 321–23. There are far too many examples of this elision of the subtitle and, hence, of the Philippines in current postcolonial studies scholarship, dominated as it is by accounts of the British empire and by scholars hailing from the Commonwealth. Most recently, Suvir Kaul argues that late twentieth-century and twenty-first-century US wars and occupations in the Middle East should be characterized as American examples of the "white man's burden." Quoting famous lines of Kipling's poem, Kaul clearly does not realize that Kipling's poem addressed American imperialism in the Philippines. The "white man's burden" is originally American and not European. Thus, no such translation or transplantation of the "white man's burden" to the United States is necessary. See Suvir Kaul, "How to Write Postcolonial Histories of Empire?", in *The Postcolonial Enlightenment: Eighteenth-Century Colonialism and Postcolonial Theory*, ed. Daniel Carey and Lynn Festa (Oxford and New York: Oxford University Press, 2009).

2. See, especially, Dylan Rodriguez's *Suspended Apocalypse: White Supremacy, Genocide, and the Filipino Condition* (Minneapolis: University of Minnesota Press, 2010). See also Paul Kramer's *The Blood of Government: Race, Empire, the United States, and the Philippines* (Chapel Hill: University of North Carolina Press, 2006).

3. For an analysis of imperial forgetting on the part of the colonized and the colonizer, see Oscar Campomanes's "The New Empire's Forgetful and Forgotten Citizens: Unrepresentability and Unassimilability in Filipino-American Postcolonialities," *Hitting Critical Mass: A Journal of Asian American Cultural Studies* 2.2 (1995): 145–200.

4. I thank Sadia Abbas for her insights about "history as stakes" in contemporary art.

5. Website of University of Michigan's Museum of Natural History, 23 September 2015, http://www.lsa.umich.edu/ummnh/about/museumfacts.

6. The Alexander G. Ruthven Museums Building is scheduled for demolition sometime in the next five years in order to make way for a new biological science building. The relocation and reconstruction of the museums are scheduled to be completed by 2019. See Kellie Woodhouse, "University of Michigan To Move Museum of Natural History," *MLive Media Group.* 21 February 2014. Web. http://www.mlive.com/news/ann-arbor/index.ssf/2014/02/photo_gallery_university_of_mi_1.html#incart_m-rpt-2. Accessed 23 September 2015.

7. I thank Bill St. Amant for this and many other observations about the design and materiality of the Philippine exhibit.

8. Quoted in Angela Miller, *The Empire of the Eye: Landscape Representation and American Cultural Politics, 1825–1875* (Ithaca, NY: Cornell University Press, 1993).

9. For an analysis of the American idea of the "Filipina savage," see Nerissa Balce's "The Filipina's Breast: Savagery, Docility, and the Erotics of the American Empire," *Social Text* 87, 24.2 (summer 2006): 89—110.

10. I write more extensively about this phenomenon in the work of the Filipino American digital media and installation artist Paul Pfeiffer in my book *The Decolonized Eye: Filipino American Art and Performance* (Minneapolis: University of Minnesota Press, 2009).

11. Estrada's solo work together with M.O.B.'s work were shown in the 2007 pan-Asian American group exhibition "Humor Us" curated by Yong Soon Min and Viet Le at the Los Angeles Municipal Art Gallery in Los Angeles, California. Estrada's solo work took up about 200 square feet of the exhibition.

12. Reanne Estrada, artist's statement, July 2006.

13. Unsurprisingly Estrada says that she is influenced by the work of Eva Hesse in the choice of degradable materials. Reanne Estrada, personal conversation with the author, May 2007.

14. Reanne Estrada, artist's statement, July 2006.

15. For studies of the relation between hygiene, racial purity, and colonialism, see Mary Douglas's *Purity and Danger: An Analysis of Concepts of Pollution and Taboo* (New York: Praeger, 1966); and Ann McClintock's *Imperial Leather: Race, Gender, and Sexuality in the Colonial Conquest* (New York: Routledge, 1995).

16. Reanne Estrada, artist's statement, July 2006.

17. Grant H. Kester, "Ongoing Negotiations: *Afterimage* and the Analysis of Activist Art," in *Art, Activism, and Oppositionality: Essays from* Afterimage, ed. Grant Kester, 1–19 (Durham, NC: Duke University Press, 1998).

18. "Stella, Frank," *Encyclopædia Britannica*, 2009, *Encyclopædia Britannica Online*, 20 April 2009 http://search.eb.com.proxy.lib.umich.edu/eb/article-9069562

19. There are some references to South Asia, but by and large "The Third Mind" focuses on China and Japan.

20. For example, in some Asian American venues, Estrada and Paul Pfeiffer have been accused sometimes explicitly of being "too abstract." Void of unambiguous, overt signs of things Filipino, their art is perceived as having nothing to do with being Filipino, of being formalist, apolitical and anti-identitarian (and, thus, "white"). In such cases, the artist's use of abstraction indicates betrayal of her "roots" or identity.

21. Interview of Reynaldo Ileto in Angel Shaw's video-documentary *Stay the Course*, work-in-progress.

22. Jenine Dallal, The Beauty of Imperialism: Emerson, Melville, Flaubert and Al-Shidyaq, PhD dissertation, Harvard University, 1996, 14. For an article-length version of Dallal's analysis of nineteenth-century American expansionist aesthetics, see Dallal's "American Imperialism UnManifest: Emerson's 'Inquest' and Cultural Regeneration," *American Literature* 73.1 (2001): 47–83.

23. I am indebted to Kimberly Alidio for drawing my attention to James's article. William James, "Governor Roosevelt's Oration," *Boston Evening Transcript*, 15 April 1899, 9.

Works Cited

Balce, Nerissa. "The Filipina's Breast: Savagery, Docility, and the Erotics of the American Empire." *Social Text* 87, 24.2 (summer 2006): 89–110.

Campomanes, Oscar. "The New Empire's Forgetful and Forgotten Citizens: Unrepresentability and Unassimilability in Filipino-American Postcolonialities." *Hit-*

ting Critical Mass: A Journal of Asian American Cultural Studies 2.2 (spring 1995): 145–200.

Dallal, Jenine. "American Imperialism UnManifest: Emerson's *Inquest* and *Cultural Regeneration*." *American Literature* 73.1 (2001): 47–83.

———. The Beauty of Imperialism: Emerson, Melville, Flaubert and Al-Shidyaq. PhD dissertation. Harvard University, 1996.

Douglas, Mary. *Purity and Danger: An Analysis of Concepts of Pollution and Taboo.* New York: Praeger, 1966.

James, William. "Governor Roosevelt's Oration." *Boston Evening Transcript*, 15 April 1899.

Kaul, Suvir. "How to Write Postcolonial Histories of Empire?" In *The Postcolonial Enlightenment: Eighteenth-Century Colonialism and Postcolonial Theory*, eds. Daniel Carey and Lynn Festa. Oxford and New York: Oxford University Press, 2009.

Kester, Grant H. "Ongoing Negotiations: *Afterimage* and the Analysis of Activist Art." In *Art, Activism, and Oppositionality: Essays from* Afterimage, ed. Grant Kester, 1–19. Durham, NC: Duke University Press, 1998.

Kipling, Rudyard. *Rudyard Kipling's Verse*. Garden City, NY: Doubleday Page, 1919.

———. *Rudyard Kipling's Verse*. Definitive edition. Garden City, NY: Doubleday Page, 1940.

Kramer, Paul. *The Blood of Government: Race, Empire, the United States, and the Philippines*. Chapel Hill: University of North Carolina Press, 2006.

McClintock, Ann. *Imperial Leather: Race, Gender, and Sexuality in the Colonial Conquest*. New York: Routledge, 1995.

Miller, Angela. *The Empire of the Eye: Landscape Representation and American Cultural Politics, 1825–1875*. Ithaca, NY: Cornell University Press, 1993

Rodriguez, Dylan. *Suspended Apocalypse: White Supremacy, Genocide, and the Filipino Condition*. Minneapolis: University of Minnesota Press, 2010.

See, Sarita E. *The Decolonized Eye: Filipino American Art and Performance*. Minneapolis: University of Minnesota Press, 2009.

"Stella, Frank." *Encyclopedia Britannica*, 2009. Web. 20 April 2009.

University of Michigan's Museum of Natural History. Web. 23 September 2015.

Woodhouse, Kellie. "University of Michigan To Move Museum of Natural History." *MLive Media Group*. 21 February 2014. Web. < http://www.mlive.com/news/ann-arbor/index.ssf/2014/02/photo_gallery_university_of_mi_1.html#incart_m-rpt-2. 23 September 2015.

14

Eartha Kitt's "Waray Waray"

The Filipina in Black Feminist Performance Imaginary

LUCY BURNS

Eartha Kitt's repertoire of international sounds includes a Filipino trans-lation of a popular Visayan folk song "Waray Waray."[1] She sings a version of this iconic regional tune that is a mix of Tagalog with Visayan words.[2] Eartha Kitt is known to have recorded music in at least ten languages, with "Waray Waray" standing in for the Philippines. Kitt performed the song in wide-ranging venues including Manila's Araneta Coliseum in 1963, and it is included in her repertoire of world music.[3] In a 2006 performance in New York City, Kitt shares an anecdote about perform-ing for Imelda Marcos, where Marcos's male entourage eventually sang along, (albeit) "out of tune"! (Holden) The song became a staple in Kitt's global selection, replete with her playful, sultry, feisty, and theatrical vocal performance. "Waray Waray" celebrates the strength of women from/of Eastern Visayas. The lyrics tell of Waray women's unflinching courage and resilience. This song is identified with a region of Central Philippines, acting as a foil to Kitt's artistic persona as one who embraced and explored female power and sexuality. It is unknown when Kitt first encountered this song and when she first sang it. Here, I am less inter-ested in tracing Kitt's discovery of the song than in exploring what made it possible for Kitt to perform in the Philippines in 1963, and for "Waray Waray" to become such a part of Kitt's recordings of music around the world. More specifically, I am interested in the far-reaching and poten-tially radical consequences of her border-crossing performance.

To articulate these consequences, this chapter tracks the "multidirec-tional cultural flows" in the geography of US cultures of empire as embod-ied in Kitt's performance of "Waray Waray" (Delgadillo). Kitt's rendition of "Waray Waray" raises complex questions about the entanglements of race, empire, and the politics of sound/vocal mimicry. I take my inspiration from Theresa Delgadillo's analysis of Eartha Kitt's version of the song "Angelitos Negros," wherein Delgadillo links the concepts of African diaspora, mestizaje, and borderlands. In this essay, I am interested in the world-making (and world undoing) possibilities for the African American performing body in Kitt's rendition of this song. More specifically, what does this song do to our understanding of Eartha Kitt's black feminist performance? And what does Kitt's black feminist performance offer to our understanding of "Waray Waray"—a song that has had multiple significations in the representational history of Waray women and Filipinas? What I hope to explore are the alliances that make possible a performance such as Eartha Kitt singing "Waray Waray," for the consequences it bears and the consequences out of which it emerges. By consequences, I gesture to the material and imaginative conditions of possibility that are created by and from Kitt's rendition of the song. Neferti Tadiar's formulation of "other Philippine Consequences" is useful here as she underscores the dynamic role the Philippines performs within a larger global economy. In her formative book, Tadiar considers the consequences of the Philippines to the world, specifically to the production/performance of a Free World Fantasy. In confronting the subservience of the Philippines to the United States, as "the intractable object of U.S. (as well as the Philippine) desire," Tadiar also argues for the burden and possibilities the Philippines has on the world.

Eartha Kitt's rendition of "Waray Waray" in the early 1960s signifies a period of transition between US-Philippine imperial relations. Eartha Kitt visited and performed in the Philippines when the country was just over a decade into its status as an independent nation. This was a new era for the United States and the Philippines as each traversed a new terrain. Rather than one of imperial administrator and its territorial acquisition, the United States and the Philippines were learning to negotiate their relationship as two self-governing states. This chapter acknowledges the crucial and shifting roles of cultural exchanges and of artists in international relations, specifically toward the normalization of US-Philippine relations.[4] What meaning might we make in listening to Eartha Kitt's singing of "Waray Waray" in the context of the United States and the Philippines forging new bonds between two sovereign countries?

Indeed, most centrally, I wish to foreground a materialist analysis of this performative act. In other words, I want to attend to material and historical conditions to make meaning of Kitt's "Waray Waray," with a particular concern toward US cultures of imperialism, US-Philippine relations, and black feminist performance. Yet my meditations on such issues hinge equally on my early captivation with the way Kitt inhabits this song. In the recording on which I base my exploration, she is barely able to pronounce some of the words. Unlike her French and Spanish song recordings, noted for her good accent and proximity to native speakers, Kitt cannot be complimented for her Filipino/Tagalog accent. Listening to Kitt sing this song prompts me to engage the politics of vocal/sound mimicry. Her performance of this song inspires a discussion of the politics of vocal/sound mimicry beyond the discourse of becoming (to sound like is to become) and being like (to sound like is to be like), and of exploitation and appropriation.[5] I resist a reading of Kitt's mistakes documented in the audio-recorded live show as incompetence and yet another evidence of American imperial amnesia. Rather the potentiality in her performance is its more disruptive refusal of binary interpretations of Filipinas. The politics of vocal/sound mimicry in Kitt's performance inspires what possibilities lie in dissonance and in approximation rather than in precision. Her rendering of "Waray Waray" provides insight into mimicry as a performance methodology that is not about mastering the other to exhibit one's virtuosity but about exploring the possibility of black feminist performance beyond the black body. The radicality of Kitt's performance is precisely on her not getting it right.[6]

Eartha Kitt's performance of this song embodies the complex management of difference by two independent yet linked nations. For the United States, during this period following World War II and the early years of the civil rights era, Eartha Kitt's international circulation provided a revised profile of America to the rest of the world. Domestically, overseas successes of black women like Kitt signaled a shifting of relations, the possibility of integration and belonging for black people in the United States through cultural entertainment and artistic exceptionality. Her rendition of "Waray Waray" provides an opportunity to further analyze the place of the international in the black feminist performance imaginary. More specifically, the place of "Waray Waray" in Kitt's recordings of global music opens up the discussion of the Philippine consequence in black feminist performance after World War II. For the Philippines, Eartha Kitt's rendition of "Waray Waray" queries the newly independent nation's strategies for managing regional difference against the image of a unified modern nation. More specifically, this song is an instantiation of the smoothing of regional differences as staged on to the shifting terrain of Filipina womanhood. How the Filipina question is constitutive to the national discourse of Filipino identity can be tracked in this regional song's reach to national status and its subsumption in national popular/folk music.

African American Performers in the World

The international performance of African American artists such as Nat King Cole, Duke Ellington, Dizzie Gillespie, and Louie Armstrong attest to the circulation of American culture during the Cold War period. In arguing for the importance of African American culture during the Cold War, Penny Von Eschen emphasizes the contradiction of the image of the United States embodied in and by African American performers on international stage. US officials supported and facilitated international tours for jazz artists such as Ellington, Gillespie, and Armstrong to redirect the image of US racism, "depending on the blackness of [the] musicians to legitimize America's global agendas" (4). Kitt may not have been officially part of this group of artists sponsored by the US government to represent the United States internationally, but her career came to its fruition at this time. State support of African American artists as representatives of American culture in the global scene facilitated Kitt's access to an international audience and performance venues, and to gaining success outside of the United States.[7] Kitt's career prior to her trip to the Philippines and recording of "Waray Waray" was a route mapped on to a larger stage of world entertainment and world politics, specifically of black nationalist politics, of racial segregation, and of US efforts to return to normalcy post-World War II. In the years following World War II, African Americans, like the rest of the American people, were subjected to a rhetoric of normalization. The US State promoted notions of cooperation and common goals to be crucial to postwar prosperity.[8]

Kitt came to performance opportunities outside the United States as a member of the highly acclaimed African American choreographer

Katherine Dunham's dance company, where she performed as a dancer, musician, and a vocalist. Her training prior to gaining scholarship at the Katherine Dunham Dance School at the age of sixteen included piano, choir singing, and theater acting.[9] Katherine Dunham, as is well-recorded, pioneered what is now known as the genre of Afro-Caribbean dance.[10] Thus, in Dunham's company, Kitt was not only introduced to ballet and modern dance techniques but also to Afro-Caribbean rituals, dance, and music. In a recorded interview, Kitt fondly attributes all she knows about dance to Dunham and to the streets of Spanish Harlem ("I was the best rumba dancer in town!").

In the 1940s, as a company member of the Dunham Dance Company, Kitt performed in Mexico, South America, and throughout Europe. She danced, played the drums, sang in the chorus, and was a vocalist. She was a principal dancer in the highly acclaimed *Bal Negre* (1946), described as "A Native Music and Dance Revue in Three Acts and Six Scenes." *Bal Negre* is an epic line up of African diasporic dance that included elements of Haitian corn-sorting ritual, rhumba, *son*, Brazilian *choros*, ragtime, foxtrot, turkey trot, waltz, the Charleston, Snake hips, the Black Bottom. It was also during her years in the Dunham Dance Company when signature pieces such as *Shango* (1945), a staged interpretation of a Vodun ritual, were performed. Kitt was one of the three in *Rhumba Trio*, a number that premiered at the Mexico's Instituto Nacional de Bellas Artes. In 1948, Kitt appeared with the dance company in *Casbah*, a movie filmed in Hollywood, California. Working with Dunham during these years of segregation, Kitt witnessed Dunham confront racial discrimination that they and their audience experienced in US cities and throughout Europe and Latin America.[11]

Kitt came to know the world outside of the United States through her work and travels with the Dunham company. In her autobiography, *Alone with Me*, Kitt laments her ignorance of global politics and her desire to know what is going on in the world. Her desire for a heightened political literacy thus may have influenced her decision to stay in Europe to pursue a solo career. It was on the international stage that Kitt came into her own as a performer, gaining the attention of internationally renown artists such as Orson Welles in the late 1940s. More offers came— theater performances, as a headliner in nightclub acts, music recordings. She found herself performing in European countries including England,

France, Russia, and Turkey. Along with these performances came opportunities to record in different languages including songs in Turkish, in French, and in Spanish.

It is well known that Kitt recorded music in ten languages, and she sang in more. Such linguistic dexterity and cultivated polyglot skills, along with her training in different dance traditions, earned Kitt the (often dubious) honor of versatility as a performer. But more specifically, her celebrated malleability underscored her racialization as a light-skinned black woman. Being cast in roles such as the Catwoman in the Batman television series (from 1967–68) is routinely read as evidence of Kitt's abilities to transcend the color line of American race relations. Instead of simply ceding to such readings of light-skinned black women as politically suspect figures, Kitt's racial malleability could equally be read as a unique and disruptive worldliness attributed to and embraced by and within African Americans' claims to world citizenship after World War II. While such an identification might be perceived as a desire to transcend race and blackness, these claims are also directed at the limitations of American citizenship. The turn to, or identification with, global belonging is among a number of political and social strategies against the continuing assault of black people and American provincialism (not exclusive of one another). Thus a claim to worldliness at this time is an act that simultaneously rejects US isolationism and is also an indictment of American racism that continues to treat and perceive black citizenry as nonequals. Black feminist radical scholar/activist Angela Davis, for example, has long insisted that the struggles of African Americans must necessarily be linked to a broader critique of empire and citizenship. With such worldviews, if you will, Kitt's worldliness cannot simply be flattened into an individual classed cosmopolitanism that sought to transcend racism by imagining a color-blind version of the world.

Catwoman Sings "Waray Waray"

For many Filipinos, this infamous folk song has and continues to showcase the so-called strength of Waray women. Or rather, the Filipino imaginary, in its nationalist fervent to manage strong regional identifications, has mobilized this song to caricature Waray women as *maton* (thuggish), as *masiga* (tough), and as *mataray* (feisty or grumpy). The tune, now considered a Filipino classic, was composed by Juan Silos Jr, with lyrics by National Artist honoree Levi Celerio. The transcription below is a translation of the song as sung by Kitt:

> Waray women will never flee,
> even in the face of death.
> She will fight even the toughest of goons,
> come what may.
> Waray Waray she is called.
> In a fight, she will not back down
> Even if you are a thug.

(Eartha Kitt translates the gist of the song: Tagalog [which she pronounced as "Togalog"]. Women of Waray Waray have muscles of steel, and we can fight any battle. But our kisses are as sweet as wine.)

> We are nature's muse.
> We are always giving
> But Waray women are different
> We do not fear anyone

[Kitt speaks here, possibly addressing the audience, the musicians and/ or the back up singers.]

> We are nature's muse.
> We are always giving
> But Waray women are different
> We do not fear anyone
> Waray women
> Are tough, wherever they are
> They put up a fight
> No matter who provokes them

> Waray Waray (men back up singers sing this part)
> Waray women will never flee
> Waray Waray (men back up singers sing this part)
> Waray women will fight til death

Waray Waray (men back up singers sing this part)
Waray Waray come what may
Waray Waray [til hell freezes over]

We are nature's muse.
We are always giving.
But Waray women are different
We do not fear anyone
Waray women
Are tough, wherever they are
They put up a fight
No matter who provokes them.

Kitt could not have been praised for her ability to sing in Tagalog, as she has been praised for her accents in her Spanish and French songs. Unlike her rendition of "Angelitos Negros," the recorded live version of Kitt singing "Waray Waray" is full of mistakes (mispronunciations, wrong word emphasis, made up words). She even mispronounces the language of the Philippines, calling it "Togalog." She plays with and off of what I hear as mistakes, creatively passing them off as scat singing as if the words are nonsense syllables. Hers is not a seamless occupation of the song through the perfect accent (or not having an accent). Rather, Kitt infuses her idiosyncratic performance persona with or into this song not to demonstrate her chameleonic voice, but to signify the potentialities of performance as it inhabits an (othered) geopolitics and racialization. Kitt's inability or refusal to linguistic verisimilitude redirects her listeners away from the (somewhat stagnant) discourse of authenticity that often charges the politics of sound/vocal mimicry.

Kitt's "Waray Waray" vocalizes Filipinas beyond the *siga, taray,* and sexually repressed *probinsyana*. She performs a playful sensuality that invites her listeners in, without the promise of a release into the languages of nationalism or universality. Writer Ambeth Ocampo was compelled to comment on this sensuality that comes through in the recording: "Listening to Kitt and reading the transcription, I can't make out what she is saying but she makes everything sound so sexy and funny at the same time, adding yet another footnote to Philippine cultural and popular history" (*Philippine Inquirer Opinion*). Prior to one of the longer instrumental breaks in the song, Kitt directs the lover-fighter Waray character that she embodies and vocalizes toward the audience and the musicians. Though not entirely clear in the recording, a back-and-forth exchange between her and the musicians ensues. She brings her sexy persona to this song, a persona that has been stylized as her Catwoman purr. A critical look/listen at performance of "Waray Waray" demystifies Kitt's particular black feminist performance, one that has become synonymous with exotic, animalistic sexuality. For many, as is well documented, Eartha Kitt's playful and rousing embrace of her sexuality refuses sedimented mythologies of black women's aberrant sexuality, situated in histories of slavery and segregation.[12] In Kitt's "Waray Waray," we encounter this playful sensuality more as a creative methodology, mobilized to interpret representations of Filipina gender formation in popular culture. The Philippine consequence in Kitt's "Waray Waray" extends black feminist performance's iconic sexuality beyond black women, refracting it onto a differently yet still racialized Third-World female body.

In listening to Kitt's "Waray Waray," what emerges as insightful (though perhaps not intentional) is another dimension of the Waray woman that breaks out of the dichotomy of the *siga* on the outside yet demure on the inside. This binary characterization of the Waray woman has been immortalized in the popular performances of the late television and film star Nida Blanca (and later passed on and reproduced in her duet performance with on-screen daughter Maricel Soriano).[13] In Nida Blanca's depiction of the Waray woman, the emphasis is on toughness. The Waray woman's rough exteriority hides a gentle, caring, and demure woman who is also ready to give her sweet love to the man who can see through her. To fully appreciate Kitt's "Waray Waray," a discussion of the song's story and its place in the Filipino imaginary must now follow.

Babae ba iyan?: "Waray Waray" and the Filipina Question

This widely known song has made in/famous the reputation of Waray women as possessing a rough shell and holding on tight to a preciously vulnerable inside. A Waray woman is always of humble background, a *probinsyana* (woman from a rural province) who lacks the refined manners of her antithesis—the *sosyal* higher class, urban-bred woman. The song insists that a Waray woman defends herself from any fight, yet her true characteristic lies in her potential to love and be loved by a man. In the mid-1950s, the song gained wider circulation through the film, *Waray-Waray* (1954), starring Nida Blanca with Nestor de Villa. The two starred as young lovers in many movies that proved to be box-office hits. Those years are considered the golden years of Philippine filmmaking, and Blanca's portrayal became a defining image for the Waray woman. The Waray woman is defined by the intersection of her gender, class, and geographic identity (*probinsyana*). Her foil, of course, is the opposite—a man, upper class, an urban sophisticate. He is cosmopolitan in contrast to her domesticated insularity. He is refined, gentlemanly, schooled, and he possesses knowledge of the world while she is crass and tomboy-ish, and she gains her knowledge from the streets, the *palengke* (public market), and her fellow service workers. His sophistication ages him as older; her crudity infantilizes her. Such a developmental character approach sets up her transformation at the end of the story. Along the way, there is some gesture toward the merits of her rawness, a conde-scending gesture toward the value of her local ways that he finds most endearing and might even teach him a thing or two about the world. These transformations, of course, are not of equal value; the entire nar-rative rests on her make over.

The script of opposites becoming ultimately compatible, through a taming of the woman and transforming her into a gentle lady, is not an unfamiliar one. It is also quite familiar that such a script flirts with the feminization of the gentleman and the masculinization of the provincial woman. At some point in the 1954 film, the Waray woman's gender is put to question: "Babae ba iyan?" ("Is that a woman?"). Here, the rec-ognizable *Pygmalion* script is deftly grafted onto the Filipino national narrative. These scripts of conversion become a place to work through the "national question"—What is a Filipino? What is a Filipina? As the Philippines, in the early 1950s, moved away from its former colonial sta-tus and into an independent state, such questions appeared in the col-lective imaginary. Both the song sung by the popular songstress Sylvia de la Torre and the film *Waray-Waray* feminized the national question, thereby illustrating gender as central to the question of national identity. While the expression of anxiety over what is a Filipino takes on the form of the woman question in this film, linking them, it behooves us not to collapse the national question with the question of gender. Gender cannot simply be a metaphor for the development of the nation. Mina Roces has argued for the parallel journeys of the national and women questions, with many points of intersection, even as Filipino feminists have cautioned against the subordination of Filipinas's equality to the project of nation-building. Denise Cruz, in her study on "transpacific Filipinas," details the complexities of Filipina intellectuals' struggle with the question of the nation and women's role during this period of normalization between the United States and the Philippines, post-World II and into the US Cold War period. Cruz argues for "the recognition the transpacific Filipinas['] role in shaping a global code of morality, ethics, and responsibility, one that is quite similar to the sentimentalized processes of U.S. cold war expansion" (26). Yet, whereas Cruz asserts how Filipina intellectuals such as María Paz Mendoza-Guazón and Trinidad Tarrosa Subido mobilized the site of the transnational to infuse their participation in "shaping the global code of morality, ethics and responsibility," the figure of the Waray insists on the place of folk and regional femininities in the future vision of this new nation. Emplacing the Waray woman within the national question and the woman question comes at a crucial time when the Philippine nation must prove itself as a new, coherent modern identity to the world.

The figure of the Waray woman also comes up against the prevailing ideal image of the Filipina at this time—María Clara. Roces argues that the icon María Clara has hovered as the ideal notion of what a Filipina is from the late nineteenth century to the late twentieth century (41). María Clara is the mortal version of *Virgen Maria*, the ultimate symbol of the sacrificial mother. María Clara is a name taken from the character in the writings of Philippine national hero Dr. Jose Rizal; his novels epitomized and sealed this ideal virgin mother in the Philippine popular memory. Against the passive and self-effacing María Clara, the Waray woman is vocal and confrontational. María Clara is "beautiful, virginal, convent-school educated, upper-class heroine, a shy, obedient daughter" (41). She endures her suffering silently; the Waray woman does not accept anything quietly. Against the demure María Clara, the Waray woman seemingly widens the possibility of Filipina embodiment. The María Clara ideal held tightly the standard for being Filipina; the Waray woman offers an alternative, even if simply to dislodge María Clara's singularity.[14] Of course, even these discussions that attempt to widen the possibilities of ideal womanhood already flatten the complexity of gender.

Other Filipina performers, particularly vocal artists who have had formidable international careers, have enshrined the Waray woman firmly in the Filipino popular imaginary. From renditions by Sylvia de la Torre, dubbed as the Queen of Kundiman, to Pilita Corrales, known as the Asian Queen of songs, to Queen of Filipino Comedy Elizabeth Ramsey, this folk song from a province in the Visayan Islands has been a staple in the repertoire of renowned singers. The film version was also revived in the 1980s, starring Nida Blanca's on-screen daughter Maricel Soriano.[15] Soriano's embodiment of the Waray woman draws its inspiration from Blanca's. Soriano, dubbed as the "Taray Queen," was the embodiment of the feisty Filipina. By the time Soriano became heir apparent to Blanca's Waray woman in the 1980s, the Waray has transformed to *taray* (feisty, sharp-tongued, possessing an attitude).[16] Soriano's personification of the *taray* on and off stage became less attached to a regional identity; by the 1980s, the icon of feistiness is an urban-reared smart-mouth who is capable of defending herself against anyone, a self-sufficient, family-supporting, working woman.

While mestiza performers like Sylvia de la Torre and Pilita Corrales were the initial songstresses attached to this song, another mixed-race Filipina, Elizabeth Ramsey, brought her brand of comedy to this song. Ramsey was born to a black Jamaican father and a Filipina mother. Her association with "Waray Waray" maintained its Visayan characterization and highlighted further its comedic potentialities. Emplaced onto Ramsey's blackness, the Waray woman's regional identity becomes racialized. Her *probinsyana* identity becomes a country-bumpkin act. Her regional difference is collapsed with her racial difference. Ramsey's racialization in Philippine media reads much like a description of Eartha Kitt. Her poverty is highlighted, as well as the strict rules by which she was raised and from which she eventually freed. Ramsey and Kitt even entered the performing and entertainment world at the same time, in the late 1950s, and came into their own in the early 1960s. Much is also made of Ramsey's petite frame, similar to the way Kitt's petite body gained attention:[17]

With a career of more than 40 years in showbiz, there's nothing faded about Ramsey, nothing diminished about her. Dark-skinned, frizzy haired, she's got the figure of an 18-year-old. Dressed in three-inch heels and a body-hugging pantsuit with a leopard spotted top, she walks with the supreme confidence of a ramp model, totally oblivious to the stares of those around her. (Lagorta)

Ramsey's "Waray Waray" is often described as an imitation of Eartha Kitt's, even though Ramsey was already a performer by the time Kitt came to the Philippines. Kitt's stamp on "Waray Waray" is also read onto Corrales. Ambeth Ocampo, as he recalls Kitt's Philippine connection upon Kitt's death in 2008, asks, "Sa kanya pala kinopya ni Pilita ang pagliyad-liyad niya?" (Was it from her [Kitt] that Pilipita copied her body bending singing posture? Who copied who? Who is the original?) The natives are copying the foreigner who copied their song. This discussion of mimicry productively illustrates Tadiar's notion of Philippine consequences that structures the principal theoretical arc of this chapter. The kinesthetic and sonar contact between Kitt and the Filipina performers bore traces in the ways they brought meaning to "Waray Waray."

Among the best known of Waray women is the former first lady Imelda Marcos. As the country's most powerful woman, her performance of the Waray navigated the necessary regional character in Filipino politics while advancing a national agenda. She even participated in the debates about the song becoming a stereotype and caricature of Waray women.[18] During the Marcos' reign, Imelda saw herself as bringing beauty to the Filipino people. She worked her appeal as a Waray woman, appearing to have come from and still of the humble origins. The Waray woman, as personified by Imelda, thus became charming and beautiful, though still rooted in her honest *probinsya* roots. Rather than squelching the pull of regionalism so strongly imbedded in Filipino identification practices, Imelda Marcos (and by extension the Marcos government) mobilized her charms to disarm the threat of strong regional affiliations against a unified nation.

Conclusion

Eartha Kitt's encounter with the Philippines at her 1961 concert was brief yet memorable, as noted in a few responses in different forms. Her concert in the Philippines inspired a poem and may have even inspired a defining performance gesture—Pilita's *liyad* (back-arching signature move)—associated with an internationally acclaimed artist. A short film titled *The Women of Waray Waray* explores US-Philippine imperial relations through a character modeled after both Eartha Kitt and Imelda Marcos. The recording of Kitt's "Waray Waray" continues to inspire citation because, for the Philippines, a country that needs to continuously articulate to itself and the rest of the world its consequence, this border-crossing performance seems a rarity.

I have labored here to consider the consequences of Kitt's border-crossing black feminist performance, the ones it emerged out of and ones that it produced. Kitt richly renders this regional song whose consequences are of national proportions. Kitt's enactment of "Waray Waray," as I have analyzed here, bring insights to vocal and sound mimicry as creative labor. More specifically, Kitt's approach to this performing "Waray Waray" challenges prevailing measures by which imitative acts are valued. There is much to be made of the imprecision and mistakes immortalized in the recording of Kitt's "Waray Waray." Her imperfect mimicry is less an act of complete transformation into the object of mimetic act. Not sounding like, in this instance, opens up a larger world of possibilities for black feminist performance.

Notes

1. Included in the album *Eartha Kitt In Person: At the Plaza Live.* Live performance recorded in 1965. Album released October 26, 1994, GNP Crescendo Record Co., Inc.
2. Filipino as the Philippine national language was made official by the Corazon Aquino administration through the 1987 Article XIV, Section 6. Tagalog became the undeclared national language because the majority of the ruling officials spoke this language. In addition, the location of the country's central government is in a Tagalog-speaking region. Filipino, the national language, negotiates the linguistic dominance of Tagalog through the incorporation of native tongues including Pampango, Bicol, Cebuano, Ilocano, as well as other languages spoken in the Philippines such as English and Spanish. For more information on the emergence of Filipino as the Philippine national language, see Pam M. Belvez, "Development of Filipino, the National Language of the Philippines," *National Commission for Culture and the Arts* website, http://www.ncca.gov.ph/about-culture-and-arts/articles-on-c-n-a/article.php?igm=3&i=207. See also Josephine Barrios, "Why Filipino and not Pilipino?"
3. Araneta Coliseum is one of the largest covered coliseums in Asia, and it opened in 1959. It holds entertainment events, including concerts, sports events, and beauty-

pageant competitions. The coliseum hosted Nat King Cole in 1961. Other US artists who have held their concerts there include Carlos Santana, the Black Eyed Peas, and The Pussycat Dolls.

4. My use of normalization to describe this period of US-Philippine relations means to invoke what is referred to as the American period of normalization following World War II and the Cold War. Within the continuing US-Philippine imperial relations, the early 1960s are years following the post-war Republic and its transitional years shifting away from direct US colonial administration. What I call normalization here is how the United States and the Philippines negotiated their new relation as two sovereign nations.

5. Scholarship on the politics of vocal mimesis and racialization have been dominated by a focus on yellowface, a performance practice likened to blackface that is an Orientalist appropriation of what is understood as Asian embodiment. Critiques of yellowface have provided language for cultural appropriation, consumption of racialized bodies by white bodies, and how colonialism, imperialism, indentured labor, and other systems of subordination have produced the conditions that facilitated racist depictions.

Scholars such as Bill Mullens, Vijay Prashad, Claire Jean Kim, Josephine Lee, and Shannon Steen and Heike Raphael-Hernandez propose a shift away from white-black, white-Asian binaries that underpin discussion of yellowface through a formulation that Steen and Raphael-Hernandez offer in their formulation "AfroAsian" and Mullens in his "Afro Orientalism." Mullens, Prashad, and Fred Ho in particular richly represent masculinist AfroAsian coalition traced in figures like Mahatma Ghandi, Bruce Lee, and Malcolm X, as well as in artistic practices like hip hop and jazz and in their invocation of the promise of anti-imperialist coalition between African and Asian states seen in the Bandung Conference of 1955. This essay benefits from the growing critical work on AfroAsian relations as it acknowledges the rare feminist critique in this existing body of scholarship. Thus, this chapter aligns with the work of scholar/artists/feminist/queer activists C. A. Griffith and H. L. T. Quan in their focus on feminist anti-imperialist politics of Angela Davis and Yuri Kochiyama. For a unique creative yet critical approach to Black-Asian relations, see Karen Yamashita's novel *I Hotel*.

6. I wish to acknowledge the work of two scholars that helped me arrive at these ideas. First, there is Daphne Brooks's discussion of Sandra Bernhardt's performance of the failure of white women's embodiment of black women. Second is Laura Kang's critique of "stereotype critiques" that dominated representational analysis in Asian American Studies in the 1990s. Both works push away from valuing what is a correct representation and provide a much more layered insight to the complexity of mimicry as a representational practice.

7. Just two years prior to Kitt's concert at the Araneta Coliseum, Nat King Cole held his concert there. He sang and later recorded a Filipino classic love song, "Dahil Sa Iyo" (Because of You).

8. Abby Kinchy's essay on African Americans and the atomic age provides an interesting perspective on how black communities in the United States were incorporated

into the project of post-World War II normalization via nuclear technology. He writes, "The atomic bomb revealed new possibilities for African Americans to pursue full inclusion in the postwar national project. In contrast to radical critics of nuclear weapons, some black leaders saw opportunities for the advancement of civil rights in the industries and ideologies of the atomic age" (30). Kinchy also situates this pro-nuclear point of view emerging within following era of attacks on anticommunist and radical politics ("African Americans in the Atomic Age").

9. Kitt spent some years in New York's High School for the Performing Arts. There she focused her studies in theater but did not have dance training.

10. Dunham is also a cultural anthropologist whose research on Afro-Caribbean culture included rituals is considered groundbreaking. Dunham put in conversation Afro-Caribbean dance with modern dance, influencing Dance Studies.

11. Katherine Dunham's much-cited vocal resistance to the racism she and her company experienced include a performance in Louisville, Kentucky, in 1944 where Dunham addressed the audience after the show to say that her company would not return until people with her skin color are allowed to sit next to people with the audience's skin color. Another racial discrimination the Dunham company dealt with was when they worked on a film in Hollywood. She was instructed to replace her darker-skinned company members with lighter-skinned ones. Other incidents of racism included difficulty in finding housing in Europe and Latin America. Consistent in the citation of these incidents is the grace and authority with which Dunham addressed discriminatory acts and challenged them. (http://lcweb2.loc.gov/diglib/ihas/html/dunham/dunham-timeline.html#stormyweather; http://fora.tv/2002/06/26/Katherine_Dunham_on_Overcoming_1940s_Racism#fullprogram. See also Clark and Johnson, *Kaiso!*.

12. For a deeply insightful essay on black women's sexuality and slavery, see Spillers, "Mama's Baby, Papa's, Maybe."

13. This excerpt is posted on Youtube by Edric Eustaquio, February 1, 2012. https://www.youtube.com/watch?v=AHznJmfHcj4. The show is *Maricel Live!* Maricel Soriano's Variety Show which aired in 1986 in the IBC network [which was turned over to ABS-CBN Broadcasting Corporation after the EDSA Revolution]

14. Writer Carmen Guerrero Nakpil once pronounced in 1964 that "the idealization of Maria Clara was the greatest tragedy experienced by the Filipino woman in the last hundred years" (cited in Roces 41).

15. Blanca and Soriano were part of an iconic television family comedy, one of the longest-running sitcoms (from 1973 to the 1990s), along with Dolphy Quizon and Rolly Quizon. Blanca played the mother of the working-class Puruntong family and Soriano played the daughter.

16. Films that depict the 1980s version of Waray woman include *Galawgaw*, the *Bote* series, and others.

17. Eartha Kitt's petite frame is immortalized in the healthy-living genre book *Rejuvenate! It's Never too Late*.

18. As an alternative to "Waray Waray," which has become a caricature of the women from Eastern Visayas, Imelda Marcos offered "*ada ada*" (there is something). She

proposed this alternative term of endearment with the intent to maintain the gesture toward a special quality of women from this region. Others retorted that *ada ada* gestures to something worse—"something askew."

Works Cited

Barrios, Joi. Appendix 2. "Why Filipino and Not Pilipino?: A Brief History of the Making of a Language a National Language." In *Tagalog for Beginners: An Introduction to Filipino, the National Language of the Philippines*. N.p.: Tuttle Publishing, 2011.

Brooks, Daphne. *Bodies in Dissent: Spectacular Performances of Race and Freedom 1850-1910*. Durham, NC: Duke University Press, 2006.

Clark, Vèvè, and Sarah E. Johnson, eds. *Kaiso! Writings by and about Katherine Dunham*. Madison, Wisconsin: University of Wisconsin Press, 2005.

Cruz, Denise. *Transpacific Femininities: The Making of the Modern Filipina*. Durham, NC: Duke University Press, 2012.

Holden, Stephen. "Fabled Feline Charms, in Fine Working Order." Cabaret Review, *New York Times*. June 10, 2006. Available at http://www.nytimes.com/2006/06/10/arts/music/10kitt.html. Accessed September 2, 2012.

Kang, Laura. *Compositional Subjects: Enfiguring Asian/American Women*. Durham, NC: Duke University Press. 2002.

Kim, Claire Jean. "Racial Triangulation of Asian Americans." *Politics and Society* 27.1 (March 1999): 105–38.

Kinchy, Abby. "African Americans in the Atomic Age: Postwar Perspectives on Race and the Bomb, 1945–1967." *Technology and Culture* 50.2 (April 2009): 291–315.

Kitt, Eartha. *Rejuvenate! It's Never too Late*. New York: Scribner Publisher. 2001.

Lagorta, Michelle ."Elizabeth Ramsey: A Thousand Laughs in a Lifetime." September 7, 2002. Philippine News Online. Available at http://www.newsflash.org/2002/08/sb/sb002386.htm. Accessed September 2, 2012.

Lee, Josephine. *The Japan of Pure Invention: Gilbert and Sullivan's* The Mikado. Minneapolis: University of Minnesota, 2010.

Maricel Live! IBC. Manila Philippines. 1986. Television.

Mullens, Bill. *Afro-Orientalism*. Minneapolis: University of Minnesota, 2004.

Ocampo, Ambeth. "Eartha Kitt's Philippine Connection." *Philippine Daily Inquirer Opinion*. January 7, 2009.

Prashad, Vijay. *Everybody Was Kung Fu Fighting: Afro-Asian Connections and the Myth of Cultural Purity*. Boston: Beacon Press, 2002.

Roces. Mina. *Women, Power, and Kinship Politics: Female Power in the Post-war Philippines*. Santa Barbara, CA: Praeger, 1998.

Spillers, Hortense. "Mama's Baby, Papa's, Maybe." *Diacritics* 17.2 (summer 1987): 64–81.

Steen, Shannon, and Heike Raphael-Hernandez. *Afro-Asian Encounters: Culture, History, Politics*. New York: NYU Press, 2006.

PART V

Philippine Cultures at Large

Homing in on Global Filipinos and Their Discontents

15

Diasporic and Liminal Subjectivities in the Age of Empire

"Beyond Biculturalism" in the Case of the Two Ongs

FRANCISCO BENITEZ

Going beyond biculturalism would seem by now to be an old call to arms.[1] Asian or American? Both linked by a hyphen? Does one situate one's identity as dominant over the other? Is the function of Asian American Studies to facilitate or critique assimilation into dominant American society? The notion of biculturalism presumes culture can be thought of as a field of communal formations of which there are two primary ones that Asian Americans deploy. What happens when identitarian moves that stipulate identity as communal belonging are questioned by diasporic and transnational transformations—themselves categories that immanently emerge out of particular contexts of struggle? What if in the age of empire the politics of belonging to any community, or even community itself, becomes the problem? In the course of this chapter, I will analyze the notion of subjection and desires for community and intersubjective responsibility manifested in diasporic and transnational subjectivity explored by writers "Chinese Filipino" Charlson Ong and "Filipino American" Han Ong.

Writing about the liminal position of Chinese Filipinos and Filipino Americans in a moment of transnational flows and diasporic displacement, these two Ongs make manifest the problematic construction of relations within and across social fields in an age of empire. Empire may be seen as a globalized ideological form that imputes to itself the legitimate juridical and sovereign source of recognition. Such a notion of empire covers the period of high imperialism that gives us multiple empires competing over a planet that has been turned into a globe—spatially mapped into boundaries and borders and temporally gridded into time zones and date lines—to the contemporary neoliberal moment of US hegemony, and the planetary expansion of liberal democracy at the "end of history." This long historical period also coincides with the march of the nation form, ultraimperialism, and the state mode of production.[2]

The idea of an imperial field, which I borrow from Puerto Rico historian Ileana Rodriguez-Silva, foregrounds the tracks and networks of flows of value, the nodes where such value accumulates, and the structures that arise from this accumulation. These nodes are produced, maintained, and managed by the state or at least the constant threat of state violence. An imperial field combines the idea of imperial formations with Foucaultian ideas of governmentality and its related ideas of "cultivation of the self" or "technologies of the self" as modes by which value is produced, extracted, and accumulated through the proximities and relations that delimit and constitute the imperial field. While still maintaining an awareness of the complex and differential concentration of power and the necessary disciplinary aspects of self-cultivation, attention to the field deemphasizes the old center-periphery frame that privileges metropolitan centers and instead alerts us to flows and movements rather than just to sites. The empire as a state disciplinary form *and* the imperial field that subtends it sometimes work together, and sometimes do not. Diasporic subjectivity requires the constitution of a community in exile, displaced from a homeland, that is constantly consolidating as a community with complex relations to both their host and home nation and states, and depends on the networks and connections generated by imperial incorporation, encounter, and exchange.

Reading selected works of Han Ong and Charlson Ong, I suggest that much which requires our consistent return to arguing against mere biculturalism comes not only from our acknowledgment of the inadequacies of bicultural categories for the interpretation of actual lived experiences, or even from our recognition of how biculturalism entraps us within the very nationalist biases that manifest as the dominant social scripts to which identities are subjected. I argue that the two Ongs suggest our constant return to the problematics of biculturalism stem from our *desire to be given* as well as to *deploy* a coherent subjectivity that emerges out of a set categories and subject positions that often reifies multicultural politics. At the same time, acts of recognition and the subjectivity that depends on them are things we *cannot not* want—even as we "unlearn" the privileges that derive from them through some form of Spivakian "strategic essentialism," or seek out the openings of Chela Sandoval's "cruising, migrant, improvisational mode of subjectivity" that produces a differential or oppositional consciousness in those deemed to lack the cultural capital of the nation-state.[3]

All community formations are imagined and all community formations require a hailing or calling together of community in narratives that generally function like myth. Subjects are positioned and their deployments into relations allow us to form communities and to find the support networks from which to launch collective resistances to the limitations these very scripts impose upon us. I suggest the question of biculturalism may be taken as a figure for how the forces of our subjection are also simultaneously the bases of our subjectivities and our sociality, for how the modes of address and scenes of our interpellation render categories like biculturalism a necessarily provisional moment in our vain attempts to make us fully recognizable to ourselves and to others. Our struggles then toward legibility are necessarily social and desire a certain communicable transparency.

We of course are not transparent but opaque, and our desires always exceed legibility. This opacity means that we are always social in our formation, the materials available to our narrations of ourselves are not of our creation but come from the world and project on to the world. Our opacity also means that something always escapes, something gets beyond our capacities to narrate our stories. Such suggestions mean neither opting for biculturalism, nor simply rejecting outright the parameters given discursive structures have created, *as if* we could somehow completely get outside the conjunctures that define us and the conditions of possibility out of which we and our senses of ourselves imminently emerge. Instead, I suggest that these conditions paradoxically sustain us, even as they constrain us. It is through this bind that I would approach the question of subjectivity in the two Ongs. Here I would like to suggest that their texts offer us insights into three different though linked and overlapping aspects of subjectivity's aporia. In what follows, I suggest that the texts foreground three problematics of subjectivity that emerge from Butlerian scenes of address, iterations of performance, and acts of interpellation: (1) that of our situatedness in particular contexts and social fields; (2) that of our search for human connection through love objects despite, or perhaps precisely because of, differential and singular positioning within these social fields; and finally (3) that of the ethical responsibility the image of the other, particularly the abject or disenfranchised other, demands from us. Perhaps then biculturalism is a name for a specific attempt to turn subjectivity's aporia into a dilemma with a pragmatic solution in a particular social field that takes into account subjectivity's juridical structures of recognition. Biculturalism negotiates subjectivity's ruptures in order to mediate them for social mobilization. I conclude with the suggestion that perhaps it is from such aporetic ruptures however that the properly political or democratic emerges.

Beyond Biculturalism

Going beyond biculturalism would seem by now to be an old call to arms that Asian American Studies scholars have been desiring for quite a while. Kandice Chuh's *Imagine Otherwise* argues quite articulately that Asian American critique demands tarrying with the negative, practicing strategic antiessentialism in our critiques of subjection. As critics, Chuh's work suggests, we uncover and deconstruct the processes of identity construction from the acknowledged multiplicity and difference of our lived realities, and we imagine otherwise than the normative structures that constrain us in specific categories and delimit our capacity to work toward social transformation. Chuh insists on the "subject-lessness" of Asian American Studies in the interest of unleashing what Lisa Lowe so long ago called its heterogeneity and multiplicity, beyond bi- or any other kind of culturalism, and to uncover work, gender, and immigration as the new subjects of cultural politics. Such a politics of heterogeneity is not, Chuh also clearly insists, the final goal as some proponents of celebrating the recognition of hybridity as a multicultural liberalism might argue. Rather social justice and transformation become the moving horizon of "a commitment to an indefatigable and illimitable interrogation of myriad relations of power and how they give, shape, and sometimes take life" (Chuh 150).

Yet despite this cogently articulated plea, other scholars have argued against a notion of Asian American "subjectlessness." Interested in the agency of an Asian American subject implicit in its construction of an identity, the editors of *Transnational Asian American Literature: Sites and Transits* juxtapose their approach to that of Chuh and Lowe. They insist that Asian American identity is founded upon and locatable in US sites and institutions, and that "Asian American" may be read "as a multiplier signifier, attributed with political, social, and cultural value particularly by US institutional forces such as state and federal governments, legal, education, and cultural systems and organizations, capitalist apparatuses, like banks and corporations, and so forth, whose significance in a literary and critical domain is at once capable of incorporating fresh immigrant subjectivities as well as recuperating historical multilingual texts" (Lim et al. 5). They argue that Asian American literature, as a textual and discursive field, belongs to a specific site and location, even if the boundaries of this site and location are flexible and porous. Asian American identity, they argue, has a capaciousness that is "constructed, invented if you will, in the way that all social-cultural identities are constructed, out of a combination of canny political agendas, individual imaginations, communal histories, erasures and elisions, provisional arrangements, and contingencies. "Asian American," in the literary sphere, offers a way of understanding and constructing identity mediated by textual power—that is, how language operates in these works as an agent for novel imaginaries and social transformation" (Lim et al. 5). As a textual construct that exerts "textual power," Asian American identity only makes sense, they argue, within a specific local site of exchange and communication, within a specific field of ideological struggle. Such localization requires an engagement with the juridical structures of recognition and the creation of stable and coherent subject positions that often flattens the understanding of oppression's intersectionality and constrains politics.[4]

I suggest that at issue in treating the Asian American condition as either "subjectless" or a "multiplier signifier" are the distinctions between subjectivity's structuration and agency's precipitates. These are legible within porously bounded social fields, registers, and particular discourses. Sovereign subjectivity appears as an aftershock of these narrative acts that allow us to organize temporal experience and create stories of seemingly coherent subjectivity in a necessarily social field or formation.

Filipino American writing problematizes the field of Asian American Studies as a field of immigrants struggling with assimilation into the dominant culture. Filipino American writing, because of its imperial history with the United States, gains "paradigmatic exteriority' to the dominant practices of Asian American studies" as Kandice Chuh reminds us. The very integrity of specific enclosed fields of communication around national boundaries becomes problematized by Filipino American literary studies because they point to imperial legacies and continuities, as well as contemporary diasporic or transnational realities of an imperial age. Diasporic theories and transnational approaches would seem to function as counterpoints to the formations that emerge from the still dominant imagined communities and their social institutions called nation-states. They index the flows across national social fields or else disrupt the connection of the nation to the state. However, the case of the two Ongs problematizes both approaches. They provide a contrapuntal vantage point from which to see the lineaments and rubrics of the nation form's putative fictive kinship,[5] and they ask about the imperial fields and histories that subtend this form.

The juxtaposition of texts written by two multiply displaced overseas Chinese authors with origins in the Philippines—both writing in English, one publishing in the Philippines and the other in the United States—foregrounds certain questions about the liminal and mobile subject's imperial provenance and ethics of intersubjectivity. In these texts, neither the Philippines nor the United States is a site of racial or cultural purity. They question our assumptions about the "purity" of origins from which notions of biculturalism stem. At the same time, they too are constrained by the juridical and structural necessity to think in terms of subjectivity, community and social fields, even if they insist on the subject as decentered and not self-sufficient. To think through community formation this way suggests we move out of thinking about identity and subjectivity *as if* it is a self-grounding, self-founding, and autonomous act of autobiography, while still holding ourselves accountable to a community that is more than just a background world to our narratives of self-formation. Identity is always implicated in sociality, and subjectivity is always intersubjective. The conditions for their emergence can never fully be accounted for, but nonetheless require some kind of ethical response. What are our "passionate attachments" as Butler might ask to these conditions that are the sources of both our subjection and our subjectivities? One could of course simply state what seems undeniably true, that what structures the performance of our identities are the conditions of uneven development, capitalism, globalization and the nation-state system, or even that subject formation *is* subjection. At the same time, something always exceeds and escapes subject formation.

Scenes of Subjectivity

Judith Butler's text on Levinasian ethics of decentered subjectivity, *Giving an Account of Oneself,* argues that the social theory of recognition depends on norms that constitute recognizability of something exchanged beyond recognition itself. Butler here focuses on singularity rather than identity. Instead of the content of recognition, she takes up the question of address in the act of exchange. The question of the scenes of address moves Butler from the question of "what can I be within the scripts given me" that was a prior concern in her work, to the question of "who are you that is demanding a response," which precedes and calls out the "I" who responds.[6] Butler's notion of the *scene* of address involves exposure to the other and the self as an "other." Here the "I" is ecstatic, in the sense of requiring a move away from the self that has been initiated by an "other" demanding a response, before it can return and recognize itself as a self.

The "I" in this manner depends on some other agency to provide recognition before the "I" can even be constituted as a "conversation partner." The "you" demands a response that triggers the process of constituting "I." The "you" in the process of initiating the constitution of the "I" carries a command or a force that is felt as a communicative power. Moreover, the "I" is exposed to the other in a singular, corporeal, and bodily manner. The relation between the "I" and the other that constitutes it is a relation of singularities of bodily existence and not endless seriality and substitutability. Butler discusses this singularity as finitude: something that we all have in common in our existence, but that does not thereby make us all "the same" in essence. It is this singularity of the material body that Butler maintains narratives generally mitigate against, by giving us a form and norms, through which we can try to identify with each other as the same—or at least link one another as proximate in a given social field. This corporeality is not fully available to narrative coherence, and its complex relationality is a source of our opacity. It functions like a real that Butler recuperates as resistant to, or at least interruptive of, the symbolic. At the same time, narrative's interruption through finitude does not alleviate the need for weaving a gathering of the community through myth or ideology. On the contrary, the terror of finitude exactly motivates and intensifies the desire and need for recognition and narrative form. Butler contends:

> The structure of address is not a feature of narrative, one of its many and variable attributes, but an interruption of narrative. The moment the story is addressed to someone, it assumes a rhetorical dimension that is not reducible to a narrative function. It presumes that someone, and it seeks to recruit and act upon that someone. (63)

She argues that the process of addressing someone does not presuppose they shall tell us the truth, or that they shall respond. Wary of narrative's will to coherence, Butler argues that the interruption of narrative suggests our inability to fully account for ourselves. Narrative closure for Butler requires a legislating body that evaluates the need for an ending: "The relationship between interlocutors is established as one between a judge who reviews evidence and a supplicant trying to measure up to an indecipherable burden of proof" (64). In a narrative according to this logic, some agent is required to take the position of this legislating body that sets the norms of recognizability and establishes the parameters for communication, and that dictates what might be called narrative or performative "competence." The issue of agents and institutions providing and desiring recognition is precisely the problem. Generally, this is the position of the social formation or institution, which might be called the state, the nation, and the community. Diasporic texts, I would suggest, foreground the contingencies by which particular moments and means by which recognition is constituted, but retain the need for recognition. What are the legislative bodies from whom we desire recognition? What are the institutions that generate the kinds of subjectivities with which we need to contend?

Reading the two Ongs, I suggest that much which seems to require our consistent return to arguing against mere biculturalism comes not only from our acknowledgment of the inadequacies of bicultural categories, or categories of thought in general, to actual lived experiences, or even from our recognition of how biculturalism entraps us within the very nationalist biases that manifest as the dominant social scripts to which we are all subjected. The two Ongs suggest to me that our constant return to the problematics of biculturalism stems also from our desire to be given and deploy subjectivity within a particular social field. Acts of recognition, and the subjectivity that comes from them are things we *cannot not* want, as Spivak keeps reminding us, even if the terms and costs of gaining them ought to always demand that we "unlearn" the privileges that derive from them. We cannot not want them because these identifications allow us to form communities, find support networks from which to launch resistances to the limitations these very scripts impose upon us. Perhaps, I suggest, the question of biculturalism may be taken as a *figure* for how the forces of our subjection are also simultaneously the bases of our subjectivities and our sociality, for how the modes of address and scenes of our interpellation render categories like biculturalism a necessary temporary moment in our attempts to vainly make us transparent to ourselves and to others—attempts that are the bases of social mobilization.

We of course are not transparent but opaque, as Judith Butler reminds us. Our opacity means something always escapes, something gets beyond our capacities to narrate our stories. This opacity also means that we are always social in our formation, the materials available to our narrations of ourselves are not of our creation but come from the world. All acts of worlding, of giving a form to our experience and conditions must take into account, even through repression, the various Others that populate this world, the Others who demand our accounting and to whom our narratives are addressed. Such suggestions mean neither opting for biculturalism, nor simply rejecting outright the parameters that given discursive structures have created, *as if* we could somehow completely get outside the conjunctures that define us and the conditions of possibility out of which we imminently emerge. Instead, our attention can shift towards the conditions and structures that create the terms of our fields of practice and the means, both affective and ideological, that we use to negotiate and live through them.

Embodied Dis/placements and the Feng Shui of Identity in *Fixer Chao*

Han Ong's acerbic *Fixer Chao* has Filipino American gay hustler William Paulinho play on the orientalist assumptions of New York elites as he pretends to be a Chinese feng shui expert William Chao. Here the interchangeability of Asian Americans as the orientalist other of a constructed occidentalism becomes the means by which William Chao's class revenge gets enacted. The deployment of markers of bounded identity, the performance of ethnicity and race, articulate for us the binds of subjectivity in *Fixer Chao*. On the one hand, William does not invent the categories and scripts that he so deftly manipulates. On the other, his capacity to maneuver anticipations of identity, the categories and markers by which social relationships gain sufficient fixity to be instrumentalized and manipulated, constitutes a certain contingent agency to William. It is through these markers of identity that William tracks and registers not only the layering of social spaces and locations that interweave class and race in New York, but also the movement from the past to the present that constitutes one of his many definitions of immigration and the American dream.

If the novel only played out the orientalist/occidentalist binary, William would perhaps be like the closeted Chinese American author Paul Chan Chuang Toledo Lin who writes "Peking Man? Woman?" in the novel. Instead, part of what makes the novel interesting is how this binary itself is also part of a social field's mapping. The novel lays out difference in order to make us painfully aware of the materiality of the infrastructure that underpins social difference, as well as the ways in which markers of identity are used to concentrate and accumulate, regulate and manage material and cultural value through status. Negotiating the social field thereby becomes a means to play the game whose rules are not of our own making. The novel suggests that the distinctions that position and constrain us within a social text, the habitus of our dispositions, also become registers through which we can mark the terrain we traverse. The objects that populate our everyday life, that we consume, exchange, and display, become markers of social distinctions of class and ethnicity. These markers of identity are revealed by the novel to have socially constructed values that nonetheless anchor our journeys through social maps. They function as registers or points in the flux between being and becoming, as we try to negotiate and measure our passage through accumulated value. Objects gain the aura of aspiration as they represent for us not only the supposed telos of migrancy, but also the yardsticks of our journeys as well as the vectors of imperial accumulation and concentration of value and power. Toward the end of the novel, when William is asked why he and his parents came to the United States, he tells us:

> They wanted a better life. This was how it always ended: at the wall conjured by those words, true though they were. What did those words really suggest except that the life being led was suddenly made intolerable by news of another life available elsewhere? News that revealed the first life for the unnecessary sacrifice that it was. The images of this good life, this better life that existed on the other side of a line suddenly drawn by knowledge, were at the same time fuzzy and vivid: it was the vividness of a foreground detail in a photograph, with the background turned out of focus and made in effect, for lack of a better word, dreamlike. So we saw objects clearly, but had no idea of their true context, what was behind them. It was only that these foreground details that we kept our eyes on represented, for us—my family and me—luxury. The idea of luxury. That was the most important thing for us, who believed so strongly in the categorization "Third World." What were these objects, these images? Wall-to-wall carpeting . . . to walk on softness, coolness. On something manufactured to go nature one better . . . that in our minds was true wealth (it would take me a long time to acquire a preference for wood floors. To see that as being out of the ordinary and therefore better). (263)

"They wanted a better life"—this articulation forms the limit, the end point of conversation, William informs us. Yet this statement, true though it might be, hides the unaccountable. News from elsewhere bringing images of luxury interrupts our immediate life. They appear to us as vivid details in a photograph whose fuzzy background makes their true context, of what is behind or structures them, unknown. The desire here for something constructed, something better than nature, provides a sense of the function social distinctions have in cultivating hierarchies and desires. The objects in the photographs, like images in advertising, become Lacanian *point de capiton* and anchor our desires along vectors already given by imperial networks. They become material objects of desires as well as gauges of our social mobility—in both cases, they foment what Tadiar might call our fantasy productions.

The haze of aspiration masks the order that structures our desires. Objects gain a fetishistic power in our subject formation whose source is linked to our differential emplacement in a social field. It is in fact in the specific and particular field or locality of exchange and recognition, in which objects' and markers' symbolic capital is deployed that give them value. Shifting our attention to the imperial field foregrounds a shift in orientation, from a systemic analysis of macro forces that is oriented to totality, to a cognitive mapping sensitive to the registers of practice and lived experience while playing on the social field. This focus on the ways that objects spatially organized constitutes a cathexis for the imperial field. It exposes the structured terrains of our subject formation and the scenes of our interpellation, to the fields of force that dictate certain social scripts for the performance of our subjecthood. At the same time, it calls attention to our libidinal investments in, or passionate attachments to, the conditions of possibility of our desires and our pregiven subject positions that emerge from such terrain. It is through photographs of the past, through news from afar, solicited by the other, that our eternal discontent impels desire for survival, mobility, and betterment.

Hsuan Hsu's thesis about "de-individualizing attraction toward one's environment" or spatial captation in the Lacanian mirror stage in *Fixer Chao* as a contrast to Bhabha's notion of colonial mimicry suggests that this moment calls into mind the mode in which "truly inclusive communities could be built" (677). Mimicry as a camouflage and environmental blending in which "a person, by inserting herself into a social space, subtly changes that space" (Hsu 677). Paulinha's capacity to "blend" is a product of Filipino racial ambiguity. Hsu emphasizes the spatial capacity of subjects to blend and affect their social field. Location and urban life is Hsu's focus in order to see how subjects emerge into visibility and links urban literature written by ethnic minorities with ecocriticism (689). Here I would like to build on Hsu's argument and emphasize the manner in which objects themselves take their place in the narratives of our identities and presence. Speaking of his friend and accomplice Preciosa's leaving:

> Preciosa's things in her empty apartment gained value from Preciosa's person, even though, William tells us, even while Preciosa lived there the whole place already had the air of vacancy, of the non-attachment Preciosa, the eternal immigrant, had with her context as she performed "some deficiency encoded into her genes, a hunger, some basic discontent. This,

being one more definition of immigrant—torn between the competing
pulls of the fiction of the promised land, on the one hand, and the fiction
of the sustaining mother country, on the other. (325–26)

Preciosa's presence, the aura that she leaves behind among the objects
and the space she once occupied suggests that affective memories are left
behind. Following Hsu, the contrast between Preciosa's objects and the
idea of luxury as mise-en-scène for a person's emergence or existential
weight allows us to ask about the scene of interpellation that subject
formation requires and the role complex and potentially contradictory
roles valuation of objects in a social map might have. The desires that
both push and pull diasporic subjects are fictions woven into a narrative
of self-construction that in turn links and sequences the routes of their
desires and migrancy.

Feng shui as the practice of putting objects in their context, their
proper placement, in their appropriate order to maximize harmony and
good fortune, becomes in this novel a metaphor for the grammar and
syntax of mapping social orders, and the way that everyday life and objects register the passing of time and movement, of the performance of
subjectivity and the way the interpellation of subjects is dependent upon
social distinctions and social maps. It draws attention to the scenes of
address of interpellation, of the situatedness of identity that constitutes
the pregiven of any subject's formation. To *Fixer Chao*'s foregrounding
of geomancy as the sensitivity to the force and vectors that constitute
the ley lines of social distinction in a specific and particular locality, I
would like to link Charlson Ong's short story, "Another Country." "Another Country" presents to us multiple scenes of interpellation to which
the sojourner must respond.

Intersubjectivity Is "Another Country"

Charlson Ong is less familiar to Asian Americanists than Han Ong. A
Chinese Filipino writer who explores the liminal position of the *tsinoy*,
Charlson Ong reminds us that categories like Filipino American have
also their own Feng shui-like characteristics. After all, we think of Han
Ong as a Filipino American, not as a Chinese Filipino American or a
Filipino American Chinese or American Chinese Filipino or any other

permutation of the three terms. The overseas Chinese, particularly when embedded in a relationship between multiple countries outside of China, constitute a counterpoint to a biculturalism that posit only two hegemonic categories. In his short story "Taking Flight," included in the anthology *Intsik*, Asian American author Paul Lim describes the experience of a Chinese Filipino entering the United States with the odd misfit of being both Taiwanese and Filipino. At the airport in Honolulu, a "big black woman" scrutinizes Wing's Taiwanese passport since he claimed to be from the Philippines. Wing's explanation of "Overseas Chinese" does not even register to the woman. In the story, he uses US popular culture as anchor points to his journey toward a liminal American-ness while news of his father's death makes him wonder about his own future trajectory and patrimony. Taiwan's own contested status makes the issue of Taiwanese versus Filipino citizenship problematic to Filipino Chinese. After Marcos's 1975 decree giving Filipino Chinese the opportunity to gain Philippine nationality has created a generation of Filipino Chinese whose biculturalism is tied to civic anxieties. Educated like Filipinos, with a certain distance from their mother tongue, they have taken cues from identitarian movements in the United States to forge their own place in Philippine society.[7] Using Asian America as a model for identity construction, these tsinoys have explored their liminal position between their Chinese heritage and their Philippine involvement. Charlson Ong is one of the most visible "tsinoy" writers. His introduction to *Intsik* outlines his belief that tsinoy movements came out of a specific historical moment that included Asian American identity politics with all of the imperial and transnational complexity this implies.

Charlson Ong's "Another Country," follows the story of Arthur, a Filipino Chinese in Taipei who works as a bilingual journalist, enlisted to translate from English to Chinese and Chinese to English for the *China Tribune*, a newspaper that had seen better days. Charlson Ong makes clear that the Chinese in Taiwan live a complex relationship with mainland China, where Arthur's boss continues to dream of past glory, of the return to the mainland as a hope that defined their existence, that made their sojourn in Taiwan and the sacrifices they made to reach it bearable. At the same time Taiwan here is described as the phantasmatic shadow of a promised "home" to the Chinese from the Philippines that no longer quite exists. Growing up in a Chinese household in the Philippines, fluent in Tagalog and *feeling* like a Filipino even though clearly tied to his father's ethnic heritage, Arthur strives to understand his father's connection to both "Amoy" or Fujian and Taiwan, his father's horror of miscegenation between the overseas Chinese *lannang* and the Filipino *huanna*. At the same time, Arthur seeks a place he can call his own, a situation in the sense of a place and circumstance, where he can belong. The title of the story, "Another Country," designates the endless search for belonging and home, as well as the geopolitical and global economic forces that renders the identity of the overseas Chinese from the Philippines, as well as the significance Taiwan plays to them, as liminal to the stable and bounded categories of China and the Philippines. The liminality of the overseas Chinese in the Philippines impels Arthur to go to Taiwan in search of a home. Finding instead in Taiwan a liminal position with regards to China and Chinese-ness, with Taiwan itself something of a sojourner's rest stop, Arthur finds himself increasingly homesick for the Philippines. This anomie he feels gets associated with sensations and memories. Instead of Proust's madeleine, however, he and his cousin Daryll fixate on memories of sexual encounters with prostitutes in Manila, both successful and failed ones. The same geopolitical realities that make Arthur's Chinese-ness an ambiguous ethnic marker, make Taiwan a receiving country of Filipino labor migration. Taiwan is itself marked as an ambiguous space of empire between the United States and China, necessitating the bilingual services of overseas Chinese like Arthur, educated in neocolonial Philippines.

The alienation Arthur feels in coming to the liminal geopolitical status of Taiwan, a place that his father ambiguously calls "home" as a temporary resting stop on the way to retaking the mainland, is reflected in the ambivalent feelings he has for Aurora, who works in Taipei illegally as a domestic. Aurora was previously a huanna, a derogatory term used by Chinese Filipinos for non-Chinese Filipinos, prostitute whom Arthur's cousin knew "biblically speaking" in Manila. To Arthur, Aurora appears similar to most other ex-patriots he comes across, she appears as a woman "trying to keep her wits, her dignity, and what remained of her prime while seeking redemption in another country" (55). Arthur's liminal and ambivalent position with regards to both being Chinese and Filipino emerges clearly when he is asked to report on a panel about the immigration of domestics to Taiwan. It is here, faced with the prejudice of the locals against the migrant workers, Arthur declares his affiliation and his allegiance to the Philippines. Here Arthur links the desires of overseas Chinese to find better living conditions, their dependence on the kindnesses of other host countries, to the desires of the transnational Filipino domestic. Against Arthur's ethical and moral plea, a discourse of debt and gratitude, of responsibility to the other, the panel insists on rationalizing the situation as simply one of economics, of labor surpluses and demand. Arthur's discourse is a discourse of love, specifically individual heterosexual love. He decides that he will build, like the sojourners, a "home" despite the social conditions he finds himself in and which the short story has been carefully elucidating for us. Arthur, finally deciding to declare his feelings to Aurora and thereby disobey his father, declares to his cousin that he has found the woman he will marry and the city, Taiwan, in which they will live and settle. One would think that the story could end in this way. Two individuals carving out a life for themselves against all that stands in their way. The story, however, does not end happily.

Visiting Aurora to declare his intention to save her even as she will now finally save him from the displaced migrant and exilic life he has known, Arthur finds Aurora servicing local policemen in order to stay in Taiwan despite her lack of a visa. In the face of his call that they become the romantic couple he had envisioned, Aurora, whose feelings for Arthur have thus far never been explored, calls Arthur a child and demands that he leave her life alone. This declaration of Aurora, pleading that Arthur leaves her alone to her own devices, is a declaration that the story leaves unrationalized. It stands as the subaltern's declaration of alterity against the narrator's assumptions about her desires. Arthur runs from the scene of this exchange and moves through Taipei now described as a dark dreamlike city that is but another country. In the moment of crisis when sides are drawn and choices are demanded, Arthur decides to care for Filipinos and show his willingness to save Aurora from her fate through his love. Despite Arthur's desire to link the situation of Filipino domestics to overseas Chinese sojourners, his gesture of good will is rejected by Aurora. Arthur's desire for a home is foiled. He thinks to create a sense of belonging through pledging allegiance to the Philippines as a marker of nationality. While clearly sympathetic to Arthur's predicament and choices, Charlson Ong leaves us with the irreducible gap between Arthur and Aurora's positionalities, actions, and decisions. Arthur is held hostage by Aurora's otherness through which he attempts in vain to create an accounting of himself.

Realizing his dependence upon Aurora's recognition, the assumed hierarchy collapses, even as the structural inequality does not. Aurora's assertion of her agency, her apparent refusal of Arthur's use of her as the abject upon which his subjectivity will be restored to him, highlights her desire for dignity in an unjust global condition. It highlights, on the one hand, the differential access to mobility among particular diasporic subjects. On the other hand, it rejects the simplistic call of moral equivalence that Arthur makes to the Taiwanese and foregrounds the constraints of the nation-state system and immigration laws in which our actions and choices are embedded. Instead of Arthur saving Aurora from her fate, it is Aurora's act of recognition that becomes important and upon which Arthur's subjectivity depends. The loved object in this case exposes Arthur's dependency and need for recognition. Aurora, and her refusal to be made into an imago for Arthur's desires, sets Arthur adrift into another country and a certain desubjectification. At the same time, the question of social justice, or responding ethically to the real and material plight of the other remains. I would like to now suggest that this contradiction or perhaps dilemma is something we can also glean from Han Ong's second novel, *The Disinherited*.

Desire and the Legacies of Ethical Demands in *The Disinherited*

Han Ong's recent novel, *The Disinherited*, follows the story of Roger Caracera, alienated from his haciendero or sugar plantation elite Philippine family, and who becomes heir to $500,000 from his father. Roger is tormented not only by class guilt about the source of his family's wealth in the Philippine sugar industry, but also by the memory of a homosexual pedophilic uncle whose inheritance he also received instead of his uncle's loved object, Pitik Sindit. Like Arthur in the Charlson Ong story, Roger wishes to salve his conscience by giving the money away. He finds that giving it away is much more difficult than it seems, particularly as he does so not in a disinterested way but as a means to reject his family and the oppression on which their wealth and social status depends. It isn't just that giving the money away does not address the underlying structural inequalities in the country; it is also that to do so means addressing why he needs to make amends at all. What in other words is his responsibility to the Philippine poor? While Ong's William Chao positions the Filipino American as a member of the underbelly of empire, his Roger Caracera asks what the relationship is between the Filipino American mobile subject and the abjection of the Filipino poor. Roger's capacity to create a subjectivity for himself depends upon his ability to relate to his Philippine surroundings instrumentally. Ong asks us about who profits from images of Philippine poverty and abjection circulated in America even as he insists that the referent of these images of abjection are real.

The issue of homosexuality, whether Roger is homosexual in his love for Pitik Sindit, his confusion about the ability to fully distinguish between erotic desire and pity based on guilt, ties social, and sexual reproduction and its queering.[8] The queering of social reproduction is tied to the issue of disconnect between Roger and his home and all that this represents. This disconnect is not "reproductive," and the film viewing in the end is the desire for reproduction faced with images of death. Instead, the disconnect denies any simplistic formation of community or a communal narrative that might suture Roger to his Filipino background even as it insists on a need for a response and responsibility to this legacy. It asks the question in other words of what kind of community may be formed when all the narratives of charity, of debt, of love and erotics even, are denied or suspended. It is interesting that it ends not in Roger's death, but in Pitik's death that arrives only as a story that commercialized filmic images bring to mind.

There are no celebrations in *The Disinherited* of cultural identity or even of the tradition of revolutionary resistance that marks the utopic impulse of many Philippine works. Here the gap between the Filipino and the Filipino American is marked as the responsibility to the sufferings of past seen like Benjamin's Angel of History, and to the contemporary Other as the impoverished multitude given form in the gay child sex worker. Watching a film about Douglas MacArthur called *Fiesta of the Damned* in the safety of New York City, Roger sees in the margins of the film's shots, the dead body of Pitik, the haunting reminder of his failure to save the abject. Even when the bodies of the dead are not Pitik's, Roger transcodes these images into Pitik's as a marker of his guilt and inability to surmount the structures that maintained the real distinctions between them. The filmic images at the end of the novel return us once again to the body as an object that gains significance from a context, from an environment. Stuck somewhere between mourning and melancholia, Roger's obsession with watching *Fiesta of the Damned* is in the name not of the future, but of the pain of the dead and dying, of the pile of disasters that have brought him to that movie theater. The satiric edge of *Fixer Chao*, that exposes the emptiness or fraudulence of elite New York life here is turned on the Filipino American formation. In the Philippine context, Filipino Americans are considered a privileged class—privileged in their social and cultural mobility. *The Disinherited* exposes this privilege as not detached from the suffering others who have a claim upon Filipino American attention.

In many ways, and as Judith Butler reminds us, the ways that we can narrate ourselves, to give accounts of ourselves, must derive from the social norms that make such accounting recognizable, legible, and communicable to the various others with whom we must relate. We must take narrative materials from the given-ness of the culture and structures in which we find ourselves embedded. These structures and norms are not only the terms by which we can create narratives that can lead to some contingent self-understanding, but are also scenes of address and interpellation. At the same time, this implicit sociality in the formation of our subjectivity necessarily implies its opacity and excess outside the terms of identities, including those given by constructions of biculturalism or even diaspora. The misfit between norms, ideas of betterment, and our lived realities propel our desire to change the conditions in which we find ourselves. Our capacity to act in and relate to the world, in other words our agency, emerges out of the binds of subjectivity. Diasporic subjectivity contains the demand for community, for intersubjectivity even as it displaces the state supported boundaries of the nation-state. To be diasporic is to be dispersed, often through political events beyond one's own choices, to be uncanny and *unheimlich* yet insistent on a ground and a home to which one can belong.

An ironic subjectivity that questions the coherence and stability of identity cannot make sense unless coupled with an awareness of the stakes in identity formation itself and the fields that this irony allows to emerge. The shifting line of inclusions and exclusionary politics, of uneven development in a neoliberal global hierarchy that leaves some unhomed and in exile, but whose feelings of generalized alienation cannot be simplistically collapsed and compared, means intersubjectivity requires and transcends biculturalism. What the two Ongs suggest to me is that creating and constituting ourselves through discursive acts implicates us in power relations that demand not only an accounting of our positionalities in the face of our exposure to the other, but also questions the imperial field that subtends transnational mobility and that demands a response to the dilemma of an imperialism and neoliberalism that postulates certain rights as universal and cosmopolitan but demands limitations on the nation-state's capacity to regulate within a bounded territory or social sphere.

What the two Ongs suggest to me is that creating and constituting ourselves through discursive acts implicate us in power relations that demand not only an accounting of our positionalities in the face of our exposure to the other, but also the questions of responsibility toward social justice, as well as the imperial field that subtends transnational mobility and the various means it deploys to produce, accumulate, and concentrate value in the hands of the few. The figure of the body in these texts demands a response to the dilemma of an imperialism and neoliberalism that postulates certain rights as universal and cosmopolitan as part of a globalized modern social imaginary, but creates limitations on the nation-state's capacity to be the forum of appeal for redress. In what space or forum can we grieve for Pitik Sindit, where his body is not on the margins of a mise-en-scène of a film about the violence of empire building? Through what social form can Arthur constitute a home free from the hierarchies of inequality that structures basic needs? What are our passionate attachments to liberal charity?

The aporia of subject formation, faced with the corpse of the other, the body of the abject or the images of these are shown in these texts as themselves limits of representation. The bodily here disrupts what Jacques Rancière might call the choreography of order of things, they introduce an interruption or a dis-sensus into the norms of recognition and makes us ask who counts or who can provide recognition. In this sense they open up the possibility for the properly political. I would argue, however, that the aporias of representation can become a dilemma about which decisions must be made beyond the narrowly literary, where the properly political still begs the question of the politics per se. The ethical questions with which reading the Ongs' texts leave us ought not be taken as a replacement for politics. The text makes us aware of the abject body's demand and its ethical force; but also of its limitations, its need to point us beyond its formal resolutions, its sense of endings, to a politics without guarantees as Stuart Hall might say. It asks us to ponder potential new social arrangements in the light of the insufficiencies of our current conjunctures, structures, ideologies, and myths of subjectivity, identity, and belonging. This might be the promise of diasporic and liminal subjectivities in the age of empire that points to our need to go beyond biculturalism.

Notes

1. A version of this paper was given at a panel on "Beyond Bi-culturalism: Boundary Making, Racial and Ethnic Performances, and the Establishment of the American Dream" in the Association of Asian American Studies 2007 conference. I would like thank Rick Bonus, Shilpa Davé, Augusto Espiritu, Anna Guevarra, Emily Ignacio, Alan Isaac, Martin Manalansan, Kristin Pitt, Chandan Reddy, and Ileana Rodriguez-Silva for their engagement and comments on the paper. All errors in spite of their help are mine.

2. See Hamid Hosseini, "From *Communist Manifesto* to *Empire*: How Marxists Have Viewed Global Capitalism in History," *Review of Radical Political Economics* 38, no. 1 (winter 2006): 7–23; and Henri Lefebvre, *State, Space, World: Selected Essays*, ed. Neil Brenner and Stuart Elden (Minneapolis: University of Minnesota Press, 2009).

3. Chela Sandoval's *Methodology of the Oppressed* (Minneapolis: University of Minnesota Press, 2000), 179.

4. See Kimberle Crenshaw, "Demarginalizing the Intersection of Race and Sex: A Black Feminist Critique of Antidiscrimination Doctrine, Feminist Theory and Antiracist Politics," *University of Chicago Legal Forum* (1989): 139–67.

5. See Etienne Balibar, "The Nation Form: History and Ideology," in *Race, Nation, Class Ambiguous Identities,* trans. Chris Turner, ed. Etienne Balibar and Immanuel Wallerstein (London: Verso, 1991).

6. Butler deploys the multiple meanings of "giving an account."

7. See Charlson Ong's own introduction to the collection *Intsik* where he cites Jessica Hagedorn's *Charlie Chan Is Dead* to critique Philippine representations of the Chinese in their midst and gestures toward identity movements in the United States: "Chinese Filipinos should take to *Intsik* in the manner that Afro-Americans and other Negores now call themselves Blacks and Rizal and his gang chose to name

themselves Indios Bravos" (*Intsik: An Anthology of Chinese Filipino Writing*, ed. Caroline Hau [Mandaluyong City: Anvil Publishing, 2000], xiv).

8. I thank Allan Isaac for bringing this point to my attention. To the extent the text is about the difficulties of patrimony and social/sexual reproduction's coupling, I leave a more sustained complex queer reading of this text for another time.

Works Cited

Balibar, Etienne, and Immanuel Maurice Wallerstein. *Race, Nation, Class: Ambiguous Identities*. London: Verso, 1991.

Bourdieu, Pierre. *Practical Reason: On the Theory of Action*. Cambridge: Polity Press, 1998.

Butler, Judith. *Giving an Account of Oneself.* New York: Fordham University Press, 2005.

Chuh, Kandice. *Imagine Otherwise: On Asian Americanist Critique*. Durham, NC: Duke University Press, 2003.

Hau, Caroline. *Instik: An Anthology of Chinese Filipino Writing*. Mandaluyong City: Anvil Publishing, 2000.

Hosseini, Hamid. "From *Communist Manifesto* to *Empire*: How Marxists Have Viewed Global Capitalism in History." *Review of Radical Political Economics* 38, no. 1 (winter 2006): 7–23.

Hsu, Hsuan L. "Mimicry, Spatial Captation, and Feng Shui in Han Ong's *Fixer Chao*." *MFS Modern Fiction Studies* 52, no. 3 (fall 2006): 675–704.

Lefebvre, Henri. *State, Space, World: Selected Essays*. Eds. Neil Brenner and Stuart Elden. Minneapolis: University of Minnesota Press, 2009.

Lim, Shirley. *Transnational Asian American Literature: Sites and Transits*. Philadelphia, PA: Temple University Press, 2006.

Lowe, Lisa. *Immigrant Acts: On Asian American Cultural Politics*. Durham, NC: Duke University Press, 1996.

Ong, Charlson. *A Tropical Winter's Tale and Other Stories*. Quezon City: University of the Philippines Press, 2003.

Ong, Han. *The Disinherited*. Farrar, Straus and Giroux, 2004.

———. *Fixer Chao*. New York: Picador, 2002.

Ranciere, Jacques. *Dissensus: On Politics and Aesthetics*. New York: Continuum International Publishing, 2010.

Sandoval, Chela. *Methodology of the Oppressed*. Minneapolis: University of Minnesota Press, 2000.

Tadiar, Neferti. *Fantasy Production: Sexual Economies and Other Philippine Consequences for the New World Order*. Hong Kong: Hong University Press, 2004.

16

The Legacy of Undesirability

Filipino TNTs, "Irregular Migrants," and "Outlaws"
in the US Cultural Imaginary

ANNA ROMINA GUEVARRA

Filipino migrants were the corporeality of contradictions
that existed in American colonial policy and practice.
—Mae M. Ngai, *Impossible Subjects: Illegal Aliens and the*
Making of Modern America

Introduction

The Philippines, heralded for its vibrant labor export economy, prides
itself as the "Home of the Great Filipino Worker." It is a moniker made
possible by a neoliberal and market-driven state that capitalizes on the
ideals of entrepreneurship, self-regulation, and "freedom" in its prized
commodities—professionals and "super" workers, whose added value is
supposed to be their competitive advantage in the global marketplace.
Despite the presence of Filipinos as agricultural and cannery workers for
decades, beginning in the mid-1920s, their role in the economic landscape
of the United States has traditionally been constructed in the image of
high-skilled health professionals. Legislations like the Immigration Act of
1965, which created occupational preference categories that allowed professionals to come to the United States was one such vehicle for this kind
of migration such as in the case of Filipino nurses (Choy 2003; Espiritu
2007; Guevarra 2010; Ong and Azores 1994; Posadas 1999). However,
this dominant representation of Filipino migration to the United States is
changing. Troubling the Philippine state's representation of the country as
a source of "highly skilled,"[1] "more than usual" professional workers, is the
growing number of undocumented overseas Filipinos. Given the numbers

of such workers in recent years, the Philippine state has no choice but to officially recognize them, even as it anxiously categorizes them as "irregular migrants,"[2] or TNTs (*tago-ng-tago*) as they are commonly referred to.

According to the Commission on Filipinos Overseas, in the United States alone, of the 3.2 million overseas Filipinos residing in the United States as of 2010, approximately 5 percent are undocumented. Studies of Filipino immigrant communities in Chicago reveal that the kind of migration that has prioritized family reunification in the last decade means that a large proportion of Filipinos entering the country are funneled in to service occupations, with little chance of mobility, primarily because migrants coming through this pathway may not necessarily carry the requisite skills or educational credentials to garner or guarantee high-paying employment (Lau 2006, 2007). Additionally, according to the Migration Policy Institute, the number of unauthorized immigrants from the Philippines has increased 40 percent between 2000–2006, which may contribute to supporting (or creating new) precarious forms of employment, such as the burgeoning informal economies of elder caregiving, as some studies show with respect to Filipinos in Southern California (Guevarra and Lledo 2013; Parreñas 2001; Tung 2003).

Yet, we know very little about this population. In the midst of continuing xenophobic anxieties in the United States, such "irregular" Filipinos continue to be made invisible, or at best, perceived as "good enough" foreign labor that can be readily (if temporarily) incorporated in the national fabric. And when they are visible, their added value as workers is often constructed in ways that pit them against and denigrate other racialized minority groups. For example, in Arizona, the hotel industry has started recruiting laborers from the Philippines because they are perceived to be "better" than Mexican workers not only because of their English-language proficiency and high levels of educational attainment but, more importantly, because they are perceived to be less likely to overstay their visas.[3] But this narrative was drastically interrupted in June 2011 by journalist Jose Antonio Vargas, whose coming out as an undocumented Filipino immigrant and "outlaw" rendered visible the TNT community.[4] While his testimony challenges the oft-cited perception that immigration reform is only a Latino issue, the responses to his coming out have also been uneven among Filipinos, raising questions about the possibilities and limits of organizing with respect to immigration reform.

In this chapter, I examine the Filipino labor diaspora and, in particular, the presence and formation of the TNT community in the United States. I explore the contradictory positions that Filipinos occupy within the US racial matrix as former colonial subjects, strategically propped up as model workers, and now perhaps again constructed as "undesirable aliens" (Ngai 2004). I analyze the meaning and significance behind the apparent invisibility of Filipinos in discursive constructions of "illegality" despite their growing numbers, and its implications for community organizing. As Mae Ngai (2004) noted in relation to earlier migrations, "Filipino migrants were the corporeality of contradictions that existed in American colonial policy and practice" (97). Their migration to the United States was defined in the context of benevolent assimilation at the same time that the anxieties about their so-called hypersexuality and possible race mixing rendered them undesirable for incorporation in US society. In the present context, Filipinos continue to occupy a contradictory position—they are model workers who provide much needed labor as well as possible "outlaws" as Vargas made concretely visible. Drawing on fieldwork I conducted in 2008–9 with undocumented Filipino caregivers in a Workers Center, this chapter addresses this contemporary predicament of Filipinos, caught between a nation that denies their "regular" existence, and one in which they remain forever foreign, "outlaws" in the eyes of both the state and the wider undocumented community. It is a predicament that provides a lens through which to examine the intersection between citizenship and community formation among these diasporic subjects. This is especially so in the context of a neoliberal landscape that seeks to govern them not only through the discourse of responsibility but also through fear and a sense of placelessness, even as it relentlessly extracts their much needed labor power. It prompts us to think through what this ultimately means in terms of organizing and mobilizing this group under the umbrella of immigration reform and what it may suggest about coalition-building efforts to this end.

The Filipino Labor Diaspora and US Imperial Legacies

The presence of Filipino workers on the global stage *officially* began in 1974 with the establishment of the country's labor code.[5] The 1974 Labor Code was created by the Ferdinand Marcos administration as a temporary stop-gap measure to counter rapidly escalating unemployment and the mounting balance of payments to the IMF and the World Bank. It was also a strategic response to the employment opportunities enabled by the 1970s Middle East Oil Boom where oil-rich countries such as the United Arab Emirates, Kuwait, Saudi Arabia, Iran, Iraq, and Bahrain sought workers for infrastructural and development projects (Asis 1992; Villegas 1988).

This labor code institutionalized the country's labor export policy by establishing what is now known as the Philippine Overseas Employment Administration (POEA), a state body in charge of managing the country's overseas employment program.

So successful has the POEA been in carrying out this task that the International Labor Organization (ILO) designated the POEA as a "model" for other labor-exporting countries (Tyner 1996). As Robyn Rodriguez's (2010) ethnography of the Philippine state highlights, the Philippine state, as a "labor brokerage" state, is instrumental not only in defining the Philippines' role as a labor supplier but also in shaping Filipino workers' sense of belonging to the nation.[6] My research further adds to this argument by showing how Filipino labor migrant streams and the ongoing foreign labor recruitment from the Philippines in general are made possible not only through the work of state bodies like the POEA but also state-licensed private employment agencies that broker Filipino workers for global markets (Guevarra 2010, 2003).

The most comprehensive figure provided by the Commission of Filipinos Overseas (CFO) reported that as of December 2010, approximately 9.5 million Filipinos are living overseas, of which 4.3 million (45 percent) are Filipinos carrying employment contracts and about 8 percent are irregular migrants.[7] In May 2010, the estimated population of the Philippines was 92 million (Philippine National Statistics Organization) and these expatriates represented 10 percent of all Filipinos. With an annual deployment of one million workers to more than two hundred nations, succeeding administrations maintained this program of development because of the contribution of overseas workers' dollar remittances to the country, which, in 2010, amounted to US$20.1 billion—a figure that represented approximately 10 percent of the country's Gross Domestic Product (POEA 2008).[8]

As I argue elsewhere (2010), the presence of the Filipino labor diaspora can be attributed to a state that fashions itself as a "manager" of labor migration. Building on a neocolonial legacy that catapulted the Philippines into a trajectory of economic crisis, Filipinos were introduced as globally exploitable human resources. This ethos of labor migration enabled the creation of political economic conditions through which the Philippine state constructed overseas employment as the most viable source of income. Filipinos were henceforth deemed the so-called Great Filipino Workers, individuals who carry a racialized form of productive labor power—their *added export value*—which the state pitches as their competitive advantage. The brokering of Filipino workers as "heroes," "mercedes benz," or "supermaids" by institutional actors like the Philippine state and private employment agencies are all emblematic of this process (Guevarra 2010).

In the context of the Filipino labor diaspora in the United States, this phenomenon is informed by the Philippines' colonial history. As a colony of the United States from 1898–1945, the Philippines was subjected to the US project of benevolent assimilation, founded on the intent to convert the Philippines from a "collection of tribes" into one ready for self-government. This process of conversion materialized in the imposition of English as a medium of instruction, the presence of the Thomasites—American teachers—in the country, and the creation of educational and training institutions modeled on a US curriculum. This process had a particular impact on the institutionalization of US nursing programs in the country, which Choy (2003) described was an essential "precondition" to the migration of Filipino nurses in the United States, providing them with a US-based nurse training and familiarity with the US work culture. This process of conversion also resulted in supporting educational exchanges between the United States and the Philippines through the *pensionados*—government scholars in the fields of medicine, education, engineering, and law from the Philippines who left for the United States between 1903–14 to receive training in these fields and then later returned to the Philippines as teachers or government administrators.

It was also during this period that the Hawaiian plantation owners turned to the Philippines for agricultural laborers. This was largely in response to the labor shortages resulting from growing labor unrest and organizing on the part of workers recruited from Japan. These "new" Filipino workers—*manongs*—initially found work in Hawaiian plantations, while a number of workers also went to California, Washington,

Oregon, Idaho, Wyoming, Nevada, and Montana as vegetable and fruit pickers, in Alaska and the Northwest as fish-cannery workers, and in New York as domestic service workers (Cordova 1983; Habal 2007; Liu 1991; Sharma 1984; Takaki 1998; Villegas 1988). But beginning in the mid-twentieth century, with the continuing decline of the Philippine economy and the ensuing demand for and/or availability of jobs for physicians, nurses, engineers, computer technicians, artists/musicians, to name a few "professions," the migration of Filipinos abroad began to surge. Following World War II and the creation of the US Exchange Visitors Program, a large number of Filipinos, of which nurses comprised the majority, also left the Philippines to receive advanced training in US hospitals (Bergaminini 1964; Ong and Azores 1994). When the 1965 US Immigration Act was passed, the migration of Filipino professionals surged even more. The 1965 Immigration Act not only abolished the 1924 National Origins Act, which imposed the 2 percent quota per nationality, but it also facilitated the entry of "professionals" to the United States. Nurses, physicians, surgeons, scientists, lawyers, and teachers from the Philippines entered the United States through the "third preference" immigration category.[9] Between 1966 and 1970, 65 percent of Filipino immigrants who entered through the professional third preference category were highly skilled professionals (Keely 1973; Takaki 1998;). Notably, the passage of this legislation was strategic for the United States, which faced its first national nursing shortage in 1965, prompting the US labor secretary to waive the labor certification requirement of foreign nurses regardless of employer sponsorship (Ong and Azores 1994). Almost a decade later, the outmigration of Filipino workers continued in the Middle East and Asia following the institutionalization of the country's labor export policy program in 1974. This labor export program further solidified the country's dependence on overseas employment as a form of economic development and a nation-building strategy.

As colonial subjects in the racially stratified social system of the United States, their presence, however, was not without contestation. Despite their value as laborers, this "racial statecraft"[10] (Baldoz 2004, 2011) subjected Filipino immigrants coming to the United States in the mid-twentieth century to a growing exclusion movement against Filipinos, a process that disallowed and barred them access to social and political opportunities such as citizenship, property, and labor rights, while imposing various antimiscegenation and alien land laws. As colonial subjects, the racially motivated violence that they experienced as immigrants was buried in anxieties about their social construction as suspect, uncivilized, immoral, sexual deviants, and labor militants who disrupted the moral and social order of the United States (Baldoz 2004, 2011; Habal 2008; Ngai 2004).

Thus, the racialization of Filipinos in America's sociopolitical imaginary is necessarily contradictory. On the one hand, their desirability as immigrants stems from their position as colonial subjects who carry the residues of America's "benevolent assimilation" project, which increases the value of their labor power. On the other hand, this very same position is also a threat, emblematic of a xenophobic state that willingly takes Filipino labor but without the expectation or promise of any social entitlements. This became evident with the Philippine independence from the United States through the passage of the 1934 Tydings-McDuffie Act, which imposed a quota of fifty persons a year from the Philippines, but also through the enactment of the Filipino Repatriation Act of 1936, which paid for Filipinos' return to the Philippines with the promise that they will not return to the United States.

Regardless, the United States continues to turn to the Philippines for labor with the recruitment of nurses (Choy 2003; Guevarra 2010) and teachers to address ongoing labor shortages in these fields. However, recent studies of Filipino migration to the United States also indicate some demographic shifts. Not only are there a growing number of Filipinos funneled into service occupations and low-wage industries, but there is also a sizeable population who are undocumented. In 2010, the US Department of Homeland Security revealed that the Philippines is among the top five source countries of unauthorized immigrants. It is this growing population that we know very little about, except that they are officially categorized by the Philippine state as "irregular migrants" and by the larger public as "TNTs" (tago ng tago)—always in hiding. It was not until the "coming out" of Jose Antonio Vargas that Filipinos and Asians, in general, were finally made visible and incorporated in America's discourse around undocumented immigration.

The Model "Outlaw?" Jose Antonio Vargas

Over the past 14 years, I've graduated from high school and
college and built a career as a journalist, interviewing some
of the most famous people in the country. On the surface,
I've created a good life. I've lived the American dream. But I
am still an undocumented immigrant.
—Jose Antonio Vargas, "Outlaw: My life in America as an
Undocumented Immigrant," New York Times Magazine

On June 26, 2011, Jose Antonio Vargas, a Pulitzer Prize-winning journalist disrupted the common discourse around immigration. First, as
a racialized immigrant figure, he interrupted the common perception
that the problem of the broken immigration system and the plight of
undocumented migrants were primarily concerns faced by Latino communities. His story made visible the reality that this is an issue shared
by other communities of color and, in this case, pointing to the Filipino
TNT community in particular. Second, as an "American dreaming" economic actor whose position and social networks endowed him with a
set of privileges and with a degree of power, he came to trouble the class-
based perceptions of who constitutes the category "undocumented."

While the overall response to his story was that of general curiosity
and intrigue, the interpretation of his story varied. While some lauded
Vargas as another necessary voice for a marginalized population who
courageously took the step that would put him at risk of deportation
and alienation from his family and friends, others characterized him as a
fugitive who had committed a series of deceptive acts. Another set of responses sought to justify his presence in the United States by highlighting his value primarily in economic terms, dubbing him a representative
of "unrecognized talent among children of illegal immigrants who are
educated, bright, useful members of American society and should be
accepted as American citizens" (NY Times, Reply All Letters, 7/10/11).
Others, however, assert that his presence only masks the economic hardships faced by "the poorest of Americans, whose stories of competition
with illegals is the saddest and most underreported story in journalism"
(NY Times, Reply All Letters, 7/10/11). At the same time, Filipinos in
the Philippines probe his sense of national allegiance, questioning his

intentions to return to his birthplace and whether he perceives the Philippines to be a good enough home for him.

Juxtaposed with these narratives, is Vargas's representation of himself and his coming-out process. First, he projects himself as a storyteller whose goal is to engage different audiences. As he explained, "We're telling our stories. More and more people are going to be coming out. And more and more people who are supporters are going to be coming out. It's so important that we're engaging them in whatever way we can, and insist, by just simply being there, that we are human beings who cannot be denied" (Chang 2012). As a storyteller, his project of engagement is rooted in his goal of making visible the range of communities impacted by the broken immigration system, as well as in terms of widening the audience for such stories. Second, he projects himself as a coalition-builder who sees the importance of summoning allies from other communities. With his story, he hopes to enable different publics/communities to identify with the condition of undocumented immigrants and take up their issues as a platform worth fighting for. As he exclaimed, "We are now at the point in this movement where we have to figure out how to broaden this conversation. How are we sure we're not just preaching to the choir? How do we make sure that white people and black people feel like this is their issue, too? If we are not doing that, then we are not doing our job" (Chang 2012). However, he also recognizes and has even apologized for the privileged position he occupies, one that affords him a tokenizing limelight in various mainstream and ethnic media outlets to tell his story. In response, he emphasizes the need to recognize the larger landscape and the shared goals among immigrant communities, even if the strategies and the means for conveying the message of social justice differ.

While Vargas's story certainly disrupts the current conversation and landscape about undocumented immigration in the United States by including other ethnic minorities like Filipinos as yet another group of implicated actors, his story and strategy also beg the question of framing, that is, the extent to which his framing of his story and call to action capture the complexities and the contradictions of the US "racial statecraft" (Baldoz 2004) and its categorization and treatment of immigrants historically. On a short video documenting the process of writing the cover story for *TIME* magazine, he states, "The question about immigration is even bigger than itself. It is the question of citizenship. It's a question of what this country is about. It's a question of how you even define what 'American' is. And that is what I'm trying to figure out." For Vargas, the process of defining this remains caught up in the narrative of the American Dream, reflecting the United States as the bastion of goodness and greatness, without adequately problematizing this cultural imaginary and the very tensions in this proclamation. For example, in his *New York Times* article, he makes a case for why he is deserving of US citizenship:

> Over the past 14 years, I've graduated from high school and college and built a career as a journalist, interviewing some of the most famous people in the country. On the surface, I've created a good life. I've lived the American dream. But I am still an undocumented immigrant. (Vargas 2012)

On the one hand, he points out why he is deserving of US citizenship and does so through the narrative of economic productivity as an immigrant success story, which the US state values, while not highlighting the contradiction in a state policy that rests on economic productivity as the primary measure of "good citizenship" yet does not seem to reward it. It is also this kind of framing that reifies and presents a limited definition of productivity that is deserving of US citizenship. In this context, he is a model American who is living the "good life," brought about by his career as a journalist. In his "Define American" video, he further reiterated: "I define American as someone who works really hard, someone who is proud to be in this country and who wants to contribute to it; I am independent. I pay taxes. I am self-sufficient. I am an American." This narrative of self-sufficiency presupposes a kind of American citizenship that is based on neoliberal principles that value self-governing and self-activating individuals who will not be a burden to the state.

But to what extent is Vargas also an exception? He himself acknowledges the fact that he has not been deported, which he attributes to the ways in which he has become a public figure, where the publicity affords him a degree of protection. But it is also because of the very fact that he is an exception to the US state-constructed figure of the deportable subject that he assumes a privileged and perhaps, a protected status. As he professed, "Coming out didn't endanger me; it had protected me. A Philippine-born, college-educated, outspoken mainstream journalist is not the face the government wants to put on its deportation program"

(Vargas 2012). In this moment, Vargas invokes race and class and while he does attempt to highlight the contradictions in his relationship to the state, he does so without historicizing this experience, especially in terms of what this means for Filipinos in general, and how the United States has historically constituted the Philippines as a colonized space and Filipinos as an ideal labor force. He is deemed as an "outlaw," yet he is not what the US state seeks to mobilize as the deportable subject whose "freedom of movement" (De Genova 2012) must be held up to scrutiny. He is a model and therefore desirable subject for the US state by virtue of his economic productivity, even if some question his integrity for not disclosing his status at an earlier point and thus, deceiving his community.

Tago-ng-Tago and the Politics of Belonging: Philip Jacinto and Myra Cordero

Until his coming out, Vargas was part of what Filipinos referred to as the tago-ng-tago community in the United States, comprised of individuals who became undocumented primarily through overstaying their visas. Their presence has contributed to the growth of precarious low-wage employment, both within informal and formal economies. Between 2008–9, I met a group of Filipino workers who work within the burgeoning gray market economy of home-care work in Southern California and whose lives are caught up within and governed by the uncertainty and insecurity that come with their undocumented status. These caregivers defy the common perception of workers in this field as those possessing low levels of social capital; instead, many of these workers had attained advanced degrees in fields like nursing, education, business, and engineering. Many of them had also worked in high-paying and high-status occupations or assumed supervisory positions in the Philippines. Their stories offer this disruption and give voice to a group who, unlike Vargas, are unable to experience the same upward mobility and are instead rendered immobile in an exploitative industry that profits from their vulnerable status. I present two snapshots of these stories.

Philip Jacinto[11] is a forty-year-old man with a degree in marine engineering. He worked as a seafarer for sixteen years. In 2005, his ship docked in the United States in Port Hueneme, and although he had just finished his contract and was on his way back to the Philippines after having been on the ship for three years, the temptation of being in the United States overcame him. He succumbed to this temptation by jumping ship with the help of his ship's security guard who facilitated his passage and relatives living in California who provided him temporary refuge and an entry point into the world of caregiving work. As with other undocumented caregivers like him, his first job was at a board-and-care facility, which was owned by Filipinos. These facilities, as is well known among caregivers, are notorious for understaffing, low wages, and deplorable working conditions. Philip ended up working in such a situation—being shuttled to work in three different locations—and managing a range of work that went beyond caregiving (for example, housekeeping and cooking).

The precariousness of his situation became evident when he was terminated without any reason; given his status, he did not have any recourse to take action against his employers. Thereafter he sought employment in a home-care agency whose unscrupulous practices involved attempting to impose a $45 deduction from the purported daily base pay of $80. His employers justified this deduction by explaining that it was necessitated because he did not have a social security number, which thereby required extra processing time, and the fact that he did not have a car/drivers license, which necessitated availing of their carpooling service. When I met him in 2008, Philip had been living in the United States for three years and seemed to have found a reliable network of friends to keep him apprised of better-paying and less labor-intensive jobs. He is quite aware of his dispensability as a caregiver and has, thus, learned how to perform a series of "added" bonuses to ensure his job security, such as giving hair cuts and massages to his clients. While he does not necessarily see the work of caregiving as a difficult transition from his seafaring work, which involved intensive work with machines, because both require a certain kind of body labor; it is also for this very reason that he does not envision it as a permanent job. As he explained, "katawan ang punuhan" (your body is your capital)—where he regards his body as that which determines his capacity to do this work, but recognizes that is also the very reason why he cannot imagine doing this work on a long-term basis because of what it demands on the body. However, he believes this to be the most viable job he can access, especially given his status.

Perhaps, in addition to the precariousness of his job status, Philip also feels the consequences of being an undocumented caregiver in the context of his separation from his family. He, like a growing number of migrant workers, is part of a transnational family, having left his wife and daughter in the Philippines while working overseas. Already quiet, Philip grew somber during the interview as he narrated his current familial situation. He left the Philippines in 2002 at a time when his wife was pregnant with their only child. At the time of our interview, his daughter was five years old. Their skype conversations often revolved around their daughter's queries regarding his homecoming or complaints about his absence at school events and her constant longing for his presence in her everyday life. In response, Philip has also constructed his absence in his family's life not only as a consequence of a faulty immigration system but also as a matter of self-determination and one that is embedded in a racialized and naturalizing discourse about Filipinos' work ethic: "For people like me, I would be grateful if I had papers. We want to live legally. We would have an opportunity to get our family so we can be happy. We are not doing this work just for our livelihood and survival. You know how Filipinos are—we are thinking about our future and not just our livelihood—unlike Whites who are working now just so they can save money for themselves in the future."

While it is in this moment that Philip makes a case for why Filipinos like him are deserving of the benefits afforded to those who carry the requisite authorization to work in the United States, it is also the moment that highlights the contradictory position he occupies as an immigrant worker who disrupts the narrative of the much lauded desirable Filipino migrant. On the one hand, he is one of the millions of Filipinos, paraded as modern-day economic heroes. On the other hand, he is also what the Philippine state categorizes as the "irregular migrant," which disrupts this narrative of heroism. Although he shares Vargas's status, his is not the story that is likely to garner sympathy from a state that is insistent on projecting an image of greatness—what the former Philippine President Arroyo would refer to as the "Great Filipino Worker." He works in a low-wage job, contributes to the so-called care crisis by being an absent father, and lives in the United States without the requisite authorization. Nevertheless, his story offers an interruption to Vargas's exceptional story because, unlike Vargas, he does not carry the class privilege or social status to garner the same kind of protection. This is also the case for Myra Cordero, a caregiver whose story I turn to next.

Myra Cordero is a forty-four-year-old woman who left the Philippines in 1992 to work as a domestic worker in Hong Kong. At this time, she worked for a family she referred to as a "royal" family, whose affluence afforded her the resources to send her children to private schools and purchase a house and a car in the Philippines. Unfortunately, these were also the resources that rendered her husband dependent and irresponsible—resulting in his squandering her hard-earned money on top of engaging in extramarital affairs. His absence as a father necessitated Myra's designation of her sister-in-law as her children's caregiver. As with many migrant parents, working overseas is based on the hope of ensuring that their children do not end up working in low-wage jobs and instead experience a wider degree of social and economic mobility. However, this was not the case for Myra; it was her daughter who supported her family and allowed for her brothers' social mobility. Myra's daughter found a job as a musician overseas, and her earnings not only enabled her two brothers to pursue nursing and computer engineering, but they also allowed her to financially support Myra when she became financially strapped.

I met Myra in 2008 where she had been living in Southern California for six years. She accompanied the so-called royal family on their visit to the United States and, like Philip, she saw this trip as a ticket to reuniting with her family who was then living in Northern California. While she boasted about the material rewards of working for this royal family, she also felt like a "prisoner" whose activities and movements were constantly monitored. Her parents, who are based in California, sought to find ways to also bring her to the United States so they facilitated a virtual introduction between her and a man named Fred who started to court her while she still worked in Hong Kong. Thus, he was the other motivation for her to make her way to the United States. Her employers decided to let her go and what she thought was going to be a blissful life with Fred turned out to be a nightmare. Soon after relocating to California, Myra moved in with Fred and his sister. Myra soon realized that Fred's sister had a temper that seemed to get triggered by jealousy and the attention that Fred was giving to her. This temper ultimately escalated to violent acts that the sister committed toward Myra. His sister lived with them for two years, and despite Myra's grievances, Fred did not intervene. Thus, Myra thought that if she and Fred moved away, this would minimize this tension or at least take Myra away from this violence. She found and paid for a house that they rented, but it was only a matter of time when the nightmare continued as Fred also engaged in similar acts of violence toward Myra. He monitored Myra's every movement, including accompanying her to work and making sure she told him every detail of her daily activity. Myra was too afraid to report him to the police because he threatened her with deportation. She asked her family for help, but they carried the same fear. So instead she was told to "just bear it." One night the intensity of his violence resulted in Myra being physically incapacitated. It was at this moment that she, with the help of other caregivers, finally decided that she needed to escape. Two caregivers helped her leave the house, with one of them providing her refuge. Myra could not get a restraining order from the police because she did not have a medical record of his attacks. So she remained in hiding from Fred, working as a "reliever" for caregivers who needed a temporary replacement while they were on leave or on their days off.

Myra's story exemplifies the heightened vulnerability and immobility that come with this status and the specific gendered dynamics at play. The fear of deportation became the primary reason Myra tolerated and stayed in this relationship, just as it was for her family who was not able to provide her the requisite sanctuary. Even in her most severe moment of despair, she did not get any support:

> I told my parents that he strangled me. I told them that I'm about to die and they didn't do anything. How will I go to San Francisco when he has my money? They would ask [Fred about the abuse] but of course he would deny it. Why would he tell them the truth? My sister was so scared because they thought that he would report me to immigration. They said that I should just put up with it. But he is going to kill me! (Interview, 2/21/09)

This particular instance only highlights the precarious status she occupies that not only renders her vulnerable to violence and exploitative work arrangements but also is exacerbated by the lack of support from her own social network. Moreover, her experiences fall outside the success story that would afford any kind of social tribute. Not only is she the "absent" parent, but also her earnings ultimately were not able to stop her daughter from also pursuing overseas work. Nevertheless, she takes pride in her work as a caregiver: "Binubuhay ang pasyente," she remarked as she described the godlike responsibility of breathing life into people. She described instances of caring that often demanded constant monitoring, lack of sleep, and backbreaking tasks–all of which also took a toll on her own health. But in recounting her experiences, her narrative is always embedded in a discourse of self-sacrifice–whether in terms of managing the emotional pain of leaving her children, or in terms of the heroic acts she commits to save her patient's lives. In the end, it is her life and health that take the toll and pay the price for caring.

Conclusion

At the end of one of my interviews, a caregiver named Marie Atienza explained that America is certainly not the so-called land of milk and honey, especially in the context of her undocumented status and its impact on the work of caregiving. She said, "Imagine when my patient dies after eight years of working with her, I find it hard to look for another job. It is good if I have a regular three-day schedule. Otherwise, I just relieve, [working as a "reliever" which is temporary work]. Sometimes there is no work. It is hard. I know a lot of agencies so I ask them if there are vacancies. But many of the agencies I know about have also closed." Like other caregivers, Marie's disillusionment with the United States does not only pertain to the isolation and loneliness that come with engaging in this work and being separated from their families. Rather, her situation demonstrates the multiple axes of vulnerability that are defined by, or get exacerbated by her undocumented status. As caregivers in this low-wage industry, these contingent workers are already vulnerable to market dynamics and structural conditions that contribute to the precariousness of their situation.

As the discourse on immigration reform continues to broaden its lenses and be inclusive of other communities, this move must also be attentive to how such inclusion is framed, what it excludes and privileges, and what contradictions and tensions are embedded in this movement and in individual communities. For Filipinos whose subjectivity as a colonized subject positions them in distinct ways relative to the US state, their participation and incorporation into this conversation must be attentive to this colonial history and its legacies. While Jose Antonio Vargas's story served as a catalyst for allowing the movement to incorporate other voices, his representation and strategy are also limited and do not seek to destabilize the very system and institution that reproduces the inequalities faced by immigrants as racialized minorities in the United States. As Lisa Lowe (1996) noted, "Legal institutions *reproduce* the capitalist relations of production as *racialized gendered relations* and are therefore symptomatic and determining of the relations of production themselves" (22). In the cases I have presented, Filipinos are no exception, and the ways in which public figures like Vargas seek to narrate their visibility as undocumented immigrants still serve to reify the terms and conditions under which the US state views immigrants—primarily as economic actors—whose labor will not only serve capital's needs, but also fulfill the state's racial project of stratification. Meanwhile, they are also somewhat abandoned by the Philippine state, which deems them to be illegitimate ambassadors of their country. One of the "reality checks" outlined in the materials designed by the Overseas Workers Welfare Administration dictated, "Iiwan mo ang pamilya mo pero dala mo ang bansa mo" (you leave your family but you bring your country with you). As Filipinos, they are supposed to carry the burden of upholding the so-called image of greatness of the Filipino worker. Meanwhile, in these scenarios, workers like Philip and Myra then suffer the consequences of these renderings—leaving them in positions of vulnerability and fear, immobility and uncertainty; whose lives are implicated in institutional neoliberal imperatives that continue to govern the ways in which immigrants get defined and become desirable subjects of the state.

Notes

1. What gets defined as a "highly skilled" or "unskilled" occupational category is, of course, highly problematic. In the case of the Filipino labor diaspora, those who work in the low-wage sector as caregivers, nannies, and domestic workers often possess advanced degrees and have worked as nurses or teachers or possess skills that would make them "overqualified" for the work or not the typical candidate for the job (for example, seafarers, engineers)

2. According to the Commission on Filipinos Overseas, "Irregular migrants" are those not properly documented or without valid residence or work permits or who are overstaying in a foreign country.

3. Paterik, Stephanie. 2007. "Resorts Tap Filipino Laborers: Recruiting Overseas Helps Fill Staffing Shortage." *Arizona Republic*, April 29.

4. Vargas, Jose Antonio. 2011. "Outlaw: My Life in America as an Undocumented Immigrant." *The New York Times Magazine*, June 26.

5. Filipinos were already working overseas even prior to the 1974 labor export policy. The first official group of laborers, the "manongs," left the Philippines as plantation laborers for Hawaii in the early twentieth century (1900-30s) as a result of a rigorous program of overseas recruitment that Hawaiian plantation owners launched to fill their labor demands and to replace striking workers (for example, the 1909 Japanese labor strike) (Agoncillo 1990; Bello et al. 1982; Cordova 1983; Eviota 1992; Liu et al.1991; Sharma 1984; Takaki 1998; Villegas 1988).

6. In my work, I examine labor brokering not only from the perspective of the state but also in its partnership with other actors such as private employment agencies and workers who are products of this work. Also, the brokering process I highlight is specifically focused on the production of careworkers and the gendered and racialized processes embedded in this (Guevarra 2003, 2010).

7. The specific breakdown of this number is as follows: temporary migrants (4,324,388); permanent migrants (4,423,680); irregular migrants (704,916). "Permanent migrants" refer to "immigrants or legal permanent residents abroad whose stay do not depend on work contracts." "Temporary migrants" are "persons whose stay overseas is employment related, and who are expected to return at the end of their work contracts." "Irregular migrants" are "those not properly documented or without valid residence or work permits, or who are overstaying in a foreign country" (http://www.cfo.gov.ph). The problem with this classification system is that some overseas Filipino workers are also under contracts but carry immigrant visas like the EB-3 that is offered to many nurses working in the United States. Therefore, a worker on EB-3 visas technically enters the United States as a "temporary migrant" but is eventually eligible to become a "permanent migrant."

8. While "remittances" refer to the "transfers, in cash or in kind from a migrant to household residents in the country of origin," The Bangko Sentral ng Pilipinas (BSP) calculates and records remittances in its balance of payment computation by following the IMF broader definition of remittances which includes the following: (1) workers' remittances or cash transfers from migrants to resident households in the country of origin; (2) compensation or wages to employees paid to individuals working in a country outside their legal residence; and (3) migrant transfers involving capital transfers of financial assets when workers move to another country and are there for more than one year (ADB 2004). However, the remittances BSP calculates take into account only money sent through official banking channels.

9. The immigration preference system is as follows (Liu 1991): first preference category: unmarried children (over twenty-one years old) of US citizens; second preference category: spouses and children of permanent US residents; third preference category: professionals, scientists, artists; fourth preference category: married children of US citizens; fifth preference: brothers and sisters of US citizens; sixth

preference: skilled and unskilled workers in occupations where labor is in short supply; EXEMPTIONS: spouses of US citizens, children (under twenty-one) of US citizens, parents of US citizens

10. "Racial statecraft" describes "how the state codified, enforced, and recalibrated immigration and nationality controls that determined the political and civic standing of racialized collectivities" (970).

11. These names are pseudonyms.

Works Cited

Asis, Maruja B. 1992. The Overseas Employment Program Policy. In *Philippine Labor Migration: Impact and Policy*, edited by G. Battistella and A. Paganoni, 68–112. Quezon City: Scalabrini Migration Center.

Baldoz, Rick. 2004. Valorizing Racial Boundaries: Hegemony and Conflict in the Racialization of Filipino Migrant Labour in the United States. *Ethnic and Racial Studies* 27 (6): 969–86.

———. 2011. *The Third Asiatic Invasion: Empire and Migration in Filipino America, 1898–1946*. New York: NYU Press.

Bergamini, Marie Carmen. 1964. An Assessment of International Nursing Students in the United States: A Case Study of the Philippine Experience. PhD diss., University of California, Berkeley.

Chang, Jeff. 2012 October. The Progressive Interview: Jose Antonio Vargas. *The Progressive*: 35–37.

Choy, Catherine Ceniza. 2003. *Empire of Care: Nursing and Migration in Filipino American History*. Durham, NC, and London: Duke University Press.

Cordova, Fred. 1983. *Filipinos: Forgotten Asian Americans: A Pictorial Essay, 1763-Circa 1963*. Seattle: Demonstration Project for Asian Americans.

Espiritu, Yen Le. 2007. Gender, Migration, and Work: Filipina Health Care Professionals in the United States. In *Contemporary Asian America: A Multidisciplinary Reader*, 2nd ed., edited by M. Zhou and J. V. Gatewood, 259–78. New York and London: New York University Press.

Guevarra, Anna Romina 2010. *Marketing Dreams, Manufacturing Heroes: The Transnational Labor Brokering of Filipino Workers*. New Brunswick, NJ: Rutgers University Press.

Guevarra, Anna Romina, and Lolita Lledo. 2013. Formalizing the Informal: Low Wage Immigrant Highly Skilled Filipina Caregivers and the Pilipino Worker Center. In *Immigrant Women Workers in the Neoliberal Age*, edited by N. Flores-Gonzalez, A. R. Guevarra, M. Toro-Morn, and G. Chang. Champaign-Urbana: University of Illinois Press.

Habal, Estella. 2008. *San Francisco's International Hotel: Mobilizing the Filipino American Community in the Anti-Eviction Movement*. Philadelpha, PA: Temple University Press.

Keely, Charles B. 1973. Philippine Migration: Internal Movements and Emigration to the United States. *International Migration Review* 7 (2): 177–87.

Lau, Yvonne. 2006. Revisioning Filipino American Communities: Evolving Identities, Issues, and Organizations. In *The New Chicago: A Social and Cultural Analysis*, edited by J. Koval, L. Bennett, M. I. J. Bennett, F. Demissie, R. Garner, and K. Kim, 141–54. Philadelphia, PA: Temple University Press.

———. 2007. Change, Community, and Politics: Shifting Agendas Among Chicago's Filipino Americans. In *American Sociological Association 102nd Annual Conference*. New York.

Liu, John M., Paul Ong, and Carolyn Rosenstein. 1991. Dual Chain Migration: Post 1965 Filipino Immigration to the United States. *International Migration Review* 25 (3): 487–513.

Lowe, Lisa. 1996. *Immigrant Acts: On Asian American Cultural Politics*. Durham, NC, and London: Duke University Press.

Ngai, Mae. 2004. *Impossible Subjects: Illegal Aliens and the Making of Modern America*. Princeton, NJ: Princeton University Press.

Ong, Paul, and Tania Azores. 1994. The Migration and Incorporation of Filipino Nurses. In *The New Asian Immigration in Los Angeles and Global Restructuring*, edited by P. Ong, E. Bonacich and L. Cheng, 164–95. Philadelphia, PA: Temple University Press.

Parreñas, Rhacel 2001. *Servants of Globalization: Women, Migration, and Domestic Work*. Stanford, CA: Stanford University Press.

Paterik, Stephanie. 2007. Resorts Tap Filipino Laborers: Recruiting Overseas Helps Fill Staffing Shortage. *Arizona Republic*, April 29.

Posadas, Barbara M. 1999. *The Filipino Americans*. Westport, CT: Greenwood Press.

Rodriguez, Robyn Magalit. 2010. *Migrants for Export: How the Philippine State Brokers Labor to the World*. Minneapolis: University of Minnesota Press.

Sharma, Miriam. 1984. Labor Migration and Class Formation Among the Filipinos in Hawaii, 1906–1946. In *Labor Immigration Under Capitalism: Asian Workers in the United States Before World War II*, edited by L. Cheng and E. Bonacich, 579–615. Berkeley: University of California Press.

Takaki, Ronald. 1998. *A History of Asian Americans: Strangers from a Different Shore*, updated and rev. ed. Boston and New York: Little, Brown and Company.

Tung, Charlene. 2003. Caring Across Borders: Motherhood, Marriage, and Filipina Domestic Workers in California. In *Asian/Pacific Islander American Women: A Historical Anthology*, edited by S. Hune and G. Nomura, 301–15. New York and London: New York University Press.

Tyner, James. 1996. The Gendering of Philippine International Labor Migration. *Professional Geographer* 48 (4): 405–16.

Vargas, Jose Antonio. 2011. Outlaw: My life in America as an Undocumented Immigrant. *New York Times Magazine*, June 26.

———. 2012. Not Legal, Not Leaving. *TIME*, June 25, 34–44.

Villegas, Edberto M. 1988. *The Political Economy of Philippine Labor Laws*. Manila: Foundation of Nationalist Studies.

17

"Home" and The Filipino Channel

Stabilizing Economic Security, Migration Patterns, and Diaspora through New Technologies

EMILY NOELLE IGNACIO

In recent years, scholars from various disciplines have interrogated what circumscribes the concept of "home." Barros (2008), a legal scholar, for example, has examined "home" as a legal concept within which lawyers must take into account the status of both the people and various structures (financial and legal), as well as the structure of the "house as property," in and of itself. Others, like Cieraad (2010), through "place attachment theory" analyze how individuals' memories affect their emotional attachment to home or places, ideas, and/or events that remind them of "home." Because of my own research on transnational movements of various peoples and images between the Philippines and other places in the world, particularly the United States (for which they once served as a colony), I have been increasingly pushed toward asking that same key question: *What does it mean to be "home"?*

I ask this especially as I have recently reimmersed myself in discussions with my colleagues Douglas Avella-Castro (2014) and Jonathan Grove (2014) about the applicability of Chela Sandoval's *Methodology of the Oppressed* in thinking about honoring the voices of Puerto Rican churchgoers, white males in Appalachia, and Filipinos in the diaspora; Foucault's ideas of what it means to be "free" in this postmodern moment; and, Toni Morrison and Bernice Reagon's (1983) musings and warnings about the difficulties of feeling "home" in this house that race, gender, capitalism, and colonization built. What *does* it mean to be *home*? Is it possible for those of us who have been negatively impacted, but have simultaneously greatly benefited, from these various oppressions to feel home, anywhere?

Although all those who have experienced various intersections of oppression can (and should, in my opinion) seriously reflect and engage in discussions about "home," for this chapter, I am thinking precisely about members of diasporas of present or former colonies whose countries are still deeply dependent on the countries that colonized them. Whether we're talking about Puerto Ricans in the United States, Algerians in France, or, in my case, Filipinos in the United States, our notions of "home," our positionalities, and our selves reflect and embody our past and present social, political, economic, and cultural relationships with this (technically, former) colonial power.

Home in the Afterlife of Empire

I have presented some empirical material related to this overall research project at an Association for Asian American Studies conference that focused on the "Afterlives of Empire." Without fail, critical Filipino Studies scholars questioned the use of the word "afterlives." Why? One of the reasons is that the Philippines has wholeheartedly accepted its place in the global neoliberal capitalist order by embracing the fact that, in order to pay down their enormous debts to the World Bank, their labor should continue to be their #1 export, cultivating a sophisticated labor-brokerage system that relies heavily on problematic stereotypes of Asian/Filipina females.

Unsurprisingly, the gender and ethnicity of the leader made no difference. Though the selling of Filipinas began in earnest by President Ferdinand Marcos and US Secretary of State Robert McNamara in the 1960s, just a few years ago, President Gloria Macapagal Arroyo met with G8 leaders and introduced herself as "the CEO of the Philippines" with "8 million workers for export." Anna Guevarra (2010) and Robyn Rodriguez (2010), especially, have written extensively on this labor-brokerage system, the Foucauldian disciplining of Filipina workers, and the creation of the notion of a "migrant citizenship."

But, as I thought about their work, I began to look at how it was that the Philippines has come to be seen by CEOs of transnational corporations, non-Filipinos, and/or people who don't identify as Filipinos as a place to obtain the "ideal worker" or to set up shop. As Guevarra (2010) and Rodriguez (2010) have stated, disciplined (in the Foucauldian sense) Filipino workers themselves serve as "bulletin boards" for this labor-brokerage system. Thus, both government agencies (such as, the Technical Education and Skills Development Authority [TESDA]) and private companies spend considerable amounts of time and money to developing these "ideal workers." Because of the feminization of certain, more open labor sectors, the Philippine government and private brokers actively cultivate this "ideal Filipina worker," drawing on accepted stereotypes and disciplining their workers to embody these stereotypes.

Similarly, it is clear to me that images of the country have to also highlight why the Philippines is the place to either set up shop (for transnational companies to outsource their labor) or to obtain these workers. Given this, I believe we should also focus on the comparative advantage the Philippines has in selling the special relationship between it and the United States to CEOs of transnational corporations, potential overseas employers, the potential Filipino immigrants alike. It is from this particular vantage point that I started to undertake this particular project. And, it is in exploring this special (neocolonial) relationship that I realized how important is this notion of "home" to this particular neoliberal project.

Background

Before I introduce how The Filipino Channel fits into this puzzle, though, I want to briefly explain why I believe that "home" is so important to neocolonialism and the neoliberal project. Mae Ngai (2004) has argued that just because the US "granted (political) independence" to the Philippines in 1934, ultimately, to prevent the "influx" of labor-organizing and race-mixing Filipino males to the United States, it does not follow that the United States wished the Philippines to be absolutely economically independent.

The United States is and has been heavily dependent on Filipino labor for nearly 120 years, and the Philippines on remittances from various countries, particularly the United States for, at least, the past fifty years. This mirrors Mexico's economic relationship with the United States. Yet, Philippine independence—particularly during a moment when countries were more open to establishing a more protectionist and "shared risk," Keynesian economic system—threatened to bring problems to this economic order. In particular, "granting independence" risks the cultivation of Filipino national pride, ideas of "difference" between the United States and this former colony, or worse, an anticolonial sentiment. Thus, while it was and is important for the United States to create and maintain the political and economic order between the United States and Mexico by producing and reproducing social and cultural boundaries between "us" versus them," for the Philippines, this boundary making and reinforcing of the political and economic relationship entails the reversal of this social and cultural order. It entails the production and reinforcement of *"sameness"*—or the creation of a "home" away from "home"—in order to contend with this growing sense of national pride, ideas of difference between the United States, and especially any anticolonial sentiment.

These notions of "home" are complex and multivalent. The home in the Philippines must appear somewhat Americanized so as to stand out as a place that's exotic, but not too exotic—so that tourists and heads of corporations or businesses (American and non-American alike) can be assured that they have chosen a place whose population knows how to operate in modernity. The home in the United States must appear like a place wherein one can "move on up"—but do so in a place that embraces and values their community, contributions, and culture—or, at least, provides an access to the Philippines in some way—via Skype, satellite TV, or, at least, accepted cultural artifacts like food items or food chains Jollibee, Goldilocks, or lumpia trucks.

Much like the "slavery is in the past" rhetoric we race scholars often hear when we attempt to talk about the continuing significance of race, those that benefit from neoliberalism and neocolonialism redefine this "special relationship" between the United States and the Philippines, creating this notion of "sameness" and a "home away from home" by focusing on "contributions" of Filipinos to the "building of the USA" that necessarily erases or (at best) downplays the violent history between the United States and its former colony. Using Joseph Nevins's (2010) language, but applied in the Philippines, the production of "sameness" effaces difference that legitimizes this colonial relationship. That is, instead of capitalizing on the construction of a "violent other" to efface violent difference, it is the construction of a "peaceful sameness," a shared history, and an American experience that pacifies the Philippines.[1]

New Technologies, Identity, "Home," and Business

How are these social and cultural representations of sameness, of "home" created, produced, and disseminated? In my book *Building Diaspora* (2005), I had written about Filipino diasporic members' use of the Internet to stay in touch with one another and to learn about "home." Here, I write about the use of another, relatively new technology that many nations with huge diasporas literally capitalize on: satellite television. I focus here on ABS-CBN's The Filipino Channel (or TFC, or, what they'd recently called themselves, The Filipino Community). This channel is one major medium that helps develop that comparative advantage of the Philippines as having the ultimate labor force by simultaneously focusing on bringing the diaspora together—on being a home away from home—*kasi kapamilya tayo* (because we are family), but it also sells the Philippines to non-Filipinos and heads of transnational corporations alike. Specifically, I focus on a now defunct, but hugely popular and long-running show, entitled *Wowowee* and the long-running show, *Citizen Pinoy*. But, instead of only focusing on how both shows serve the needs of the diaspora, I would like to simultaneously talk about how they serve the needs of the Philippine nation as well.

As I stated before, and while it sounds crass, the emigration policy is one of the most effective ways for the Philippines to repay its debts. Thus, if we look at the relationship between the Philippines and "the West" from a very strict, neoliberal business vantage point, President Arroyo was right to consider Filipino labor her most lucrative export, in addition to using American colonization as a comparative advantage to increase tourism and court transnational corporations to the city centers.

Managing a balance between this lucrative emigration policy and attracting transnational capital is, actually, a complex task, especially in an era where less-developed countries are competing with one another for potential "host" countries' and transnational corporations' attention and where neoliberal economic policies reign. That is, the Philippines has to appear stable so as to attract more transnational corporations and foreign capital either to its shores or as sponsors for their humungous labor force, but it cannot be so stable because it risks being considered more costly than their competitors in terms of labor.

To be blunt: in neoliberal economic thinking, to remain competitive against other developing countries aiming to attract the same transnational corporations' interests in their labor both abroad and locally means that the Philippines must continue to keep its currency value low. This continues to contribute to a plethora of problems, not least of which is making it nearly impossible not only to pay down their debt to the World Bank. According to the World Bank, as of 2013, the external debt owed in US dollars was $60,608,594,000. The Philippine Central Bank reported that, in this same year (2013), remittances of Overseas Filipino Workers totaled $25.1 billion, which greatly supported local economies and also accounted for 8.4 percent of the GDP. This is but one reason why the Philippines *must* continue to depend on foreign investment in the form of remittances and tourists. While it is true that Filipinos have, increasingly, been deployed to the Gulf Region, such as Dubai, and other countries where English is not a primary language, many emigrants and contract workers—as well as tourists—reside and work within so-called Westernized countries.

This is where The Filipino Channel and online spaces come in handy. In order to accomplish the above goals, the Philippines must present itself in a "safe" way, especially to Westernized, English-speaking transnational corporations and countries with strong currencies like the United States, Canada, Australia, and England. They absolutely must do this to convince employers of successful transnational corporations and heads of state that their laborers can serve their companies and citizens effectively. But, post-September 11, 2001, many nations (not just the United States) started to change their immigration laws, such that it is more difficult to obtain visas, other than those which grant temporary migration status. Again, with respect to the Philippine government, so long as their workers can obtain good paying jobs outside the nation and send remittances that will help pay the debt, all is well.

With respect to families, however, this is problematic. Like any other immigrant group, Filipinos would much rather obtain permanent visas, either through employment opportunities or via family reunification provisions, to ensure that they can provide for themselves and their families in the best manner possible. This is where the program *Citizen Pinoy* is pivotal to the discussion.

Citizen Pinoy: Success and the "American Dream"

While it is true, especially post-1965 in the history of the United States, that many Filipinos have tried to immigrate permanently to the United States, many have done so using circuitous routes. My parents, for example, came independently to the United States via student visas. They'd married in the United States, but because my father's visa was to expire, they applied for working visas in Canada. After gaining work experience in Canada, they applied for working visas to the United States and were able to immigrate there as permanent residents that allowed them to, after seven years, naturalize as citizens. As in anything, timing is everything. At the time, suburbanization in the United States left many city centers devoid of essential workers, especially in the high-service sector (Barlow 2003). Thus, my parents, who were lab technicians, were recruited to work in hospitals in Chicago's inner-city neighborhoods—but this was after I was born in Canada. Technically, then, I am a first-generation, Canadian immigrant of Filipino descent.

Before online communities and satellite television, immigrants from various countries learned of these measures much as they do now: through ethnic newspapers and other media and word of mouth (especially, via their places of work and ethnic organizations). With respect to Filipinos in the United States, Rick Bonus (2003), Sunny Vergara (2010), and others have written extensively about this. *Citizen Pinoy* is one program on The Filipino Channel that continues this tradition. Here, every weekend, lawyers (particularly Michael Gurfinkel) explain the ever-changing (especially post-9/11/2001) policies in a multitude of countries, and they briefly provide explanations of who might still be able to emigrate under said law. In addition, the program highlights success stories, especially by those who were able to emigrate to the United States.

Again, although there are Filipinos all over the world, some in nations whose currency is stronger than the US dollar, the goal for many Filipinos is to emigrate and settle in the United States. Thus, even though this is a global program, *Citizen Pinoy* and the lawyers' corresponding website (http://www.gurfinkel.com/) has a tendency to focus on bringing people to the United States. In fact, Gurfinkel's main selling point is that he and his office's main goal is "to be of service to the Filipino community" (The Filipino Channel press release, February 2007) and that they have been "fortunate to help thousands of people solve their immigration problems, be reunited with their families, and be able to live the "American Dream" (gurfinkel.com/).

Thus, there are three law offices, two in California (in Los Angeles and San Francisco) and one in New York City.

Obviously, this particular program is pragmatic in nature and addresses how and where Filipinos can obtain visas. But, by highlighting the various, unique ways for our family members to emigrate to more developed countries, and the focus on "success stories," particularly an unproblematic acquisition of the "American Dream," *Citizen Pinoy*, deploys the "special relationship" between the United States and the Philippines in that it actively constructs the United States as Filipinos' "home away from home" to reinforce neoliberal economic policies and maintain the neocolonial relationship between the United States and the Philippines.

As each story unfolds, no one questions that leaving the Philippines is essential to the financial stability of the whole family. In other words, it leaves unquestioned the need to split up the family for the good of the family and nation. As Anna Guevarra (2010) has noted, emigrating Filipinos have been well socialized to be the *bagong bayani* of the Philippines. In 2015, The Filipino Channel's self-identification tag that was often shown at the beginning of each program contained various descriptors of the Filipino community; the first descriptor that was highlighted and proudly displayed was *bagong bayani*.

Of course, then, this leaves little room for discussing how to *remain* home in the Philippines and/or how the Philippines may be able to become economically stable while keeping families intact. In other words, *Citizen Pinoy* and other programs, simply focus on *maintaining* stability and relationships with people "back home" or within "the homeland," which, obviously, leaves unquestioned the dependency on emigrants to strengthen the nation. This art of maintaining relationships—and leaving unquestioned the distance—between members of the diaspora and those back home is especially prominent in the second program that I examine in relation to the question of home.

On *Wowowee*: The People's Show

Wowowee was, technically, a game show within which various members of the audience were called to participate. Much of it, though, resembled a very long variety show, as various performers are called to the stage to dance and/or sing to a myriad of songs. For two and a half to three hours, six days a week, members of the diaspora watched host Willie Revillame bound across the stage, yelling "WELCOME TO YOUR SHOW!!!" and then perform songs (while surrounded by scantily clad mestizas, of course) in Tagalog or a mix between Filipino and usually American English words or, sometimes, songs that contained either Taglish or Englog words. Here, though, without explicitly focusing on emigration and the American Dream, this show highlighted the continuing special relationship between the Philippines and the United States. It also displayed the strong tourist industry through focusing on tourists—of Filipino and seemingly non-Filipino descent alike—in each show.

For example, in a typical episode, the initial MC was a hip-hop, b-boy DJ, mixing Tagalog songs with James Brown's "I Feel Good," while very light-skinned Filipino women in red miniskirts gyrated about the stage. Meanwhile, the cameras panned the audience, focusing on people of various phenotypes holding up placards that read Bohol, Bataan, England, Seattle, New York, California, Virginia, Honolulu, highlighting tourism from both within and outside the country. Other placards displayed "thank you" messages either from people greeting their family members abroad or from people acknowledging family members housing them during their vacation.

As in other variety shows around the world, often the show's laughs were made at the expense of people in the audience who do not fit the standard beauty ideal. To be sure, this show and other programs on The Filipino Channel could and should be analyzed through a variety of angles—race, culture, beauty standards, and nationalism. However, for the purposes of this chapter, I concentrate on how it, literally, brought the diaspora together in one room, and, through its choice of contestants and the chosen family stories, connected and sutured particularly very sad stories that illuminated the hardships people face at home, stories about the lack of good employment prospects and the other conditions that have propelled people to emigrate in order to give back to the homeland especially via remittances.

The real story and reason for the success of *Wowowee*, then, is that it truly, openly reflects the state of Filipino families, labor sectors, and economic policies. On nearly every single show, cameras pan the audience and focus upon the placards they hold. Most often, the camera operators especially focus on those holding signs that indicate that person (or family) is visiting from another country. Although many others hold placards indicating the island, province, or neighborhood in the Philippines from which they came, most often, the camera operator sweeps by those audience members.

While it is true that US game shows (for example, the *Price is Right*) also pride themselves in attracting a global audience, having this global audience represented in the studio as both spectators and participants is of central importance to *Wowowee*. While watching *Wowowee*, especially seeing all these placards and hearing the personal experiences and/or hardship stories of the contestants, it is impossible to forget that many families are split between countries, that family members in the Philippines (particularly those with children) have a difficult time surviving solely on their salaries, that people abroad (though they may be suffering) cannot possibly be suffering in the same way as those in the motherland, *and* that the Philippines greatly benefits from tourism.

Thus, this show is so powerful because it spurs those overseas Filipino migrant workers to give back to the homeland in some way. Presumably, viewers remember to send something home to family members. How the show impacts diasporic members has not yet been systematically studied, but it has undeniably spurred them to donate money to the program. Indeed, one US newspaper commented:

> The show is known for occasionally bringing on contestants in traditionally low-wage jobs: housekeepers, janitors, farmers. Filipinos working overseas give money to the show, knowing that the cash prizes will go to the less fortunate.
>
> Critics of the show call it exploitative of the poor, as they're expected to share their hard-luck stories, while sometimes being made to look silly in the various contests.
>
> But others say it's inspirational.

"The show helps a lot of indigent people. It's very touching," said Wandy Opao, who keeps the television set in his Filipino restaurant in Atlantic City tuned to *Wowowee* daily.

By emphasizing audience members from outside the Philippines, the show also highlights the importance of tourism, particularly how adept the Philippines is at welcoming tourists to their "home." Most of the shows on The Filipino Channel (including various *teleserye* or TV series) display the hospitality of Filipinos and their ability to make tourists—particularly from Western countries—feel at home in this exotic, tropical paradise. It does not matter whether the audience member is of Filipino descent; the camera operator and the host take a considerable amount of time during each show to capture and shout out the names of the countries from which these audience members came. Although it does not happen in every episode, the hosts often do make the point of choosing people who belong to non-Asian/ Pacific Islander races to participate, and (though the host does highlight the country from which they came), they are given a warm homecoming and shown that in the Philippines, we are, truly, one family. Or, in the network's words, *talagang kapamilya tayo* (we are one family).

The reason that I am putting so much emphasis in this is because, as I stated earlier, I believe it is crucial to cast a critical eye on digital diasporas (whether via the Internet or satellite TV), not only as a way for members of the diaspora to keep in touch with family back home, or even as a way for Filipinos to keep up with Filipino news and pop culture. Instead, it is important to see how the medium itself carefully articulates "home" (both abroad and in the Philippines), our "homeland heroes" (*bagong bayani*) as "migrant citizens," and very specific images of the diaspora (that is, success stories and homecoming warmth) to promote the two industries—labor and tourism—that boost the GDP and somewhat keep the external debt from increasing too much.

After acknowledging the realities of pacification, maintaining neo-colonial relationships, and the fallacies of the "afterlives of empire" for former colonies, it becomes necessary to ask ourselves some very difficult questions—especially with regard to "home" and emigration policies to "places like home." These following questions are, of course, not new. But, they are questions we should ask again and should remain as guideposts for thinking about the diaspora and its futures.

The first is: while it is true that new technologies and this program indisputably have the capabilities to immediately impact members of the diaspora, should we also simultaneously address, as we started to do here, how transnational mediums (that is, satellite television, Internet groups, and social-networking tools) frame stories of "home" and the diaspora such that it is difficult to talk about and take time to analyze critically the reasons *why* the diaspora exists and is growing?

That is, instead of merely *servicing* members of the diaspora, would it be also fruitful for us to offer a program that critically assesses, in a positive manner, how the diaspora and Filipinos have not been served through these arrangements? Could there be a medium to discuss creative ways to simultaneously pay down external debt while developing the infrastructure such that the Philippines is not as dependent upon emigration and/or an industry that creates mostly low, service-sector jobs?

Should we also be asking ourselves how our remittances, the tourist industry, and other industries can be used to help people (rather than the government and transnational corporations), especially since *kapamiliya tayo*? How then can a focus on and redefinition of "home" help us, such that we can contribute most effectively to our nation, our world, industry, and families while keeping our families well provided for and intact?

Finally, how can we use our new technologies effectively to create a good, open, critical dialogue to answer these questions and generate more that may move us to better understand the construction and maintenance of "special relationships" and relations that undergird capitalism?

These questions, of course, bring up huge arguments and problematics because they force us to confront policies, practices, and laws that we unwittingly support. As someone who was trained in implementing and assessing the efficiency of neoliberal economic policies and as someone who has been and is currently seeing the effects of these neoliberal economic policies on her own family members, students, neighbors, immigrants, and families of immigrants of various races, ethnicities, and documented statuses, I urge all of us to try to continue to be judicious and critically expansive, not only in our use of these technologies to advance our individual interests but also for a more equitable "home" in the world.

Notes

1. Many thanks to Douglas Avella-Castro for helping me clarify my thoughts regarding the importance of this production of "sameness" in legitimizing—and strengthening—the "special [neocolonial] relationship" between the United States and the Philippines.

Works Cited

Avella-Castro, Douglas. 2014. Critical Reflections on and in "the Field": The Study of "Religion" and the Methodology of True (Reflexive) Praxis in Puerto Rico.

Barlow, Andrew. 2003. *Between Fear and Hope: Globalization and Race in the United States.* New York: Rowman and Littlefield Publishers, Inc.

Bonus, Enrique. 2000. *Locating Filipinos.* Philadelphia, PA: Temple University Press.

DuBois, W.E.B. 1989. [1903]. *Souls of Black Folk.* New York: Bantam Books.

The Filipino Channel. 2007. "The New Season of Citizen Pinoy." Press Release, February 16, 2007.

Grove, Jonathan K. 2014. Unmarked and Unheard: Voices of Working-class White Men in an Appalachian Borderland.

Guevarra, Anna. 2010. *Marketing Dreams, Manufacturing Heroes: The Transnational Labor Brokering of Filipino Workers.* Piscataway, NJ: Rutgers University Press.

Ignacio, Emily Noelle. 2005. *Building Diaspora: Filipino Community Formation on the Internet.* Piscataway, NJ: Rutgers University Press.

Jones, Steve G. 1997. *CyberSociety: Computer-Mediated Communication and Community.* Thousand Oaks, CA: Sage Publications.

Lindio-McGovern, Ligaya. 1998. "Peasant Women, Foreign Debt, the IMF and the GATT." *JSAWS* 4, no. 1 (December 22).

Ortiz, Eric. 2008. "'Wowowee'—What's the Attraction?" *Press of Atlantic City,* July 12, 2008. Available at http://www.pressofatlanticcity.com/186/story/203953.html

Rheingold, Howard. 2000. *Virtual Community: Homesteading on the Electronic Frontier.* Boston, MA: MIT Press.

Rodriguez, Robyn Magalit. 2010. *Migrants for Export: How the Philippine State Brokers Labor to the World.* Minneapolis: University of Minnesota Press.

Turkle, Sherry. 1997. *Life on the Screen: Identity in the Age of the Internet.* New York: Simon and Schuster.

18

"Come Back Home Soon"

The Pleasures and Agonies of "Homeland" Visits

RICK BONUS

"You are not Filipinos," Tita Ruby, our local guide in the Philippines, said to me and to some of my students, as we were on our way to the airport to fly back to Seattle.[1] "But you must come back home [here] soon," she added, rather quickly but in what seemed to sound like a contradiction. Her saying this put a hesitant smile to our faces, for it was a moment that captured what all of us have been dreadfully anticipating since the night before, to say goodbye to a place we called home for the past four weeks, and then to be simultaneously reminded that this is not our home. Tita Ruby was right. Even though some of us who identified as Filipinos by blood or by birth comfortably imagined the Philippines as "home" (or, at least, a second or alternate "home"), our US citizenship bluntly excluded us from being designated as "Filipinos," which Tita Ruby had no trouble telling us. But then again, she also invited us back, as her special reference to "back home" signaled what later to me implied a willingness on her part to perhaps reconsider or complicate her initial exclusionary gesture.

It was a contradiction that we as a class, for two study-abroad trips to the Philippines, had been ruminating on even before we left Seattle and had continued daily on site in Manila and beyond. The meanings of home, homeland, and nation, the definitions of belonging and loyalty, the practices of collectivity—what do all of these have to do with identity, history, and globality as they are all instantiated and convoluted by travel? In this chapter, I offer ethnographic accounts and analyses of two summer abroad trips to the Philippines that I led in 2007 and 2011, under the auspices of my school, the University of Washington, and with the collaborative participation of several universities and organizations in the Philippines.[2] On these trips, I took with me a total of thirty-one students, out of whom sixteen identified as Filipino Americans (all but two were children of recent immigrants; eight were women; eight were men; all were between the ages of eighteen and twenty-five). Twelve of them were traveling to the Philippines for the first time.

In the narration of selected accounts, both personal and participant-based, and based on observations, journal entries, and extended interviews before, during, and after the trips, I pay close attention to the contradictions of identity and community produced by the social encounters of travel that occurred within the specific contexts of historical and contemporary conditions of unevenness and inequality rife between the United States and the Philippines.[3] Since traveling occurs not in a vacuum, but in the interstices of origins and destinations, and the worlds of time and space that connect and disconnect them, it has the potential to produce displacement in the ways it can expose, decenter, or contradict previously held realities or hidden assumptions about selves and others (Brettell 2003; Kaplan 1996).[4] As it happens, it has the capacity to complicate the processes and contradict or limit the terms by which we are able to see ourselves in relationship to the places where we come from and go to (Gupta and Ferguson 1997; Keith and Pile 1993; Louie 2004). In this chapter, I probe how specific instances of schooling abroad for US students in the Philippines enable such contradictions to be experienced firsthand both as the expressions of the limits of transnational identity and community formation as well as the generative locations for a critical transnational consciousness and practice that attempt to circumscribe the continuing effects of social inequality between and across these nations.

My students had little difficulty comprehending the vast social, political, and economic differences between the Philippines and the United States so much so that even though their required readings emphasized the historical foundations of such difference, which colonization secured and contemporary imperialism sustains (San Juan 2007), they were not the meat of our course. Rather, these differences were treated merely as entry points for ruminating on what Vicente Rafael (2009) originally referred to as "the afterlife of empire," which I adopted for the two courses I taught—to have the students explore the conditions of "what happened next" after the Philippines declared its independence from both its Spanish and American colonizers.[5] In our courses, I asked my students to see the country not so much only through the rudimentary lens of colonization history and its aftermath, as if they were only identifying relics frozen in time, but to find ways to recognize and track the currency of US colonization in the moment of their experience. Students were, thus, provided opportunities to understand how colonization continues in its nonofficial formation, and how this contemporaneity of colonization in the Philippines is precisely the condition that makes possible all aspects of their study-abroad trip. This is the subject of the first part of this chapter.

Corollary to the study of colonization's afterlives, our classes in the Philippines pored through the conditions and complications of transnationalism—the phenomenon of having multistranded political, social, and economic relationships between at least two countries—as a significant element of modern-day globalization and, to some extent, as lived experience for some of the participants (Basch, Schiller, and Blanc 1994).[6] The principal location of inquiry for this theme centered on definitions of "home" and their related or overlapping issues with identity, belonging, nationhood, and community—what I thought initially to be an easy matching of concept with practice especially for students whose personal experience with transnationalism before our trip was immediate and familiar. I was wrong. While constituting "home" in multiple locations was easy for many of the students, including me, we were struck at how Philippine locals had quite a different attitude with regard to how we were too quick in our embrace of our own transnationality. How did we assume so brashly the ways in which our First World privilege dictated how transnationalism had to be practiced? What lessons can be learned from practices of transnationalism that depend on or reinforce uneven global conditions? The second part of the chapter discusses this.

In many respects, by the time our classes were winding down, and this was apparent in the two study-abroad instances I describe here, it became more and more clear that our privilege and advantage as members of the First World that is the United States defined how we thought about colonization and transnationalism, and how we were somehow assisting in the perpetuation of the structural inequalities brought about by these two. Such anxieties made us rethink our deep but questionable attachments to the Philippines, they encouraged us to look for pleasurable activities to distract us from our troubles, but they also motivated us to find productive ways to engage with our predicaments. Students and I were insistent on finding lessons here—lessons that did not make clear appearances to us as they were happening during those moments, but lessons learned later, of horizontal comradeship and cross-national community alliances that can be made possible in unequal spaces and during flashes of "homeland" encounters. The third and last part of the chapter covers these.

Did Tita Ruby say "come back home soon" only because she was tired of us and just wanted to be cordial? Was she perhaps relieved that finally she'd be done with having to take care of us, now that we were on our way out? Or was this simply her reminder to us that, in some complicated way, and in this colonized and transnational moment and location, the Philippines *is* but *cannot* be our home at the same time? I looked at my students, who smiled back at me. That was all we were able to express then.

A Present Past

In constructing the syllabi for these summer-abroad trips to the Philippines, my intention was to enable the student participants to explore and experience issues of colonization, postcolonization, and transnationalism as they are lived by Filipinos (and as gleaned from our observations and interactions with them). This was our principal goal. But in advancing this course mandate, I also wanted the students to engage these issues relative to themselves, either as individuals who may discover empathetic insights into the psychic effects of colonization on other individuals (from their points of view as knowledgeable and interested observers), or as members of the collective known as "American students," whose presences themselves mark in palpable forms the very colonization histories that we were studying.[7] "I guess we cannot just be regular travelers, huh?" remarked one student. "No," I said. "Our presence there will most definitely be read in relationship to who we are as Americans, the privileges we enjoy and represent to them, and possibly, the desire that many of them have to be in our shoes." "Literally," someone else muttered.

These were things I wanted students to be prepared for prior to our actual trip, for not only did I assign a hefty packet of reading materials for them to pore over, but also I led a couple of workshops with them on the nature and critical comprehension of structural privilege. I wanted them to be conscious of and ruminating on their positions and contexts of advantage, to be able to link structural societal arrangements of opportunities and values with their individual lives and the neighborhoods they grew up in, and to have some competency in stringing the relationships between knowledge and power and their connections to issues and practices of social justice and transformation within and outside of their school. In addition, I wanted them to grapple with the histories of the rise of the United States to a global power at the turn of the twentieth century in which the acquisition of the Philippines (along with Hawai'i, Guam, Sāmoa, Cuba, and Puerto Rico) became the US imperial project's key component. These were heavy readings that compressed what could have been a whole year's work, but I think the workshops that we did made the readings even more meaningful. On these two trips, right before leaving the United States, I was bursting with ambition and giddy with excitement!

Unexpectedly, on the ground, and on both trips, I was quite disappointed!

At the top of things that my students wanted to attend to days upon landing were not issues of power and privilege; they wanted to visit shopping malls, restaurants, and massage salons. Instead of ruminating on the latest incarnation of US colonization, they desired and reveled at the ease by which they could obtain liquor or get into clubs and bars without being carded. And what I was hoping to be difficult discussions about what it means to be an American tourist in a Third World country turned out to be intermittent remarks about how wonderful it was that many places in the Philippines seemed to be conveniently designed for the touristic consumption of people like us. Instead of anticipating that they would be bothered, I was amazed at how my students were so delighted that everyone spoke English and that they readily understood all the public business and transportation signs around them. They would never get lost there, and they felt quite pleased and secure in their new surroundings.

I thought these were not going to last for long, and when in the first trip they did, I was half worried that our course was rapidly falling apart. The other half of me, however, felt a bit resigned, and I remember telling

myself that this is how experiential classes abroad happen. They sometimes do fall apart (Lempert and Briggs 1996). Until one thing occurred
the week before our program ended. This event stood out as something
that provided a bit of a wrinkle in our easygoing tour and gave the students and me opportunities to question, at the very least, our fraught
presence as privileged visitors in the Philippines and amidst all the
pleasures we were experiencing. This happened in Olongapo, the site
par excellence of US military might on the islands, with its remnants of
housing facilities, now that the forces have been driven out and the bases
converted into recreational and residential spots for tourists.[8] We stayed
in three of their rental houses, and as part of our scheduled activity, we
were supposed to be led by our local coordinator into a tour of the "red-
light district" in Olongapo. Along with a tour, and without consultation
with me, students were promised opportunities to engage in conversations with some of the sex workers. This irritated me tremendously,
for so many reasons. First, I was not sure that it would be appropriate
for my students to observe and communicate with sex workers without
thorough preparation and discussion. Second, I thought it was unethical
to subject sex workers (or any other subject of study) to conditions that
might expose them to judgment or ridicule. And third, we hadn't asked
if the students felt all right with this.

I immediately scheduled a conversation with all of the students and
the coordinator. Following our discussion, half of the students decided
to go. The other half stayed with me. The tour group left us in our rentals
and went ahead with the local coordinator leading them. As excerpted
from one of the student's journals, here are some thoughts about why
some students stayed:

> Tonight, we decided to stay with Professor Bonus and not go to the clubs
> to see the prostitutes. That is disgusting! First of all, what are we expected
> to learn from them? That they sell their bodies for money? Don't we know
> that already? What's the point of talking to them? It's just so ridiculous and
> also insulting for the Filipinas who will be ashamed probably when they
> talk to us. Wow. Americans are merciless. We are why they are prostitutes.
> They service our soldiers. And now, they still do it because we make them.
> There's nothing for them to do. And now, we even bother them. They can
> use this time to work or do something else instead of talking with us and us

wasting their time, all good for us, for our benefit, not really for them. We treat them like animals in the zoo. Shame! Shame! Shame!

I recall talking with these students for a long time that night, anguishing with them about the ways in which our trip was both possible and pleasurable for us but exploitative for the Filipinos, how we could be so quick and smug about determining our objects of study without interrogating beforehand the potential effects of our study on others, and, of course, how and why we had to learn these lessons only by interacting with those who were part of the local sex-work industry. This was quite ironic, especially for all of us participants who seemed to be so critical of the continuing consequences of US colonization in the Philippines. It was also interesting that those students who chose to stay were women. By the time the other students came back from their trip to the sex-work district, I was still conversing with those who stayed behind, but it was too late to have a mutual and serious conversation. Besides, some of them appeared tipsy to me.

In our full-class discussion we had the next night, the local coordinator and I led a dialogue about what transpired. Those on my side were eager, although sad and angry at the same time, to explain to the rest why we stayed behind. "How could you?" one of my students, Myra, said. "How much does it take to understand that what you guys did was wrong?" These admonitions were promptly responded to by a student from the other side, Miguel. "What's wrong with talking to these women? They are workers who were okay in talking with us. We learned a lot from them."

> Myra: "And pray tell what you learned, Miguel."
> Miguel: "We learned about why they do what they do. We learned how this is difficult for them. But they also try to enjoy. And they try to be nice. For their kids. They need to make a living for their family."
> Myra: "Well, that's sad. But didn't you know that already? Why bother talking to them? That's kinda rude. And why [do this conversation] in the bars where they were working? That's dirty."

Myra began crying, which caused everyone to be quiet. After a few minutes, our local coordinator spoke:

I know this is a hard one to bear. And I'm sorry that . . . what this has caused us. This is my country, and I just wanted you to see my country for what it is, dark spots and all. I want all of you to experience what it means to be like that. Or, at least, observe and see for yourself what it means to work like that.

It was, indeed, a tough night for my students and for me and our coordinator. I encouraged the students to write in their journals about this, and in the remaining class sessions we had until the end of our trip, we shared verbally many of the things we wrote. We collectively expressed concern about our split opinions regarding the sex-worker interviews, and even though we could not reconcile then what we felt with what the other side did, we brought into our conversations the force of colonization not only appearing as "fact" in the Philippines and present in the bodies of their sex workers, but colonization acutely and palpably personified by us Americans.[9] "It is amazing to think that we think of colonization as existing out there, like, out here in the Philippines," Myra remarked. "But come to think of it," she continued, "we represent it. And we are it! We have the power to make choices, to judge them, to say what is good or not for them. And we don't even remember that it was because of us that they're like this."

Or, to put it in another way, we were there because it was our colonization of them that this trip was planned and possible.

But it was not as if this particular set of events led to some kind of triumphant transformative outcome for this first study-abroad trip to the Philippines that I led. I wanted the students to experience something different, which they did, and I planned to have them learn about the history and current experience of colonization in ways that would change them or cause them to be reflective. I am not so sure about whether they were qualitatively transformed, but I tend to think that at the minimum, their comprehension of colonization is now much more nuanced and complex after their trip with me. This comprehension, particularly of colonization as it is lived on site and in the present, and in relationship to the violence it perpetuates upon women's bodies, is something that many of my students, both Filipino American and not, expressed as a reason for them to connect and stay connected with the Philippines. At the end of their trip, and now as I read through their journals, everyone found ways to imagine some kind of connection between themselves as Americans and the people they just visited, the Filipinos. These included some kind of affinity because of blood connections, some measure of attachment (as in, "I care about what happens to Filipinos because I feel responsible for their life"), some kind of shared temporal proximity (as in, "our histories are bound together"), and a good measure of recognition of spatial commonalities (as in, "our cities look the same; they have McDonald's and Starbuck's there too") that students have identified as enough to make them feel like the Philippines is also their "home." We shall see in the next section how this gets to be pleasurably experienced but anxiously questioned.

Finding and Losing a Home

"Why do you think this is your home now?" I asked Angelo, a Filipino American participant during my recent trip there. He responded:

> Of course this is home. My parents and everyone else . . . my old ancestors . . . are from here. And everyone looks like me, haha, black hair and all. Weird, huh? I've never been here before, but it feels kinda like home. I love it here, and I don't stand out, haha! Everyone looks like me everywhere! It feels strange. But it's a good kind of strange, haha.

"Why strange? Would you entertain the idea of moving here?" I continued.

> Oh no. Haha. Maybe just for visiting. My life is in Seattle. I have everything there. Here, I'm so like a . . . I don't know . . . I'm so spoiled here. But yeah, people will find out [soon enough] that I'm not from here, and I'll be leaving soon. I don't think I'll stay here. And my mom said I should not give up my U.S. citizenship. But I want to visit all the time. I want to stay longer next time.

Narratives like these exemplify not only the centrality of the practice of multiply defining locations of homes in view of the contemporary realities of globalization and transnationalism, but in figuring these definitions as practices that are mediated along multiple vectors of histories, identities, and experiences (Levitt and Waters 2002). Andrea Louie's ethnography, in *Chineseness Across Borders: Renegotiating Chinese Identities in China and the United States* (2004), shows the profound participation of the media, schools, social and state institutions, as well as local communities in shaping the composition and tenor of such processes of constructing "home." As indicated by Angelo's thoughts, a good sense of blood or ancestral attachment is key to how he is able to imagine the Philippines as his "home." But it is not as simple as that.

Angelo's conversation with me (and himself) about making sense of his trip to the Philippines, as it was happening, points to a multilayered web of connections and considerations that he was negotiating and articulating as they were quickly being revealed to him. Moving to the Philippines? That sounded frightening to him. And to think that he just said that the Philippines is his home. Give up his US citizenship? He cannot let that happen. Visit the Philippines from time to time? Of course. But just to visit. These thoughts appeared contradictory to me at the time Angelo was saying them, but looking deeply now at my field notes, it is not hard to think about multiply regarded homes as principally possible only through the advantages brought about by one's privilege. Angelo is able to travel, and travel freely, because he has the resources to do so and holds US citizenship status. This was also true with regard to the other Filipino American participants in this recent trip. They, like Angelo, demonstrate the ease by which their US identities enable them to define the Philippines as their home as if it were simply a choice (staying or leaving) borne out of convenience, not out of necessity or limitation. Tita Ruby was quick to point this out:

> Lucky kayo kasi you all can travel. You can go back and forth, ganyan. Kami dito, walang pera. Kaya . . . kahit na sabihin ko e yung Amerika second home ko, hanggang pangarap na lang.

> (You're all lucky you all can travel. You can go back and forth, you see. Us here, we have no money. That's why . . . even though I can say that America is my second home, it's only through dreaming about it.)

This is precisely the reason why people in the Philippines like Tita Ruby tended to scoff at those of us in the trip who overplayed our flimsy demonstrations of "the Philippines, my home" without acknowledging our privileged status as US-based transnationals. And it was not a stretch for both locals and us visitors to regard this as yet another nasty manifestation of colonization-in-the-present and, worse, as the annoying incarnation of the all-too-familiar rude, overprivileged group of Americans masquerading as innocent tourists. Before this particular trip, I conducted classroom discussions of the different ways in which we could address all these histories of US-Philippines relations within the contexts of colonization and imperialism, as gleaned from our readings. We collectively ruminated on how we may interact with the locals and how the locals might regard us, given all these historical contexts. We decided that, at least on the level of attitude and public behavior, we should refrain from acting obnoxiously and that we should try as much as we can to use our privilege for the benefit of others. These were easier said than done.

On the ground, it was a challenge for many of us and the locals to handle sameness and difference. Sifa, a student who is mixed Filipino and Samoan by birth, remarked, "It's so easy here to think we're all the same. Because I look like them. They even [mistakenly] talk to me in Tagalog. But, of course, we're not!" While the local coordinators regularly warned the students to always keep an eye on each other and on their possessions for fear of kidnapping and theft, I repeatedly told my students to stop taking pictures of people without their permission and to try learning a bit of Tagalog so that the locals do not need to adjust to them all the time in terms of speaking in English with them. We would often think that just because we were US people, we could do whatever we wanted, so this attitude irritated our local guides. The students of color in the group seemed to occasionally forget that their skin color, which frequently marked them in the Philippines as non-American, surreptitiously works differently in the Philippines. Sometimes, people would mistake them as locals and would not bother with them. Other times, their US identity, once found out, trumped the color of their skin, in which case, they would be treated so nicely. They did not expect this. But they were elated about this ability (that locals afforded them) to free themselves from the disadvantage brought about by the color of their skin, as they are wont to experience in the United States. Still, many of them also thought that their US status reinforced hierarchies between the United States and the Philippines and deprived them of some kind of freedom to mix well with the locals, or to be counted as "the same." Once they talked, or even in the ways they dressed and walked, they got surprised when people found out that they were foreigners. One of the locals comically said to us, "*na-aamoy namin kayo!*" (We can smell you!)

Indeed, if there was a chance that these study-abroad participants could feel "at home," despite their feelings of immediate connectedness during the short length of time they were in the Philippines, that chance was slim. This was not only because of their limited visit; it was because their chance was mediated by the difference in social status that they commanded in each of the two countries. In the United States, they were minoritized persons of color whose identities were largely structured by race. In the Philippines, their privilege as US citizens was magnified, for it seemed that their overall social status as US-based people, regardless of their skin color, enabled them to be seen as people with high value to a good extent. Angelo thought at first that this was great, being an object of some sort of desire and envy. "They like me," he said. "They want to get married to me." So I asked, "Well what's wrong with that? Don't you want that?" He replied:

> I don't want to be seen like that! They like me only because I'm American. They like me because they want what I have. That's not a good thing. And besides, they know I'm not really "with it" for good. You know what I mean? They know I'm not serious about being here, you know? 'Cause I don't have everything here, and I have everything there. What they want is to be like me. They want to come to the states and be Americans. They want that because they're poor. It's okay. I will help them if they come.

Being in the Philippines, at least for Angelo, offered but a glimpse of home that can only exist in fantasy and could easily be complicated by the more practical aspects of not "having everything," the prospect of losing citizenship from a high-status country, and the ambivalence that he felt about people's desire of him and what he represents. Home, as Louie argues, is negotiated in multiple locations and contexts, as much as individuals in relation to groups construct it. Along with the students, I helped in proposing an idea to them that, especially for those who have families there who they were seeing either for the first time or after a long time, this trip was going to be some kind of a "homecoming." There were sixteen Filipino American students (from both of the trips) who wondered with me, "How is homecoming possible for those who have not been [or have rarely been] to the Philippines?" We came to and left the Philippines with many answers to this.

My students defined home in multiple ways; of course, as the vast literature on home suggests, particularly in relationship to globalization, migration, mobility, and transnationalism, home is whatever it is you define in the contexts of your and your groups' histories, experiences, and processes of identity formation (Ahmed 2003; Levitt and Waters 2002). Home can stay in the mind as much as it can stay in solid space, it can be the past or the future appearing in the present, and it may not necessarily only be put into words for it to be adequately and appropriately understood. My students learned about the Philippines through my lectures, the books and essays we read, the videos we watched, the stories from their families and friends, the frequent media appearances of celebrities such as Manny Pacquiao and Lea Salonga, the Filipino cable channels when they received them, and through the rest of the wide and deep array of histories and images passed to them by the many virtual and social communities and nations they are members of or that they interact with. Each of them had their own particular construction of what this place is, and when we finally got there, their constructions of "home" grew even richer and more complex as they encountered quite a dazzling profusion of images, smells, tastes, noises, feelings, words, embraces, and emotions—stuff they have never encountered before. This is reminiscent of Mary Louise Pratt's (1991) notion of a "contact zone"— the intermingling of diverse cultures in a particular space, which can be both discomforting and simultaneously energizing.[10] Because we were seen as visitors, we found our local contacts to be hospitable and generous with everything they could offer. They wanted us to "feel at home."

Even though my students understood that "feeling at home" is different from "being at home," they were nevertheless enticed to develop a strong regard for this new home of theirs. This was expressed in their journals, in my conversations with them, and in their attitudes and actions for the rest of the trip and beyond. As the days progressed, they were walking the streets by themselves, they became more comfortable in doing things by themselves, and they were speaking louder, until, that is, when the local coordinators and I took notice, and we began scolding them. "Home" in the Philippines was something that these students warmly embraced and took as their own, perhaps as a way to enjoy a new aspect of their transnational life, one that seemed to be seductive precisely because their hosts were willingly assisting them, their skin color (for at least half of them) did not seem to place them at a disadvantage, and because their First World privilege became intensified. But our hosts, including our local coordinator Tita Ruby, knew too well that this wouldn't last long, as we were sojourners and not exactly returnees, and that it was about time for us to return to our "real" homes and lose this one. It was as if it was up to us to resort to other ways to think of home, if we were to make sense of this study-abroad trip's significance to our study of colonization's afterlives in relation to who we are.

Small Alliances

The first Philippines study-abroad trip that I led focused on a set of activities and lectures that aimed to immerse students in the nation's major historical events and contemporary conditions. In doing this, the aim was to encourage the students to acquire some facility in tracing the significant transformations of the country from colonization to modern globalization, and to have the students experience in some form the processes of such transformations as they are occurring in sites like schools that are reviving the teachings of indigenous music and the former US military bases in which exploitative conditions of sex tourism have persisted. For the second trip, which happened four years later, I decided to plan for a trip that was more intentionally hands-on or, at least, proactive about determining what the students might want to do with the knowledge that they learn on the field regarding the Philippines' colonization histories and their afterlives. That is, having learned from making the students simply listen to lectures and interview locals, and finding out on site how disappointingly limited, self-serving, and facile these activities were, I vowed that this next trip should devote some time and effort to making the students useful to locals. I thought that with a "service" component in this study-abroad course, students will be able to not only complement the academic and touristic activities they have with much more meaningful service-oriented activities, they will also be able to find ways to ruminate on the prospects of engaging with the afterlives of colonization through the more positive dynamics of collaborative work. I wanted this trip to entail some measure of personal and collective transformation for the students and those we were about to interact with.

During this trip therefore, our itinerary was packed with activities that provided students with substantial materials to work through national and local histories, as well as to engage with experts on cultural and performing arts that our university host/partner is famous for having.[11] But I was personally more interested in our planned "service" activities, so I highlight two sets of those activities here to offer what I claim are examples of grounded, productive approaches to a transnational-themed study-abroad program. Like many other small-scale pedagogical projects that aim to be transformative in their emphasis, these activities were experimental and limited in their scope and depth. Much of the work on these attempts needs further improvement, so I use this ethnography to simply highlight what I think are critical points to consider in the conduct of study-abroad programs like this with a view toward expanding the spaces for deeper conversations about transnational alliances (Lewin 2009).

Dorothea, one of the student participants, told me, "This hard labor sucks!" She was referring to the labor of having to load, carry, and distribute bags of sand to different parts of a housing construction site we visited. It was the setting for one of our service-oriented activities, one of several locations that the international organization, Habitat for Humanity, has identified as part of its worldwide campaign to address the housing needs of those in poverty. By volunteering to work side by side with the housing project's future residents, I thought it would be a good experience for students to literally have a hand in laboring for and with those who were not as fortunate as they. Dorothea later continued:

> I know, we were complaining so much, huh. It's just that we're not used to this. But its still good experience. Something different. Something that makes us humble . . . and thankful that we do not have to do this everyday. Imagine? If I did this everyday, I'd die. I think of my uncles and cousins [in the United States] who do this, so now I get it when they look so tired all the time. Hard labor sucks! But if you're poor, you gotta do what you gotta do, ya?

We worked on this Habitat site in Pasig city, some nine miles east of where we lived in Manila, for about six hours that day. And that's all we could take! During the hour's bus ride back to our apartment, nobody opened their mouths to talk due to sheer exhaustion. Everyone was hungry and thirsty. We didn't get the opportunity to interact much with the housing project's participants, including the other volunteer students from our university partner who joined us for this day, but I thought it was alright that we did more work than talk. We did not need to process with them our "good deeds" for the day. And the students didn't seem to mind that at all.

In some respects, we were already "practiced" in what we just did, for a few days before, we were assisting in the planting of seeds for a vegetable patch in our university partner's community-development project called "Munting Paraiso," which I translate as "Little Paradise." The Philippine Women's University was also in yet another partnership with a large international but Philippines-based organization called Gawad Kalinga (I roughly translate this as "Bestowal of Care"), and the community we visited was located in Trece Martires city in Cavite province, some twenty miles south of Manila. Our activity also took place for only a day, and it involved meeting the community leaders and members, interacting with their youth through a musical performance program, and helping some of the elders in tending to their small farmlands. The labor here was not as intense as the one we experienced in Pasig. But all of the students wanted more. Alvin, one of them, said to me:

> It's too bad we just came here [to Cavite] to plant for a short time, and that's it! I hope they did not get mad at us. I thought it's too bad they spent more time teaching me how to plant, instead of me helping them all the time. Yeah, we should do more. We should go back and do something more for them. You know, we learn from them, but they also get some from us. That's nice when we're useful.

I felt the same way. I saw how students were enthusiastic to be of service to others, and I thought that these experiences gave them a taste of how it is to be beneficial, even in small ways, to other people whose lives were intertwined with us within contexts that were unequal, in the past as well as in the present. We already were devoting many parts of our trip to pleasing ourselves, from shopping to eating, and from simply observing classrooms to visiting museums, churches, and community centers. Many students and I felt it was about time that others make use of us. It was unfortunate that this farming activity in Trece Martires was not as carefully planned as I hoped it should have been, and that we were in this community for such a short period. But I thought it was also worth doing, considering that it deviated a bit from how regular study-abroad courses were done in my school and that this was a learning experience that someone like me would find useful in planning for similar trips in the future.

There were other short service-oriented trips that we did in this class. We had a day trip to a local shelter for abandoned and abused women and children where students led small group activities with the young residents, we participated in a collaborative learning session on indigenous musical traditions with university students, and I cofacilitated with my students a workshop on globalization and schooling with hundreds of university students on our site who actively sat and participated in class with all of us. These were activities that were designed to pay attention to how study-abroad participants learn lessons not through traditional methods of teaching and not only by themselves but also through experiential ways of learning outside of classrooms and in collaborative sessions with others from the visited sites. The "others," in this special instance, were those who were our course's objects of study whose interaction with us (the "others," from their perspective) enriched our class in extraordinary ways. Said Dorothea:

> I liked how our class made us talk to everybody, and not just talk to ourselves. I hope I can be classmates with them longer, like for the rest of the trip! 'Cause I wanna keep in touch with them. I want to do things with them and I want to continue what we started. The farmers, the students, the community, the kids. . . . I want to keep going at it with them.

At the beginning of this trip, I admonished all the students to focus on what they could give, not what they could take. I told them that whatever it is that they will learn or get out of this trip, they are guaranteed to be realized because that's the nature of study-abroad programs. "You will learn on any trip no matter what," I told them, and that they do not need to worry about whether any kind of learning was going to happen or not. So, I said to them that instead, they ought to think of ways to give or share whatever it is that they could, and to think of things beyond giving money or gifts in kind. I told them to give of themselves, and since they were giving from a position of privilege, that they should find ways to make this kind of giving meaningful to others beyond having it just meaningful to themselves. In these activities, students were thus encouraged to work while staying conscious of the contexts of inequality (so that they are mindful of their privileged status) as much as within the prospects of what working together in cross-national alliances could entail (so that they are not immobilized by such unequal conditions and positions). These activities were small-scale, minimal, and felt shallow to some, but I thought they were appropriate experiments on how the study of the afterlives of colonization can have a service or "give back" edge to it. "Someone else benefited besides just us, for a change," I remember telling this to the students over and over again.

As a teacher, however, I did not want to impress to my students that they accomplished a lot, nor did I intend to have our hosts feel like either this was all we could do or that this was enough for them to feel very grateful for, as they were always respectfully inclined to do. I just wanted the students to perform some kind of physical and intellectual communal labor in collaboration with the community members, students, and teachers we briefly visited in places where we could be made useful. On site, I purposely did not ask the students to reflect deeply on these service activities because I thought that doing so would just make them feel good about themselves while forgetting that they need to think more about others in places and moments where they came to at an advantage. Only in hindsight, during the last remaining days we were in the Philippines, when we had conversations about the highlights of our trip, did many of the students choose to bring up the community-service work they intermittently performed during our course, among an array of many other activities we did. I remember one of the students who paid close attention to these service work experiences, Suli, who wrote in her journal:

> I don't mean to be corny, but I thought it was a good way to bond with the people. That planting thing we had, the house building, and the babysitting in the orphanage. We clearly did not communicate well

with words, but we had some kind of interaction. My [local] partner [in Cavite] . . . she even invited me to her house . . . and I really felt humbled. My family in the states, we're poor. But when I saw her house, I felt like I was rich. But that didn't matter. I just thought that, for a moment, people who are not equal were working together. And then, I was more touched when she said she hoped I'd visit again soon.

It was this injunction to "come back soon"—uttered by locals over and over again in many of the places that we visited—that caught many of us not so much by surprise, as by a pleasant but melancholy feeling that we were at once welcomed and also reminded that this ought not to be our last encounter with them. I frequently thought that they were just being courteous to us, and Tita Ruby validated this to me, saying that guests in the Philippines are always invited to come back. But then, on several occasions, and on the last day of our trip, she did tell us, "come back home soon," something that made many of us, especially those of us who identify as Filipino American, feel pleased and anguished about.

Conclusion

My US students who took a study-abroad trip to the Philippines with me definitely experienced the pleasures that can be expected from a summer outing into the tropics. As their journal entries gleefully recorded, they undertook many opportunities to enjoy what they were discovering on their field trips, they were able to mostly afford what they desired to consume, and they marveled at the beauty of their surroundings, the sumptuousness of the food they ate, and the friendliness of the locals. They were awestruck by the kindness and hospitality of most everyone they encountered. Plus, they were also traveling as a group, and this made them form strong bonds of friendship with each other, with me, and even with our drivers, local coordinators, and other staff members involved in the business of our trips. There were US-identified stores and restaurant chains that all of us recognized very quickly. It helped that everyone spoke English. For the students of color, it was a relief to not stand out in the crowd and convenient that they did not have to adjust to a dominant culture that they did not identify with. They had a pretty good sense of the transnational condition that they were inhabiting momentarily. For Filipino Americans, especially, it was not that hard to feel "at home." They felt embraced by a culture that felt unexpectedly very warm and familiar to them in the strangest of ways.

But the force of such welcoming and enjoyable encounters equally, if not awkwardly, coincided with a plethora of disorienting and anxiety-provoking images, feelings, and confrontations. In Manila, students were surprised at the preponderance of US consumer icons and products, at the ubiquity of billboard ads that hawked the latest American movies, and the great extent to which hip-hop was part of the urban music scene. They felt a good measure of discomfort as they encountered locals who they thought were mirror images of themselves—who spoke like them and dressed like them—yet were poorer, openly desiring and desperate for a better life (in the United States), but quick to label them as foreign. These reminded the US students of all the privileges that they had even in a country that was not their own, and of their own country's abundant and continuing, though undesirable, historical and current imprints on the Philippines. For the students who identified as Filipino Americans, it was disappointing to see so many things "American" in this nation that they were (problematically) expecting to be more "Filipino," and it was regretful that the place they called "home" could exist only as a romanticized fantasy in their heads. They were confronted by both the pleasures and limits of their newly experienced transnational identity.

The pleasures and agonies that students experienced while traveling to the Philippines and returning to the United States coexisted as expressions of a moment and space of transnationality whose currency is simultaneously a reason to celebrate as well as a condition to be struggled with. Students and I marveled at the possibilities of quicker-than-usual travel times to and within the Philippines (for those who can afford them), the ease by which we can continue interacting with our hosts through the Internet long after our trip is done (for those who have access to it), and the seemingly endless prospects of constructing and maintaining multiple residences, friendships, and alliances across an ocean. At the same time, we struggled, and continue to struggle, with the ostensible impossibilities of a stable and secure set of homes elsewhere, of relationships that are long distance, and of communities that are not equal to each other, the very stuff that we struggle with domestically. These struggles are both products and productive of yet larger sets of histories, cultures, and conditions of colonization and its afterlives that span across these two nations.

In the meantime, and as we learn in and from these trips, these experiences of struggle may well teach us that they can also be generative of practices that approximate and engage with the unequal conditions traversed by modern transnationalism. When given opportunities to be of service to others, these experiences show the positive extent to which US students and their local counterparts and hosts welcomed the departure from classroom work, the setting aside of books and readings, and the application of ideas, concepts, and thoughts regarding, say, the continuing consequences of colonization or the persistence of inequality among social groups, into practice. So long as these service activities are integrated into a broad range of other activities that make possible, in the case of these study-abroad programs, the comprehension of globalization, transnationalism, and mobility as historically and locally situated, they are experiments that can well elicit a more meaningful collaboration of those from similar, yet different, places. Small-scale projects that bring communities of privilege and underprivilege to work together may have limited utility and short-range consequences at the outset, but they can also generate renewed interest and room for improvement for those who care about this kind of work, they can be seedbeds of and laboratories for the potential uplift and transformation of all its participants, and they can actualize the prospects of what could be a more ethical, productive, and just condition of transnationalism.

Notes

1. "Tita Ruby" is a pseudonym. All the names mentioned in this chapter are also pseudonyms.
2. These included the Tagalog On Site Program, the University of the Philippines, and the Philippine Women's University (PWU). The curricular design of both trips was done in collaboration with members and affiliates of these institutions, but I led the overall conceptualization, direction, and implementation of all the activities within the trips in my capacity as a member of the faculty in the Department of American Ethnic Studies at the University of Washington (UW).
3. For key analyses of Filipino American identity and community formation in contexts beyond travel, see Bonus (2000), Espiritu (2003), Isaac (2006), Manalansan (2002), Mendoza (2001), Okamura (1998), Pido (1986), Root (1997), Strobel (2001), Tiongson, Gutierrez, and Gutierrez (2006), and Vergara (2009).

4. The scholarship on travel in relation to identity, migration, and transnationalism is vast and place- or group-specific. I would like to thank Martin Manalansan for sharing with me relevant parts of his bibliography on this subject.

5. Rafael, a colleague and professor at UW Department of History, originally planned and advised me on the overall themes and emphases of the first Philippines study-abroad course, which I inherited, refined, and eventually conducted as my own class.

6. The phenomenon of transnationalism, especially as experienced by second-generation children of immigrants, is a trend that's being closely monitored by social scientists and policymakers. See Levitt and Waters (2002).

7. For a similar account of Filipino American youth struggling with US and Filipino identities and positionalities in the Philippines, see Mendoza (2006).

8. Olongapo was once the location of the US Subic Bay Naval Station from 1901 to 1991, when the Philippine senate terminated the naval station's existence and turned it into the Subic Bay Freeport Zone.

9. The paradoxical issues of prostitution relative to the political-social economy of tourism in the Philippines are amply analyzed in Ralston and Keeble (2009).

10. Pratt (1991) writes, "I use this term to refer to social spaces where cultures meet, clash, and grapple with each other, often in contexts of highly asymmetrical relations of power, such as colonialism, slavery, or their aftermaths as they are lived out in many parts of the world today. Eventually, I will use the term to reconsider the models of community that many of us rely on in teaching, theorizing and that are under challenge today" (34).

11. The PWU, a nonprofit educational institution founded in 1919, is home to the world-renowned Bayanihan Philippine Folk Dance Company.

Works Cited

Ahmed, Sara. 2003. *Uprootings/regroundings: Questions of Home and Migration*. Oxford, UK: Berg. Print.

Basch, Linda G, Nina G. Schiller, and Cristina Szanton Blanc. 1994. *Nations Unbound: Transnational Projects, Postcolonial Predicaments, and Deterritorialized Nation-States*. Langhorne, PA: Gordon and Breach. Print.

Bonus, Rick. 2000. *Locating Filipino Americans: Ethnicity and the Cultural Politics of Space*. Philadelphia, PA: Temple University Press. Print.

Brettell, Caroline. 2003. *Anthropology and Migration: Essays on Transnationalism, Ethnicity, and Identity*. Walnut Creek, CA: Altamira Press. Print.

Espiritu, Yen L. 2003. *Home Bound: Filipino American Lives Across Cultures, Communities, and Countries*. Berkeley: University of California Press. Print.

Gupta, Akhil, and James Ferguson. 1997. *Culture, Power, Place: Explorations in Critical Anthropology*. Durham, NC: Duke University Press. Print.

Isaac, Allan P. 2006. *American Tropics: Articulating Filipino America*. Minneapolis: University of Minnesota Press. Print.

Kaplan, Caren. 1996. *Questions of Travel: Postmodern Discourses of Displacement*. Durham, NC: Duke University Press. Print.

Keith, Michael, and Steve Pile. 1993. *Place and the Politics of Identity*. London: Routledge. Print.

Lempert, David H, and Xavier S. Briggs. 1996. *Escape from the Ivory Tower: Student Adventures in Democratic Experiential Education*. San Francisco: Jossey-Bass. Print.

Levitt, Peggy, and Mary C. Waters. 2002. *The Changing Face of Home: The Transnational Lives of the Second Generation*. New York: Russell Sage Foundation. Print.

Lewin, Ross. 2009. *The Handbook of Practice and Research in Study Abroad: Higher Education and the Quest for Global Citizenship*. New York: Routledge. Print.

Louie, Andrea. 2004. *Chineseness Across Borders: Renegotiating Chinese Identities in China and the United States*. Durham, NC.: Duke University Press. Print.

Manalansan, Martin F. 2003. *Global Divas: Filipino Gay Men in the Diaspora*. Durham, NC.: Duke University Press. Print.

Mendoza, S. Lily L. 2006. "A Different Breed of Filipino Balikbayans: The Ambiguities of (Re)turning." In *Positively No Filipinos Allowed: Building Communities and Discourse*, ed. Antonio T. Tiongson, Edgardo V. Gutierrez, and Ricardo V. Gutierrez, 199–214. Philadelphia, PA: Temple University Press. Print.

———. 2006. *Between the Homeland and the Diaspora*. Manila, Philippines: University of Santo Tomas Press. Print.

Okamura, Jonathan Y. 1998. *Imagining the Filipino American Diaspora: Transnational Relations, Identities, and Communities*. New York: Garland. Print.

Pido, Antonio J. A. 1986. *The Pilipinos in America: Macro/micro Dimensions of Immigration and Integration*. New York: Center for Migration Studies. Print.

Pratt, Mary L. 1991. "Arts of the Contact Zone." *Profession*: 33–40. Print.

Rafael, Vicente L. 2009. "The Afterlife of Empire: Sovereignty and Revolution in the Spanish Philippines." In *Colonial Crucible: Empire and the Forging of a Modern American State*, ed. Alfred McCoy and Francisco Scarano, 342–52. Madison: University of Wisconsin Press. Print.

Ralston, Meredith L, and Edna Keeble. *Reluctant Bedfellows: Feminism, Activism and Prostitution in the Philippines*. Sterling, VA: Kumarian Press, 2009. Print.

Root, Maria P. P. 1997. *Filipino Americans: Transformation and Identity*. Thousand Oaks, CA: Sage. Print.

San, Juan E. 2007. *U.S. Imperialism and Revolution in the Philippines*. New York: Palgrave Macmillan. Print.

Strobel, Leny M. 2001. *Coming Full Circle: The Process of Decolonization Among Post-1965 Filipino Americans*. Quezon City: Giraffe Books. Print.

Tiongson, Antonio T., Edgardo V. Gutierrez, and Ricardo V. Gutierrez. 2006. *Positively No Filipinos Allowed: Building Communities and Discourse*. Philadelphia, PA: Temple University Press. Print.

Vergara, Benito M. 2009. *Pinoy Capital: The Filipino Nation in Daly City*. Philadelphia, PA: Temple University Press. Print.

Kimberly Alidio holds a PhD in history from the University of Michigan. Essays have appeared in *American Quarterly* and *Social Text*. Poetry recently or will appear as a Fact-Simile Editions broadside and in *Everyday Genius*, *Horse Less Review*, *ESQUE*, *Bone Bouquet*, *Lantern Review*, *Make/shift*, and others. She lives in Austin, Texas, where she teaches history at St. Stephens Episcopal School, writes and dramaturgs for the Generic Ensemble Company, and works on a book of scholarly essays entitled *Colonial Cosmopolitanism*. She blogs at www.kimberlyalidio.tumblr.com.

Victor Bascara is Associate Professor of Asian American Studies at the University of California, Los Angeles. He is the author of *Model Minority Imperialism* (2006).

Francisco Benitez is President of the Philippine Women's University in Manila. He taught comparative literature at University of Washington, Seattle, and holds a PhD in comparative literature from the University of Wisconsin, Madison.

John D. Blanco is Associate Professor at the Literature Department at University of California, San Diego. He is the author of *Frontier Constitutions: Christianity and Colonial Empire in the 19th Century Philippines* (2009).

Rick Bonus is Associate Professor of American Ethnic Studies at the University of Washington, Seattle. He is the author of *Locating Filipino Americans: Ethnicity and the Cultural Politics of Space* (2000), co-editor of the anthology, *Intersections and Divergences: Contemporary Asian American Communities* (2002), and writer of essays on the cultural politics of difference, media representations, and multicultural education. His forthcoming book is based on an ethnography of Pacific Islander students and their allies whose college experiences become generative sites for critiquing and transforming university schooling. He is former president of the Association for Asian American Studies.

Lucy Burns is Associate Professor of Asian American Studies at the University of California, Los Angeles. She is the author of *Puro Arte: Filipinos on the Stages of Empire* (NYU Press 2012).

Richard T. Chu is Associate Professor of History at the University of Massachusetts Amherst. He is the author of *The Chinese and Chinese Mestizos of Manila: Family, Identity, and Culture 1860s-1930s* (2010) and editor of *More Tsinoy Than We Admit: Chinese-Filipino Interactions Over the Centuries* (Quezon City: Vidal Foundation, 2015).

Denise Cruz is Assistant Professor of English at the University of Toronto. She is the author of *Transpacific Femininities: The Making of the Modern Filipina* (2012) and the editor of Yay Panlilio's World War II memoir, *The Crucible: An Autobiography of Colonel Yay, Filipina American Guerrilla* (2009). Additional publications have also appeared in *American Literature, American Quarterly, American Literary History, Modern Fiction Studies,* and *PMLA.*

Robert Diaz is Assistant Professor in the Faculty of Liberal Arts and Sciences and the Faculty of Graduate Studies at OCAD University in Toronto. His first project analyzes queer Filipino/a embodiment and its relationship to nationalism and redress. Diaz is also currently editing *Diasporic Intimacies: Queer Filipinos/as and Canadian Imaginaries* (under contract with Northwestern University Press), which brings together artists, scholars, and community workers in order to examine the contributions of queer Filipinos/as to Canadian culture and society. His research has appeared or is forthcoming in *Signs: Journal of Women and Culture in Society, GLQ: Journal of Lesbian And Gay Studies, Women and Performance, The Routledge Companion to Asian American and Pacific Islander Literature,* and *Plaridel.*

Augusto F. Espiritu is Associate Professor of History and Asian American Studies at the University of Illinois Urbana-Champaign. He is the interim head of the Department of Asian American Studies. He is the author of *Five Faces of Exile: The Nation and Filipino American Intellectuals* (2005). His next book is a comparative intellectual history of the Philippines, Puerto Rico, and Cuba under United States (neo)colonial rule, focused on the pro-Spanish, racial/cultural ideology of *hispanismo.*

Kale Bantigue Fajardo is Associate Professor of American Studies and Asian American Studies at the University of Minnesota, Twin Cities. He is the author of *Filipino Crosscurrents: Oceanographies of Seafaring, Masculinities, and Globalization* (2011). He is currently writing a book entitled, *Following Filipinos: Sailors, Travelers, and Migrants – or – A Pinoy History of the World* and a memoir called *North-Star-Lone Star: Reflections on Translocal Transgender Fathering.* Kale divides his time between Minneapolis, Minnesota; Austin, Texas; Portland, Oregon; and Malolos, Bulacan, Philippines.

Julian Go is Professor of Sociology at Boston University, where he is also a Faculty Affiliate in Asian Studies. His recent books include *Patterns of Empire: The British and American Empires, 1688-present* (2011) and *American Empire and the Politics of Meaning: Elite Political Cultures in Puerto Rico and the Philippines During U.S. Colonialism* (2008). He is also editor of the journal *Political Power and Social Theory.*

Anna Romina Guevarra is Associate Professor and Director of Asian American Studies at the University of Illinois, Chicago. She is the author of *Marketing Dreams, Manufacturing Heroes: The Transnational Labor Brokering of Filipino Workers* (2010) and co-editor of *Immigrant Women Workers in the Neoliberal Age* (2013). Her current book project explores the relationships between technoscience, globalization, and care work through the lens of Filipina *cybraceros*, workers in the Philippines who operate tele-education robots to teach English to South Korean children.

Emily Noelle Ignacio is Associate Professor at the University of Washington, Tacoma. She is author of *Building Diaspora: Filipino Cultural Community Formation on the Internet.* (2005)

Martin F. Manalansan IV is Associate Professor of Anthropology and Asian American Studies and Conrad Professorial Humanities Scholar at the University of Illinois at Urbana-Champaign. He is an affiliate faculty in the Gender and Women's Studies Program, the Global Studies Program, and the Unit for Criticism and Interpretive Theory. He is the author of *Global Divas: Filipino Gay Men in the Diaspora* (2003, 2006), which was awarded the Ruth Benedict Prize in 2003. He is editor/co-editor of several anthologies, including *Cultural Compass: Ethnographic Explorations of Asian America* (2000) and *Queer Globalizations: Citizenship and the Afterlife of Colonialism* (NYU Press 2002), *Eating Asian America: A Food Studies Reader* (NYU Press 2013), as well as a special issue of *International Migration Review* on gender and migration. His current book projects include the ethical and embodied dimensions of the lives and struggles of undocumented queer immigrants, Asian American immigrant culinary cultures, sensory and affective dimensions of race and difference, and Filipino return migration.

Martin Joseph Ponce is Associate Professor in the Department of English at Ohio State University. He is the author of *Beyond the Nation: Diasporic Filipino Literature and Queer Reading* (NYU Press 2012), as well as articles in *GLQ: A Journal of Lesbian and Gay Studies*, *Journal of Asian American Studies*, *Modern Language Quarterly*, and *Philippine Studies*, among other venues.

Dylan Rodriguez is Professor and Chair in the Department of Ethnic Studies at University of California, Riverside. He is the author of *Forced Passages: Imprisoned Radical Intellectuals and the U.S. Prison Regime* (2006) and *Suspended Apocalypse: White Supremacy, Genocide and the Filipino Condition* (2009).

Robyn Magalit Rodriguez is Associate Professor of Asian American Studies at the University of California, Davis. She is the author of *Migrants for Export: How the Philippine State Brokers Labor to the World* (2010). Rodriguez's research, which has focused primarily on contemporary Philippine labor migration, has appeared in several dozen scholarly journals including *Citizenship Studies*, *Identities*, *Philippine Sociological Review*, *Signs*, and *International Labor and Working Class History*, as well as a number of edited anthologies. A longtime Filipino immigrant-rights advocate, Rodriguez currently supports the organizing efforts of Filipino caregivers in San Francisco.

Sarita Echavez See is Associate Professor of Media and Cultural Studies at the University of California, Riverside. She is the author of *The Decolonized Eye: Filipino American Art and Performance* (2009).

Neferti Tadiar is Professor of Women's Studies at Barnard College. She is the author of *Fantasy Production: Sexual Economies and Other Philippine Consequences for the New World Order* (2004) and *Things Fall Away: Philippines Historical Experience and the Makings of Globalization* (2009).

CPSIA information can be obtained
at www.ICGtesting.com
Printed in the USA
FSHW021255050819
60732FS